William H. Thomes

The Belle of Australia or who am I

A novel about the discovery of Australia

William H. Thomes

The Belle of Australia or who am I
A novel about the discovery of Australia

ISBN/EAN: 9783743382046

Manufactured in Europe, USA, Canada, Australia, Japa

Cover: Foto ©ninafisch / pixelio.de

Manufactured and distributed by brebook publishing software (www.brebook.com)

William H. Thomes

The Belle of Australia or who am I

THE

BELLE OF AUSTRALIA

OR

WHO AM I?

THE LIBRARY OF CHOICE FICTION

THE

BELLE OF AUSTRALIA

OR

WHO AM I?

WILLIAM H. THOMES

Author of "*The Gold Hunters of Australia,*" "*The Bushrangers,*" "*The Gold Hunters in Europe,*" "*Life in the East Indies,*" "*A Slaver's Adventures,*" "*Running the Blockade,*" "*A Whaleman's Adventures,*" *Etc.*

ILLUSTRATED BY F. CHILDE HASSAM

CHICAGO
LAIRD & LEE, PUBLISHERS

Contents.

CONTENTS.

PART I.

PASSAGE AND ARRIVAL AT MELBOURNE IN SEARCH OF FAME AND FORTUNE, AND WHAT WONDERFUL ADVENTURES HAPPENED TO ME THE FIRST DAY OF MY ARRIVAL IN THE CITY. — A CRAZY FRENCHMAN AND HIS PACKAGE. — MY DOUBLE.

PART II.

THE MEETING IN FRONT OF THE CLUB-HOUSE. — WHO AM I? AND WHAT HAVE I DONE? — A FRIEND OF THE FAMILY. — AN OLD ACQUAINTANCE ON THE POLICE. — MISS KITTY AND THE DIAMOND RING. — NO EXPLANATIONS RECEIVED OR WANTED.

PART III.

MISS KITTY AND THE DIAMOND RING AGAIN APPEAR. — A PROMISE TO BE SILENT. — MR. KEBBLEWHITE AND HIS HOME. — HOW MR. MURDEN SURROUNDED ME WITH PITFALLS. — USELESS DENIALS. — THE FIRST VISION OF MY FUTURE WIFE; AND A PLEASANT ONE IT IS.

PART IV.

AN EMBARRASSING POSITION FOR A YOUNG MAN. — MR. KEBBLEWHITE AGAIN GETS ANGRY, AND ONCE MORE CALLS FOR HIS PISTOLS AND NULLA. — NO TIME FOR EXPLANATIONS. — A SAD WEDDING, AND A COLLATION AND DRINKING. — I LIKE MY NEW MOTHER-IN-LAW, AND SHE RATHER LIKES ME. — MR. KEBBLEWHITE GIVES US A SPECIMEN OF HIS VOCAL POWERS.

PART V.

A SHORT PRIVATE INTERVIEW WITH MY WIFE. — I MAKE SOME EXPLANATIONS, WHICH ARE NOT WELL RECEIVED. — A PLEA FOR PARDON, AND A REFUSAL. — LEAVING THE HOUSE BY THE AID OF A TREE. — MR. MURDEN AND HIS PLAIN TALK. — A LONG FAREWELL.

PART VI.

A JOURNEY, AND A MOUNTED POLICEMAN'S HALT. — THE NOISES OF THE FOREST. — A CUP OF TEA AND THE KANGAROO. — THE QUAKER AND HIS QUESTIONS. — OLD WEBBER AND HIS BLOOMING DAUGHTER. — AN INDUCEMENT. — MIKE GIVES ME A SOLEMN WARNING.

PART VII.

ON THE ROAD TO BALLARAT. — A SHORT NAP, AND A LIVELY BLACK-SNAKE. — LOST IN THE BUSH. — AN AUSTRALIAN CRY FOR HELP. — THE TORTURED CHINAMAN. — A RESCUE. — AN ENCAMPMENT FOR THE NIGHT. — A FLYING CHINAMAN. — THE BLACK FELLOWS AND THEIR FEAST. — A TERRIBLE VISITOR. — ON THE TRAMP.

PART VIII.

BALLARAT AND ITS MINES. — HOW THREE OLD PIRATES SOLD A CLAIM AND MYSELF AT THE SAME TIME. — HOUSE-CLEANING MADE EASY. — A NEWSPAPER'S ACCOUNT OF MY WEDDING. — MISS KITTY STUCKLY MAKES ME AN UNEXPECTED CALL, AND WANTS TO TALK OF LOVE, BUT I DECLINE TO LISTEN. — THE ARRIVAL OF MR. MURDEN AT MY SHANTY IN THE NIGHT, AND WHAT HE SAID.

PART IX.

MR. MURDEN EXPRESSES HIS OPINION QUITE FREELY. — KITTY'S DISAPPEARANCE. — THE NUGGETS OF GOLD, AND HOW MUCH THEY WERE WORTH. — A SALE OF THE MINE. — MY WIFE AND HER FATHER, AND HOW THEY WENT AWAY. — A SCHEME TO CAPTURE FLORENCE AND HER FATHER BY BUSHRANGERS. — MIKE WANTS TO FIGHT SOME ONE.

PART X.

A DISAGREEABLE NIGHT RIDE. — FINDING THE TRAIL. — THE BLACK TRACKER THROUGH THE BUSH. — THE BUSHRANGERS' CAMP. — THE SUDDEN ATTACK. — A HAND-TO-HAND BATTLE. — THE CHINAMEN'S BLOOD DELIRIUM. — A VICTORY. — THE HIDDEN TREASURE. — FLORENCE RECOGNIZES HER HUSBAND, AND IS VERY FAR FROM BEING SATISFIED.

PART XI.

AFTER THE FIGHT. — ARRIVAL OF THE POLICEMEN, AND MR. MURDEN PUTS IN AN APPEARANCE, AND EXPRESSES HIS VIEWS. — MY OLD SHIPMATE. — SOME THINGS ARE EXPLAINED, AND OTHERS A MYSTERY. — THE HIDDEN TREASURE. — A BOLD PROPOSITION. — A WOOL SPECULATION. — FLORENCE IS OBDURATE. — SMITH'S HOME, AND ANOTHER FEMALE CRANK. — A BOLD CLAIM FOR A HUSBAND.

PART XII.

THE BURIED TREASURE. — A BOX OF GOLD. — THE RETURN TO BALLARAT. — SELLING OFF. — FAREWELL TO THE MINES. — A BIG SPECULATION IN WOOL. — A HASTY SUMMONS. — FACE TO FACE WITH A LORD AND A DOUBLE. — MY MOTHER'S ARRIVAL, AND HER STORY. — TWIN BROTHERS. — FLORENCE MAKES HER CHOICE, AND IS HAPPY. — GRAND EXPLANATIONS. — MR. KEBBLEWHITE OPENS SOME WINE. — MIKE'S CAREER. — A GENERAL CLOSING UP. — THE END.

MY FIRST APPEARANCE IN MELBOURNE.

PART I

PASSAGE AND ARRIVAL AT MELBOURNE IN SEARCH OF FAME AND FORTUNE, AND WHAT WONDERFUL ADVENTURES HAPPENED TO ME THE FIRST DAY OF MY LANDING IN THE CITY. — A CRAZY FRENCHMAN AND HIS PACKAGE. — MY DOUBLE

IN the year 186-, a long time after the great gold discoveries in Australia, I needed money, and was anxious to work for it, so determined to take passage in the ship *Iowa*, Captain Crescent, from San Francisco, where I had not met with much success in mining, bookkeeping, or trading. For one hundred dollars Captain Crescent agreed to land me on the shores of Hobson's Bay, Victoria, provided I should do some writing for him on the passage, settle his accounts, listen to his yarns, and energetic oaths, regarding his treatment by commission houses and boarding-house keepers, sailors, and runners of the Golden City. I kept my promises, and the master of the ship was faithful to his word; but I fear that I heard more first-class profanity on that sixty-days' passage than was good for a young man of nineteen, who had been tenderly reared by a loving mother, and who had been in the habit of associating with men who did not swear, except under great provocation. Who I was, and why I was seeking my fortune on the shores of the Pacific, will be revealed in the course of this true and minute history of my early life. Of our passage from San Francisco I will say but little, for a more disagreeable voyage I never experienced, as our men were ignorant and brutal, hardly one of them knowing the duties of a sailor, many of them shanghæ'd from the shore during a drunken stupor, while the officers were impatient, cross, and tyrannical, and gave their orders with blows, and the latter usually preceded the former. The ship was a floating hell, yet as a passenger I suffered but little discomfort, and was on friendly terms with master, mates, and crew, and never failed to lend a helping hand in dressing a sailor's wounds, when a scalp was laid open with a belaying pin, fid, capstan bar, or marlinspike. I was looked upon as the surgeon of the vessel, and had free access to the medicine chest, and thus was enabled to soothe many a poor fellow's pain, which might have gone unrelieved for all the officers cared.

"Angus," said Captain Crescent one morning at breakfast, the fifty-ninth day of our departure from the Golden Gate, "if the wind holds I shall land you on Australian soil tomorrow forenoon. We are making ten knots an hour, and Hobson's Bay is just two hundred miles distant."

"I hope we shall see a good deal of each other while you are in port," I replied.

"I hope not," was the gruff response; and then, looking up at the tell-tale compass over his head, growled out to the steward, "Go on deck, and tell that swab at the wheel that if he does not keep the ship on her course I will come up, and belt him over the head with a rope's end. —— him! where is he going to?"

The steward delivered the order, and returned to the cabin to wait upon the table.

"No, Angus," the master said, after the tell tale had showed that the vessel was once more on her course, "I hope we shall part in Hobson's Bay, and that when we again run afoul of each other it will be in China, or the States. Blast the countries where gold is dug out of the earth by the shovelful. It spoils sailors, and makes a captain an old man afore his time."

"I thought you intended to take in a cargo of wool for the London market," I remarked.

"There's just where you fools yourself, and so does all the men on board. Lord! how the scamps would cut and run if the anchor was down over night. I've kept this thing kinder quiet like, to keep the boys in good humor, but now I don't mind tellin' yer that if there is no cargo for me all ready, then up goes the helm, and I 'm off to China, for tea."

"How are you to know?" I asked.

And I saw that the chief mate began to look a little glum, as though disappointed.

"My ship's number will be displayed at the fore, and the signal station will repeat it, and then a tug will come off, and bring instructions from the firm I am consigned to. If wool is cheap and plenty, then down goes my mud-hook. If not, I 'm off to China for the same firm."

"And how am I to get ashore?" I demanded.

"In the tug, with all yer dunnage, unless yer want to go to China with me. I a'n't mean, and won't charge yer a dollar for yer passage."

The mate hastily left the table, with a troubled face. The master chuckled.

"——— him!" he said, "I believe he 'd desart with the rest of 'm jist as quick as wink. O Lordy! won't it be fun to see the faces of the loblolly cusses, if I have to square away, and make for China, through Torres' Straits."

The idea so pleased the captain, that he laughed until he was purple in the face, and small streams of coffee spurted all over the table, until I felt that I was undergoing a warm shower bath.

"Get all yer dunnage ready, Angus," said the captain, as soon as he recovered breath, "and be ready for a sudden surge, for time will be money tomorrow, if this wind holds. Damn that feller at the wheel, he 's off his course agin. I 'll belt his blasted head off!"

He bolted from the cabin, and in a few seconds I heard cries of pain, and felt the ship jar, and then heard the sharp crack of a spar, and, when I went on deck, saw that the "belting" of the man at the wheel had resulted in a sudden luff, and the carrying away of the foretopmast studding-sail boom.

"——— yer!" roared the now thoroughly angered master, "I 'll make yer pay for that spar. I 'll take it out of yer wages, as sure as you 're a sogger. Send another man to the wheel, and let this jemmy ducks help get up another boom."

The sailor's face was bleeding as he walked forward, and there was murder in his eyes as he passed to the leeward of the mainmast.

"Keep quiet, Jack," I said, as he passed me. "I will come forward and dress the cuts, as soon as the old man goes below."

He growled his thanks; but if the master had stood where I was standing he would have felt the blow of a sheath knife in his side. or I am much mistaken.

I dressed the man's head and face in the course of the forenoon, and my patient muttered his thanks, and said that he would not forget a good turn, and would remember a bad one for a good many years.

The next morning, just at daylight, the captain opened the door of my stateroom, and shouted, —

"Come, rouse out of this. Land is in sight, and by four bells we shall be in the bay."

I threw on my clothes, and ran on deck. It was broad daylight by the time I stood alongside the captain, on the heel of the bowsprit, and saw for the first time the dark shores of Australia, relieved here and there by patches of white sand, and bold, savage-looking rocks, where many a noble vessel had left her ribs before the era of light-houses and reliable charts.

"Well," asked the master, with a grin on his mahogany-colored face, "what do yer think of yer new home?"

"Wait until a year from now, and I will answer your question. Now I am too much occupied with thoughts of the future to reply."

"Ah," snarled the master, "the more yer see of the place and people the less yer will like them. Most of the men were transported for crimes, and, damn me, if I don't think they deserved all they received."

"Surely," I remarked, "there must be some good, honest people in Australia."

"There may be, but I have never heard of them."

And, with this parting snarl at some of the most enterprising and hospitable people in the world, the master walked aft, and left me to ruminate on the prejudices of seamen, and the beauty of the coast, and the dark-blue water through which we were passing at a rapid rate, followed by schools of porpoises, and flocks of sea fowl, the latter nearly coming on board, in their eagerness to scrutinize the ship and the people moving about the decks, while they darted with the swiftness of lightning at every bit of matter that was thrown overboard, in the hope of receiving a morsel of grease or meat for breakfast.

We ran along the coast until seven bells, and then a pilot-boat came out from behind a bold headland, and stood along on the wind, so as to intercept us.

"Blast him," muttered the captain, "I know the way in, but I must take him, I suppose. In with the topmast studding-sails, and stand by to brace up the headyards, so as to lay the maintopsail to the mast. Rig in the booms, and unreef the geer, Mr. Mallet. We sha'n't want any spare canvas for today, at least."

In half an hour's time the pilot-boat was alongside of us, and sent us a red-headed, grisly old fellow, with a squint in one eye, and a small hump on his back, the effect of bending over yardarms in English seventy-fours, during gales of wind, when reefing and furling had to be done in a hurry, or a dozen blows of the cat on the bare back rewarded the last man off the yard.

"Cap'en," growled the old pilot, as soon as he touched the deck, "have you got a bloody piece of 'bacca to give a mate what a'n't had a chaw for the last twenty-four hours? and while you is about it jist tell the steward to fetch a tot of grog. Put yer helm up, and let her slide. Well yer foreyard. Steady as yer go. How long afore breakfast will be ready?"

The steward brought the old fellow a tot of grog, and a hand of navy plug tobacco, and once more we headed for the dark rocks that guard the entrance to Port Phillip and Hobson's Bay.

The pilot knew but little about wool, and cared less. He said that there was a rousing lot of gold being parbuckled out of the mines at Ballarat, and other places, and there was some good strikes all round, but he did n't pay much attention to 'em, as piloting was good enough for him, at his time of life.

"I should think it would be," muttered the captain. "A hundred dollars for taking the ship in, and another hundred for taking her out. What are gold mines alongside of that?"

We ate breakfast, and then I packed up my baggage, — a hammock and a clothes-bag; and while I was thus occupied the captain entered the cabin.

"Angus," he said, "how much money have yer in yer lockers? Enough to take care of yer till yer finds somethin' to do?"

"Yes, sir; I have just one hundred sovereigns in a belt around my waist."

"Well, that a'n't none too much. Them fellows will steal the teeth right out of yer, if they gets the chance. You have been a pretty good boy on the passage, and so here 's fifty dollars. I refund yer half of yer money. Yer may want it, and the owners won't miss it."

I thanked the captain for his kindness, and took the gold; for I was not sure but that I had earned it during the passage.

"And, Angus," said the old man, "do yer think yer will go to the mines?"

"Yes, sir, if I can't find a good situation in Melbourne. I know something about digging gold, and quartz mining, and, perhaps, I may find a fortune in the country if not in the city."

"And what will yer do if yer meet with some of them bushranging thieves? The country is full of 'em."

"I have a nice revolver, and know how to use it."

"Bah! a revolver a'n't much agin a dozen bloody scoundrels what would cut yer throat in no time for a York shillin'. Tell yer what I'll do, Angus. I've got a repeating rifle; fires seven shots as quick as wink, and can do sure work, too. Yer shall have it, my lad; and may it do yer some good when yer want a steady hand and a cool head. Here it is. Yer see that it all comes apart. Well, now stow it away in yer bag, and no one will dream that it is there."

I was delighted with the gift, but made some show of refusing it. The captain, whose heart seemed to expand as the time for parting came, insisted on my accepting the present, and, to the captain's kindness and forethought, I am now enabled to write the various changes of my eventful history, for more than once has that little repeating rifle, weighing not more than six pounds, stood between me and death, when ambushed by the natives of Australia, or the still more cruel bushrangers, who murder for the sake of shedding blood, and rob when they can't use the proceeds of their expedition.

The signals were run up to the fore, and were answered from the signal station on the borders of the bay, on a high bluff that overlooked an immense expanse of water. In a few minutes we saw a steam tug coming toward us at a rapid rate.

"Now we shall know all about our fate in a few minutes," the captain said. "Pilot, had n't we better wait for that fellow here? I don't want to go nearer the anchorage than I can help, unless obliged to."

"Sartainly, cap. Anything for a quiet life, as the convict said, when they gagged him for using too much lip. Brace up the foreyard, haul up the foresail, round in the cross-jack braces. Put yer helm to port. So, steady. Gently with her. Ease off the spanker sheet a little, or you'll have the old hooker comin' round on another tack. She works like a pilot-boat. Most of the Yankee clipper ships do. So. Well, all. Stand by to give 'em a rope, and see that the d—d thieves don't cut off a fathom, when they cast it off."

And, while the pilot was thus handling the ship, and giving advice, the old *Iowa* came to the wind, with her maintopsail to the mast, and remained stationary, as a tug ran alongside, and a person, whom I took to be the skipper, hailed, —

"Is this the *Iowa*, from San Francisco, to call for orders?"

"Yes. What news for us?" asked Captain Crescent.

"Here's the papers. Yer can see for yerself," was the answer; and he passed up a package on the end of a boat-hook.

The captain broke the seal, and read the note that was addressed to him. The mate and second mate drew near the "old man" with anxious faces. They wanted to know the destination of the ship.

"Holy Moses!" cried the master, "this is good enough for me. No wool, and no freight. We're off for China and tea."

A suppressed groan escaped from the mates, and they looked at each other in despair, while the crew, who caught the bad news from the elated expression of the captain's face, clustered together, and seemed to meditate mutiny.

"Skipper," shouted Captain Crescent, to the master of the tug, "I want yer to land a passenger for me, and here's a plug of tobacco to pay yer for your trouble."

He flung a package of navy plug to the deck of the tug as he spoke.

"All right," was the answer. "Pass over his dunnage, for I'm in a hurry. I've got to tow a bark down the Yarra at twelve."

Some of the men passed my hammock and clothes-bag over the side, and then I shook hands with the captain and mate, and, as I did so, the latter whispered, —

"Wish I was goin' with yer. We're tired of this bloody old hooker, and every one on board."

"So 'long, my lad," said Captain Crescent. "Hope ye'll make yer fortune, and won't be cleaned out by the bushrangers. Take care of yer money. Better bank it as soon as possible, for them people on shore will steal if they has a chance."

I passed over the side, the line was cast off, and the tug steamed away, while the ship wore short round on her heel, braced sharp up, and stood out of the bay.

"So yer a Yankee, a'n't yer?" asked the skipper of the tug, as we steamed along, after I had waved a farewell to the old ship, which I must confess I left with a heavy heart.

"What makes you think I am a Yankee?" I inquired.

"Wall, yer looks like a cross between a Frenchman and a Yankee. Whar is you going?"

"Melbourne."

"Know any one thar?"

"Not a soul."

"What is yer goin' to do when yer gets there?" the skipper asked.

"Don't know. Have n't made up my mind as yet."

"Wall," continued the skipper, as he gnawed off a huge chunk of the tobacco which Captain Crescent had given him, "if yer is a cross between a Yankee and a Frenchman yer 'll own half of Melbourne in less than ten years. They is jist the awfulest coves to get on that we has around here."

We steamed on past the shipping lying at anchor at William's Town, with the flags of all nations flying, and, to give variety to the scene, I noticed two English frigates, and a French seventy-four, just outside of the peaceable merchant vessels.

"I 'm going up the Yarra for a tow, and will land yer at Melbourne in less than half an hour. Ever here afore?"

"Never. All seems strange and new to me. I think I shall like Australia."

"Don't be too sure of that, lad," growled the skipper. "Many coves has thought the same thing when they has arrived from a long voyage, but they has changed all that in less than a year. When I fust came here I thought the place was a paradise; but afore one month I wished myself and the whole country in a red-hot — Wall, never mind whar. Whar are yer goin' now, yer South-Spain booby?"

This last remark was addressed to a fishing-boat, or yawl, which was attempting to cross the bows of the tug, and required the skipper to shut off steam, or run the fellow down.

"I 'd like to smash 'em," the irate skipper said, as he passed the boat, the inmates of which saluted us with ironical cheers, and some gestures which would not be considered polite in fashionable society, or among the crème de la crème of Beacon Street and Commonwealth Avenue.

I must give our tug's crew the high praise of saying that to all the insults and gestures they returned word for word, motion for motion, and oath for oath. I had heard profanity in the mines of California, and in the gambling hells of San Francisco, but for original, utterly utter swearing that which I listened to on the Yarra-Yarra (the meaning of which in the native tongue denotes flowing flowing) surpassed all previous experiences in God-defying expressions

"The miserable, ticket-of-leave sons of the devil!" growled the skipper. "I shall have to fetch 'em some day. Human natur can't stand it much longer. These blasted cusses has the right of way, and they knows it, but I shall have to fetch 'em some time. Go ahead, and let 's get up the river some time today. Oh, how I should like to, but I s'pose I should have to pay for it; and yet how much better for the place if sich rats was drowned as they deserve."

In a few minutes the skipper recovered something of his good-nature, and resumed his subject, broken off by the encounter with the fishermen, who were now far astern.

"Yes, sir," he said, "the first few months I was here I did wish an earthquake would swallow up the whole island, but now I feels quite content with my lot."

"What has produced such a change in your disposition?" I asked.

The skipper looked at me rather sharply, while the man who was steering the tug, and had heard all of the conversation, turned away his head so that his superior could not see the grin that spread all over his face, from ear to ear, as he tried to suppress a hearty laugh.

"Never yer mind what has changed me," the master said. "If yer had to do the work that I did once, yer 'd cuss the day yer was born."

And then the man, with a scowl on his sun-burned face, walked aft to see about his tow-line.

"He vos transported for ten years, and had to work on the roads all that time," whispered the wheelman, as soon as the skipper turned his back. "He vos a hard one, and no mistake. But he 's all right now, and vould n't steal from his brother unless he had a gallus chance."

"What was he transported for?" I inquired.

"Oh, vell, he mashed a shipmate's head, and took all his chink. The man he died did arter a vile, and so the big vigs sent him out here to mend the roads, and, I tell yer, he was kept at it pretty vell till he got his ticket-of-leave, and ven his sentence vas hout he jist staid here. But he 's all right how." The man at the wheel was silent for a moment, and then asked, "Say, has yer got much chink in yer pocket?"

"No, very little."

"All right. I vos in 'opes yer had lots, so that yer could tip the boys some beer. But I say, youngster, mum is the word, yer knows."

"Yes, certainly."

"And if I vos you, you know, ven the skipper recommended me to go to a certain boarding-'ouse, yer know, don't yer see I 'd go to some other, yer know. But mum is the vord, yer know. But 'ere ve is, right alongside the bark vot ve is to tow down the river, and I thinks they is all ready for us."

The engine stopped, and we run alongside of a small English bark, that did not draw more than ten feet of water aft, and was lying at Queen's Wharf, a nice looking pier, that was just opposite a wide street.

"Pass up the gentleman's dunnage," cried the master of the steam-tug; and, while the men were doing so, he asked, "Do yer know where to go? Do yer want a nice, quiet boarding-house, where the cost won't be much, and the lush and grub is first-class? If yer do, say the word, and I can put yer on the track of a bully place, kept by a widder woman, what would just coddle the life out of a fine-looking youngster like yer. She 'd keep yer away from the gals."

"Thanks," I said, remembering the warning of the wheelman, "I shall go to some hotel, and look about me for a few days, before I settle down in a boarding or lodging house."

"All right, mate, have it yer own way. I has taken a fancy to yer, and would like to help a good-looking, decent lad like yer. That face of yern will lead yer in some bad mess with the girls afore yer has been ashore twenty-four hours, unless yer has some old mother likely to ballast yer with good advice."

I blushed and laughed at his flattery, and, had I not been warned by the wheelman, would have taken the skipper's advice, for I now more than half suspect the fellow gave me a dose of romance because he thought that there was a good field to practice on a greenhorn who did not know the ways of the country.

Had I listened to the master of the steam-tug, had I but asked the names of the former and latter, gone to the boarding-house which was presided over by the careful old widow, much embarrassment would have been spared me, and I could then have referred with confidence to the statements which I had to make that same evening. But I did nothing of the kind, and so was the innocent and careless means of producing a state of affairs which even romance has hardly ever equaled by the most vivid imagination. Fate willed it otherwise, much to my regret at the time, and to my own unhappiness and that of others. Who could have supposed, seeing me land on Queen's Wharf, that bright summer morning in November, that before midnight I was to be united in marriage to the Belle of Australia, the handsomest young lady that ever walked the streets of Melbourne or Sydney, rich, proud, disdainful of all common things, who had rejected scores of lovers, and whose heart had never been touched by the arrows of the god of Love, so far as was known by society?

My baggage, what little I had, was removed to the wharf, and then pitching a two-dollar-and-a-half gold piece to the thirsty deck hands, bade them drink my health, or spend the money as they thought best. They seemed to think that beer was the right thing just at that time, for all hands left the tug, and rushed to the nearest saloon at the head of the pier, much to the disgust of the master, who swore at the men, and at me, in no measured terms. I did not hear the conclusion of his peppery remarks, but hailed a drayman, who was sitting on his team laughing at the skipper and crew, and throwing in a word or two of slang when an opportunity offered, and asked him if he wanted a job.

"Yes, and some beer at the same time," was the ready answer.

"All right. The job first, and the beer afterward. Pile those duds on your cart, and let us be off."

"Whar to?"

The skipper stopped swearing to listen to the directions, but I was determined he should not know my destination, so replied, —

"Oh, put on the baggage, and I'll tell you when we get off the wharf."

The man loaded the few effects which I owned, and then I mounted on the dray, and up the pier we rattled.

"Stranger here?" asked the driver.

"Yes."

"Yankee or Frenchman?"

"Yankee."

"Thought so. If yer had said luggage should just took my Bible oath that yer was French. Only Yankees says baggage. Get up, yer lazy devil; are yer goin' to sleep?"

The last remark was addressed to the horse, which had stopped as though exhausted at the prospect before him. Every rib in his body was visible, and his coat was like the quills on a porcupine, never having felt brush or cloth.

"Where can I find a cheap hotel?" I asked, as we moved along through the crowded streets.

"Yer means a chop house, where yer can lodge, and grub when yer likes. That's what yer means, I s'pose," the drayman said.

"You have caught my meaning. Name the place."

"Well, there's the Hen and Chickens. The lush is good, and the charges is moderate."

"Is the hotel located in a nice place?"

"Well, I should think it was. Near Collins Street, the banks, and all the swell places."

"Are the charges moderate?"

"A crown a day for a slap-up room, and the grub hextra. It's a paradise for them what has the blunt, and the lush is good, and no mistake."

"What do you mean by lush?"

The man looked at me in a contemptuous manner, as though I was a little too green to converse with an enlightened citizen of Melbourne. At length he answered, —

"I s'posed that any blessed fool knowed that lush meant drink. Where in the devil's name did yer come from?"

"San Francisco," I answered. "They have as big rascals there as can be found in Melbourne, but I don't think they call drink lush."

The fellow's face clouded for a moment, then he said, —

"Great place San Francisco. Have a cousin there. P'aps yer know him. Darky Dunder. He's in the crimping line."

"Crimping hair?" I asked, without a smile on my face, and as grave as a judge of the Supreme Court of Massachusetts when he is not certain on a law point."

"Crimping the devil! No, he gets sailors drunk, and then ships 'em afore they knows it, and when they wakes up they is on the 'bounding blue,' as the poet says. Is yer a poet?"

"No."

"Well, yer kinder looks like one. I had a cousin once what was a poet. O cracky! how he could jist sling the words and beer at the same time. He was a pot boy in Lunnon."

"Where is he now?"

"Dead. Drank too much swipes, and seed things; and one day he said the devil was arter him, and he jist slashed a razor across his throat, and that settled him."

The remembrance of his cousin's fate set the fellow to musing, and, while he held his tongue, I admired the broad streets, and stately buildings which we passed, and, just as we turned a corner, a nice-looking gentleman, who was waiting for us to move, looked up at me, smiled, and actually took off his hat, and bowed to me in the politest manner.

I knew that he did not know me, but I returned his bow, and smiled in return. I was not to be outdone in politeness.

"Thought yer was a stranger here," growled the driver.

"So I am."

"Strangers don't have the richest man in Melbourne bow to 'em, and take off his hat as though yer was one of the tip-top swells."

"Some mistake," I replied.

"I believe yer are givin' me sour beer," was the response, which, as near as I could understand, meant what we call "taffy."

Just then an elegant carriage, with a driver and footman, in livery, came along, and a fine-looking old lady, glancing out of the window, saw me, smiled, and then bowed, and waved a lace handkerchief in greeting.

I responded to the salute with a bow, and a flourish of my hat, which was really a nice Panama, that no person need to have been ashamed of.

"Well, I'm blowed!" gasped the driver. "If this 'ere thing keeps on I'll tell yer what I means to do."

"Well, tell me."

"I'll drive right up to the Government 'Ouse, that's what I'll do. A cove what has rich old gals like that bow to 'em, a'n't the kind of chicken for a cheap lushing crib."

"Yet I do not know the lady, and assure you that I never saw her before, as far as I am aware."

"Not know her? Does yer mean to tell me that yer don't know the lieutenant-governor's wife when yer sees her?"

"I never saw the lady before, I am certain."

The driver gazed at me in silence for a moment, and then muttered "sour beer," whipped his horse, as if in revenge for my conduct, and, after a while, asked, —

"Well, shall it be the Government 'Ouse or the Hen and Chickens?"

"First tell me," I responded, "can I obtain a clean bed and civil treatment at the Hen and Chickens?"

"No better in Melbourne. They is on style there, and would n't take in a cove like me 'cos I don't dress well enough; and then the lush is about " —

"Never mind the lush. You have told me that before."

"And I'll tell it to yer agin and agin, if I wants to. When a place keeps good stuff it had oughter be advertised. There is lots of poor liquors sold here, and, if yer is on the drink, yer 'll find it out afore a great while."

By this time we were in such a crowded thoroughfare that I did not relish being perched on the team, so slipped off, and told the man that I would follow him to my chop house, as I imagined that I could see the city to better advantage from the sidewalk.

"All right," he responded. "I thought yer would sicken of me afore long."

I walked along the sidewalk, and met many well-dressed gentlemen, some of whom stared at me in a very bold manner, and two or three raised their hats quite respectfully, and would have stopped and exchanged some words with me, had I not hurried on, being fearful of losing sight of the dray driver.

Of course all this attention was a puzzle to me, but I thought that it was a genial custom of the city to show a little courtesy to strangers, and that all whom I met recognized me as such. In fact, one old gentleman, with a sharp face, thin, upright form, tall and dignified, a grizzly mustache and goatee, stopped directly in front of me, and said in French, with a smile, and a shrug of his straight shoulders, —

"Bon jour, monsieur."

"Bon jour," I responded, for I did not want to disappoint such a smiling and courteous gentleman, a Frenchman of the old school, and, perhaps, a member of the old régime.

"Je suis content de vous voir ici," the stranger continued, and bowed quite low, and raised his hat, and swept it through the air like a broadsword.

Thanks to my dear mother, who had learned the French language while living abroad the first few years of her wedded life, I had acquired some knowledge of the tongue, and, therefore, knew that the French gentleman had said that he was very much pleased to meet me.

"Merci, monsieur," I answered, "vous êtes très polis."

In the mean while the confounded drayman was disappearing, and I saw him grin at me as though he was delighted at my being interrupted.

"Bon jour, monsieur," I cried, as I tried to pass him, but he put his hat on his head, laid one long, bony hand on my arm, and whispered, —

"Attendez, monsieur. Je vous dis."

"But, confound it, I can't wait," I said, "and as for telling me 'attendez,' let it go for some other time."

"Ecoutez moi," smiled the gallant Frenchman. "When married you is to be on the day much hurry you is. Hey. Bien, think I should. Hey?"

"Yes, naturally," wondering what the old fellow was driving at.

"Your fiancée, sweetheart, yours. Hey?"

"Oh, yes," I replied. "Je vous comprend."

"C'est bon. Good it is. Nice girl, little. Petite. Hey?"

"Certainly. Never saw a nicer lady in my life," and again I attempted to dodge him, but was unsuccessful.

I thought the old fellow mad, or love-cracked on some girl, and would humor him to the best of his bent.

In the mean time, the drayman had coralled his team in the gutter, and gone in to a saloon for a glass of beer. He could not pass one without stopping. His horse dropped its head, and went to sleep, for which I was thankful, for I feared the Frenchman would hold on to me until an earthquake shook him to some other part of the city.

"Oui," murmured the Frenchman, "très petite. Très jolie. Hey. Oh, milord, lucky is you. Dame. Twenty years myself younger I take her. Vot you calls cut out. Hey. Bonne girl. Wants title all the time. Parbleu. S'il vous plaît, mad you is not. Hey?"

"Non, sans doute."

"Diantre, blame her do not I, when a bon garçon like you for her love does ask, and makes her a lady to be. Hey?"

"Well, I should be surprised if she did not strike her flag under the circumstances."

And then I saw that blessed drayman come out of the beer shop, and wipe his mouth with the back of his hand.

"Non, non," gesticulated the Frenchman, with a wave of his hands, and a movement of his shoulders that made me fear the bones would crack. "Non, a Frenchman strike never a woman, and Englishman should Frenchman like follow. You such things vil do not. Hey?"

"I would die first," I answered.

Then the lunatic seized my hand in both of his own, and pressed it most fervently.

"Bon milord. Mille merci, I better know you would not. She dear to me, very. Friend's daughter, old."

"Yes, I know. Bon ami, and all that."

"Alors, go you, monsieur, to the house of your fiancée?"

"Well, not just at present. I have other fish to fry."

"Poisson! Vot? Vot de debil de poisson to do vid de fiancée? Hey?"

He stared at me in silence for a moment, and then a smile broke over his white, thin face.

"Ah, oui. De poisson for de dinner. Oui. It now I see. It is bon. Go you now where?"

"To my hotel," with a grand air.

"Vel, milord, vil you for me take von little ding your wife for?" the crank asked, with a bland smile.

"No, not today."

And I attempted to pass the old gentleman, and join the drayman, but the Frenchman would not permit me to do so.

"Attendez, milord. C'est dommage, hurry you. Hey? The bonne petite vil expect some dings her old ami from. Oui. Disappoint her vil I not. Jamais. Prenez le vite."

And, as he spoke, he thrust into my hands a small package, and then, with a simple, "Au revoir, monsieur. Pas besoin de me remercier,' and away he went.

"Hold on," I said, as I ran after him. "Arretez. Wait a moment, will you, and listen to me? There is some horrible mistake in all this. I am not what I seem. You have lost your tête. Your head is gone. Regardez vous, monsieur, for a moment. What are you giving me? I am a stranger, but I will not take you in. Will you stop a moment?"

"Tonight, see you will I," was all the Frenchman would answer, and into Collins Street he went, as I thought, and entered the doors of the Melbourne club house, and I lost sight of him.

"Decidedly," I said to myself, "this city is full of cranks, and that Frenchman is the boss of them all."

Putting the package, small and compact, not larger than an under-sized orange, in my pocket, I walked hastily toward the drayman, but found that he had returned to the saloon, and was having some more beer. But he soon came out, and, when he saw me, remarked,—

"Yer is the swell what did not know people here. Oh, yes. Sour beer."

"If you keep on drinking you will smell like sour beer," I replied; and then the true-hearted Briton turned on me in his wrath.

"Did n't yer say that yer knows nobody? and did n't I wait for yer while yer gabbled with that old Frenchman? and did n't yer make a motion for me to go in and have a drink, and that yer 'd pay for it?"

I did not answer the charge, and the fellow continued,—

"And a'n't yer goin' to pay me an hextra shillin' for waitin'?"

"Yes, if you proceed, and say no more about it."

"All right. Yer a'n't a bad sort of swell, if yer do salts the truth a little when yer wants to."

We turned into Elizabeth Street, and then stopped before a plain, three-story house, with a sign board, on which was painted, in bright, pretentious colors, a red-and-yellow hen and a brood of chickens.

"'Ere yer are, sir," said the drayman. "This is the old Hen and Chickens, and I 'ope yer 'onor won't forget to give a willin', 'ard-workin' man a pot of beer."

"Wait until I see if I can get accommodated here," I replied, and passed into the tap-room, where I encountered the head waiter, a bald-headed man, with immense shirt collar, and hair so red and stiff that he could have cooked a dinner by merely putting kettles on his shoulders, and splitting his beard and the hair around his temples for kindling wood.

"Can I engage a room here?" I asked, as the waiter came toward me, and beamed warmly upon me.

"Room, sir? Yes, sir. Vot kind of a room, sir?"

"A sleeping-room, quiet and comfortable."

"For 'ow long, sir? Yes, sir, if you please, sir."

"I don't know. It may be for a day, and it may be for a month. I am undecided."

"Vell, sir, ve hexpects our guests, them vot is not known to us, sir, to pay in adwance, sir. No hoffence, sir, 'cos none is intended."

"I am ready to comply with the custom. Show me the room, and let me see what it is like."

"Yes, sir. Vill yer follow me, sir? Bill, look out for the bar a minute."

I liked the room. It was clean, and large enough to accommodate me, and my belongings. The bed was not bad, and seemed to have had fresh sheets put on that very morning.

"A crown a day," hummed the head waiter.

"I will take it. Let the boots bring up my luggage at once."

"Yes, sir, and a shillin' to me for showin' yer the room."

"Anything more?"

"A shillin' to boots for bringin' up yer luggage."

"What else?"

"Vell, the chambermaid should n't be forgotten, sir."

"Anybody else?"

"Vell, sir, ve vill think of some other little hextras arter a vile."

"Don't be modest, my friend. Remember when you get a guest squeeze him all you can. It looks so English-like that I should grow homesick unless a waiter was continually asking for fees. But go and send up my traps, and here is your shilling, and one for boots," and then the waiter rubbed his bald head and left me.

But I had to go down-stairs, and pay a crown to the drayman, and to stand the beer, but at last I was settled in the house as a lodger. But still I wanted an American luxury,—a warm bath, a comfortable shave, and a thorough shampooing. The head waiter had heard of some kind of a bath in Great Bourke Street, where people got scalded for a reasonable sum. He did n't know about it personally. He never bathed. "It vos n't 'ealthy in that part of the vorld. Vould I please to order dinner?"

No, I would not dine until I had bathed and shaved and dressed.

Then I thought of the package that the crazy Frenchman had forced on me, and of the money which I had in a belt around my person. I opened the package, and, to my surprise, found that it consisted of an exquisite jewel-box, made of pure gold, and contained a pair of diamond ear-drops, that were so brilliant and large I almost dropped them, so astonished was I at the unexpected sight. I ran to the door, and locked it, as soon as I had recovered from the effect of the first emotion, and then examined the jewels at my leisure. They were steel-blue, a color so rare and valuable, and must have weighed six carats each, and cost, as far as I could judge, in the neighborhood of twelve thousand dollars, while the box in which they were inclosed, a beautiful specimen of art, and made of solid gold, must have been worth more than a thousand dollars.

What to do with the jewels I did not know. They had been thrust upon me in the most mysterious manner, and in spite of my remonstrances, yet I knew if they were found upon me, and I could give only my weak explanation, that the law would make short work of me. I thought the subject all over, and then determined to conceal the box on my person, and when I went to bathe to keep a sharp lookout for the crazy Frenchman, and return the casket to him in spite of his refusals to take it. Then I re-covered it with paper, and went down-stairs, feeling very serious, and rather anxious for my personal safety.

"Where is the proprietor of the Hen and Chickens?" I asked of the head waiter.

"Vell, sir, 'e 's gone to a 'oss trot, or a prize fight, I does not know vich. If yer vants to leave some dosh vid 'im I 'll take care of it."

"I think a bank would be the best place. Some of my money might be wagered on the wrong horse, or the weakest man."

The waiter stared at me, but did not reply. He slowly drew a glass of beer, and drank it, and then nodded his bald head and grinned, as much as to say, "You see that I 'm a good patron of the bar when the proprietor is absent."

I went in search of a bathing establishment, and found one on Market Square, where I astonished the proprietor, who happened to be a barber, by asking for a shave, hair trimming, shampooing, and a warm bath.

"My hyes," the fellow said, "I thinks some von is habout to get married. I 'm not in that line meself, sir, but I likes to see the young ones kinder mix up like ven business is good. It vould be a pity to cut off too much of that curly 'air, sir. It is wery nice, sir, wery, and the ladies always goes for a gent vot 'as 'air like yours, sir. Dark-brown, and wery fine, and wery curly, sir. As nice a 'ead of 'air as ever come in this establishment. I keeps the best in Melbourne, sir. Stranger 'ere, a'n't yer, sir?"

"Yes, somewhat."

"I thought so, sir. Vell, yer just come to the right place, and no mistake. Nice smooth skin for a razor. It's a pleasure to shave sich a cheek as you 'as. Don't shave hoften, does yer, sir?"

"No, not more than once a week."

"Thought not. Now if you vould let me take off that slight mustache, sir, it vould grow wery thick in the course of a few months. It is light, and no mistake, but it can be made to grow vid a little of my 'air sprouter. Honly a crown a bottle, and it vill last you six months. The governor-general uses it every mornin', and vould n't do vithout it, on no account votever. His vife jist hankers arter it all the time, and all the ladies of the city has it on their tables."

"Let the mustache alone," I managed to say.

"All right, sir. I know that some vimmen like a man all the better if he has but a feeble mustache. They says that a 'eavy one tickles 'em too much ven they is kissed. Don't care for sich things meself, but some men does ven they is young. They gets all hover it ven they gets their hyes open, sir, as the sayin' is. Now ve vill have a crack at that 'air. Wery nice 'air, and I 'll be wery careful of it. It's sich 'air as the vimmin likes. Now some of my customers has 'air like marlinspikes, yer know, and it is no pleasure to me to cut sich 'air. But yours is so different. Quite harristocratic 'air, sir, and no mistake. Some sich 'air, sir, as the nobility has, sir."

"If you won't say another word about my hair or mustache I 'll give you an extra shilling," I said.

"Vell, sir, the temptation is wery great, and I 'll try and hearn the extra bob. But ven a gent comes into my shop vid such a fine "—

"Remember," I cried, "you are on dangerous ground."

"So I am, sir. I 'll keep my mouth shut, sir, about the 'air, sir, and yer shall have no cause to complain."

And the fellow really kept his word; yet I can't say that I was greatly offended at his words, for youth does like flattery as well as old age. My hair was trimmed and washed, and then a warm bath made me feel like a bridegroom, as the barber said.

I paid the man a crown, and asked him where was the best and safest bank in Melbourne.

"Vell, sir, they is hall slap bang up, but the safest of hall, sir, is, I think, the Horiental, on Collins Street. Jist turn to the right, and then to the left, go ahead a vile, and there yer is. Yer won't take any of my "—

But I left him while he was extolling his hair invigorator.

I had placed my sovereigns, one hundred of them, in a bag, for convenience sake, while the casket of diamonds I secured in my bosom, underneath my clothes, so that no one could steal it from me, even if I was asleep, without disturbing me. The jewels were too valuable to run any risk by carrying them in my pockets.

I had to make several inquiries to find the Oriental Bank, in spite of the clear directions of the barber, but at last I found the building, a massive structure, that would have reflected honor on any stone palace in State Street, Boston. I had no difficulty in making a deposit, and in writing my name, so that, if I drew a check or draft, the cashier would know that the signature was all right.

By the time I had concluded my business it was two o'clock, and I felt as though a good dinner would not come amiss, for I had eaten nothing since an early breakfast on board the *Iowa*.

I sauntered along the broad, nice streets, filled with wagons drawn by six and eight bullocks, some by horses, and quite frequently a mule team, of extra pretensions, loaded with wool, hides, fire-wood, vegetables, and fruits, and driven by men who were armed with whips, six yards long, and short handles, not more than a foot and a half in length, but which were used with terrible force in the hands of the half-brutal-looking stockmen. Sometimes I saw a native black, with only a rag tied around his waist, trotting beside the oxen, and punching them with short spears, if the beasts did not move as fast as was required by their owners. Three or four times I met well-dressed gentlemen, who took off their hats, and bowed quite low to me, and would have stopped and spoken if I had shown a disposition to exchange compliments, but I had seen enough cranks for one day, and thought that the people of Melbourne would let me alone, and not be quite so civil, when my foreign air was worn off a little. So on I walked, and raised my hat when other people did, not wishing to be outdone in civility, and at last gained the shelter of the Hen and Chickens, and the head waiter, with his hair and face redder than ever, the effect of drinking beer in the forenoon, took my order for dinner, and gave me a nice piece of boiled mutton (the national dish), and some very good vegetables, one of them new to me, and closed the entertainment with a pot of half-and-half, a bit of cheese, and a very good pudding, for all of which I paid four shillings.

"If yer please, sir," the waiter said, as I paid him, and dropped thrippence in his hand, as his fee for service. "shall I send to the Royal Victoria Theatre, and get yer a seat for tonight? Great attraction, sir."

"What is the attraction?" I asked.

"Vy, sir, the Belle of Australia is to be married this 'ere afternoon, and she goes to the theatre in the hevening, and the governor-general is to be thar, and hall his haids, and the ladies, and hall the swells of the city. If yer has a hevenin' suit of clothes yer can get in, but, unless yer has, it's no go."

I had an evening dress suit in my clothes bag, but they had not seen the light of day for some time, and must be fearfully wrinkled, and I told the waiter so.

"Oh, never mind that, sir. Jist give 'em to me. I knows a cove vot vill take out all the vinkles, and make 'em as good as new."

"Well, come up-stairs, and get them, and be sure and secure me a seat. By the way," I asked, as I started for my room, "who is the Belle of Australia to marry?"

"Oh, a great swell. He's a Hinglish hearl, sir, I'm told, and vorth no end of money."

"Well, he's a lucky man, to marry so handsome a girl, and she's lucky in obtaining a title and so much money. Hope I shall see her tonight at the theatre."

"You'll be sure to, sir. Oh, she's a beauty, and no mistake. Hall the young men swear by her, she's so awful lovely."

I smiled, and went to my room, and, after giving the waiter my dress suit, to be restored to its original freshness, and requesting him to furnish me with a white necktie, and a light-colored pair of gloves, I felt so sleepy that I laid down, and went to sleep, and did not awaken until six o'clock, when I found my clothes at the door, all ready, and looking quite nice, in spite of a long voyage.

I dressed, and went down to the coffee-room, where I had a cup of tea, received my ticket, and a remark from the head waiter that I looked "wery much like a bridegroom, and that he vished I vas."

"There won't be a better lookin' swell in the theatre than vot you is," he asserted; and I did not contradict him, but the fellow received half a crown for his trouble and flattery. "'Ere is a vite rose for yer buttonhole. The chambermaid she sent it vid her regards. Blest if she ha'n't taken a shine to yer."

I thanked the girl, and went into the street to look at the city by gaslight, as the curtain did not rise until eight o'clock. I walked around, a light shawl over my shoulders, and, when I came in front of the Melbourne club-house, stopped to admire the building. It was then twilight, but on each side of the entrance two great lights showed the surroundings as plain as day.

Just as I stopped a light covered team drove up to the door. It was drawn by two dark horses, which looked as though they could trot, and, while I was admiring the animals, the door of the Melbourne opened, and three men came down the steps. They passed close to me, and the middle one, a young fellow, glanced at me, and started back, and I must confess that I was also astonished, for the youngster looked very much like me, as far as I could judge. Then one gentleman said, —

"For God's sake, my lord, do not hang back now. Your life, your future happiness, and everything, depends upon you. Get out of the city as quick as you can. Go to Gelong by land. This team will drive you all night, and in the morning you will be safe. I would not give a shilling for your life if you are found in the city tomorrow morning. That old Frenchman will carve you into mincemeat, and the brother and father riddle you with bullets. No one can ill treat the Belle of Australia and live. Every hand will be against you, and your death will be only a matter of hours, not days. Now go. Think of your mother, the countess, and go. We will send everything to you at Gelong, and keep your secret. Get out of the country as soon as you can, and don't return to it."

"But, doctor, I did n't mean to throw off like this, you know," cried the person who was addressed as "my lord." "Of course I can't marry her, but, —— it, you know, I like her, and was only having a little fun."

"Will you go, my lord?" cried the others; and they forced him into the vehicle, and struck the horses, and they were off like a shot.

The two gentlemen stood gazing after the carriage, until the sound of the horses' feet had died away. Then they whispered together for a long time, and at length turned to enter the club-house. As they did so, their eyes fell upon my face, and one of the gentlemen threw up his arms, and uttered a loud, wailing cry.

"My God!" he said, "he has come back to death and dishonor."

"WILL YOUR LORDSHIP PROMISE TO MAKE NO ATTEMPT TO ESCAPE?" ASKED THE CHIEF.

PART II

THE MEETING IN FRONT OF THE CLUB-HOUSE. — WHO AM I, AND WHAT HAVE I DONE? — A FRIEND OF THE FAMILY. — AN OLD ACQUAINTANCE ON THE POLICE. — MISS KITTY AND THE DIAMOND RING. — NO EXPLANATIONS RECEIVED OR WANTED.

THE gentleman who accompanied the one who threw up his arms, and uttered the exclamation, did not seem so excited as his friend. He merely removed the cigar from his mouth, and said in a quiet way, —

"I'll be —— if I'd insure your life, my lord, for a premium of dollar for dollar, pound for pound. I've seen simpletons, but you beat my time. I have done the best I could for you. I can do no more. What is the use when you will not take advice?"

"I was not aware that you had given any advice," I remarked, as I lighted a cigar, and, leaning against the iron lamp-post, smoked quite contentedly a weed which I had brought from San Francisco, and, therefore, felt assured that it was a good one.

The gentleman who claimed to have advised me, shrugged his shoulders like a Frenchman, and looked at his ardent friend, a man old enough to be his father, and simply said, —

"What more can I do?"

"A great deal. You can aid me in saving this willful young gentleman. He is like his father in some respects, and in others he is entirely different. Oh! but I did love his father, and he loved me. We were shipmates at one time, on board the old *Asia*, a seventy-four-gun ship, of her blessed majesty's navy. He was the first lieutenant, and I was the surgeon. We were at the battle of Navarino together, and I stood by his side when three of our ports were knocked into one by a marble shot from a battery of the accursed Turks. Thirteen men were killed by that shot, and his lordship and myself narrowly escaped death at the same time. He was like a brother to me the three years we were together, and now, after so many years, I can't desert the son of the nobleman who was my fast friend, and stood by me when I needed them. Help me, Mattocks, to save him."

"I 'll be —— if I do any more for him," was the bluff rejoinder, as he blew a cloud of smoke from his mouth. "You have told your yarn, now let me tell mine, and see if I am right in refusing to do more."

He removed his cigar from his lips, took a step nearer to me, so that he could have a good look at my face, and then slowly and deliberately said, —

"My lord, you must listen to me for a moment."

"Drive on," I remarked. "I am paying all attention to you."

"Three weeks ago you landed at Melbourne."

"Did I?" I asked, and then added, in an undertone, "I wonder who in the deuse I am, anyway?"

"Yes, my lord, you did. You brought letters of introduction to many people. One to me."

"Is it possible?"

He did not notice the interruption, but continued, —

"We introduced you to the best society in Melbourne."

"Never mind all that, Mattocks," cried the surgeon, whose name appeared to be Haverley Haverley. "Of course his lordship is accustomed to good society. We do not have many earls visit us in Australia, and when they come make much of them."

"But I do mind, doctor, and I must unburden my thoughts in my own way. Let me proceed. Your lordship is listening?"

"Yes;" but I was wondering if I was not half asleep, and dreaming, for the gentleman appeared very earnest.

"I was particular to make everything pleasant for you," continued Mr. Mattocks. "You were known to be an earl, rich, young, and not bad-looking."

I bowed at the compliment, and smiled at the eager-looking gentleman, who did not appear to appreciate my politeness.

"You were well received everywhere. All the best houses in the city were open to you."

"Especially the Hen and Chickens," I muttered.

"Imagine my surprise when I saw that you were bound to make the warmest kind of love to every pretty girl you met."

"Young girls were born to be made love to," I answered. "They like it, you know. They would feel offended if we did not flirt with them."

"Don't be too hard on his lordship, Mattocks," pleaded the surgeon, who was such a friend of my father's, although I did not believe that the worthy old gentleman had ever heard of him, but, strange to say, my father was a lieutenant in the navy, but it was the United-States Navy, and he had served as first lieutenant on board of a seventy-four, but it was the old *Ohio*, now lying at the Charlestown Navy Yard, and not the English ship *Asia*, broken up for all that I know.

"I am not too hard on his lordship," Mr. Mattocks retorted, turning to his friend. "I am speaking the truth, and even your partiality must not prevent me from saying all that I feel."

"Be gentle. Remember he has Scotch blood in his veins, and is a lord."

"I know that he has Scotch blood in his veins, and that he is an earl of the united kingdom of England and Scotland. I know that he is worth millions of pounds," Mr. Mattocks continued.

"Just one hundred sovereigns," I whispered to myself. "They must be counting my money by half-pence."

"I know that he has a yearly income of three hundred thousand pounds," Mr. Mattocks said.

"Well, these men are the craziest cranks that I ever met," I muttered. "Melbourne must be full of them."

"But, knowing all this, I shall speak my mind freely," Mr. Mattocks snarled.

"For God's sake be quick about it, so that we can get his lordship out of the city before there is much of a stir," urged the surgeon.

"You may take all the trouble yourself to get him out of Melbourne. I have done my duty, and that duty ended when I helped him into the carriage that was to take him on his way to Gelong. If he meets with disaster now it will not be my fault."

Then Mr. Mattocks turned to me, and addressed his remarks to my surprised ears.

"Your lordship is rich, as I have said. Your income is enormous; but all the gold that you can command would not induce me to repeat the task which I have so recently undertaken. I have been cursed by fathers, scolded by mothers, and d—d by brothers, all on your account."

"What have I done that should cause such a commotion?" I asked, and the question did not soothe the gentleman.

"O my God! He asks what has he done!" cried the excitable Mr. Mattocks, turning to his friend.

"Merely the animal spirits of a young man," said the surgeon, in a soothing manner.

"Animal damnation!" roared the gentleman. "Has n't he made love to more than a dozen of the handsomest girls in Melbourne?"

The surgeon nodded, and tried to seem sad; and then he sighed, and looked me full in the face to see if I was conscience-stricken. But I was not suffering much just at that moment.

"Has n't he praised them, and complimented them, kissed them when he had a chance, and gave all the fond hope of being a countess, as the wife of the Earl of Afton?" demanded Mr. Mattocks.

So I was the Earl of Afton, was I? I was glad to know who I was after all this talk and bluster.

"You, Haverley, know how the girls run after him, and how he run after the girls."

"All young people do the same thing," said the surgeon soothingly.

This surgeon appeared to be a wise man.

"Yes; but all gentlemen would not have done what his lordship has. You know what he is suspected of doing as well as myself. Was it fair to lead a young lady along, to pay her compliments, and make her promises, and then laugh at her prayers for lawful justice?"

"It would be wrong for any man to do so," I remarked, in a calm and collected manner. "I am not guilty of the charge."

"Then report lies. We only know of one case at the present moment," said Mr. Mattocks. "We shall hear of more in the course of time, I dare say."

"Heaven forbid!" I ejaculated.

"I am glad to see that you feel some of the shame which scandal has whispered in this city, while you have been here. But now I come to the meanest part of your career."

"What?" I asked, "do you intend to tell me that there is more to come?"

Mr. Mattocks looked at me with as much contempt as a genuine British merchant dares to bestow on one of the nobility.

"Yes, my lord, there is more to come."

"Then be quick about it, for I am on my way to the theatre, and fear I shall be late."

At these words both men started back with perfect bewilderment stamped on their faces, as though they had not heard aright.

"*You* go to the theatre?" they gasped. "Do you mean it?"

"Yes. I have a ticket and secured seat in my pocket."

"And you will go without the Belle of Australia in your company?" they demanded.

"Yes. What is the Belle of Australia to me? She cares no more for me than I do for her."

"My lord, my lord," cried the surgeon, "the people would tear you limb from limb if you dared to do such an outrageous act."

"Why should the people treat me in that manner? I have done nothing to deserve it."

"One word, and I'm done with such a *sang-froid* young man," cried Mr. Mattocks, dashing his cigar to the pavement, and kicking it into the gutter, with an imprecation that was not polite. "Listen to me for a moment. Give me a chance to speak, or I shall burst with rage," the younger gentleman continued, gaspingly.

"Good Heavens, man, I have n't prevented you from talking. In fact, I have n't been able to get my oar in edgewise since you commenced the conversation."

"Patience, Mattocks," said the surgeon. "His lordship is considerate, I 'm sure."

"—— his lordship!" roared the excited man. "I wish that I had never seen him. But he shall hear me, and hear me now, in spite of his attempts to put me off. Listen to me if you can."

"I am listening. Fire away," I said.

"You have made love to a dozen or two young ladies of Melbourne," Mr. Mattocks cried.

"A few moments ago you said the number was twelve. But the more the better, if they are all pretty," I answered. "A man can't have too much of a good thing, and I'm sure a pretty girl is one of the best things of this world. Lord! I love them all, the fat and the lean, the rich and the poor, the blonde and the brunette, the dark haired and the golden, the blue-eyed and those with dark, gazel-like optics. All are alike to me."

"I believe you," Mr. Mattocks sneered. "Your career in Melbourne has shown it from the first night that you arrived, when you kissed Colonel Cracker's daughter in less than an hour after an introduction."

"Well, if the lady did not object, whose business is it?" I asked.

"None of mine, but if you should happen to meet the colonel tonight he might horsewhip you," Mr. Mattocks said.

"That is hard. The daughter would not like that," I remarked.

"My lord," cried Mr. Mattocks, "do you not know that the lady now hates you with an undying hatred?"

"For what reason?" I asked.

"You know the reason. Did you not tell her that you loved her?"

"I don't recollect of doing so."

The excitable crank expressed his disgust with an emphatic gesture, and continued, —

"Then you heard of Miss Florence Kebblewhite, the Belle of Australia."

"*Santissimo!* what a funny name. Florence is pretty though. I like that. But Kebblewhite! Who would marry a Kebblewhite? Could n't the legislature or the city council change it?"

Only a smile of contempt from the younger crank.

"You would have an introduction. I introduced you. You made love to her," the young man continued.

"Naturally. Did n't you say that she was pretty?" I asked.

"She was cold to you, and did not like your forward, impertinent manner," Mr. Mattocks remarked.

"All put on, Mattocks. She was bound to catch me, and so played the proprieties, thinking that I would bite the hook a little harder and quicker. Girls know how to do those things. The fact of it is, Mattocks, you don't understand woman's nature. Now I do," I said, with provoking coolness, for I meant to let these gentlemen see that, if they were playing a neat little game on a stranger, he could equal them, and, at the proper time, turn the laugh against them.

Another gesture of disgust, and the crank continued, —

"At last you swore that you loved her better than all the world, and would make her your wife, and a countess, at the same time. Her father pressed the lady to accept you, and she did, only after careful consideration."

"Bosh, Mattocks. Don't lay it all on the old man. You know the lady wanted to be a countess all the time. Give the old gentleman a fair show. He has enough to answer for without that charge."

"The wedding day was appointed, and you were to be all ready. It was to be a private marriage, only the friends of the family present. The announcement nearly broke my heart;" and Mr. Mattocks almost sobbed.

"Ah, Mattocks, this is all news to me. You love the lady, it seems," I said, quite tenderly.

"I did love her, and should have won her, if you had not put in an appearance."

"And now you want me to leave the city so that you can have a clear field?" I asked.

"No, a thousand times no. She is lost to me forever. Had you but adhered to your word, — had you married her, — I should have been content. But you did not. You did not put in an appearance, and basely said that you had no idea of marriage. It may have been fun for you, but it is death to the lady. You came to the club this evening in your dress-suit, and said that your mother, the dowager countess, would never forgive you if you made a *mésalliance*. You asked us to help you out of the bad position in which you were placed. I despised you, but, at the entreaties of my friend, and your father's friend, Doctor Haverley Haverley, I consented to aid you. I have done my duty; and now, my lord, if tomorrow you are riddled, like a sieve, with bullets, at the hands of the lady's friends, do not blame me. Your life is not worth an insurance, even in a grave-yard office. Farewell, my lord, for we shall never meet again as friends."

He raised his hat, and bowed, and was turning away, when I said, —

"One moment, Mr. Mattocks. Who do you think I am?"

"Angus Mornington, Earl of Afton, Baron Midlothian, and half a dozen other titles. Good-night."

Heavens! the man had pronounced my full name, for I was Angus Mornington. But I was not an earl or an Englishman, but an American, and a native of New England. Surprise rendered me speechless. Who was I? and did I bear such a close resemblance to some person, that I was mistaken for him? Or were these gentlemen merely having a little fun at my expense, such as is often practiced in Boston and New York, when a foreigner is green and fresh to our practical jokes?

The last suggestion I considered the proper one; but how could these people have learned my name? I had not registered it at the Hen and Chickens, and only given it at the Oriental Bank when I deposited my little fortune.

"There is where they learned it," I thought, and made a firm resolution not to be frightened out of the city by the loud talk of two strange gentlemen, who would laugh at the joke in the club house, as soon as I departed from Melbourne, in hot haste, to escape danger.

"You see, my lord," said the elderly doctor, "what your imprudence has brought upon your head. You have lost a good friend, and now I am alone, and doubt if even I can save you from the vengeance of the lady's friends."

"Doctor," I replied, lighting a fresh cigar, "has n't this joke gone far enough?"

"A joke, my lord?"

"Yes, a joke. You see that I do not scare worth a cent."

"I know that you have your father's courage and imprudence, but you have not his great sense and good judgment, if you think this is a joke. But come with me, and I will find a refuge for you until this unfortunate affair has blown over. It will be no joke to me, and to you, if you are seen in the city tomorrow, let me tell you."

"I will run all the risks. Do not be anxious about me. I can take care of myself. I shall be armed, and the man who lays a hand on me in anger, will repent it," I said boldly.

My French and Yankee blood began to assert itself, as I thought of the trick which was being played on me.

"O Angus, Angus," pleaded the old gentleman, "do be advised by me. When your lady mother wrote to me that you would visit Australia, and begged me to keep a watchful eye on you, I promised her that I would do so. I protested against your engagement to Miss Kebblewhite, you remember, for I knew that the countess would not approve of her father, and his antecedents, but you would not listen to me. You pretended to be in love with the lady, and would win her. You did win her, and were to wed her this very afternoon. At the last moment you changed your mind. You had seen another fair face that attracted you more than the Belle of Australia. At least, this is the only supposition that I can entertain at the present time. Do you love another more than Miss Kebblewhite? Answer me without the least hesitation."

"No, to tell the honest truth, I am not in love with any one, and never have been," I answered.

"My God! how like his father," exclaimed the doctor, with a gasp. "From one fresh face to another, all through his life."

"Was my father fond of pretty faces?" I asked in a bantering tone, for, in truth, I had heard that my respected parent was a little wild in his youth, but then he was a naval officer, and gentlemen of that class are not saints in foreign ports, where dark eyes and hair predominate.

"You are like him in every respect except one, my lord."

"And that one?"

"Is honor, my lord."

The doctor spoke in slow, severe tones, and I had no doubt that he was firm in his belief. I was not in the least offended.

"The Earl of Afton, your father, would not have pledged his hand, and then forfeited his word. He was too much of a gentleman for that. You will pardon my plain speaking, will you not?"

"Certainly. But let me make one suggestion, doctor."

"Yes, a dozen, if you desire, my lord."

"The Earl of Afton would not have scrupled to deceive a lady if he had not pledged his hand?"

"It ill becomes a son to blacken his father's memory, my lord."

"Answer the question, doctor. Do not luff up into the wind like that. Steer a straight course when the channel is wide."

"My lord, I decline to answer the question," said the doctor, with a slight gasp, as though I had him at a disadvantage.

"Very well. One more question, if you please. Will you answer it?"

"Perhaps. Let me hear it, my lord."

"Would the old Earl of Afton have married Miss Kebblewhite had he been in my place?"

"No, you know he would not. He never would have disgraced his family by such a *mésalliance*. The idea of the Earl of Afton contracting a marriage with a lady whose father was a "—

He stopped short, and bit his lips, and looked a little confused.

"Go on," I said, for I saw that he held back some important information.

"No, my lord, I will not go on. It is clear to my mind that you have suddenly learned something of the past life of the lady's father, and that your proud blood will not permit you to wed one who would only dishonor the long line of distinguished ancestors which your house can boast of. No, my lord, I shall say no more."

"But you must. You have already said much, and it is better to say more. Continue."

"Tell me then," the doctor cried, as he seized my hand, and pressed it warmly, "you decline the marriage because you fear to contaminate the noble blood of the house of Afton?"

I looked as dignified as possible, and withdrew my hand from his grasp. It would not do for a real earl to shake hands in too familiar a manner with a plebeian surgeon.

"If such is the case, if you have heard the truth,— and I swear to you, my lord, that I did not learn of it until this very day,— then I forgive you for the course you have pursued. But you will break the heart of the loveliest girl in Australia. Even she does not know of her father's previous unfortunate life."

"Oh, let us hope that she will recover. Girls mope for a while, and then look for another lover. Miss Kebblewhite will prove no exception to the general rule."

"You misjudge her," the doctor said. "She is the most ambitious girl in Melbourne. Mattocks would have married her a year ago if she would have had him, and I tell you he is a great catch, rich and young, and not bad-looking."

"Then you will not tell me about the stain on Mr. Kebblewhite's past life?" I asked.

"No, my lord, for you already know it, and I am not a retailer of scandal. But come with me, and let us seek a place of safety. In a week's time I can get you out of the city. I know a house where you can keep quiet until the storm blows over. Come, my lord. I do not blame you as much as when I first met you this evening. But, in Heaven's name, let the girls alone in future. They will be your ruin, as they have been the ruin of many older and better men."

Just as he uttered these words a servant of the club house came down the steps as though he was in a desperate hurry. Seeing the doctor, the domestic ran toward him, and said, —

"O Doctor Haverley, one of the members of the club has a fit, and is black in the face. I was sent to find you. Do come at once, or the poor gentleman will die."

"Here, my lord," cried the doctor, "get under the shadow of the wall of the building, and wait for me until I return. I will not be gone long. Do not venture to enter the house. If that old Frenchman should find you there he would kill you. Keep your face covered up, and attract no atten tion. Your safety must be assured at all hazards. Don't stir from here until I return. Promise me that."

He did not wait for a response, but ran up the steps, and then I heard the nearest clock strike eight, and the curtain of the theatre was to rise at that hour.

"Well," I said to myself, "if I am to see the play I had better be moving. I think that I have heard enough of the Earl of Afton, and the Belle of Australia, for one night. Good-by, doctor, I 'm off," and walked in the direction where I supposed the Royal Victoria was situated. I was not exactly certain as to the street, but I remembered that I turned out of Collins Street into Russell Street, and then, not knowing just where to go, stopped under a gaslight, and waited until some one should come along who could give me the desired information. In a few minutes a stout, active, soldierly-looking man, with a dark face, and close-cropped hair, a person who looked to the right and to the left as he walked, who seemed to see everything and every one who passed, as if by intuition, came along with a quick step, and, just as I was about to speak to him, he stopped in front of me, and fixed his snapping black eyes on my face. Then, without speaking, he raised a little ivory whistle to his lips, and blew three distinct blasts. I heard them answered up the street, down the street, and around the corner in Collins Street, but, as the whistling did not concern me, I paid no attention to it. The man with the black eyes, and a cap on his head, that looked like those which soldiers wear when on fatigue duty, for it was cocked on one side of his head, in a rakish style, stared at me in a bold, yet respectful manner, until at last I lost a little of my usual patience, and said, —

"Well, my man, you will be certain to know me the next time."

"I know you now, and shall always recognize you wherever we meet. I am one who does not forget a face, no matter how much it may be changed," was the black-eyed man's answer.

"A precious gift," I replied; "and now will you do me the favor to direct me to the Royal Victoria Theatre? I fear that I shall be late for the first of the performance, as I have missed my way."

"I could direct you to the theatre, but it would be useless," the stranger said, in a short, abrupt manner.

"Why useless? The doors are open, and I was told that there was to be a remarkably good performance tonight."

"Because, my lord, instead of visiting a theatre this evening, you are going with me," and the dark man smiled grimly.

"How? What do you mean?" I asked.

"Just what I say, my lord. You are going with me," and the man's eyes snapped ominously.

"And who in the devil's name are you?" I asked indignantly.

He turned back the lappel of his vest, and there I noticed a large gold badge, studded with diamonds, an elegant and costly jewel as I ever saw before or since.

"Well, sir, and what does that signify to me?" I asked.

"Simply that I am the Chief of the Melbourne police."

"And how does that concern me? I have committed no crime," but just then I happened to think of the diamonds in my bosom, and the gold casket, and my spine began to grow cold, and my blood to tingle.

"Crime!" ejaculated the Chief. "Humph! that depends upon the light in which men view it."

"Well, name mine, if you please. If I am to accompany you, at least let me know on what charge," I said quite boldly.

"Will you remove your hat for a moment?" the Chief asked.

"Certainly," and did as requested.

The sharp-eyed man gave me a glance, and then removed his cap, and stood before me bare-headed, with every mark of respect on his stern, strong face.

"My lord," he said, "you will pardon me for doing what is strictly my duty."

"Oh, botheration!" I cried, in a fury. "Here is another crank. There are more cranks to the square acre in Melbourne than any place that I was ever in."

The Chief did not appear to notice my burst of rage. He seemed to have expected it, for, still standing before me uncovered, remarked, —

"I would have spared you this humiliation, my lord, had it been possible, but I had my orders to look for you, to find you, and detain you."

I glanced over my shoulder to see if I had better bolt for it, but the Chief seemed to divine my thoughts. He simply said in a calm tone, —

"It is useless, my lord. Do not attempt it."

He waved his hand, and then I saw two police officers standing on the opposite side of the street, and two more on each side of me, not six feet distant, alert, and quite strong enough to contend with a youth like me. They did not advance, but appeared immovable as statues, waiting for orders.

"Promise me one thing, my lord," the Chief said.

"What is it?" I asked, a little sullenly, for this thing was growing monotonous.

"Pledge your word as a nobleman that you will make no attempt to escape."

"And I can't go to the theatre?" I demanded.

"No, my lord, that would not be safe for your lordship. The people would be enraged at the sight of you, without the Belle of Australia by your side."

"Confound the Belle of Australia!" I cried. "I am tired of hearing her name."

"That is a matter that does not concern me. Your lordship should have thought of that before you promised to marry her."

"I have made no such promise. I don't know the lady. I don't want to know her. I'm no lord. I am an American citizen, and won't be imposed upon."

The dark-eyed man smiled in a peculiarly exasperating manner, as he said, —

"My lord, when I have seen a face once I never forget it. I have seen yours a dozen times before tonight. Once at a reception of the lieutenant-governor's. Your evasions will not suffice with me. I should know you even in the bush, twenty years hence. There is no mistake. You are the Earl of Afton just as much as I am Chief-of-Police Murden."

"Murden, Murden," I cried, "it seems to me that I have heard that name before."

"It is pretty well known in Australia," answered the Chief. "I have been on the force for twenty-five years, and some Americans have been pleased to mention my name in a couple of books published about this country. I will confess, however, that they have exaggerated my services in more ways than one."

"Name the books," I said. "Let me see if you are the Murden of my romances and dreams."

"Well, my lord, if you press me I will say that 'The ——— ———,' and 'The ——— ———,' are the works I allude to. But I did not suppose that you had ever seen them."

"Indeed I have, and am glad to meet with such a good representative of an Australian policeman. I would like to talk with you further on the subject."

"Not tonight, my lord. We have too much business on hand. Some other time I'll spin a few yarns for your entertainment. And now will your lordship promise me to make no attempt to escape?"

"Willingly, for I suppose it would be of no use," I answered; and the

Chief smiled, as he put on his cap, a little more rakish than before, and then looked very serious.

"Not of the slightest use, your lordship. Six men have their eyes on you, and will continue to watch you until I give the signal for a retreat, or a let up."

"Then make the signal. I have given my promise."

The Chief raised his hand, and the policemen seemed to slink out of sight as rapidly as they had appeared on the scene.

"Now what would happen if I should make a bolt for it?" I asked.

"You could not run ten rods without falling into the hands of my officers. Does your lordship think that I am a fool to put implicit trust in any man? I am not to be caught by young birds, or old ones. See here."

He put the whistle to his lips, and blew a slight blast, and in an instant two officers were at my side, and another in the rear, while echoing whistles were heard all along the street.

"I am satisfied," I said.

"People generally are when they can't help themselves," and the Chief smiled a confident, self-satisfied smile, as though he had the power in his hands, and was determined to make it felt.

"Do you renew your promise, my lord, that you will make no attempt to escape?"

"Willingly, for I see that it is useless."

"I think your lordship is a gentleman who will keep his word in some respects, but, after the experiences of the other night, it is well to be cautious, and be on my guard."

"What of the other night, Mr. Chief? Please explain."

"I know your lordship was a little over the bay, if I may so express myself, but that was no reason why you and others should pelt one of my men with eggs, at two o'clock in the morning. It may be fun for you, and English ways, but it is not Australian customs."

"Good heavens, Mr. Chief, you have made a mistake," I said. "I did nothing of the kind."

The Chief smiled quite amiably.

"Smithers," he cried, "come here."

The man on my right promptly stepped forward, and made a military salute, and then awaited orders.

"Smithers, do you recognize this gentleman?"

"Yes, yer 'onor. 'E 's one of the bloods vot pelted me vid heggs the huther night, vile I vos on my beat."

"You are sure this is the gentleman? Look at him attentively."

"Cock sure, yer 'onor. I 'd know 'im among a thousand, and swear to 'im on a stack of Bibles as big as the station-'ouse. Beside, 'e hoffered to fight me for a sovereign."

My namesake appeared to have made things lively in Melbourne, and, confound him! I had to endure the disgrace, and did not have any of the fun.

"You hear, my lord," the Chief said.

"I am afraid that I do. I have met another crank, it seems. Have you any more of the same species? If you have, bring them on, and let us hear them all at once."

"I does n't bear the swell any ill vill," the officer cried, with a good-natured grin. "I grabs 'im, yer know, ven he hoffers to fight me, and jerks 'im to the station-'ouse in double-quick time, and all 'is friends did n't get 'im away from me, neither. I 'its two or three of 'em vid my club, and the rest jist dropped their little game, and left. But this swell comes down 'andsome, and the inspector lets him hoff, 'cos some of the big bloods of the city puts in a plea for 'im. Oh, 'e is a trump, 'e is."

"How much did he give you for soiling your uniform?" asked the Chief.

"Fifty pun, yer 'onor, and a big lush of beer for all in the 'ouse; and 'e drinks vid us, and sings some pretty lively songs, and raises the devil ginerally, and at last the inspector sent 'im to 'is 'ome in a 'ansom, vid a man to take care of 'im till 'e vos sober. Oh, 'e is von of 'em, yer 'onor, but he is as liberal as a prince."

This was all news to me, and I saw that it was quite useless to deny that I had created a riot in the streets, got drunk, offered to fight a policeman, sang songs, and raised a first-class commotion. I sighed as I thought of all these things, and wondered if I should ever awaken from what I thought must be a troubled dream.

"That is all, Smithers. Fall back," the Chief ordered.

The officer saluted, and retired, but he grinned at me as though he would like to have another egging match, and a fifty-pound note for damages.

"Your lordship sees that you have made quite a sensation in Melbourne during the short time that you have been here," Mr. Murden remarked.

"Yes; but still I am not a lord. You will not believe me, and I am tired of denials."

The Chief smiled, and his black eyes glittered as he put his hand in his pocket, and drew out a diamond ring.

"Does your lordship recognize this jewel?"

He handed to me for examination a magnificent solitaire diamond ring. My blood began to congeal again, as I thought of the diamonds concealed in my bosom. I gave the jewel a hasty glance, and simply answered, —

"I have no recollection of ever seeing it before."

"Be careful, my lord," the Chief said, in a tone that sounded threatening. "Look again. Make no mistake."

Once more I examined the ring, and saw that it was a brilliant of the first water, and at least four carats in weight, and must have cost a large sum of money.

I knew that there was some trap in the question the Chief was putting to me, but I could not for the life of me see how I was to avoid falling into it. He held the thread, and I was groping in the dark.

"Well, my lord?" the Chief asked, after a long pause, still watching my face attentively.

"I know not what to say," I answered.

"Then say nothing, for all that you utter might be used against you some time or other."

"How? Do you mean to intimate that I stole this valuable jewel?" all my blood boiling at the unjust suggestion.

"Stole is a harsh expression, my lord. I make no such charges. You know how you came in possession of this jewel, and you also know how it left your custody."

"I swear to you that" — I stammered.

The Chief shrugged his shoulders, and gave me a look that stopped my torrent of denials.

"My lord," he said in a voice that was meant to be firm, and to show that he was not trifling, "do not try to convince me that ever since you arrived in Melbourne you have been in a state of intoxication, and, therefore, unable to distinguish between right and wrong."

"I was never drunk in my life, sir," I responded, as proudly as my nature would permit under the circumstances.

"Then, in the name of all the saints, how do you explain about this ring?"

"I can't explain. Will you do so?" anxious to have him show his hand.

"Yes, quite willingly. A day or two after you were engaged to the Belle of Australia" —

"Oh, ——! can't you leave her out?" impatiently, for the Belle popped up at every point.

"No, my lord, for she is one of the principal characters after yourself."

"Well, go on. Every few minutes she appears on the scene. Every way I turn I am confronted by that young lady."

"No wonder. When a man engages to marry a beautiful young girl she usually confronts him at every step in his future life."

"Such is, unhappily, the case, I have been given to understand. Well, go on."

The street where we stood conversing was nearly deserted, but the few people who were passing were waved off by the Chief, if disposed to arrest their steps, and see what attracted the officer's attention.

"As I said before," resumed the Chief, after he had told several young men to move on, or he would know the reason why, "a few days after you were engaged to Miss Florence Kebblewhite you gave her a curious seal ring, with your family coat-of-arms engraved upon it. You are following me, my lord?"

"I am trying to, but am still bewildered."

"When you put it on her finger, you noticed this valuable diamond, and admired it. It was but natural. Most men would."

"I should think so," I murmured.

"She was pleased at your admiration, and asked you if the Earl of Afton's family jewels had anything to compare with it. You said that she should judge for herself some time, and then the lady begged of you to wear the jewel for a few days. You put it on your finger, and, from that day to this, Miss Kebblewhite has not seen her diamond."

"And she is naturally anxious to have it returned. Give it to her by all means," I said hastily. "Some girls would shed oceans of tears at the loss of so beautiful a gem."

"She is not anxious, my lord. She cares nothing about the diamond compared to yourself. She does not know that a complaint has been made on account of the ring. She still believes in you, and imagines you true and generous and noble."

"A thousand thanks for her confidence. I begin to think more of the Belle of Australia than I did an hour ago. She must be a noble-hearted girl."

"My lord, she is the pride of the city. She is as pure as she is beautiful. Even you, my lord, know that."

The Chief snapped his eyes at me as though he meant more than his words implied. Then he continued, —

"No, the lady made no complaint, but her brother did."

"She has a brother then? Is he a big fellow, with a fist like a top-mall?"

"This afternoon at six o'clock," the Chief continued, "her brother came to my office, and said that you had not shied your castor into the ring at three o'clock, as per agreement and articles. That is," the Chief said, with a slight cough, to hide the fact that he had used the slang of the prize ring, "you had not come up to time, you had flunked the fight, and all bets were off until the referee decides what shall be done. You follow me, do you not, my lord?"

"I am close on your heels. Proceed."

"The brother feared that you had drank too much, and gone to sleep, forgetting your engagement. But at the hotel no one had seen you; at the lieutenant-governor's residence no one knew where you were. Her ladyship said that in the forenoon she had seen you on a dray, and that you seemed jolly, but sober. A Mr. Haley reported that he had seen you on a dray, and you appeared to be under the influence of liquor. Another person saw you drinking beer with a drayman. Monsieur Allete, a French gentleman of uncertain temper, said that he met you in Collins Street at eleven o'clock, and that you were impatient to leave him, so that you could dress, and be prompt in the ring at three. He stated that he handed you an elegant pair of solitaire diamond ear-drops, in a gold jewel-box, for the bride, who is his idol, and will inherit all his immense wealth."

Cold shivers began to run down my spine again. I feared that the Chief would lead up to those diamonds.

"You still follow me, my lord?" the Chief asked.

"I am trying to, but feel a little staggered at that last blow. However, I shall soon rally, and face you once more. Go on."

"Then the brother mentioned, in an incidental way, that you had his sister's ring, a present from her father on her sixteenth birthday, a jewel that cost one thousand pounds, in London."

"It is worth it," I said quite heartily.

"This information which I had received," the Chief said, once more exposing the *pénchant* of a real police officer, "together with other information I had secured, set me to thinking. I had obtained some pretty strong hints where your lordship has passed a number of evenings the last two weeks. I thought I could get on your track by going to a certain house, and having a personal interview with one Miss Kitty Stukely, a young — well, girl, if you will. I don't blame your lordship for being pleased with her face. It is a handsome one, and she was the best-formed ballet girl in 'The Black Crook,' when it was played here last season. She came from England, and has never returned home, and never will."

"Don't wander," I said. "Stick to your subject, Mr. Chief."

"I will. I fear that I was a little groggy, but now I am all right. Well, Kitty was glad to see me. We are good friends, and nothing more, and I asked after your lordship. She had not seen you since last evening when you called. While she was talking with me, I noticed this ring on her finger. My lord, my lord, it was a vile, disgraceful thing for you to do."

"What?" I asked, suddenly awakening to my peril.

"To take a jewel from the pure, and noble-hearted Belle of Australia, and place it on the finger of your latest mistress."

"It is a lie, a damnable lie. I am incapable of such an outrage. Not for all the gold in Australia would I insult a true lady in such a dastardly manner. Good God, man, what do you think of me?"

"I think," said the Chief, his voice low but firm, "that you are like many other noblemen who have visited us. You suppose that we have such reverence for the old country, and titles, that any disgraceful act that you may commit will go unpunished. My Lord of Afton, this time you have met your match, and, unless you fight foul, you will have to marry Miss Kebblewhite before the moon is two hours higher."

"In the name of Heaven listen to me, Mr. Murden," I cried. "I do not know who I am; I half believe either you or I to be a crank. I am not a lord. I am an American. Save me from such a fate as a forced marriage with a lady, who will curse me when she learns that she has been deceived. I will not submit to it, I tell you. Think of your American friends, those who wrote about your wonderful adventures in hunting bushrangers. For their sake save me, and get me out of this accursed city, where every other man is a crank, or else I am one."

"My lord," responded the Chief, in a cold, harsh tone, "you have pitched your ring, and must enter it, and put up your maulies like a man, or take the consequences. I can't save you. I would not if I could. Do not think for a moment that your strange, improbable story is believed. I am too old a hand to swallow such stuff as you have put before me. You must marry the lady or die, for all the traps of Melbourne, with me at their head, could not preserve your life. You would be hunted for under every sun, and in every country, and death would be the ultimate result just as sure as you stand here, the proud Earl of Afton, and I stand here as simple Mr. Murden, the Chief of the Melbourne police."

I could only utter a groan of anguish at the prospect before me. Mr. Murden paused a moment, and then continued,—

"I would do all that is in my power to aid an American, for the sake of the three gentlemen who were, for some years, my best friends, and whom I loved most dearly. I told you that I never trusted a man fully. I make an exception in favor of the three Americans who came here some years since, in search of fortune, and, thank Heaven, found it in abundance, as I have good reason to know. Those men I relied on, believed in, and, when I was in a tight place, they never shirked, but helped me out. At my side, behind me, or in front of me, they were just the same. Their word was sacred as the Bible. Their promise as good as an oath. And now let me speak still plainer, Earl of Afton. For all of your proud position, for all of your wealth, for all of your coronet, and title, I tell you that I had rather have one of those unknown Americans for my friend, had rather shake hands with him, than to call you an associate, or to let my hard palm rest against yours."

What could I reply to such a torrent of words? I could say nothing, and do nothing. The more I denied my identity, the more contempt I was likely to experience at the Chief's hands.

"And now, my lord, you will pardon me, if you please, and if you do not please, for my frankness, and let us once more turn to business."

"Willingly. It is useless for me to deny anything. I will listen to you. I know not who I am."

"As I said before, I saw this ring on Miss Kitty's finger, and recognized it from the description which the younger Mr. Kebblewhite furnished. It is not usual for a girl in her position of life to wear a brilliant that cost one thousand pounds."

He paused, and looked at me with his sharp black eyes, but I did not answer. I was almost speechless.

"I took the jewel from her finger, and asked of whom she obtained it. She hesitated for a moment, and but for a moment, for Kitty is honest, even if she is weak, and then she told me that a gentleman named Angus — she did not know the rest of your name, or suspect your position in life — had placed it on her finger three or four evenings since. At first she supposed the stone but paste, and of little worth, but when she learned that the diamond was real, and of great value, she became frightened, and feared that it had been stolen by the giver. You are paying strict attention to my words, my Lord of Afton?"

"Yes," I muttered, seeing the pit that the Chief was digging beneath my feet, and, detective like, he was calmly waiting until my supports were knocked from under me, and I should fall in.

"Now, my lord, I believe the girl spoke the truth, but you deny that you loaned her the ring, or gave it to her. Did I understand you aright, my lord?"

Not a movement of my face escaped his keen gaze.

"Man or devil," I cried, "can't you let the matter drop where it is? Return the ring, and say no more about it."

The Chief smiled. He liked the compliment. It was a tribute to his sagacity.

"No, my lord, the matter has been placed in my hands. I mean to bring it to a speedy conclusion. I never let go my grip when I have once fastened on my prey, and, in this important case, I mean to fight it to the bitter end, and justice shall be done."

"And if I deny that I gave the poor girl the ring, or loaned it to her, what then?" I asked.

"Cannot your lordship surmise?"

"I think I can. The idea is worthy of you," I answered, in an indignant tone.

The Chief flushed, and his eyes showed the temper that he tried to control by an effort. For a moment he was silent. Then he spoke,—

"We will not bandy epithets now," Mr. Murden remarked, sneeringly. "The *gentleman* who would take a valuable diamond ring from the hand of a pure girl whom he is about to marry, and bestow it upon a common — Well, well, let us not be too hard upon poor Kitty. She is not quite as bad as that, just now. But your lordship will see that all the civilities and courtesies of life are not embodied in your own person. I do not wish to speak harshly to you, but remember this, my lord, that a police officer may be as noble in the discharge of his daily duties as a peer of Great Britain, and that his word is just as good until he is a convicted liar."

"Do you mean to intimate that I have told an untruth?" I demanded, hotly indignant.

"I intimate nothing, my lord, so do not square off at me. It won't do here. I am the Chief of the Melbourne police, and not private Smithers, who is satisfied, after an insult, with a present of fifty pounds."

"Pardon me, Mr. Murden," I said, "I had no intention of assaulting you, but it is hard to be called a liar, and not retort in a forcible manner."

"Then keep your maulies down, and don't look fight, unless you mean it. You are a high-spirited lad, and a handsome lad, and I should be sorry to make a mark on that fresh face of yours, on your wedding night. The Belle of Australia would never forgive me, for, woman-like, she would declare it was all my fault, and that you were a lamb, who could do no wrong

4

Oh, damn! don't I know them? I have been scratched often enough to understand them, at my time of life."

"Are you a married man, Mr. Murden?" I asked; and the Chief smiled a grim smile, as though he saw the joke, and did not think it so bad.

"No, I am not married, my lord. I have no time for domestic bliss, and such nonsense. I'm a widower. Now I'm wedded to my duties. But all this has nothing to do with the business which I have on hand. Whether I am married or single can concern you but little, or any other man. Let us return to Kitty, and the ring, for time is precious just now."

"Well, what more have you to offer?" I asked.

"Me? Bless your lordship, if such a thing were possible, I have nothing to offer. It is for your lordship to make suggestions, not me."

"Then let me understand you quite clearly," I said. "If I deny that I gave the ring, or loaned the ring, to the girl, then she goes to"—

I hesitated, for the word seemed harsh and cruel.

"To prison, my lord. That is the ticket," and the Chief smiled grimly, as though the word had no terrors.

"Can nothing be done to save her from such a wretched fate?"

"Yes," and the Chief lighted a cheroot, one of Manila's first quality, and handed one to me.

"Name the course which must be pursued, and, if it depends upon me, she shall be saved."

"That is well spoken, my lord. Answer me the first question, and then we will lead up to the others in the course of events. Now then, were you *over the bay* when you gave Kitty the ring?"

"Over the bay?" I stammered.

"Yes. Intoxicated I mean."

"No, sir. I was never intoxicated in my life, as I told you before."

The Chief whistled, and shrugged his broad shoulders. He counted that as lie number one on my part. I could see that he did by his dark, expressive face, and twinkling eyes.

"Question number two," he said, in a calm tone, as though I was before a French tribunal: "Did you give her the ring, or loan it to her, when perfectly sober?"

"I refuse to answer the question," I cried. "I do not wish to criminate the girl, or any other person. For God's sake, Mr. Murden, why will you not believe me when I tell you that only this morning I stepped on a tug boat in the bay, and came up the river soon afterward."

"The name of the tug-boat, if you please."

"I do not know it."

"The name of the master then."

"I did not learn it. I did not ask it. I should know him if I saw him once more."

"Is the ship at anchor in Hobson's Bay?"

"No, she braced up her yards and left, just as soon as I was landed on the tug."

"Give me the names of the parties to whom the ship was consigned."

"I do not know them. Some firm at the bay, I think."

The Chief laughed, as he took off his cap, and made me a low bow.

"Earl of Afton," he said, in a mocking tone, "you will pardon me when I tell you that, without exception, you are the most audacious and magnificent liar in Australia at the present time. Why, you could give points to a bushranger, and beat him at his own game. In all of my long experience on the police I never met but one man who could equal you. That was a fellow named Steel Spring. I captured him once, and he got fifteen years at hard labor. His time has recently expired, and he has, so I have been informed, again taken to the bush, and is in the vicinity of Ballarat. How I wish that I could lay hands on him, and get up a first-class lying match. I would wager two to one on you, and rake down the boys in a manner that would astonish them."

I thought of my poor dear mother, who had always taught me to speak the truth at all hazards, and under all circumstances. I thought of my noble-hearted father, wounded before the walls of Vera Cruz, while in command of a United-States ship, during the Mexican war, and how he had loved me, and then I could no longer stand up under the vile accusation. My head drooped lower and lower, and, had I not clung to a lamp-post, I should have fallen on the sidewalk, while tears fell from my eyes, and a heavy sob broke from my overcharged heart, and reached the quick ears of Mr. Murden, who sprang forward, and threw his strong right arm around me, and held me up.

"My lord, my lord," he cried, with more of pity in his tones than he had displayed during the interview, "I did not dream that you were so sensitive to mere words. I thought that you were hardened to everything in this world. That your life had been so wild that not one single tender spot was to be found in your heart for man or woman. Pardon me for misjudging you, my lord. Let me assist you. Take a drop of brandy. Smithers, come here quick."

"Yes, yer 'onor," and the officer, who had stood at some distance from us during all the conversation, ran toward me, flourishing his club, as though some hard work was to be done in breaking heads.

" Put up your club, you damn fool! " roared the Chief, "and give me your flask of brandy. I know you always carry one."

"Yes, yer 'onor, 'ere it is, and nearly full."

" Take a drop. It will do you good," whispered the Chief; and it did, for it sent the blood dancing through my veins, and once more my manhood asserted itself, so that I shook off the arm of the Chief, and again stood erect, like an innocent boy.

" They seem to think that the touch of common people is pollution," I heard the Chief mutter, as he released me, and once more assumed the hard tones and face of the police officer.

" My lord," he said, " I have apologized for my rude words, and that is all I can do in the way of an atonement. But you will admit that they were justified by all the facts of the case. No one but a nobleman or a fool would have invented such a cock-and-bull story, in the hope of deceiving the Chief of the police force of Melbourne. But I now look on you with a milder eye than before. You have a heart, and you will not let little Kitty go to prison. Of that I am sure. Now to the proof. Come with me. Smithers, take your flask, and be careful how you drink while on duty, or some day you will find that you have been cut off from the flower of the force. You and Dick follow me. The rest of the squad can return to the station house, and report for duty."

"Where do you wish me to go?" 'I asked, still faint, but once more hopeful.

" Before I conduct you to Mr. Kebblewhite's, for a wedding, or a settlement of some kind, we will have an interview with Miss Kitty. Her mouth must be kept shut, and you will not offend your sweet wife, I hope, by ever speaking of the way and manner in which you disposed of the ring. As for me, I could ruin half the married men in Melbourne, if I desired, so your lordship need not fear of my squealing on your little game. Come, my lord."

He gave me his arm, and looked as if he meant that I should take it whether I wanted to or no.

" Some man would feel proud like, you know, to be seen walking down Russell Street with a live earl leaning on his arm. Pull your hat over your face, if you please, my lord, and bring that shawl over your chin. That's right. Now no one will recognize you, and we sha'n't have a confounded row on the street if we meet some of the Belle's friends. Yes, some people would give a pound or two to have you take their arm, but I a'n't proud. I want your arm in mine so that you won't attempt to waltz down the street without me. There must be no skipping out as far as I am concerned. You are listening, I suppose?"

"Yes, sir; but, as I promised not to escape, or attempt it, the precaution is useless."

"Ah," chuckled the Chief, "never met but three men in my life whom I fully trusted, as I said before. The Americans I spoke of. Those who wrote the books, and introduced me in a tip-top manner. Ah, those were men, and no mistake. But here we are at the house, and Kitty is at home. I see a light in her window. I told her not to have company tonight, and I warrant you she has obeyed me. Courage, my lord, and speak the truth, and all will be well with the girl hereafter."

We stopped before a small house, and the Chief turned to the two policemen who were following us.

"Smithers," he said, "you and Dick hang around, but out of sight. Come, my lord," and he gave a gentle knock on the door of the house where Miss Kitty, whom I had never seen, or heard of, resided, and whom I was to face for the first time on a serious charge, and, for the life of me, I could not see how I was to disapprove of it, and still afford escape for the girl and myself, unless she repudiated me as her friend, and of that I had great hope, in fact, the only hope of turning the tables on the Chief, and his eternal sarcastic grin of delight at his supposed smartness.

"O ANGUS! DEAR ANGUS! I HAVE BEEN SO UNHAPPY." THE YOUNG LADY CRIED, AND PUT HER WHITE ARMS AROUND MY NECK.

PART III.

MISS KITTY AND THE DIAMOND RING AGAIN APPEAR. — A PROMISE TO BE SILENT. — MR. KEBBLEWHITE AND HIS HOME. — HOW MR. MURDEN SURROUNDED ME WITH PITFALLS. — USELESS DENIALS. — THE FIRST VISION OF MY FUTURE WIFE; AND A PLEASANT ONE IT IS.

AS Mr. Murden knocked on the door, just light enough to attract the attention of the people inside, I would have drawn back, but the Chief held on to me like a devil-fish.

"No, no," he whispered, "none of that. Don't you dare to attempt it just now. It will be dangerous for you. Beside, it would be of no use. You go in first, and give no intimation that I am near you. I will follow, as soon as I have overheard a little of your private conversation. Do you understand me?"

"Yes; but it is cruel and cowardly," I answered.

"Not so cowardly as to give a girl a ring that did not belong to you. Ah, my lord! Think twice before you speak of mean deeds, and cowardly conduct," and the Chief snapped his eyes at me.

The door was opened by a frowsey woman, stout and full-chested, with a face that betokened love for bitter beer and rum. She would have spoken, but the Chief put his finger on his lips, and motioned her to be silent. She looked a little frightened at sight of the officer, but received me with a grim smile, just as though I was an old acquaintance, whom she had met quite often.

"Enter that first apartment on the left," the Chief whispered. "Do not knock, and do not close the door. You hear me?"

"I 'opes, Mr. Murden, that there's no row 'ere. I'm an 'onest vomen if there hever vos one," sniffled the frowsey one, wiping her fat nose with the back of her hand.

"If you speak above a whisper I'll strangle you," the Chief said. "Go to your kitchen, and keep quiet. No harm is intended you, just at present."

The woman waddled off, and left us alone in the entry. I delayed following my instructions, for I dreaded what the result would be, and feared it.

"Go on, my lord. I am waiting for you. Let the girl speak first, if you please. I am a little bit curious to hear what she will say," and he motioned me toward the apartment.

He gave me a gentle push, and I opened the door and entered a pretty little chamber, with a neat carpet, lace curtains, and a bed, that was covered with a white French quilt, pillow shams over the pillows, and a bouquet of fresh flowers on a table, at which was seated a young girl, not more than sixteen years of age, dressed in white, with bare arms, and very scant garments around a pretty and white pair of shoulders, exposing a bust that would have been appreciated by a painter or sculptor. In fact, she was in what the French would call decidedly *décolleté* costume, although I have seen much freer exposure of the person at a select ball or party in New York or Boston. She was as handsome a picture, as she sat there by the table, reading by the light of a student lamp, as I had ever seen, and for a moment I did not wonder that my "double" had surrendered to her charms, and even given her the diamond ring, or anything else that she asked for. Her auburn hair fell over neck and bust, and revealed a face that was singularly fair, with the reddest of lips, and teeth that were small and white, and wonderful in their evenness and regularity. She looked up from a paper that she was reading, and, as soon as she saw me, gave a glad cry, and sprang toward me with outstretched arms, and a smile of delightful sweetness over her fresh, pink-and-white face, and there was no paint on it, either.

"O Angus," she cried, "I am so glad to see yer 'ere this hevening. I did not expect yer. Yer said that yer did not intend to call. Yer dear, naughty boy, to give me such a delightful surprise," and then, confound her impudence, she put her white, well-formed arms around my neck, and pulled my face down very gently, and kissed me a dozen times on the lips, cheeks, and eyes, before I recovered my presence of mind, or made an attempt to resist her glowing welcome, disagreeable as it was to me.

"Heavens!" I thought, when I had recovered my breath, "here is another crank, and the most dangerous one of the lot. What would my dear mother say to all of this, if she should know it?"

"Angus," the little girl said, "yer don't kiss me as though yer cared for me heny more. And yer don't seem a bit glad to see me. I don't believe yer 'as given yer chickabidy a thought all day. Now then, one good one. That's a dear. I'm hawful glad yer 'as come. I 'se somethin' to tell yer, vot vill surprise yer. That old Murden, the Chief of Police, vos 'ere this wery hafternoon, and took away the diamond ring vot yer gives me a few days ago. 'E said that there was some mistake about it, and that hall vould be hexplained ven the proper time arrived. Vot did the old rat mean, Angus? Yer gave me it, did n't yer? Hanswer me that, vont yer?"

"That's the very question I want him to answer," said the deep, quiet voice of Mr. Murden, who entered the room just at this moment.

The girl withdrew her arms from my neck, and fell back, astonished at the Chief's appearance.

"Yes, Kitty," Mr. Murden cried, "the old rat is here, and wants that question answered. It is an important one for you and this gentleman," and then he smiled, one of his exasperating smiles.

The girl gazed at me, and then at the Chief, as though she did not exactly understand his meaning.

"Look here, Kitty," Mr. Murden remarked, "I am disposed to be your friend, but I must have straight-forward answers. The law demands it."

"Don't give me heny of yer *sour beer*, Mr. Murden," the girl said, with a pout, that was quite pretty, even if it was a little vulgar, and disrespectful to the Chief.

"I am in earnest, Kitty, if ever I was in my life. Pay attention to what I say," the Chief remarked, quite composedly.

"All right, old 'un, go ahead," she answered, and made a face at him, when she thought that he was not looking at her.

But he had eyes like a hawk, and noticed it, although he did not display any tokens of anger.

"Your face is pretty enough, Kitty, without those contortions, which do not improve it. Now be serious for a moment. Do you recognize this gentleman? Be quite careful before you speak."

"Do I vot? That 'ere is a big vord, and I can't swallow it 'hole, Mr. Murden."

"Do you know this gentleman?"

"Ah, now yer talks. Vel, I should think I did," and Kitty laughed quite merrily.

"What is his name?" demanded the Chief, seriously.

"Angus, and I loves him," was the prompt answer.

"Never mind the love just now. Try and forget that part of the farce."

"I can't, and I von't," she answered, in a determined tone, and then put her arm around my neck, and looked at the Chief triumphantly, as though daring him to part us. I would have removed her arm, but did not feel like wounding her pride and devotion, she was so loving and confiding.

"You are sure that his name is Angus? and that you have seen him before?" the Chief asked, and his eyes were looking at me so firmly that I could make no sign of dissent. "You can swear to him?"

"Swear to 'im? Vy, I could jist get up and 'owl that 'e is 'im at heny time of the day or night. Don't I know my Angus?"

Again I felt I was going down hill, as though sliding on an avalanche, and that I should land at the bottom a wreck, or else the husband of a lady whom I had never seen, cared nothing about, and could not love. I thought at the time that one state was as bad as the other, and ruin was preferable to matrimony.

"You see that Kitty recognizes you," the Chief said, with a grim smile. "She is not mistaken, for the eyes of a woman in love are sharp, when fixed on a young and handsome man."

I did not answer, but let him enjoy his triumph as he pleased. I could say nothing in my own defence that would have the least effect on his mind, or that of the girl. They were determined cranks at best.

"Now, Kitty, a few more questions, my good girl, and we are done. When did you first meet with Mr. Angus, as you call him?" the Chief asked.

"At a free-and-heasy on Market Square, two veeks ago. Ve spoke together, and 'e stood for the beer, and then valked 'ome vid me. He jist talked beautiful, he did, and I grew wery fond of 'im."

"You hear?" the Chief said, nodding to me, and again that exasperating smile appeared on his face.

"Yes, I hear," I answered despondently.

"And you do not desire to ask her any questions?" the Chief demanded, now quite radiant.

"No," I said, in a low tone, sad and sick at heart. "It would be useless, I know. You will not believe me."

"Angus," the young lady said, with a look of deep anxiety on her face, "is yer in trouble on my account? Vot does the *traps* (police) vant of yer? Vy is that old Murden axin' hall of these 'ere questions for?"

"Be quiet, Kitty, and old Murden, as you call him, will explain all things in due time. I 'm not so very old, Kitty, that you should throw it in my face," showing that the bold, bad man had one weak spot, like the rest of mankind, and womankind, likewise, for that matter.

"Vell, Mr. Murden, I honly spoke a jokin' like, yer know. But I was so fearful of Angus, that I did n't know vhat I said."

"Your friend is in no danger just at present, Kitty, but his safety depends upon your answers, and I need not say that your safety is in some measure involved with his own. Now answer me, and be true to yourself. Did Mr. Angus give or lend you a diamond ring?"

"Vy, 'e puts it on my finger three or four nights ago, and did n't say nothin' about my returnin' it. I s'posed 'e give it to me, till yer calls this wery hafternoon, Mr. Murden, and axed me for it," and Kitty's face glowed like an innocent girl's.

"Is this statement correct?" the Chief asked, and looked at me so fixedly that I had to drop my eyes, and think for a moment about the trap into which I had fallen, through his devilish mixture of cunning and good-nature.

If I denied the story the poor girl was threatened with prison, although I half believed it was only a bluff. The Chief held a strong hand, and would not let me see his cards unless I came up to his terms.

"Angus, yer know I speaks the livin' truth, and 'opes to die if I don't," Kitty said, as I hesitated. I could not break her heart even to save myself.

"Yes, she speaks the truth," I cried, and then added in an undertone, "And may Heaven forgive me for lying to save a poor girl from prison, for some man's crime."

Kitty put up her lips, and kissed me as a reward for my words, while Mr. Murden smiled in such an exasperating manner that I wanted to punch his head.

"You put the ring on her finger, did you?" the Chief demanded, and his eyes went through and through me.

"Yes," quite boldly this time, for I was becoming desperate, and did not care how soon the farce, or tragedy, was concluded.

"And you did not request her to return the ring to you since you put it on her finger?" persisted the Chief.

An anxious look from poor Kitty, and a stern one from the Chief.

"No," I stammered, with a guilty look.

"You are sure, sir?"

"Quite sure," I answered very softly.

"Then why did you deny that you gave or loaned the ring to the girl when we were on the street?"

"Did I do so?" I faltered.

"My Angus vould n't do any such thing," interrupted Kitty, confident of the integrity of the man to whom she was clinging so affectionately, and so eagerly.

"Silence, girl," said Mr. Murden, in a low, determined tone. "Your punishment is soon to come, you poor thing."

"Perhaps I had forgotten the circumstance," I cried, grasping at any loophole for escape.

"You know better, my lord. You know that you have committed a mean, contemptible action in giving this poor girl a ring that you had taken from the hand of a true and pure lady. Men do not give away diamonds that cost a thousand pounds, and forget all about the circumstance, even if they are wealthy."

Kitty's eyes began to glitter, and her face grow pale. Jealousy was tugging at her heart, to add to my other troubles, which, God knows, were already heavy enough for a young man of nineteen to bear.

"Vot?" she said, starting back, and sitting down on the bed so suddenly that she nearly rolled over on the other side, and thence to the floor. "Do yer mean to tell me that there is another voman vot howns that ring?"

"Listen to me for a moment, Kitty," the Chief said. "If you give way to any yelling or temper I swear to you that I will lock you up."

"Yer hold willian," the girl began, but a look from the Chief, as black as a thunder-cloud, stopped her.

"It is useless for you to go off into a tantrum," the Chief continued; "so let me warn you. Keep quiet, or I 'll summon one of my men. This gentleman and you must part tonight, and never meet again."

A moan from Kitty, and a rocking of her body to and fro on the bed.

"You do not know who he is. He has concealed his name and position in the world from you," Mr. Murden said.

"I love 'im! I love 'im! I don't care if 'e is a sweep, I love 'im," moaned the girl.

"Don't be a fool, Kitty, but act like a sensible little woman. In two hours from now this gentleman will be married to the Belle of Australia."

"I 'd like to scratch 'er hyes out. Oh, 'ow I 'd like to scratch 'er," and then she rolled over in a dead faint, and looked as white as death, but her fingers and heels were active even if she was unconscious.

"You see what a d—d mess you have made of it," said the Chief, just as though I was to blame for all that had occurred. "I should have thought you knew better. What do you do when women go off like that? Souse them with water? Here 's the jug. Now then."

But Miss Kitty did not wait for the deluge. She suddenly sat bolt upright, and said in a tone of voice that was quite firm, if not cheerful,—

"'Old yer 'and, yer hold willian, and don't drown me. O Angus, is this true?"

"It is true, Kitty," the Chief said. "I never deceived you. He is to be married tonight. Hereafter if you should see him on the street, or anywhere, you must turn away your head, and no longer recognize him. Do you hear me?"

"I von't," was the sullen response, and a shower of tears.

"You will find it for your interest to do so. Money will be given to you if you follow my advice," the Chief promised.

I wondered where the money was to come from. I was worth just five hundred dollars, and that was not a large sum to bribe a girl who had expensive tastes.

"I vont 'ave 'is money. I 'll throw it at yer 'ead if yer hoffers it to me. I vant 'im, and not 'is money," and the tears rolled down her cheeks, and she tried very hard to suppress her sobs.

"One more word, Kitty, and then I am done with you," Mr. Murden said. "This gentleman has wooed you under a common name. He is not for the like of you. He is a nobleman, an English lord."

"I don't care vot 'e is. I should love 'im just as vell if 'e vos no more than a common trap."

"We can spare no more time here," the Chief cried impatiently. "We must move along. It is near nine o'clock, and we shall be late."

"O Angus, vill yer leave me?" asked Kitty, and stretched out her arms.

"It is I who force him to go," said the Chief, in the hope of aiding me.

Kitty sat for a few minutes with her head cast down, and tears flowing freely from her handsome blue eyes.

"Must it be so, Angus?" she asked.

"I shall have to obey Mr. Murden. He has me in his power as well as yourself. If I say that I did not give you the ring of my own free will and accord, he arrests you for larceny. I have said that I gave it to you, and you are safe."

"Right you are," chirped the Chief; "and now put the ring on your finger, where it belongs, and swear by all the saints that it has never left your possession, if a certain person should question you on the subject. I am a man of truth, and never lie, if the truth is just as available; and, although I am not overpoweringly enamored of your personal character, my lord, still, to save the happiness of a most estimable young lady, I will never mention this matter, and I am sure that you will keep a close mouth, if you know when you are well off. As for Kitty" —

"Yer let me alone, Mr. Murden," moaned the girl. "Yer has done mischief 'nough for one day and night. Yer is always up to some diviltry. I 'ates yer!"

"As for Kitty here," resumed the Chief, not noticing the interruption, "she will keep as mum as a detective that is not paid to furnish information. She knows me, and I can rely on her silence. That ring is a valuable one, and a little romance has been connected with it. Look on the inside, my lord, and you will see the engraving, 'Florence, 16.' It was a birthday present from a father to an only daughter, just one year ago. I need not tell you how that father would swash around, and how the young lady would tumble, if they knew of this little transaction. Beside, there is a brother, a stout fellow, some twenty-five years of age, and he knows how to handle his maulies, and to shoot quite well. He is a blood that will stand no nonsense when his sister's name is concerned. Come, my lord. We must go."

He slipped the great, blazing diamond on the little finger of my left hand, and lightly touched me on the shoulder, and motioned toward the door, as though in a hurry to depart.

Kitty started from the bed, and came toward me, her arms open, and her head still down, to hide the tears that flowed from her eyes.

"I promise hevery thing," she said, "if it is for 'is 'appiness."

"It is, Kitty," the Chief remarked, more mildly.

"Let 'im hanswer me," the girl cried, and raised her head in a queenly manner. "Yer speak, Angus, and hanswer me yerself."

"You hear what Mr. Murden says. It may be for my happiness. God knows, I don't. There is some cruel mystery connected with this matter, which I am unable to fathom. Good-by, Kitty."

I held out my hand.

"Give me one last kiss, a good one, and then go," she cried, and put up her white arms.

"Don't you do it," cried the Chief, with some visible alarm. "A jealous woman is like an old man kangaroo. She will scratch the life out of you while you think she is surrendering, and about to be good. Keep her at arm's-length."

I paid no attention to the warning, but put out my arms, and let the girl rest for a moment on my breast. Then I bent my head, and kissed her red lips, a long, lingering kiss, and when I had finished I felt her whole weight rest on my arm. Poor Kitty had fainted.

"Tumble her on the bed," cried the Chief, "and let us be off before she comes to her senses. I'll send the old woman to look after her. Oh, confound it! why can't women take to love as children do the measles, in light doses; break out for a while, and then recover, and get all ready for another attack, equally as harmless."

Instead of bundling the girl on the bed in an unceremonious manner, I laid her down with gentleness and reverence, and then bent over and kissed her pale lips for the last time.

"Well," muttered the Chief, "I don't see but that you can kiss a woman like other men when you get started. I began to think that you were coming the Joseph game, for the sake of throwing minute particles of our sandy plains in my eyes. However, I give you my word that I shall say nothing of all this at the next house where we have to make a call."

He opened the door leading to the entry, suddenly, and there found the old woman listening at the keyhole.

"I thought as much," Mr. Murden remarked, and, seizing the old female by the ear, led her into the room, and pointed to Kitty. "Look to the girl," he commanded, "and see what you can do for her. Do not let her out of the house tonight. You hear me, and understand?"

The woman nodded, and rubbed her ear.

"Keep your eyes on her all night, and don't let her slip away. We shall have rows enough in a little while without the girl putting in her oar, as she might do unless looked after. Remember, I shall have the house watched all night, and if you disobey me the worse for you."

The Chief motioned for me to pass on, and followed me to the door closed it, and then we stood on the sidewalk. He put the little whistle to his lips, and blew a gentle blast. Smithers and Dick emerged from the obscurity of a dark alley, and came toward us.

"Dick, go for a hansom," Mr. Murden said. "Smithers, find the officer on this beat, and tell him to shadow this house all night, and to let no one leave it, unless it is a matter of life and death. If Miss Kitty should make a move, lock her up until morning, when I will dispose of her."

The two officers saluted, and left us to do the bidding of the Chief.

"Now, my lord," said Mr. Murden, "you may as well brace up, for you have a devil of a job before you, and no mistake. All that has passed is mere child's play compared to what you will have to encounter. What are your plans?"

"I have none," I said. "I shall tell the truth."

"Bosh! how do you intend to account for your absence when you face a beautiful girl, dressed for a wedding, and some confoundedly ugly relatives?"

"Deny that I am the Earl of Afton," I stammered.

"My lord, don't be any greater ass than you can help, or that Providence intended you should assume during your minority. That cock won't fight here in Melbourne, and you should know it by this time. We Australians may not be noble by way of birth, but we are not altogether such blasted fools as you would have us believe. Now listen to me, and be attentive. You want to live, don't you? A man with an income of three hundred thousand pounds a year, and millions of ready money, lands and castles in Scotland and England, does n't want to kick the bucket when he is only nineteen years of age, does he?"

"No, it does not strike me that he would. I should think he would find life very pleasant."

"Well, you pipe that lay, and see where you land. Old Monsieur Allete, a fiery Frenchman, who can fence like an angel, will be there."

"I should like to see an angel fencing," I remarked. "It would be an angelic sight. Did you ever see an angel?"

"Now look here, my lord, don't you be any funnier than you can help just now, because you will want all of your wit, if you have any, to get out of the worst scrape that you ever encountered in your life. Come, what yarn will you reel off to the old man Kebblewhite, and his amiable daughter, her brother, and a dozen old women, who would hang by the neck every man who did not marry at the age of twenty, and dared to look at any other woman beside his wife ever after? Let us have your plea, and, if it is consistent with truth and honor, I 'll swear to it, for the sake of helping you along in the world. I don't want to lie, I despise a liar from the bottom of my heart, but sometimes it is necessary that men should make common cause with each other, and thus protect themselves from their mutual enemy, woman, who is bound to get married at all hazards, at all times, and in all places, and to be the biggest toad in the puddle, if she can only freeze to a male in time, or before a rival girl has a chance. Come, my lord, your plea."

"If I deny that I am the Earl of Afton, the consequences will be serious, you think?" I asked.

"I know what they will be. The old Frenchman will spit you on his rapier, the brother will shoot you down like a dog, old Kebblewhite will bang you over the head with a native's *nulla*, and crack your skull, the women will go into convulsions, and all the young bloods of Melbourne will take a hand, and end your days, if you get through with the relatives with life in your body. By the way, are you a good shot?"

"Excellent, with pistol or rifle."

"Can you fence?"

"I'll warrant that I could even hold the Frenchman in check. I have had foils in my hands since I was eight years of age. My father gave me lessons, and he was a pupil of the best swordsman in France."

"That may be, but, dash it! the nulla would fetch you, unless your skull is as thick as boiler iron, and I begin to think that it is. No, no, my lord, none of those excellent qualities will save you. You would have to fight too many men. Some of them would fetch you. Let me think. Ah, now I have a plan."

"What is it?" I asked eagerly, for I thought that he would let me escape.

"It is this, my lord. Most of our young swells knew that you were to be married this afternoon."

"Did they?"

"Yes; and they also knew that the wedding was a private one. They thought that you should have been swung off at St. Paul's Church, with a big audience, and all the fuss and tumult of a public execution. You follow me, my lord?"

"I am trying to. Lead on."

"Well, then, some of the young swells put up a job on you."

"What kind of a job?" I asked.

"Well, my lord, that I will explain if you will only have patience to listen to me for a moment. Here comes the hansom. I hear it rattling around the corner. I must be brief. The young fellows put up a job on you in this way. They drugged your wine, and let you sleep until I found you at a young gentleman's residence, where you had been carried while stupefied. Owing to the tearful pleadings of the young swell and his parents, I agree to keep everything secret, and not reveal his name. You do not know it, and never will. I have bathed you, soda-watered you, walked you up and down, until the fumes of the opium wore off, and now here you are, all right, and repentant. What do you think of my scheme, my lord?"

"Mr. Murden," I said, "you told me some time this evening that you were acquainted with a celebrated bushranger, named Steel Spring."

"Yes. What then?"

"You also said that he was a celebrated liar. That none could surpass him."

"Yes; and he is just what I represented."

"Don't you think you and he could have a meeting, and see which is the most proficient in yarning? I won't say lying, for I don't want to hurt Steel Spring's feelings, if he should ever hear of my remark."

"Bosh!" cried the disgusted Chief, "don't be foolish, and think it is smart. I compared you to the bushranger, so your idea is not original. I have invented the only plan by which all things can be made smooth, the lady's wounded vanity healed, and the rest of the relatives satisfied. Will you accept the theory, or not?"

"Must I marry the lady at any rate?"

"Of course. That is part of the programme. No marry, no safety."

"I can't deceive a pure young girl like Miss Kebblewhite," I said, in a dejected tone.

"Yes, d— me if I should n't think your conscience would trouble you by this time, my lord. It is as elastic as a boomerang, and you never know when and where it is going to strike, after it once gets going. Oh, yes, you have a conscience, you have, and Kitty, and other girls, and the diamond ring, know all about it."

"Let events take what course they will," I said, with a sigh of real regret. "I have done all that man can do to avoid my fate. Do as you please with me, but be assured I shall speak the truth."

"I hope, my lord, you will not exert yourself unnecessarily over such a difficult task;" and just then the hansom drove up, and Smithers reported, and received orders to follow us with Dick, as soon as the latter returned.

"I may not want you," the Chief remarked, "but, when a man will insist in saying that he is n't himself, but somebody else, it is just as well to have a few police officers around. Keep near the house, and wait for the usual signal before you come near me. Now, my lord, put on the armor of your ancestors, and infuse some of their brass into your face, for you are going to have a devil of a time, or I 'm much mistaken."

"Var to, Mr. Murden?" asked the driver of the hansom.

"You know where Mr. Kebblewhite lives, on Victoria Parade?" the Chief asked.

"Vot is yer givin' me, sour beer, Mr. Murden? Don't I know the old cove vot vos formerly an old " —

"Silence, you scoundrel!" roared the Chief. "Your tongue is too free. Keep it in check, or I 'll find a way of shortening it."

"Beg pardon, sir. No hoffence, sir, honly yer knows he vos."

'Drive on to the gentleman's house, and hold your jaws together. Now, away you go, and don't sleep on the road."

The man did not go to sleep, or allow his horse to slumber. He was just ten minutes on the way; the most mauvais quarter hour that I had ever experienced in my life, for I was all of a tremble, and my throat was parched with thirst.

"Courage, my lord. We 'll meet them like men. Why, all the young swells in Melbourne would dance with joy if in your blessed shoes. Ah, here we are.' Come, my lord, please to dismount, and take my arm. So, that is well. Call at the office and get your pay tomorrow, unless his lordship has a couple of crowns. Ah, that is all right. Let us be generous on our wedding night. Brace up, and smile just a little."

I looked at the house, as we walked up the path to the front door. It was an immense mansion, built of stone, and three stories high, with a broad piazza all around the front side, while vines and flowers were growing in profusion in every direction in the grounds, scenting the air with their fragrance. A large gaslight hung over the door, showing the hard, carved wood of the latter, and the big silver door-plate, and bell-handle, pride and arrogance being displayed in their size.

"Nothing mean about this house, is there, my lord?" asked the Chief; "although I suppose it will not compare with some of your castles. Well, this will answer for us poor colonial people. We shall do better some time, I dare say, as we get rich, and free, and old."

I was too much agitated to reply. The Chief touched the bell very lightly, and the door was almost immediately opened, by an old, gray-haired servant, in livery, and white favors on his coat, and a large bunch of white flowers in one of his button-holes.

"Velcome, my lud. Ve 'as been wery anxious about yer, and the poor young misses 'as just about cried 'er pretty hyes out of 'er 'ead. I told 'em yer 'd come to time, but no von vould believe me."

This was my reception by the servant. It was a warmer welcome than I expected or deserved.

"Where is your master, Harry?" asked Mr. Murden.

"Vel, sir, 'e am in the dinin' room vid the rest of 'em, a lushin' down the drink, and 'e is in a wery precious 'umor, yer 'ad better believe. But valk in, my lud, and I 'll tell 'im that yer is hall right now."

We entered the drawing-room, dimly lighted with gas, but I could see that it was exquisitely furnished, with French carpets, and old Persian rugs. On the mantels of white marble were choice Sèvres vases, a magnificent clock, and the walls of the room were covered with oil paintings and choice engravings, while in a corner was a beautiful grand piano, opened, and music on the rack, as though some one had recently been playing. The furniture was covered with blue satin damask, and the curtains were of the same material, and heavy white lace.

"Not bad, my lord," whispered the Chief. "I should not object to being the son-in-law of this establishment, with a pretty wife thrown in, just to make everything pleasant and comfortable."

I did not answer him. My heart was in my mouth, as the common saying goes, and it beat so rapidly that I feared the Chief would hear it, and note my agitation.

"You have not forgotten your lesson, have you?" Mr. Murden continued, as we heard a movement in the dining-room. "If the old man has been *lushing* to any extent he will be in a —— ugly mood, and no mistake. Here he comes, and may Heaven have mercy on your soul, or head, it does not matter much which."

The door of the drawing-room was thrown open with a crash, and in walked a stout old gentleman, with the stiffest gray hair, and the reddest face that I had seen in Melbourne, excepting the head waiter at the Hen and Chickens. He looked to me like a dangerous crank, and so I found him to be before I had done with him.

"Vy is n't this 'ere gas turned up?" the old lunatic roared, as he entered the room. "Yer 'Arry, vot the bloody thunder do yer mean by not puttin' on the light, so that ve can see vot is afore us?"

"I hobey horders, sir," was the reply. "Yer tells me vot to do, and I does it. Yer tells me to save the glim, and I does it, and then yer gives me a bloody good dressin' down ven I does do it. Vot is the huse of grumblin' at me hall the time?"

"Silence, yer scoundrel!" roared the master of the house, who I supposed was my respected intended father in-law, Mr. Anderson Kebblewhite, dressed as for a party, with swallow-tail coat, white vest, black trousers, and patent leather pumps. "If yer makes any more remarks to me, if yer gives me any more back talk, I 'll jist bundle yer hout-of-doors, or crack yer 'ead vid a nulla," the master said, in a tone of voice that was not comforting to his young listener, and prospective son-in-law, and I did feel a little timid in his presence.

Mr. Murden gave me a significant glance, as though to warn me as to my future fate, unless I was quite careful in all my dealings with the excitable old gentleman, flush with wine and disappointment.

The old servant, who did not appear to be very much alarmed at the loud talk and threats, having heard the same thing many times before, turned up the gas, and lighted some wax candles on the mantles, and then Mr. Kebblewhite and I stood looking at each other. His face was hard and stern, his eyes sharp and deep-set, with a little shade of cunning in them, but, with all his pride of wealth, and all his fierce aspect, I could see that he was uneasy and anxious in the presence of one whom he supposed to be of the aristocracy of the United Kingdom of Great Britain.

"Vell, I 'm —— if yer 'ave n't harrived at last," were the gentleman's first words, for I was in hopes that he would see that I was not the distinguished person he was expecting. "Vell, sir, vot 'as yer to say for yerself?" he continued. "A man vot is not on time for 'is vedding don't deserve a vife, and sich a vife as my own little gal, good enough for a prince, I can tell yer, sir." Then he glared at me as if daring me to doubt his word.

"Yes, or a hemperor," the old servant interrupted, standing at the door, and surveying the scene with fatherly interest.

"I 'll break yer blasted neck, if yer don't light hout of this! 'Ow dare yer put in yer woice, yer scoundrel, ven I 'm haddressin' his ludship?" asked Mr. Kebblewhite.

"'Cos 'e 'ad no business to keep us hall a-vaitin', and let the grub get hall cold. It a'n't ship-shape, and yer knows it. But, as 'e is a lud, yer puts hup vid it. Yer 'd punch the 'ead of heny one helse vot dared to do so, and put a slight on my young misses, vot is good henough for a hemperor, and no mistake about it."

Mr. Kebblewhite made a move as though he was about to throw a prayer-book at the head of "'Arry," and the latter, who knew his master's moods, and the precision of his aim, left the room, and then, turning, peered around the casement of the door, so that he could dodge like a loon at the first flash of the heavenly volume.

During all this time I had not spoken a word, or made the slightest movement, while Mr. Murden, who stood near me, seemed to tremble as though convulsed with an internal volcano, but when I glanced at him he was stuffing a silk handkerchief into his mouth, to prevent the shrieks of laughter which wanted to find vent.

"Pardon me, yer ludship, but I must 'ave discipline in this 'ere 'ouse. If I did n't the scamps vould run away vid me in less than no time. Mr. Murden, yer is velcome 'ere, and more velcome 'cos yer 'as brought the vandering sheep vid yer. Now, let us hunderstand hall about this hunfortunate business. Vy vos not yer ludship hup to time? Vot did yer keep us hall vaitin' for? Vy vas my little gal hall neglected from three o'clock till now?"

The stout, hard-faced old man stopped to get breath, and, to my surprise, I saw tears in the sharp, cunning eyes, and he did not try to conceal them, but wiped them away with a white linen handkerchief. Good Heaven! this man, whom I supposed so hard, and without feeling, loved his daughter as dearly as a person who had better early advantages in the way of education. I liked him all the more for his sentiment, so plainly expressed. He had a heart, and that heart beat warmly for his daughter, even if he was a boor.

"Mr. Kebblewhite," I said, speaking for the first time, "I know that you will pardon me when" —

"One moment, your lordship," interrupted Mr. Murden, with a significant look at me, as though to warn me that I was about to commit a blunder in denying my identity. "Perhaps it would be better that I should explain to Mr. Kebblewhite all that has happened since his son brought me information that your lordship had turned up missing, as we say in the force. The fact of it is, Mr. Kebblewhite, young bloods will be young bloods, and the boys rather played it on his lordship last night. They gave him a late supper, and a little more wine than he should have taken."

"Ah, is that hall?" the master of the house exclaimed, with a sigh of relief, and the frown left his brows.

"Not quite all, sir. In the last glass of champagne which his lordship drunk, were a few drops of a sleeping potion."

"The —— scoundrels! I 'll punish them for this. Mr. Murden, yer must take charge of this matter, and prosecute them to the extent of the law."

"That, sir, I can't do. I have promised to hush the matter up, to prevent scandal to his lordship, and to your family. Think for a moment, and you will see that my course is best."

"Perhaps it is, but I 'd like to 'ave a clip at 'em, jist the same. Now I s'pose 'is ludship is hall ready to be married? Vell, ve 'll send for the parson, and 'e 'll be 'ere in no time. I knows it, 'cos 'e promised to keep at 'ome hall the hevening. 'Arry, send the coachman for the minister at vonce; and tell Florry that 'is ludship is 'ere, and that 'e 'as hexplained, and that 'e vill be married at vonce."

"One moment, Mr. Kebblewhite," I said, taking a step forward, and speaking as firmly as I could, although I knew that I trembled.

"Your lordship will remember that there is no chance for words at this late hour. All explanations have been made," cried Mr. Murden, with a dangerous look in his eyes, and a warning gesture.

"No, now is the time for explanations, here in the presence of Mr. Kebblewhite, the father of the young lady whom you seem determined that I shall marry," I said quite firmly.

"Your lordship has had a fair warning," whispered the Chief. "Don't blame me if there is a collision on the down grade."

Mr. Kebblewhite stared at me, and I heard him mutter, "Forced to marry my precious gal," and his hands began to work, and his eyes to glitter with a dangerous light, while his face whitened with passion, and his lips moved convulsively.

"Stand by to douse all sail," the Chief groaned. "Oh, be warned, be warned in time."

"I will not be warned. I will tell all. I will not lend myself to the base, infamous scheme that I see before me."

"Go on, or I 'll be cussed if I don't strangle yer!" Mr. Kebblewhite roared, white with passion.

"Do so if you will, sir, but I am not the Earl of Afton, I am not a lord, I am not an Englishman. I am something far better than either: I am an American sovereign."

"'Arry," roared the enraged master of the house, "'Arry, bring me my pistols, and my nulla. I 'll kill him as sure as there is a God in 'eaven. Hall the law in Hostralia sha'n't prevent me!"

Luckily for me, Harry, the servant, had gone to give orders to the coachman, for I heard the carriage roll out of the coach-house, and on the gravel walks. This gave time to Mr. Murden to spring forward, and place a hand on Mr. Kebblewhite's broad shoulders, and in a measure restrain him from anticipated violence.

"Come, sir," the Chief said, very sternly, "I'll have no murder committed here in my presence. If you call for pistols again, or your club, I'll whistle in my men, and walk you off to the station-house in bloody, double-quick time now I tell you."

"Yer vould dare to do that?" roared the master of the house, foaming with passion.

"As the Chief of the Police of Melbourne, I dare do everything and anything, and fear no man, or his power, or his money. I will save you, and I will save the reputation of the Belle of Australia, and I'll save and shame his lordship, the Earl of Afton, who now denies his rank, for the sake of shirking what he thinks is a *mésalliance*."

The old man made a movement as though he would break away from the Chief's grasp, and come at me, and inflict some injuries with his bony fists.

"Don't be rash, Mr. Kebblewhite. We don't want any revival of old accounts here just now. I know all your past history, but his lordship does not, and shall not from me. Lay your finger on his lordship tonight, and all Melbourne will blaze with but what few really know. Keep cool. There will be time enough for violence if all other means fail. Will you promise me?"

"Yes; but I'd like to put my 'ands on 'is —— white throat jist for a minute; only for a minute."

"Do you think that would do any good? Do you suppose that the Earl of Afton would make a countess of your daughter after you had assaulted him? Remember, above all things, that Miss Florence loves this gentleman, loves him with all her heart, with all the strength and purity of her good and great nature. She will believe in him, and not in you, just as soon as he puts an arm around her, or presses her hand. Your word will be of no consequence in comparison with his, your paternal tenderness will not weigh as a feather, when her lover speaks to her in honeyed words. Come, listen to reason, man. Your daughter shall be married tonight, and we'll have a drink of champagne to the health of the handsomest couple in Melbourne, or Australia;" and Mr. Murden released his hold of the excitable gentleman, and waited for an answer.

Mr. Kebblewhite weakened. His eyes lost their fire, and his face once more flushed, while his fingers ceased to clutch and move, as though working around my slim throat.

"You see what you have narrowly escaped," the Chief whispered over his shoulder to me, while Mr. Kebblewhite had turned away. "Be warned in season, or I may not be able to save you a second time."

"Give me your plan," said the master of the house. "I 'll be patient, but now, by hall the saints in the calendar, 'is ludship shall marry Florry, and this wery night. I might 'ave let 'im hoff if 'e 'd cried baby, and howned up like a man; but now 'e 'll marry 'er, or 'e 'll face me and a dozen huthers. I 'll not 'ave Florry insulted by a lud, or heny von helse, vile I 'ave strength."

This was pleasant for me. I had explained time and time again that I was not a nobleman, but it was of no avail, and what to do I did not know. I must marry or die.

"My lord," said the Chief, "will you please to give me your full name?"

"Angus Mornington," I responded.

"Mr. Kebblewhite, I see you have a book of the peerage on your centre-table. Look among the peers, and you will find the name of Angus Mornington, Earl of Afton, and Baron Midlothian, aged nineteen," the Chief said.

"Yes, it is 'ere," was the reply.

"So I supposed. Now you know that his lordship arrived here from China in Her Majesty's frigate *Carrysford*, Captain Lord George Pollock. This was some three weeks ago."

Mr. Kebblewhite nodded his head in response to the question of Mr. Murden.

"Well, our friend here, the Earl of Afton, brought letters of introduction to the lieutenant-governor of Victoria, and I was present at a reception at the government house, and heard his excellency introduce his lordship to the legislature as the Earl of Afton."

"Vell, —— it! so vos I," cried Mr. Kebblewhite. "I seed the thing as vell as yer."

"I am aware of it, sir; and now I ask you if the captain of a frigate, if the governor of a province, could be so deceived as to entertain an impostor?"

"No, a thousand times no," was the prompt response.

I saw that the cunning Chief had got me into a very narrow path, and that there was no chance for me to turn aside, and save myself from destruction.

"Your lordship hears all that is said?" asked the Chief.

"Yes, I hear everything."

"Now, will your lordship please to hold up your left hand just for a moment?" the Chief said.

I wondered what he was driving at, but did as requested.

"Mr. Kebblewhite, please to examine the diamond ring on his **lordship's** little finger. You can see it glitter from where you stand. Do you recognize it?"

"Of course I do. I give it to Florry on 'er birthday, von year ago."

"You knew that she had lent it to his lordship, I suppose?"

"Vell, yes, she tells me that 'e 'as it, but I s'posed it vos hall in the family in time, and so did n't mind it wery much."

"You do not suppose that his lordship would part with that ring for a moment, do you?"

"Vell, I 'd mash 'is blasted 'ead if 'e did, that 's vot I 'd do!" was the angry growl, and a look that told what a poor chance I should have if the old gentleman had a native club, or heavy nulla, in his hand, at the time such a suspicion was raised in his mind.

"Does not this ring prove that he is the same person to whom your charming daughter plighted her troth?" asked the Chief, in a tone that was quite soothing.

I saw the point to which the Chief was leading up, but, for the life of me, I could not prevent it. He was as merciless as fate, marching onward with but one purpose, and that was to accomplish his will, and my unhappiness, or destruction. Which would it be? Time only could tell.

"Of course it does. Vot do yer hax that 'ere question for?" demanded Mr. Kebblewhite, in an angry tone.

"I have a motive," was the Chief's reply, in a quiet manner, and a look at my face, with such a glance of triumph, that I wanted to strike him, but if I did I knew that I should get the worst of it.

"Vell, hout vid it," the gentleman of the house cried.

"Your lordship will please to pay marked attention to my next question," Mr. Murden said, and turned toward me, and looked so stern, that I knew the moment, when I had got to lie and be safe, or tell the truth and be killed, had come. "Your lordship is positive that the ring which you now wear on your little finger has never left your possession since Miss Kebblewhite placed it in your hands, some few days since?"

"If I thought it 'ad, —— me if I vould n't bust 'im hall to pieces!" roared the old gentleman, and he took a step toward me, but I did not move, or put myself on the defensive. Mr. Murden laid a hand on the broad shoulder of my proposed father-in-law, and restrained him.

"Be quiet, sir," he said. "I am conducting this case, and doing it in regular supreme-court style. You just wait for the gentleman's answer before you put on your fighting rig, and step into the ring. I am umpiring this little game, and will have no interference. It is going to be a fair fight, or all bets will be off. Please to answer the question, Earl of Afton. Your lordship has had plenty of time to think of it in all its bearings, and know as well as I do what the result will be."

He gave me such a look, that, if I had had my revolver in my pocket, I would have drawn it, and defied him. But I was alone, unarmed. All were against me, and it was useless to struggle with my fate. I did not dare to say that the ring had but recently come into my possession, and from the hands of a young girl like Kitty, whose reputation, I judged, was none of the best in the city. I felt the hot tears of anger and mortified pride well from my eyes, but the Chief knew no pity. He was hard and stern as some of the rocks on his native coast, and would have an answer.

"Well, my lord, are you still under the influence of the opiate you imbibed last night, that you do not speak? We wait for a reply."

"The ring has never left my posesssion since the time I first received it," I answered, and glanced at the face of the Chief to see how he enjoyed my evasion.

To my surprise he actually smiled, as though pleased at the way in which I had escaped telling a base falsehood.

"You hear his lordship," Mr. Murden remarked, turning to Mr. Kebblewhite. "Are you satisfied, sir?"

"Vell, I s'pose I 'd haught to be. Blast it hall, a lud should n't lie, but I s'pose they is like huther men, and 'as their little veaknesses. Yer vould n't mind jist puttin' yer 'and to the Bible, vould yer, my lud, and swearin' to that 'ere?"

"There is no occasion for that, Mr. Kebblewhite," the Chief remarked. "We have established two things. First, that this gentleman is the Earl of Afton, and, secondly, that the ring has never left his hand since it was loaned him. ——— it, sir, we must give the nobility a little liberty, or what is the use of having such a class? I am satisfied with my evening's work, and should think that you would be, sir. No one could have managed the case so shrewdly as you have. You have not offended his lordship, and your daughter will have a husband, and be a countess."

"Vell, now, Murden, I do believe that I 'as done vell. I 'as kept my temper, and I ax 'is ludship's pardon if I 'as said any little thing vot vos 'asty, yer know."

The old gentleman bit quite keenly at the little bit of flattery which the skillful Chief had thrown to him, and the latter had the impudence to snap his eyes, and wink, at the manner in which he was leading along the master of the house.

"Vill yer ludship be seated?" asked Mr. Kebblewhite, for I had remained standing all the time I had been in the room, and really felt a little faint and weak after such a trying ordeal as I had gone through during the evening, in-doors and out on the streets.

I was glad of the permission, but the quick eyes of Murden saw that I was pale and trembling from agitation, and dismay at the prospect before me.

"Your lordship had better drink a glass of wine. Mr. Kebblewhite, the promised happiness of your noble son-in-law is too much for him. Will you ring for a glass of wine for his lordship, and one for myself? I like champagne if it is well *frappé*. Better bring a bottle and goblets. I am as thirsty as though I had passed through a sirocco, or dust storm."

The old servant came to the door as the bell was touched.

"Miss Florence 'ad gone to bed for a good cry, sir, but she 's hup, and vill dress agin as fast as possible. She 's jist ravin' 'cos hall the horringe blossoms is vilted, as though I 'd heny thing to do vid that. I 've told the gardener to pick some more, and now vat does yer vant?"

"Bring me a bottle of champagne, yer himpertinent scoundrel. Tomorrer yer goes," the fiery master of the house thundered.

"Go var, sir?"

The gilt-bound prayer-book was raised, but the old man was ready to skip as he uttered a protest: —

"I tell yer vot it is, sir, the dinin'-room is the place to lush in. That French moorsur is jist pourin' down heverythin' that is on the table, and 'e 'll be drunk afore the veddin', yer see ef 'e a'n't, hunless yer puts a stopper on 'is throat."

Mr. Kebblewhite made a motion with the holy book, but the old servant dodged as usual. He soon returned with the wine, as cool as the Chief desired, and then three full goblets were poured out.

"I propose," remarked Mr. Murden, "the health and happiness of the Earl and Countess of Afton. Long may they live to enjoy each others' society."

"And hall the little Haftens," said the enthusiastic Mr. Kebblewhite. "The fust boy shall 'ave a gift of ten thousand pounds, and the fust gal honly five thousand. I 'as long been hanxious to connect my family wid a *syphon* of the haristocracy."

The Chief looked at me, and nearly laughed, as he said, —

"There is but little difference after all between a syphon and scion. I rather think that the former is the strongest word, and so will not shut it off."

Mr. Kebblewhite did not seem to understand what the Chief meant, for he glanced at Mr. Murden as though an explanation was needed, but none was given, and the wine was swallowed, and really did me an immense sight of good, for it revived my spirits, and put some strength into my frame.

"Von more glass, and then ve 'll let in some of the company," cried Mr. Kebblewhite. " Ve 'll 'ave a pleasant little party vile Florry is fixin' hup. Don't be hempatient, yer ludship. It is hall right now. My vord for it."

The wine being finished, Harry received orders to let the company who were in the dining-room, feasting on the wedding breakfast, so called, come into the drawing-room, and be formally presented to the great guest of the evening, and the most important person in the house, not even excepting the prospective bride.

I heard them trooping along, and braced myself for the meeting. First came the French gentleman, Monsieur Allete, escorting a Mrs. Victoria Kebblewhite, a very tall and thin lady, about forty-five years of age, who was an aunt of the bride. Then there was Judson Kebblewhite, the son, a stout, good-looking fellow, who escorted no one, because his mother was up-stairs helping Florence to dress, and there were no young ladies present that he cared to pay any attention to. There were about twenty people in all, and they came forward, and bowed to me very low, and then trod on each others' toes and heels, while backing out of my presence, and jostled each other, and poked one another with their elbows, and whispered, and stared at me in the wildest fashion, and as though I was a great and mysteous curiosity, and they feared I might make a rush, and bite some one. All but the Frenchman, who had met me on the street, and gave me the casket of diamonds. He was not abashed in the least, for he rushed forward, and exclaimed, —

"Ah, parbleu. See you again do I? You bin whar? Alors, you my diamonds take. Do vid them vhat? Laissez moi voir."

"Come, come, Moorsur Allete, don't let 's 'ave heny of that 'ere lingo 'ere tonight. 'Is ludship vants to 'ear the real hold Hinglish, and not heny of Johnny Crapeaud's nose-talkin' stuff, vot no von hunderstands. The queen's gab is good enough for me," and Mr. Kebblewhite waved the French gentleman aside, but he would not take a back seat at the dictation of the host. He was bound to have his say, and I did not blame him, when such valuable jewels were at stake.

"Milord, regardez moi. Me look at quick. I diamonds to you give, for the fiancée. Ah, ——! vous dites, hey?"

"Oh, jist shut hup, vill yer," cried Mr. Kebblewhite. "Yer act like a bloody fool in the presence of this distinguished company. 'Is ludship don't vant no furreners a 'owlin' round 'im tonight."

But Murden had caught the word diamonds, and hastened to put in a word.

"Let Monsieur Allete speak," he pleaded. "I don't know much about the French lingo myself, but his lordship should know something of it, if he has been through Eton. Now, monsieur, do I understand that you met his lordship on the street this forenoon, and spoke to him in French?"

"Oui. — Yes, that is."

"And he answered you in French?"

"Certemont," with great assurance.

"And you gave him some diamonds to take to Miss Kebblewhite?"

"Diantre, yes."

"And is this the gentleman?" pointing to me.

"Imbécile, of course," with a shrug of contempt.

"You are sure?" persisted Mr. Murden.

"Tais tor," with a shrug of his shoulders, and turned his back on the Chief.

"What does Monsieur Allete say?" asked the Chief, turning to me, and smiling so pleasantly, that I replied, without a moment's thought, —

"He says that you are a fool, and wants you to hold your tongue."

"I think your lordship is the one who received the diamonds," was the smooth response, and no show of annoyance. "Another spoke in your wheel if you still seem disposed to deny that you are the Earl of Afton."

"Yes, the diamonds. To me give, milord. They is for une jolie femme. Your fiancée. Comprend vous? Have them now she should. To put her pretty little ears in. It is bon. Sans doubte. Pardix, a little affair overlook you."

I turned my back to the company for a moment, and drew out the precious package from my bosom, and handed it to the Frenchman, but he bowed and smiled, and shrugged his shoulders, and refused to accept the casket.

"No, pardon, milord, I to you give to put in the ears of ma petite chere amie. Do it you will."

"Let me see the jewels for a moment," demanded the suspicious Chief; and he took the box, and opened it, and then all the glorious beauty of the valuable stones was seen under the gaslight, sparkling like the stars on a cold, frosty night. A murmur of admiration was heard in every part of the drawing-room, and even Mr. Kebblewhite was kind enough to be polite, and utter a few words of thanks.

"They'll pay for hall the lush 'e 'as drunk this night," the old servant said, he having entered the room, and got a peep at the diamonds over the shoulders of the company.

"You did not mention the jewels to me," Mr. Murden remarked, as he returned the casket, and there was a look of disappointment on his face, to think that there was a secret in which he had no part.

"Now, s'il vous plait, give to her the diamonds, and compliments of mine;" said the gallant Frenchman; and, just at this moment, there was a stir at the door, and in the hall, and a vision of loveliness, dressed in white, with a wealth of golden hair floating over the handsomest pair of shoulders that ever delighted the heart of man, with just such a form as an angel is supposed to possess, slim, *petite*, and as graceful as Venus, darted toward me, and threw her white, beautifully formed arms around my neck, rested her sweet face on my bosom, and put up her red, thin lips for a kiss, as she murmured, —

"O Angus, dear Angus, I have been so unhappy all the evening because you did not come to me; but now all is explained, and all is forgiven, and I love you just as well as ever, and I do hope you will love me a little. Will you, dear?"

MR. KEBBLEWHITE AGAIN CALLS FOR HIS PISTOLS AND NULLA.

PART IV.

AN EMBARRASSING POSITION FOR A YOUNG MAN. — MR. KEBBLEWHITE AGAIN GETS ANGRY, AND CALLS ONCE MORE FOR HIS PISTOLS AND NULLA. — NO TIME FOR EXPLANATIONS. — A SAD WEDDING AND A COLLATION AND DRINKING. — I LIKE MY NEW MOTHER-IN-LAW, AND SHE RATHER LIKES ME. — MR. KEBBLEWHITE GIVES US A SPECIMEN OF HIS VOCAL POWERS.

IT was a wailing, appealing, tender, and touching cry, that simple one of —

"O Angus!"

A man must have had a heart of stone to have resisted it, especially when it was fortified by such a charming little girl as had entered the drawing-room, thrown her arms around my neck, and sighed out, —

"O Angus!"

As the young lady laid her golden hair upon my bosom, and looked up in my face with all the beaming tenderness of her pure eyes and soul, I surely thought that she would discover I was not the Angus of her true, fervent love. But no, she was just as demonstrative as though I had been the proper man, the hero of her hopes and her dreams, her ambition and confidence.

She put up her sweet lips, — a rose-bud of a mouth, — with the gleaming of white teeth behind them, and, while the tears were falling from her large blue eyes, veiled by lashes so long and dark-brown that they swept her white cheeks, she nestled still closer in my unwilling arms, and whispered, —

"Kiss me, dear Angus."

Good Heaven! Here was a real crank, and the most fascinating one that I had encountered in Melbourne. I did not dare to follow her request, although I did permit my arms to encircle her supple waist, and to hold her close to my wildly beating heart. But to kiss such lips as those, when the wealth of good things was intended for another, even if he was unworthy, was something I did not dare to undertake, much as I wanted to.

"Angus," she whispered, while the company present pretended to turn their backs on us, and engage in mutual congratulations, so that we could have a moment's private conversation, "you do not kiss me, and yet if you only knew how I have cried since three o'clock this afternoon. Oh, when you did not come at the appointed hour I thought that I should die with mortification and shame. I feared that you had repented of your promise, and no longer loved me. That you did not think me worthy to be your own dear little wife, and a countess. I know that I have spoiled what little beauty I had, and that my eyes are red with tears, but now you are here my weeping shall cease, and my eyes shall be as bright as the diamond I gave you the other day. You know, dear, that is not my comparison, but your own. But you flattered your Florry when you uttered such idle sayings. But I forgive you for being late. I have learned all about it. You will never dine with such wild young men again, will you? Harry, an old family servant, heard Mr. Murden explain to papa, and came to my chamber, and told mamma and I all about it. He listened at the door, and caught the words, and I was so delighted that I forgot to reprimand him for his fault and impertinence. It is a way he has, but then he has been in our family so long that he does just as he pleases, and says that it is all for love of me. He does love me, I know, for he has watched over me since I was born. But you do not speak to me, dear Angus, and you have not kissed me even once since I entered the room, and your arms," she concluded, with a pretty little blush.

She put up her sweet lips, and then I yielded. Man may struggle and strive to break through the meshes of a pretty girl's love, but he often fails, unless a cold and iron will is inclosed within his breast.

"Here are some of the good things of this world within my reach, and why should I not take them?" I asked myself. "These kisses were not intended for me, and I am obtaining them under false pretences, but the real owner is a mean, pitiful scoundrel, and does not deserve such treasures, and I think that I do, for I could love this little darling better than all the world, and with a love that would endure all changes and reverses."

Thus I reasoned, because I wanted to be convinced that I was justified in the course I was pursuing. Had the lady been old and plain, with lots of false hair and teeth, I could have reasoned very differently, I suppose, had I tried.

But I bent my head, and kissed the red lips that were within my reach. The hot blood bounded through my veins, and my face flushed painfully, as our lips met, and, as the first tasted so good, I did not scruple to take a second, and even a third. I forgot that I was not a lord, but a poor young fellow, with a fortune to make, and that I had no business to hold the lady in my arms, or to press her pure lips; but men often get absent-minded in such matters.

"That will do, Angus," laughed Miss Kebblewhite. "I only said one, you know, and you have taken three. Well, only one more then, for you see all the people in the room are looking, and poor mamma will have a fit if I do not keep within the proprieties. But you still love me, dear Angus?"

This last in a whisper, and only intended for my ears. Ah! how musical was her voice.

"Now for it," I thought. "She knows her lover's voice. She must be accustomed to it, and will see that I am not the person she supposes. "Dear Miss Florence," I said, and expected to see her start from my arms, but she did not, only nestled a little closer to my beating heart, "no one could see you, and not love you, no one could converse with you, and not admire you. Happy will the man be who wins you for a wife."

"Why, you are the one who has won me, you are the one who will have me for a wife. Are you happy at the thought, Angus?"

"I should be if"—I stammered, and then stopped.

"Ah, I know you fear that your mother, the Countess of Afton, will not like me, and will not think that I am suitable for an earl's bride, but I shall strive to make her love me, and prove worthy of the proud position which I am to occupy. Do you think I shall make a nice countess, and a pretty one? If you say yes you shall have one more little kiss; mind, only a little one, for that horrid Chief of Police is looking at us as though he would devour you, or is it me?"

She put up her smiling mouth, and gave me the coveted kiss, even before I had answered the important question.

"Dear Miss Florence," I said, "this lovely head does not need a coronet to add to its beauty. It would be admired in any part of the world, and there are no peeresses who can compare with you for nobleness, and goodness, and real loveliness, and angelic beauty."

"How kind of you, Angus, to speak such sweet words to me. There, as a reward, you may put your arms around my waist once more. I do not care if people are looking. In a few minutes you will be my husband, and I shall be your little loving wife, and the Countess of Afton."

How could I prevent a sigh from escaping from my overcharged bosom as I listened to her innocent anticipations. I could do nothing to dispel the illusion under which she was laboring unless I was prompt.

"Dear Florry," I whispered, "you are dear enough to be the wife of a sovereign, and if I occupied the most exalted position on the face of the globe, I would gladly share it with you. But you would not love me unless you thought I was noble, and could give you a position in the world." I meant to warn her very gently.

"I think I should," she answered, after a moment's hesitation. "I know that I love you now, but still," with an artless little smile, "I want to be a countess, and wear a coronet, and make all the girls of my acquaintance turn green with envy when they hear of my presentation at court, and read that the young Countess of Afton has excited quite a ripple in society by her entertainments, and her diamonds, and equipages. Oh, won't we be happy, Angus?"

"My own little darling," I said as soon as I could recovered my breath, for I did not see how all those luxuries could be supported with the five hundred dollars I had deposited in the Oriental Bank, "do you not think that you would be far happier if you should choose some one for your mate in your own station in society? Come, give up all ideas of this marriage, and win the love of some good man who will be worthy of you, die for you if necessary, and will never let his passion cool with age."

"What do you mean?" she asked, and turned on me in indignant surprise. "Do you mean that you want to give me up? That you are sorry you are to wed a merchant's daughter? Are you already tired of me? Is this the love that your lordship professed to feel for me, and hurried the day of the wedding, when you knew that no young lady can get her *trousseau* ready in less than three months?"

This last reflection appeared to be a little more grievous than all others, and there were symptoms of an eruption which I would have willingly quelled.

"Vot is the matter now, Florry?" asked the father, hearing his daughter's voice raised a little louder than usual, and seeing that she was agitated by some strong emotion, for tears again made their appearance.

"O papa," the young lady cried, "his lordship is asking me to release him from his engagement."

"Vot?" roared the old merchant. "Do I 'ear aright? 'Arry, bring me my pistols and my nulla! Quick! I'll kill the —— rascal as sure as I 'm a gentleman of Melbourne."

"One moment, Mr. Kebblewhite," said the Chief of Police, stepping forward. "We do not want pistols and clubs here on this happy occasion. Miss Kebblewhite has misunderstood his lordship."

"Sacre nom de Dieu," roared the Frenchman, "right hear do I? No noces. From the hook slip would he? Non, non. Carve him will I first. Dam! The meaning tell to me of this. Vit!"

"Keep quiet, all of you," said the calm, powerful voice of Murden. "Do not show a pistol or a particle of violence here. I'll do all the fighting that is to be done, and am capable of performing my share when there is occasion. Listen to me for a moment," and as the Chief advanced, he whispered to me, "My lord, you are a dead man unless you are guided by me."

"Oui, to the Chief ècutez," cried the Frenchman, waving his arms, and displaying some passion. "To him listen. Tout. —— the language Ingleese. I spit on it with contempt, much!"

In the mean time, Florence, who was frightened at the tumult which she had raised, woman-like, rushed to my arms to shelter me, and protect me from violence in case it should be offered.

"Put your arms around me, and hold me," she said. "No one shall harm you except through me."

God bless the dear little girl. Even in her distress and anxiety she thought of her love and lover.

"There is a misunderstanding here," the Chief said. "I can explain it in a few minutes. Miss Kebblewhite, have I your permission?" and he bowed very low to the lady.

"Yes, sir," she answered, and looked up at my face with a sweet smile on her own, all doubt having vanished.

"Can I speak for your lordship?" the Chief asked.

"Yes," I said, for I knew he would speak at all events, even if I did not consent.

"I accidentally overheard a part of the conversation which has occasioned all this excitement," Mr. Murden went on to say. "His lordship simply told his betrothed that he feared she would be happier to marry one in her own circle, for that he was not worthy of so much grace and beauty, such innocence and sweetness. Am I right, Miss Kebblewhite?"

"I think you are," she answered promptly.

The complimentary terms had struck her as being very appropriate, and she listened to them with pleasure.

The crafty Chief knew how to win the confidence of women, and keep them in subjection.

"Parbleu, is dat all?" muttered the Frenchman. "All fool lovers say de same ding ven court they do. Bah! Me say dat ding five hundred million dimes, and, damn! not married yet am I. Too much do I know to catch fox old like me. Elle a beaucoup de douceur, and husband do want. Dat is all right. He is here. He take her, but foolish nonsense he speak first. All men the same do. Make sick me."

We all waited until the Frenchman had finished his oration, and he was tolerated because he was immensely wealthy, and it was understood that Florence, his favorite, was to inherit his money, made in the wholesale spirit and wine trade, and still in business on Collins Street.

"My lord," said the Chief, "you have no idea of breaking the vows which you have given Miss Kebblewhite?"

"If he has, he must meet me tomorrow morning, and give me satisfaction," said the younger Mr. Kebblewhite, speaking for the first time.

"And me vid der rapier or der broadsword," cried the Frenchman.

"And I'll pepper 'im vid a shot gun afore 'e leaves this 'ouse," the old servant kindly remarked, to help make everything pleasant and lively.

"And I'll blow 'is brains hout on this carpet, if they is noble brains," yelled my proposed father-in-law, for the sake of keeping the pot boiling, as the boys used to say in the country, when at play. Oh, they were all an amiable set of cranks, and disposed to make the evening a pleasant one for me.

"Mr. Kebblewhite," I said, as soon as I could be heard, "I love your daughter so much, even in the short time that I have seen her, that I would give all the world, lose all the world, for her sake. I never loved a woman before. She is the first one to touch my heart, and now that I have seen her, held her in my arms just for a moment, I shall never love another."

"What a blasted romancer," I heard some one mutter, and I had an impression that it was Mr. Murden, and that he was addressing his conversation to me, but I could not be sure, for Florence once more clasped her arms around my neck, and murmured, —

"O Angus, my noble lord, my husband, my lover, I never doubted you in the least. Not even when you did not appear at the proper hour did my confidence wane."

"These people are not inwited 'ere in *wain*, now I tell yer," Mr. Kebblewhite said, with a slight misunderstanding of his daughter's meaning. "I 've made hall preparations for a veddin', and a veddin' ve 'll 'ave afore many 'ours, now I tell yer. Ve vill 'ave no child's play 'ere."

"O father," remarked his son, "I do wish that you would aspirate your vowels when you are in company like the present. Think of his lordship."

"His ludship be " —

He was about to utter a profane word, but thought that it might not sound well, so changed the subject, and said that he 'd exasperate every person present if they did n't mind what they were about, and that he had but one way of talking, and that was the real old-fashioned English way, and that was good enough for him, or any other British merchant.

"But, by gar," remarked Monsieur Allete, "vous talke, talke all de time, and do nuthin'. Q'ue volez vous? Is a veddin' tonight ve to have here?"

"'Ere 's the parson," announced the old servant. "If the rest of yer a'n't ready 'e is at heny rate."

Florence started, and turned her sweet blue eyes on my face so beseechingly, that I could do no more than give back an answering smile, while at the same time I was more anxious than herself as to the terrible ordeal that we were to pass through. I could see no way to retreat. All protestations were treated with contempt, as merely the efforts of a man to escape from vows which he had nearly repented of.

"Are you sure that you love me, Angus?" she asked as a final appeal, not that she doubted it, but because she wanted to know that she was loved for herself alone, and hear the vows repeated.

"I am now positive of the fact," I answered, and, as I looked at her pure, girlish face, and her exquisite form, I felt that I spoke the truth; and any good young man would have said the same.

"And one word more," she cried. "When we are in other climes, in a different circle of society from this which has always surrounded me, you will not feel ashamed of your little Australian bride?"

"She will always be the 'Belle of Australia' to me," I answered, and felt every word of it; and, oh! how I did wish that I was acting a real character instead of an imaginary one, and that I was an earl, and a rich one at that, for the sake of the angel who stood beside me, with a timid, trusting look on her face. Then I should have been happy.

"Thank you, Angus," she said, in her simple *naïve* manner. "You see that I have all confidence in our future happiness. It is such a favorable omen to know that you never loved any one but me. I don't believe that all noblemen are so good as you, so pure and constant."

"I don't think they are, pet, not as a general thing. But you see I am a little different from the real nobility of Europe."

"I believe you," and I really think that she did, to judge by the expression of her sweet face.

"One moment, Florence," I said. "Before the ceremony takes place just answer me one question. I have answered yours quite frankly. See, the minister is drinking a glass of wine. In a minute we shall stand before him. If I should not prove to be all that you expect of me as to rank, will you pardon and pity me, and believe me when I tell you that I did not expect to obtain your hand in this manner?"

"Yes, certainly," looking at me with wondering eyes, yet still smiling confidently.

"And do you think, dear Florence, that you would love me even if there was no title to tempt you?"

"I love you, Angus," was the reply. "Do believe me, it is not the title that I aspire to, although it is not to be slighted, for wealth and rank are the passports to society, and from society to real, elevated happiness, such as the common people cannot appreciate."

"But if I belonged to the common rank, Florence?" I faltered.

"I should still love you, so ask me no more questions. Time will tell that I am right."

"Yes," I muttered bitterly, "time will tell that I am right in gauging your heart, and that you are wrong. But fate is urging us, and, much as I have struggled against it, I see no way of escape except by giving you my hand and heart at the same time, and let the future take care of itself. I have done the best I could."

"Florry, dear, are you all ready?" asked a meek little woman, with a white, anxious face, who now came forward in a timid manner, and bowed as though half frightened at her own temerity in being so familiar with a lord.

This was Mrs. Kebblewhite, my prospective mother-in-law, and I rather liked her looks, and thought that if her stout, red-faced husband was half as refined, and as gentle, that I could even then explain matters, and thus escape the catastrophe which I could see in the dim future. She was not the person to yell for pistols and a nulla every time her will was crossed. She would have listened to me, believed me, and pardoned me, and, perhaps, in time would have consented to a happy union with her precious child, whom she dearly loved. I could see that she did in every glance of her gentle eyes, and every movement of her purring hands, as she smoothed Florry's white robes, and re-arranged the bridal veil and orange-blossoms, resting on the wealth of golden hair, the crown and glory of the dear girl's head. She reminded me of my own dear mother, and I imagined how those two precious old souls would have enjoyed a wedding in which they were both equally interested, had they been brought together under ordinary circumstances, such as usually exist under matrimonial inclinations. How they would have gossiped, and told about the peculiar traits of their children, and been as happy as the parties most interested.

"I am all ready, mamma," the daughter answered. "Are you ready, Angus?"

She looked up in my face all smiling and blushing, but saw the cloud that was passing over it, and said, —

"Why, Angus, you are shedding tears. This should be an evening for joy, and an occasion for smiles. Have I offended you in any way?"

"No, dear, you are perfect in every respect."

"Then shall we go to the clergyman? He is awaiting us, dear."

"If you are willing, Florence."

She looked a little puzzled, for I held back, in the hope that something would turn up to save me from a fate which I desired, yet dared not encounter.

She leaned lightly on my arm, and we had taken one step forward, when Monsieur Allete, who had been drinking wine with Mr. Kebblewhite and the clergyman, suddenly thrust out his arms, as though repelling half a dozen swordsmen at the same time, and said quite sharply, —

"Arretez. Stop that is. Forget you all?"

Here was a brief respite, and I hoped that his sharp eyes had discovered that I was an involuntary impostor.

"Vot the bloody thunder is the matter now?" sharply demanded the father of the bride, his anger overcoming his choice of expressions. "''Arry, bring me my pistols and nulla. There's a goin' to be trouble 'ere if this thing keeps on, now yer can jist believe me."

"Pardonne moi, mademoiselle," the French gentleman said. "Forget you some leetle dings?"

"'Urry hup, 'Arry," roared Mr. Kebblewhite. "I know I shall 'ave to kill somebody. I feel it in my bones."

"Yer feels it in yer 'ead, more like," was the cool reply of the old servant, as he stood on the threshold of the door, and did not seem disposed to obey orders unless those orders were to his liking. "Yer 'as lushed too much tonight, that is vot yer 'as. Now jist keep quiet, and give the young kids a chance to do a little chinnin'."

Mr. Kebblewhite sought for the prayer book, but the clergyman was looking at it, and the master of the house could n't very well snatch it out of his hands to hurl at the head of the old servant, and the latter knew it, so stood his ground, and looked at us with such a patronizing and gracious air, that I should have laughed heartily under other circumstances. But to smile now was as much out of place as at a first-class funeral. Beside, Mr. Kebblewhite was looking at me, and, confound him, he might get hold of a pistol, after all, and do a little random shooting at his proposed son-in-law, whom fathers do not always love as well as they do their daughters-in-law.

All eyes were turned on Monsieur Allete, and even the smooth-faced clergyman, dressed in Episcopal robes and bands, looked from the prayer-book to the Frenchman, as though anxious to know what was to happen next. If I hoped for a respite I was doomed to be disappointed, for the French gentleman remarked, in a tone that was intended as a reproach, —

"The diamonds buy I for noces, mademoiselle. Love her do I. Why wear them not she in her leetle ears pink? Hein."

"Oh, you dear old ami," cried Florence, "did you think that I would be married without your charming gift? I shall not give you a kiss after I am wedded for doubting me. Here, as a reward, you shall put the jewels in my ears, and kiss my hand."

"I vill do it vid pleasure much, my child. I fear that forget me you do in the hurry of the affair tonight."

Now I am more than half convinced that, in the delicious anticipation of a wedding, Florence had nearly forgotten the beautiful gems, but, woman-like, she got over the difficulty in such a sweet, natural way, that the Frenchman was mollified, and smiled his appreciation by undertaking the task of removing the pearl ear-drops, and replacing them with the great flashing diamonds in the little pink ears.

"Oh, is that hall?" asked Mr. Kebblewhite. "I thought it vos somethin' helse. Yer need not bring the pistols and the nulla, 'Arry."

"I don't hintend to," was the satisfying response. "Yer may call for 'em 'til yer is black in the face, and then yer von't get 'em. I don't put pistols in the 'ands of men vot 'as been lushin'."

With the gentleness of a lady, and the gallantry of a Frenchman of the old régime, Monsieur Allete changed the ear-drops, and then Florence held out her white gloved hand for the expected salute.

"Ah, ma chere amie," he said, as he pressed the little hand to his lips, "may life to you be bright as de diamonds, and may sorrow all fly like de gleam of de jewels, ven de light strike 'em full in de face. Now go you to your fiancé. He look already jealous of de old friend of de leetle girl, vot used in his lap to sit, and eat de bon bons."

Florence smiled on her old friend, and returned to my side. I was not jealous, but I did look my disappointment when I found the reason of Monsieur Allete's interruption. He, like the rest of them, labored under the same delusion that I was a lord.

"I wonder if there will be another interruption?" Mr. Murden said to one of the friends of the family, in a half whisper, intended for my ears. "It seems to me this affair looks like a fight where one is afraid and the other dare not come to the scratch."

I gave the Chief a look that was intended to wither him, but he did not seem to mind it in the least. His nature and sense of delicacy had been strongly perverted by being brought in contact with bushrangers, ticket-of-leave men, and other bad characters. What effect could a boy's scorn have on such a man? He was tough as steel.

"Now, Florry," whispered the mother, who had taken advantage of the stay of proceedings to have a little private cry on her own account, "now, darling, be brave, and in a few minutes it will be all over. Now, precious, bear up."

She might have made some kindly suggestion to me, for I needed advice much more than her daughter, who did not seem particularly overcome at the prospect before her. The mist from her deep-blue eyes had gone, and her bright smile was visible in place of tears. I think that women go through with the terrible and harrowing ordeal of a wedding with much more fortitude than a man. I do not know why it should be so, but it certainly is the case. I suppose it is because man is occupied in thinking how he is to obtain the money to keep up that kind of costume, and pay his board bill, and woman does not bother her head over such earthly subjects on the day of all days in her life.

"Now, Angus," whispered Florence, "I am quite ready, dear. Slow step, you know, and hold up your head, as though you were proud of me, and I am to look down, as though timid and blushing. Oh, how I wish we were in a crowded church, and the organ was playing, and every one was admiring me, and saying how handsome she is, and what a sweet pretty dress, and how nicely it does fit. Made in Paris, at an immense expense, you know, and all real lace."

Not a word about the poor devil of a bridegroom. I gave one glance at the windows, to see if I could make a bolt, but Mr. Murden, confound him! guarded one, as though suspicious of my object, and Mr. Kebblewhite the younger, and the old gentleman, the others, while the Frenchman was near the door, with a very determined expression on his face, and looking equal to a struggle. There was no hope for it, and I shuddered as if expecting some one to say every moment, "And may God have mercy on your soul."

We moved along, and knelt at the feet of the clergyman, on soft hassocks, and I felt a little dazed as the minister said,—

"Angus Mornington, Earl of Afton, Baron Midlothian"—

"No, no," I said hastily. "Call me simply Angus Mornington."

"Vell, I 'll 'ave to kill somebody arter hall," roared Mr. Kebblewhite. "'Arry, bring me my pistols and nulla this time sure."

No one paid the slightest attention to Mr. Kebblewhite. They all seemed too much astonished to heed his repeated calls for pistols and club.

"If you wish to be married as Angus Mornington simply, it can be done, although I prefer to use your lordship's titles," the minister said.

"Never mind the titles. Call me by my proper name. I prefer it to all others," I cried.

"Very well, my lord. Angus Mornington, do you take Florence Kebblewhite for your lawful, wedded wife? to cling to, love, endower?" and there was a lot more of useless words, which I do not recall at this late day, but even then I thought of the five hundred dollars which I possessed, and wondered what my wife would think of that for an endowment, in case there was a settlement of property. I know that I answered yes, when my dear little bride poked me in the side with her elbow, to awaken me to the fact that it was necessary there should be a response. She must have rehearsed the services to have been so well acquainted with them, and without her prompting I should have blundered in the most shameful manner.

"*Then I pronounce you man and wife.*"

I heard the words, and my wife gave my hand an extra squeeze, to reassure me, and then there was a mist before my eyes, and I realized that I was on my feet, that a pair of warm white arms were around my neck, and that a bright, happy face was turned to mine, and that a sweet, pleading voice was saying, —

"O Angus, my husband, my lord, my love, will you not kiss me now that I am all your own dear little wife, your countess?"

I do remember that I kissed her sweet lips, and that I heard the sturdy voice of Murden saying, —

"Quick, a glass of champagne for his lordship! The heat of the room is too much for him. He is a little faint. Great joy and happiness are as bad as guilt and misery for some people's natures. Men are often faint on such blissful occasions."

The wine revived me. It was cool, and gave me courage to turn my thoughts from the crime I had just committed to the company who surrounded us, and offered sincere congratulations. The first to come forward was my respected father-in-law, who kissed his daughter, and offered me both of his hard, large hands.

"My lud," he said, "now yer is really von of us. I vanted a syphon of rank connected vid my family, and now 'ere yer is."

"O papa," remonstrated the blushing bride, "you mean a scion, not a syphon."

"I knows vot I means," was the answer. "There a'n't much difference between 'em, 'cos they is both given to the vaist," and the old man chuckled at his joke, as he pointed to one of my arms which was still around his daughter.

One by one the company came forward, and offered their congratulations. I seemed to be in a dream, and could not realize that in just twelve hours from the time I had landed at Queen's Wharf I was married to the Belle of Australia, and she was justly entitled to the appellation, for a more charming picture than that which she presented, as she stood by my side, smiling and blushing, was rarely ever seen in the city of Melbourne. Several times I pressed her little hand to be convinced of the reality of the scene, but as each pressure was returned I knew that it was no dream, and then I wondered how it was to end, and whether so much happiness on her part, and admiration and sudden love on mine, would not result disastrously for us both. How I wished that I was all she fancied me, and that I could give her rank and wealth.

"My lord," said the deep, emphatic voice of Murden, "I too wish you and your countess all the happiness that can be encountered in this world of disappointments. You have won a prize such as is rarely met with," and, as Florence smiled and bowed to the flattering speaker, he said in a low tone, "and to me are you indebted for this. I hope that you will always remember it. Some time I may go to England, and, if I do, I shall call and pay my respects to your lordship, and charming wife."

Did the Chief suspect me, and did he know that I was only playing a vile part? Had he hurried on the nuptials for some secret purpose of his own? No, I could not believe it, for his face looked frank, and his eyes did not have a suspicious glitter. He imagined that I was a real lord like the rest of them. He would not have dared, occupying the position that he did, to countenance such a gross fraud.

"*When* I am in England I shall be glad to see you," was the quiet reply, and the Chief retired, and gave place to Monsieur Allete, who was too much affected to even talk as good English as he knew how.

"Milord," he said, "and Madame la Countess, me heart bust all up in happiness dat wish you I. By and by more shall I say to you. But now, I silent am. I am tuant to you, hey? To speak be not afraid."

"You can never be tedious to my — well, wife," I said after an effort, for it seemed an effort to utter the word under the circumstances. "She will always remember you with gratitude and affection, and I am sure that I shall," and I added in an undertone, as I looked at the active form of the French gentleman, and his classic, severe face, "when I get beyond the reach of your small-sword."

"Assez," he replied, with a smile, and a wave of his significant hands. "I am no queteur, and dat learn you some day, hey? Je ne veux pas more speak now. I proud shall be of your friendship," and he kissed Florence's hand, and retired from our presence by a backward movement, as though he had been paying his respects to a princess, and knew all the ceremonies of court life.

"Come, 'Arry," shouted the master of the house. "the 'hole thing is hover, and now tell the cook to send hup somethin' 'ot for us. Ve is hall starved, and I 'm as dry as a dust storm. Even 'is ludship looks as if a glass of vine vould do 'im good."

"Vell, yer don't mean to tell me that yer is goin' to *skoff* some more at this 'our of the night?" asked the servant who stood on the threshold of the door, and beamed on us his blessing, and smiled and grinned in the most imbecile manner.

"I 'll *skoff* yer," was the reply. "Vere did yer pick hup sich vulgar vords as that?"

"Yer knows as vell as me vere ve 'eard 'em fust. Ven ve vos on the old *Bombay Castle.*"

Mr. Kebblewhite looked the anger that he felt, for he strode toward the old servant, and the latter disappeared down-stairs, to hint to the domestics, who had all been in the hall to see the ceremony, that it was advisable to get a late supper as soon as possible, and to *frappé* some more champagne.

Mr. Murden gave me a sharp look when the servant spoke about the *Bombay Castle*, but I paid no attention to it, as the matter did not interest me, only so far as I had often heard that that ship was once famous for her India trade, and for landing convicts at Botany Bay, after long and tedious passages from England. There was a deep, remarkable silence in the drawing-room for a few minutes. Even Mrs. Kebblewhite, with her white, patient face, looked startled, and glanced anxiously at her sweet little child, as if fearful that she would notice all that was going on, and had been said. But Florence seemed as unconscious as myself, and then her brother came up, and led her away from me to a distant part of the room, where they conversed in a low tone, and so for a while I was left without a companion to speak to. I strayed around the vast drawing-room, looking at the pictures, the rare Sèvres china, the Japanese objects of art, until at last I seated myself at the grand piano, and ran my fingers lightly over the keys. The movement seemed to surprise every one, for all stopped talking, and looked at me as though awaiting further developments. I dashed through several little pieces which I could play very well for an amateur, and then recollected a song which I had often heard sung in the *Bohemian Girl*, and, as it expressed my feelings more pointedly than anything else, I sang it to an audience that was as attentive as even a lord could wish for.

> "When other lips and other hearts
> Their tales of love shall tell,
> In language whose excess imparts
> The power they feel so well,
> There may, perhaps, in such a scene,
> Some recollection be
> Of days that have as happy been,
> Then you 'll remember me.
>
> "When coldness or deceit shall slight
> The beauty now they prize,

> And deem it but a faded light
> That beams within your eyes;
> When hollow hearts shall wear a mask
> 'T will break your own to see,
> In such a moment I 'll but ask
> That you 'll remember me."

"Une bon chanson," cried the Frenchman, and there was generous applause, but, before I had concluded, I felt a warm arm around my neck, and a dear little golden head was pressed close to my face.

"O Angus," Florence said, "you never intimated to me that you could play and sing like this. How cruel to hide such talent from me."

"Because, sweetheart, our acquaintance has been too recent for you to discover all of my good qualities, if I have any," I sighed.

"But you told me at one time that you did not care much for music, and knew but little about it."

"Do you recollect the exact date, dear?"

"Several days since, when I offered to play for you."

Thank fortune there were two accomplishments in which I excelled my mysterious double. I could sing, and had a nice tenor voice. It seems he was not a musician.

"Ah, pet," I remarked, "I should be but an ungrateful husband not to be willing to listen to your playing and singing forever. To see you, to hear your voice, to feel the pressure of your little hand is too much happiness for any man."

"Not too much for you," she said, as she nestled by my side on the piano-stool, so that I was obliged to put an arm around her slender waist, to prevent her from slipping off. "You deserve more than I can give. I wish that I were ten times more beautiful, if it would make you any happier, and love me any better, you, who are so noble and good, pure and true."

I saw the Chief looking at me, and I imagined that his lips in their movement formed the word "Kitty," but he uttered no sound.

"I could not love you better than I do, Florence," I answered. "You are far too good for me, and some time you will acknowledge it, and, perhaps, the time is not far distant."

"Never," was the emphatic answer. "I am very proud of my young husband, and now that I know he is a musician of no mean skill, more proud and pleased than ever. We will practice many duetts together, Angus, will we not, dear?"

"Perhaps, sweetheart. In the coming years there may be such happiness granted to me. The past has not been always kind. God grant that the future may be more cheering. I wish so for your sake, dear Florence."

She did not speak, but allowed her slim fingers to wander over the keys of the piano. Then she said,—

"You are gloomy and sorrowful tonight, Angus. I thought husbands were usually joyful on their bridal eves. But you are sad, and I have seen tears in your eyes more than once. Am I to blame for your melancholy?"

"Yes, dear."

"In what respect, Angus?" while a look of pain passed over her sweet face.

"Your beauty, darling, your goodness, your trusting innocence, and the fear that the time will come when scorn will take the place of smiles, and tears the place of love in your bright eyes."

"You speak of impossible things, Angus, so change the conversation, if you please. It is not to my liking. I am your lawful wedded wife, and nothing can change my love, or shall diminish it, but one thing."

"And that one thing, pet?" I asked, as I held her very close to me.

"Never mind it now. I will tell you some time."

"The present is the best, little wife. I wish to be guarded in the future."

"If, in the fashionable world in which we shall move," Florence said, in a low, grave tone, "you should see a face fairer than mine, and should be attracted to it, and should love it better than you now love me, I should grieve, Angus, but I should not hate you, or pester you with complaints and wild recriminations. But I should sorrow and die, dear husband, and, dying, bless you for what you had been, and what I should expect of you in the world to come, when we met never to know the pain of parting."

She laid her golden head on my shoulder, and I heard a little sob, but the next moment her eyes were cleared of their dampness, and a pleasant smile was lightning all over her sunny face.

"No more, Angus. Let us speak of music. Tell me, dear husband, who taught you to play so well?"

"My mother, pet."

"Your mother, Angus?" she asked, in a tone of astonishment.

"Yes, darling."

"And who taught you to sing opera music?"

"Still my mother, pet."

"The countess must have devoted much time to you, husband dear. She must be a skillful musician."

"My mother is a proficient artist," I answered, quite careful not to give the good lady the title to which she had no right.

"And you were an apt pupil, Angus."

"Yes, dear, I have always loved music. I can play as well on the harp, as I can on the piano, and I can torture one with a violin occasionally."

"Is it customary for ladies of rank in England to instruct their sons in certain branches of education?" was the next question.

"I think not, sweetheart."

"But your mother is an exception to the rule, Angus. The countess must be a remarkable woman."

"My mother is a good woman. Shall I sing you a little song in praise of mothers, pet?"

"I wish that you would, Angus."

"Then do not press me quite so closely, and I will obey you. I shall have to improvise an accompaniment, for the lines have never been set to music, and the words are stray ones, without an owner that I know of. Listen, dear, and note your own mother's face, and see if she appreciates my singing," and then I sang, —

> "There are words that speak of a quenchless love
>   Which burns in the hearts we cherish,
> And accents that tell of a friendship proved,
>   That will never blight or perish;
> There are soft words murmured by dear, dear lips,
>   Far richer than any other;
> But the sweetest word that the ear hath heard
>   Is the sacred name of mother.
>
> "O magical word! may it never die
>   From the lips that love to speak it;
> Nor melt away from the trusting hearts
>   That even would break to keep it
> Was there ever a name that lived like thine?
>   Will there ever be such another?
> The angels have reared in heaven a shrine
>   For the holy name of mother!"

As the notes of the song died away, I heard a sob at my elbow, and turning saw Mrs. Kebblewhite with a handkerchief to her eyes.

"My lord," she said, "I have feared all along for Florry's happiness, when placed in your keeping. I opposed your marriage with her, but was overruled by my husband, but now, after hearing you sing that song, I am satisfied you are a good man, and will love her as she deserves. God bless you for that song, and noble sentiment, my lord. A thousand times blest is he or she who reveres a mother, and is not ashamed of her. My lord, may I kiss your hand?"

"No," I answered, as she would have bent her sweet old head and face to salute my hand. "God forbid that you should do so. Rather let me kneel at your feet, and kiss yours, or, if that does not suit you, let me put my arms around you, and kiss your forehead and cheeks, and thank you a thousand times for your kind words, and to say to you that if ever Florence is really mine, of her own free will, she shall never hear ought but words of love and tenderness from me."

She looked a little puzzled, but a remark from Mr. Kebblewhite turned the current of her thoughts.

"Sing, my lud, somethin' about us poor old daddies, vot 'as to find the cash ven our gals is vedded. Ve is ginerally neglected ven the spoonin' is hover. But don't mind me. I can stand it, and I is too 'appy tonight to complain."

As all the company were listening to the master of the house, and laughing at his remarks, as in duty bound, I took the occasion to kiss my mother-in-law, and in so hearty a manner that even Florence looked a little surprised, and laughingly remarked that her mother had lost a daughter, but gained a very demonstrative son, and if I kissed the old lady in such a hearty manner every day, she should feel a little touch of jealousy.

"Remember, my lord," said Mrs. Kebblewhite, "from this moment I am your friend; and I hope that I shall always be a dear one. Come what may, in me you will find a true mother, and I shall love you next to Florry."

"There 's somethin' 'ot on the table," Harry announced. "Ve is hall ready for yer."

"Ah, that is good news," Mr. Kebblewhite said. "I am 'ungry, and I dare say 'is ludship is a little peckish. Moorsur Allete, vill yer give yer arm to my good vife? and the rest of yer can foller his ludship and lady. Now then, come on, and don't shilly shally."

The old gentleman led the way to the commodious dining-room, where we found the table well covered with a collation, and wine in abundance. It was plain to be seen that my father-in-law was determined to make a night of it, but I had no idea of indulging in a drinking bout, and, in spite of the utmost urging, refused to partake of more than a smiple glass of champagne.

7

I wanted to have all my senses under full control for the path which I had determined to pursue, as soon as I had a private interview with Florence. I dreaded the moment, but trusted in the honesty of my intentions and frankness to carry me through in triumph.

Florence was as cheerful and happy as she had been all the evening. When she slipped away from the table, the clock on the mantel was striking half-past eleven. She gave my hand a little pressure at parting, and I felt a chill strike my heart, as I thought how soon that young, sweet face was to be clouded with sorrow and surprise, grief and despair.

No one noticed her departure. Monsieur Allete was singing the *Marsellaise* in his native tongue, and Mr. Kebblewhite was anxious for him to conclude, so that he could hurl defiance at the land of France, and all the world, by yelling *Rule Britannia*, in such a boisterous manner, that all the cats and dogs in the neighborhood were awakened, and had several fierce fights in back yards, to the scandal of the neighbors, who knew that Mr. Kebblewhite was to have a daughter married that day, and, as they had not been invited to the wedding, thought such howling and attempted singing a disgrace to the Park, and that the police ought to interfere, and take Mr. K. and all his company to the station-house.

Fortunately for my ears, I did not have to hear the whole of *Rule Britannia*. The old gentleman was red in the face with exertion and wine, and the Frenchman was the picture of calm, deep despair, when Mrs. Kebblewhite, standing near the door, made a signal that I could not fail to understand. I delayed noticing it as long as possible, and then quietly arose, drained one more goblet of champagne, and left the table.

Mr. Kebblewhite, with his eyes closed, and every vein in his forehead swollen like whipcords, was shouting forth to the world that Englishmen would never be slaves, not if they knew themselves, so did not notice me, but the Frenchman sighed as he saw me move away, gave one melancholy smile, and then appeared to devote all of his energies to the polite entertainment which his host was furnishing. Young Mr. Kebblewhite had gone to the smoking-room, and the rest of the company did not relax their attention to the fruits and wines which were spread before them. Even Mr. Murden did not look up as I passed him. He pretended to examine the bubbles in his wine glass.

"My lord," said Mrs. Kebblewhite, with a faint, melancholy smile, as the tears filled her gentle eyes, "Florence would like to speak to you, if you can spare her a moment's time."

I felt all my blood rush to my face, and it seemed for a moment as though my heart ceased to beat, and that I should fall at the lady's feet insensible. She noticed the sudden change, and said hastily, —

"My lord, you are faint, you are ill, I fear. Shall I call some one to your assistance?"

"No, no, do not mind me. I am accustomed to such spells. It will soon be over. Do not call any one. I wanted to speak to you for a moment. You are kind, and remind me of my own blessed mother."

"How I wish that she were here tonight to share your happiness," the good lady remarked.

"God forbid that she should be here to witness my misery!" I cried, and then, noticing the look of pain on the lady's face, I added, "I do not mean that your daughter is not loved by me. I do love her so dearly, so truly that even you cannot complain."

"Then why are you not happy? You are married. You are young and wealthy, and can purchase all the pleasures of the world if you desire. Be a true and good husband to my child, and we shall all be happy, — you as well as the rest of us."

"Can't you understand me?" I cried, taking her hands, and leading her to the other end of the drawing-room, where no one could overhear us, and where we could look out upon the Park, and the bright moonlight.

"No, I do not understand you, my lord," with a wondering look, as though she feared I was insane, or had suddenly lost my senses through drink.

"I know that you think me mad," I said, "but rest assured I am not. I am just as sane this moment as you are. O mother, mother, see me here on my knees at your feet, begging your pardon, and praying for one word of consolation, one word of encouragement, at your hands."

"My lord, do not kneel to me. Arise, and tell me all your troubles. What consolation can I afford? Have you been imprudent and reckless in the past? Then atone for it by the future, as even the blackest sin can be washed away by repentance and deep humiliation."

"Thank God, O my mother, if you will let me call you such, no serious crimes can be charged to me. Your daughter is the first one that ever moved my heart, or whom I ever loved."

"Here, be seated on this sofa, and let me know what is oppressing your mind and heart. Confess all to me, and be certain of an advanced pardon. Call me mother, if you will, and be assured you shall have a mother's love, and a mother's sympathy."

She led me to a sofa, and, as we seated ourselves, the dear old lady took one of my hands, held it for a moment in both of her own, and then asked, —

"My lord, answer me one question before I attempt to console you. Is this repentance, this unhappiness, the result of anything which you have heard concerning my husband's previous life?"

"No, mother, I know nothing about his previous life, and care but little for it," I answered.

"Would it make any difference in regard to your course toward my daughter if you had heard something not forgotten to this day, although the deed was committed years ago?"

"No, I love Florence dearly. All surroundings are forgotten when I think of her sweet face."

"Then Mr. Murden has not imparted the information which, as Chief of Police, he possesses, concerning my family, or, rather, the head of it?" she asked.

"No; he merely spoke of Mr. Kebblewhite as a merchant, and a man of good standing in Melbourne."

She seemed to breathe a sigh of relief as I answered her questions, and once more her white, thin hand sought mine, and clasped it quite firmly, and then she would have raised it to her lips had I permitted her to do so. I like to kiss a lady's hand, but to have a lady kiss mine is a little too much for endurance.

"Now, my lord, you have answered all of my questions in a frank and noble spirit. I feared that you had learned some facts which I could have wished had never occurred, or at least had been forgotten. The memory of the people of Melbourne is long, and those who seek for a higher station in life are not forgotten by men who have not the ambition or the ability to rise beyond the level of the common herd of the city."

"Will you not tell me of this stain which you say rests upon Mr. Kebblewhite's name?" I asked.

"No, my son. You will learn of it some day, I have no doubt, and that will be time enough to embitter a portion of your life."

"And Florence, does she know the great secret?" I demanded.

"No, thank God! the dear child is still in ignorance of the blot that rests upon our now good name. It has been kept from her, and I hope will be until the day of her death. She is proud and loving, and it would crush her to the earth. Your strong arm and heart must support her, my lord, if she should be enlightened before she leaves her home for your own."

"My own dear mother," I said, after a moment's pause, "I, too, have a secret, and a more dreadful one than you can impart. This evening you said that you would be my friend. Do you still adhere to that resolution?

Do you still say that under all circumstances you will be a mother to me, and a friend at all times?"

"I have seen nothing to change my views. In fact, my lord, I can say with more confidence than before, that I am your friend, and your mother."

"Then cease to call me a lord, for I have no right to the title."

"How, my lord? Do you speak in jest, or in earnest?"

"In most serious earnestness, I assure you."

"But I have seen you in the house a dozen times, and you were introduced to Florence at the goverenor's ball as the Earl of Afton, and by the governor himself, as well as Mr. Mattocks."

"Nevertheless, my dear mother, I am not a lord, and I never entered this house until this evening. I never saw your daughter until she entered the drawing-room in her bridal costume, and then I fell in love with her at the first sight."

"My lord, are you sane?" the lady asked.

"Perfectly, and very unhappy; but I will do justice to your daughter, and to you, even if it breaks my heart."

"And your name?" asked the startled and bewildered woman.

"Angus Mornington."

"Why that is the name of the Earl of Afton. Pray, my lord, do not be merry at the expense of an unhappy woman, whose head is almost turned by the events of the evening."

"God forbid that I should trifle with your holy feelings, but Angus Mornington is my name, and under that name was I married to your daughter. She is my lawful wife, but still I solemnly vow to you that I will not take advantage of the events which have forced me to be her husband."

"Impossible," Mrs. Kebblewhite exclaimed. "You must be deceiving me, and for a purpose."

"I swear to you that such is not the case. Do you think that if I was the Earl of Afton I would be here, talking with the mother, when I could be with the daughter, my wife, whom I dearly love?"

"And the earl, who resembles you so much,—did you ever meet with him?" asked the mother, who appeared to see that my reasoning was good.

"Only for a moment. I saw a man this evening who was enough like me in feature, form, and height to be my twin brother. He was hurried into a carriage, and told to leave the city, and never return. He was addressed as 'my lord' by his companions."

"Why did you not explain everything as soon as you entered the house?" asked the mother, tears making their appearance on her pale cheeks.

"Simply because your amiable husband called for his pistols and a nulla, and would not listen to me for a moment when I explained. Even the Chief of Police shared in the deception."

"Angus," said Mrs. Kebblewhite, trembling, while she made desperate efforts to prevent her agitation, "I am not entirely convinced by your words, yet I do not believe that you would deceive me willfully. If my daughter is not a countess, who is she, in Heaven's name?"

"The wife of an American citizen, madame, and an honest man."

"Are you rich?"

"No, I am poor, unfortunately."

"If you were rich all might be well. Mr. Kebblewhite could be brought around to view you with favor when he found that it was too late to object. He hates Americans."

"Then we are equal, madame. I detest an Englishman who does not prefer a good man as the husband of his daughter, to a *blasé* noble, who makes love to every woman he meets, and then flies when a wedding is talked of."

"It will break Florry's heart," moaned the mother. "Oh, what can I do? Oh, what can I say? Let me call Mr. Kebblewhite, and explain all to him."

"And have him riddle me with his pistols, and pound me with his confounded nulla. No, he must know nothing of all this. To you and Florence I confide it. In one half hour I shall leave this house, and never return, unless as a rich man to claim my wife. If I do not come back at the end of a year, or less, let her obtain a divorce, and be free to marry one more worthy of her."

"Oh, cruel, cruel fate for my poor child," moaned the unhappy mother "Oh, harsh, unfeeling man to leave her as you intend to on the night of her nuptials."

"Because it is death for me to remain. In a day or two the deception would be discovered, your husband would murder me, and your daughter despise me. I prefer death to her contempt and scorn, but I will not meet both. Give me a brief interview with my wife, and then good-by, perhaps forever."

The good woman put her arms around my neck, kissed my forehead, and then, with tears flowing from her eyes, said, —

"Go to her. She is in the front room; the one over this. God bless you, O my son, for I feel all a mother's love for you, and always shall. But my heart will break when I think of Florry."

"GOOD-BY, DEAR FLORENCE," I SAID, AND KISSED HER WHITE HAND.

PART V.

A SHORT PRIVATE INTERVIEW WITH MY WIFE. — I MAKE SOME EXPLANATIONS, WHICH ARE NOT WELL RECEIVED. — A PLEA FOR PARDON, AND A REFUSAL. — LEAVING THE HOUSE BY THE AID OF A TREE. — MR. MURDEN AND HIS PLAIN TALK. — A LONG FAREWELL.

MRS. KEBBLEWHITE had informed me as to the location of my wife's apartments, but, as I started for the broad hall and stairs leading to the chamber, I felt so dazed at the thought of the interview, that I staggered, and would have fallen, had not the kind lady lent me her arm for a support. For a moment I was motionless, and tried to collect my wandering senses, so that I could carry out to a final conclusion the course which I had marked out. Then I was aroused by the lady saying, —

"Angus, my son, you are not equal to the task. Rest here until you are more composed. You are faint and pale, and all of a tremble. Think better of your purpose, and forego this interview so painful to you and to Florence."

"No," I said, with an effort. "I must do my duty. O mother, for I must call you by that dear name, bless me, and pity me, for I need both in this hour of utter wretchedness."

She laid her thin white hand on my head, and I saw her lips move, and I knew that she had granted my request, and was blessing one whom she would have been proud to call her son under other circumstances.

"Go," she whispered, "and may God bless you, my dear boy, be you nobleman or plebeian."

I gained courage from her simple words, and was leaving her, when she asked, —

"Are you sure, Angus, that you can trust yourself alone with Florence? Do you not fear that you will yield to her tears, and rare beauty? A man must be very firm to withstand both."

"My mother taught me to be honorable and truthful above all things. I have not forgotten her early teachings. I will not prove false to them at this late day. Do not fear for me or Florence. With your blessing, and your confidence, I can endure much, and suffer much."

She sighed, and wiped the tears from her eyes, and motioned me to leave her. As I passed from the drawing-room, I saw Mr. Murden, the Chief of Police, near the hat-rack, as though searching for his cap. He looked up as he saw me, and a smile of peculiar significance passed over his stern, dark face. Had he played the part of an eavesdropper, and heard all that occurred between Mrs. Kebblewhite and myself? I thought that such was the case, for he looked at me very intently, and said, —

"Good-night, my lord, and pleasant dreams. I hope that I shall have the happiness of again meeting you at some distant day. This has been an evening of rare enjoyment to me, and to your lordship am I indebted for all of it."

I did not answer him. I was in no mood for banter, even from Mr. Murden. I bowed, and would have passed on, but just at that moment he seemed to have found his cap, and came near me.

"Remember," he whispered, "not one word about the diamond ring, and Kitty. You can rely on me to keep your secret, and to see that she does not disturb your honeymoon. I will put a detective on her track, and keep her away from this house, and from you, until ready to leave Melbourne.

There is no fear of discovery, I think, if you are not too confiding, and I do not suppose that you are one to blab everything to your wife. Good-night, my lord," and he bowed low, as he opened the outer door, and glided out of the house into the moonlight, and I heard his footsteps on the gravel walk, and a faint blast from his whistle.

I paused at the foot of the hard, polished stairs, as brilliant as a mirror, and wondered how a Chief of Police could have such consummate impudence as to talk to an innocent man in that manner. Just as though Miss Kitty had been anything to me or I to her. Mr. Kebblewhite was still in the dining-room with the Frenchman and the rest of the guests; and my respected father-in-law was roaring out, in tones so deep and awful that the gas flickered in the chandeliers, and the very foundations of the house seemed to shake, and the roof to rise, the noble and ear-splitting ballad of, —

" There she lay, hall that day,
In the Bay of Biscay, oh! "

I imagined the keen anguish of Monsieur Allete, and mentally thanked Heaven that there were people just as miserable as myself for the time being, although I did hear roars of applause at the conclusion of each verse, and I judged that the party was very drunk to encourage such wretched travesty of singing. Even the cats and dogs were again awakened by the noise, and renewed their yells, and barks, and fights, with much animation, and a proportional amount of profanity from the neighbors, who once more voted Mr. Kebblewhite a mean pig, and a person who would rob a Chinaman, if he had the chance.

" You still hesitate, Angus?" asked Mrs. Kebblewhite, who came to the door of the drawing-room, and saw that I had ascended but three steps of the stairs.

" Yes, mother, but I will hesitate no longer," I answered in a resolute tone.

I set my teeth together as though about to submit to a surgical operation, and up the stairs I passed, with a strange fluttering at my heart, and a cold perspiration standing on my forehead. At the landing I met a pretty little girl (one of the housemaids), who seemed to have been stationed there to welcome me, and to point out the apartments which my wife occupied. I recollect that I stopped suddenly, and looked at the blushing and smiling little thing, who courtesied, and stole a timid glance at my face, and I thought she deserved a reward for her politeness and vigilance.

"O my lud," she said, "'er ladyship is in that front room, and she is wery himpatient to speak to yer."

"Thank you, child," I remarked, although she was older than myself, and then I placed a sovereign in her hand, and, as she looked up with a grateful smile, and a blush of pleasure, bent down, and kissed her sweet lips. I was not accountable for the act, for I did not know what I was doing just at that time, my mind was so distracted.

"O my lud, that vos wery sweet and kind on yer part," the girl said. "Yer can 'ave two for a sov. if yer vants 'em."

The temptation was strong, but I recollected that I was a husband, and a very unhappy one, so waived my right, and knocked at the door of my wife's apartment.

"Come in," a gentle voice said, and, opening the door, I stood in the presence of Florence. She had laid aside her heavy satin dress and laces, and now her white shoulders and arms were covered with a blue silk *peignoir*, cut loose, but not so as to conceal her exquisite form, and the roundness of her arms and neck. Her hair, so beautiful and luxuriant, and rich in hue, was unconfined by comb or pins, and fell in a shower of burnished gold all around neck and shoulders, and far below her slight waist. She was seated in an easy-chair as I entered, but arose, and came forward to greet me with outstretched arms.

"I was fearful that papa's singing was more attractive than your wife," she said, with a pleasant little laugh, as though she did not believe her own words. "When papa once commences on his sea ballads he never knows when to leave off, and is offended if his listeners are not as pleased as himself. I feared that he would bore you, so sent for you. Forgive me, will you not, dear Angus, dear husband?"

She put her arms on my shoulders, and laid her fair head on my bosom, and looked up with such a gentle, winning smile, that I feared for my good resolution, and once more grew faint and sick at heart.

"You do not speak to me, Angus," she said, after a moment's silence, finding that I did not respond to her caresses. "Have you so soon tired of your little wife?"

"No, Florence, I should never tire of you, dear," and I kissed her pure forehead, and held her for a moment to my heart, and wished I was what I seemed.

But such happiness was not for me, and, with a groan of anguish, I released her, and stepped back.

"Why, what is the matter with you, Angus?" she asked, her large blue eyes filling with tears at my sudden coldness. "Are you ill? Has papa's champagne disagreed with you? or are you sorry that you have given me your name, so distinguished through a long line of illustrious ancestors?"

"If I had descended from the royal family of Great Britain, I should feel proud of your love, Florence, and proud that you were my wife," I answered. "But"—

"Yes, but what, you silly boy?" with a glad light in her beautiful eyes.

"But I am not what you suppose me to be, sweet one, and, in spite of your scorn and contempt, I am about to enlighten you on your marriage relation."

"Am I not your lawful wife?" she asked.

"Yes, dear, I think you are."

"And"—

She hesitated for a moment, as though she would find the right word, repugnant though it might be.

"And am I your only wife, Angus? Have you deceived me in that respect?"

"God forbid, darling. I never loved before I loved you. I never wedded until your little white hand was placed in mine. I would not exchange you for all the women in the world. I would not lose you for all the gold of Australia."

She uttered a glad cry, and sprang toward me, and threw her arms around my neck.

"O Angus, my lord, my husband, I will hear of no more explanations. You love me, you are my own, and no power shall take you from me. If you have been guilty of boyish follies, I forgive them, and do not wish to hear of them. I want no confession, except the confession of your love, no repentance, except the thought that we had not met sooner, no kisses, except those you bestow, as I am certain that you would not care for any lips but mine."

I winced a little, and hoped that the little girl whom I had met at the head of the stairs would forget all about my confounded fit of momentary abstraction, when I was not accountable for my doings.

"Florence," I said, "you are a brave little darling, and deserve happiness, and as good and kind and loving husband as I should make; but, my dear, you must hear me, and pay strict attention to my words, for they are important."

"Yes," she answered, and looked up at me with a half-frightened expression on her face.

"I have no follies to answer for," I continued, "but I have a confession to make."

"No, no, I will not hear it," and she put her white hands over her little pink ears.

"My dear, you must not be childish in this case," I said, as sternly as I could. "Come, sit down here, in this large easy-chair, and let me, standing by your side, tell you all that is on my mind, and how cruelly you have been deceived."

"No, no, I will hear nothing, Angus. Do not make me unhappy by speaking of things which do not interest me. You are doing all this to tease your poor little wife, and it is not kind. How would you like to have me pester you by telling you of my old beaux? Would you be jealous? Do you really love me enough to be jealous of me, Angus? Oh, that is so jolly. Why, you silly boy, I never loved any one until I loved you, although I have flirted a little, just a little, you know, for the innocent fun of the thing."

"And how much with Mr. Mattocks, darling?" and I smiled a little at her eager face.

"Oh, you are there, are you, Angus? This accounts for the grave face, and sober brow. You have heard in some way that Mr. Mattocks paid me marked attention at one time, and would have married me, I think, if I had encouraged him to make a proposal. But I could not love him, and he saw it, and, like the gentleman that he is, soon ceased to make only the most formal of calls. Still I think he is friendly, and do not believe that he would speak of me in any other way than as a good and pleasant young lady."

"I do not doubt it, deary, but I never heard of your flirtation with Mr. Mattocks, or any other man. After you have listened to me, you will, perhaps, regret that you did not take him instead of waiting for me."

"Never, Angus," and she put up her red lips for a kiss.

I was just weak enough to respond to her mute appeal. I was sorry, but could not help it, and resolved to be firmer the next time.

"One more," she said, as I seated her in the chair, and sat down at her feet, on a hassock, in obedience to her commands.

Ah, well, it was not worth disputing about one little kiss, even if it was so precious to me. I knew that it would be a long time before I should get another supply, if I pursued the course which I had determined upon, but I began to fear that I should waver and fail in my purpose.

"My dear Florence," I said, taking her hand, and kissing it very tenderly,

"I want you to pardon me for what I have done, and to believe that I was forced by circumstances over which I had no control to come here tonight, and unite your fortunes with mine."

"Sir, my lord!" a little bitterly, and a surprised and grieved look.

I knew that she would put on the dignity, but I did not think that she would display so much feeling when she heard my plain, blunt words.

She withdrew her hand from mine, and looked at me with an offended air.

"Do I understand you, Angus, that you would not have married me of your own free will?"

"Not tonight, love."

She started up, and covered her face with her hands, but I could see the tears stealing down her cheeks, and knew that her pure heart was wounded at my words.

"Florence," I said, as I once more attempted to take her hand, and console her, "I am pained to grieve you, but I must tell you all. It is to save you many days of misery and reproach that I now speak."

"You do not love me, you are ashamed of me, because I am not of as noble birth as yourself. O Angus, how can you treat me in such a heartless manner?" and she firmly resisted my efforts to take her hand, or to put an arm around her slight waist.

Here was a pretty position for a young bridegroom, who loved his wife most devotedly, would be unhappy while absent from her side, and yet would be very miserable if he dared to remain with her, and let the deceit go undiscovered for a few days. For a moment the thought flashed through my mind to run the risk of detection. If I resembled the earl so closely why could I not declare that I was his lordship, and so let the future take care of itself? But no, I had promised Mrs. Kebblewhite that I would be true to my manhood, true to her daughter, and true to the pledge which I had given before I entered the chamber. I banished all unworthy thoughts as suddenly as they had appeared, and resolved that I would not deviate from the moral teachings of my respected mother. I would do nothing that would cause her to blush for her only child, great as the temptation might be, and, Heaven knows, never was man so tempted before, it seemed to me at the time.

"Dear Florence," I said, as she repulsed me, "you say that I do not love you. O my love, my wife, if you could but see my heart, and know the pain that it gives me to speak to you as I do, you would pity me, and help me bear the heavy cross that is now weighing me down, and crushing out all that is joyous and bright from my young life," and then I felt the tears flow from my eyes, much as I attempted to restrain them.

She heard me in silence, but, as I proceeded, she removed her white hands from her eyes, and looked at me with a more pleasant glance, and then ran toward me, and threw her arms around my neck, and once more nestled her fair head on my bosom.

"O Angus," she cried, "you do love me. Tell me that I am not mistaken, that your heart is firmly mine, and that you are not ashamed of me because you are a great lord, and I only a plebeian."

"My darling," I said, "the tears which you now see in my eyes are proof positive that you are loved so dearly that no other woman will ever find a lodgement in my bosom. O sweetheart, I could even now fall down and worship you, happy if you but bestowed a single thought on me, happy and content with an occasional smile, and doubly happy if you would but lay your hand on my head, and call me the best and dearest friend in the world. Do not doubt my love, Florence. It is fixed and immovable. It is not a changeable, boy's love, but that of a strong man, and as a man I must resist it."

"What do mean, Angus?" and she started back, and looked at me with renewed surprise.

"The first time I saw you, when you entered the drawing-room this evening, dressed in all your bridal finery, and looking like an angel of beauty and mercy, your bright eyes pierced my heart like a dagger, and I felt you were one whom I could love forever and forever, and, dying, bless. O sweet! when I felt your white arms around my neck, and knew that you were a living, breathing woman, and not a visitor from heaven, I could not realize that there was a man in all the world so base as to trifle with your affections, or to deceive you."

"Trifle with me? deceive me?" she asked, in a trembling voice. "Angus, what do you mean? You speak in a mysterious tone and manner, as though some great wrong had been perpetrated. What wrong have I suffered except your failure to appear at the appointed bridal hour? and that you know, dear, was not your fault, but a silly joke on the part of some young men. I have forgiven you for all that, because I know that you will be more guarded in the future. Come, dear, clear your brow of its clouds, and let me see you smile once more, as you can smile when you are happy. You know when you asked me to be your wife I hesitated, because I did not know my heart, and I did not love you then, Angus. I confess it now, dear husband; but I was ambitious, and I wanted to be a countess, and to wear a coronet, and large diamonds, and to be at the head of fashionable society, and have all the young girls of my set envious of my good position and fortune. You know what I said to you, Angus, when you asked for my hand?"

I did n't know because I was not present at that important interview. How I wished that I had been there, instead of the other fellow. I made no reply, and she continued,—

"I told you that I did not love you then, our acquaintance had been so recent, but that I esteemed you, and would try and love you as soon as I became your wife. I did love the title, Angus, and it was very wrong in me to seek it, but now I love you, dear, and even if you had no title, I should still love you. Are you satisfied, you silly boy?"

"More than satisfied, darling. It shows me what a treasure you are, and what a noble heart you possess."

"And, Angus," she continued, with a pretty blush, "do you know, dear, that since I saw you this evening, I have learned to love you very dearly. You appear so manly, and yet so gentle, so respectful and tender, and not as one who presumes on his rank. I have noticed a difference, love, and yet I do not know how to account for it. Will you always be as you are tonight, Angus?" and her lips were put up for another kiss, and I had to give way to the temptation.

"Yes, dear, I hope to be. In your presence even a savage would be deferential."

"You are kind to say so; and now let me kiss away those tears, for you have been crying, Angus, and you can't hide it from me. Why should you weep when you say that you love me, and are happy?"

"I did not say that I was happy, Florence. I said that I loved you, and in loving you I am unhappy."

She looked a little puzzled, but once more she laid her head upon my shoulder, and I put my arm around her waist.

"My dear little wife," I continued, after a moment's pause, thinking of the best way to break the news to her as gently as possible, "when you pledged this dear little hand you thought it was to a lord that it was given, did you not, love?"

"What an absurd question. Of course I did. Who else should I give it to?"

"Look at me well, little wife, and see if you can have been mistaken."

She laughed, as she looked at my face.

"You provoking boy," glancing up, and smiling, "do I not see the same brown eyes, the same curling brown hair, the same tiny mustache, — you know it is not very ferocious, Angus, but it will grow in time, if you pay strict attention to it, — the same clear skin, without the least vestige of a beard, and lastly, but very important, the same white, even teeth? Now, sir, how is that for a description of a husband? The wrinkles will come, and the hair will turn gray, and fall off, but I shall always think of my husband as I see him tonight, handsome, young, and noble, and may he love me in old age, if we live, just as well as he says that he loves me tonight, with youth and health at his command."

"Your description is flattering, darling, and I feel proud of it, yet I am not the man who asked for your hand some days since."

"I do not like such foolish jests," she said with an offended look. "They are not in good taste at the present time. I pray you, my lord, to postpone them for some more fitting occasion."

"There is no time more suitable than the present, love. Would to Heaven that it were a jest, or a dream. Then, indeed, should I be happy, because all could be changed in waking. I am serious, Florence. As God is my judge, I never asked your hand in marriage, as God is my judge, I never saw Miss Florence Kebblewhite, the Belle of Australia, until she entered the drawing-room, dressed as a bride, this evening."

She broke away from my arms, and retreated to the other end of the apartment, moaning, and wringing her hands.

"O Angus," she sobbed, "what cruel words you utter. As though I would give my hand unsought, as though I would wed a stranger. Have you lost your senses? or does the fumes of the wine still linger in your brain?"

"Dear Florence, hear me with patience. I am not insane, neither am I under the influence of liquor. As I hope for God's mercy, as I hope to meet my own dear mother in heaven, as I trust to stand by your side in paradise, and ask your forgiveness for all the wrongs I have inflicted upon you, so do I declare to you, in this sacred place, your bridal chamber, that I never saw you until this evening."

"O my God, have mercy upon me, a poor, unhappy girl!" she exclaimed, and fell upon her knees, and buried her face in her hands, and sobbed so piteously, that I feared once more for my good resolution.

I went to her, and tried to raise her, but she repulsed me with all her strength. I waited, standing near her dressing-table, until the first burst of emotion had passed, when she looked up, and asked, in a constrained tone, —

"Have you any more revelations to make on your bridal eve? Come, sir, let me hear the rest of this strange romance. I will be calm, quite calm, sir."

"It is a romance, Florence, but a very eventful and truthful one. God knows what mysterious influence sent me to this city, and caused me to land here this morning. I resemble some one who is rich, young, and powerful, but who he is I do not know, except that he is called the Earl of Afton."

"And do you mean to tell me that you are not the Earl of Afton? that you are not Angus Mornington?" she demanded in a haughty tone.

"I am not the Earl of Afton, but I am Angus Mornington, as my father's name was before me."

"It is a lie!" she said, with startling distinctness and abruptness. This was not polite or courteous, but it had the merit of being quite frank, if not true. She was angry, and did not choose her words just at that moment.

I began to feel that I had made a slight mistake in not taking the two kisses from the lady's-maid at the head of the stairs instead of only one, as I really had done. A man never knows his own advantages and disadvantages until he is reminded of them in a forcible manner, by being called a liar.

"You do me a great injustice, Florence," I said, after a moment's pause, to allow her to recover her temper and composure. "I would not deceive you for all the world, and, because I do not wish to do so, I have made this explanation."

"And do you mean to tell me that I am not the Countess of Afton?" she demanded, looking up a little fiercely.

"I must answer 'No' to that question."

"Who am I then?"

"My wife, dear, Mrs. Angus Mornington."

"And who are you? Where did you come from?"

"I am an American citizen," I answered, quite proudly.

"O Heaven," she moaned, "I have married only a Yankee instead of an earl."

I again felt that I had not received the value of my sovereign, which I had generously presented to the lady's-maid, and regretted the lost kiss. Husbands don't like to be called hard names.

"You speak in tones of reproach, Florence; but it is far better to be the wife of an American citizen, with a name unsullied by vice and crime, than to wear the coronet of a dissipated nobleman, who did not love his promised bride sufficiently to keep his appointment at the altar. Forgive me, dear, for speaking harshly, but I feel as proud of my title of American as you could feel at being **a countess.**"

She did **not** answer **me,** but arose to her feet, and paced the chamber, wringing her hands, and uttering vehement exclamations.

"Why," she asked at last, stopping, and facing me, with a look in which love and disappointment strove for the mastery, "did you not explain all this before the wedding? Answer me that question."

"Simply because, every time **I** attempted to do so, your amiable parent **called for his pistols and a nulla, if** you know what that is, I don't. **He thought that I was shirking the union, and even you** would not listen to me **when I** attempted **an explanation. Do you not** remember, my dear, that such was the **case?**"

"**I** don't know, I **don't understand. I am all in a daze** at this moment, **and do not** realize what **to think or believe. Oh, it is** impossible **that you can be what you** represent. **Angus, tell me that it** is all **a comedy to try my love and pride, and** still **I will forgive you.**"

"**Would to Heaven** it **were, Florence.**"

"And **I am really your wife?**"

"**Yes, my lawful wife. Did** you not notice that I told the **clergyman I** was to be married as **Angus** Mornington, and not to refer to **titles, for I** wanted **none,** and had none."

"**Yes, I remember now, but, as I** had never been married before, I thought **it** was the custom."

"You will know better next time, Florence," I said a little bitterly, for it seemed that **she** did love titles after all.

She looked **at me in a** wondering manner, as though she did not quite comprehend me, and **then** her eyes fell upon the diamond ring which I had **restored to her at the ceremony, and** with which I had wedded her in regular Episcopal style.

"**Look at this,**" **she said.** "**By this** diamond **ring do I** convict you of subterfuge and deceit."

Now I was in **for it,** sure enough. **I had** not thought of the ring **all the** evening, or since I had restored it to her.

"**Angus,**" she said, and her voice was more sorrowful and **tender,** "I allowed you to take this diamond from my finger the day that you placed this signet ring on mine. It was an exchange of tokens of love, or at least of confidence. Your ring has a crest, and the monogram 'A. M.' on the seal, and the Latin motto of '*Ut quocunque paratus*,' or, in other words, 'prepared for any event.' Is that motto the one which your house adopts when one of its members wishes to deceive a poor girl?"

I was silent. How could I tell her what had been the fate of the ring since it had left her little finger?

"This ring," she continued, holding up her left hand, "was given to me one year ago, when I was sixteen years of age, as a birthday present from a father whom, although he is rough at times, and does not use good English, I love and respect as my father, for he loves me dearly. No one had ever worn that ring but myself, and yet I felt such confidence in you, that I allowed you to take it, and to carry it away. I have not seen it before tonight since I loaned it to you. Now, sir, if you are not the Earl of Afton, if you did not receive my pledge, how does it happen that you are in possession of a jewel that cost my father one thousand pounds, and which has my name and age engraved on the gold surroundings?"

She looked at me with flashing eyes, as though she had caught me in a lie, and was rather proud of it.

"Florence," I said, as I extended my arms to gather her in an embrace; but she moved backward, and motioned me to keep my distance, a motion that was a little disdainful and cold.

"Go on, sir," she said.

"Florence," I resumed, "I did not think of the ring, or the explanation which I must make. My darling, I would spare you all this, but I must justify myself in your eyes, no matter who is injured. I know that your pride and self-respect will be hurt, but far better all this, than that I should suffer from your displeasure. The ring was not given to me, but to the man you call Earl of Afton. This evening, on the street, the Chief of Police, Mr. Murden, accosted and saluted me as a lord. I thought he was a crank, as other people had done the same, and feared that all the citizens of Melbourne had gone mad. I denied that I was the Earl of Afton, but he refused to believe me, or to listen to me, while I reiterated the truth. At last, dear, he spoke of the Belle of Australia, and intimated that I had been guilty of a mean and contemptible trick, in not keeping my engagement to marry you at three o'clock. You are following me, Florence?"

"Yes, — continue," with a face that was very white now.

"I denied that I knew you, or had ever seen you, and said that I was on my way to the Victoria, in a dress suit, to see the lady and her husband, who were expected at the theatre, and for whom great preparations had been made. All that I could say had no effect, and at last found that I was virtually under arrest for the alleged offence of taking your ring, and not returning it. This charge was made by your brother, in revenge for the mortification which you had experienced in not being married at the appointed time."

"I knew nothing of this," she said, with a trembling lip, and a disdainful toss of her pretty head. "I desired to urge no man to marry me against his inclinations, not even the Earl of Afton."

How much I admired her in her queenly *rôle*. Never had I loved her so well as now, when she stood before me with just enough disdain on her pretty face, to make it light up like a picture. I began to feel that I had done wrong on my way to her chamber, and hoped that the lady's-maid would never boast of my little wandering weakness, a mere aberration of mind, which time and a good wife would cure.

"Go on, sir," she said, seeing that I hesitated, and was steadily regarding her. "Go on, and let us hear the conclusion of this strange story, or, rather, fable, as I can call it no less."

"It seems that your brother was determined to bring the Earl of Afton to an account, and put the Chief of Police on his track. By some strange misconception he stumbled upon me, and, to prove that he was right, drew from his pocket that diamond ring which you now have on your hand. O Florence, let me spare you the rest of my strange story. I would not bring a blush to that dear face for all the diamonds in the world."

Of course this was not exactly correct, because men are not so particular as all that when conversing with their wives in private, but I thought it sounded well, and would touch her heart and feelings, and that she would respect me the more for it.

"Go on, sir. There are men who should blush for their conduct as well as we poor women, or, perhaps, we should blush for them, as they are incapable of such manifestations of modesty."

I wondered if she had peeped through the keyhole, and seen me at the head of the stairs. But I rejected the idea as unworthy of the sweet lady, although, as a general thing, men can't be too careful as they brush through the world, and meet some of its rough corners.

"You still insist that I shall continue my story, Florence?" I asked.

"Yes. I will hear all that you have to say, sir. Go on," she said desperately.

"The ring, Florence, had passed from the finger of the Earl of Afton to that of a girl of Melbourne, named Kitty Stukely, a handsome, showy young woman, who lives somewhere on Lonsdale Street, I think."

She gave a gasp, and I thought that she would faint, but she leaned on the back of a chair, and this steadied her slight form, and it again grew firm and defiant. I waited until her faintness had passed, and resumed,—

"It seemed that his lordship loaned, or gave, the ring to the young woman a few days after he had received it from your hands."

She drew the glittering diamond from her finger, and threw it to the opposite side of the chamber, with an expression of deep disgust on her burning face, as though the jewel had contaminated her hand by its contact. I felt more proud of her superb and regal beauty than ever, as I witnessed this display of passion and haughty pride.

"I was informed that there were but two things for me to do," I resumed. "The Chief said that he first noticed the ring on the hand of the girl at a *free-and-easy*,—if you know what that is, I do not,—on Market Square, one evening, and he was suspicious that it had been stolen. He took it from her this afternoon at her house, and, on questioning her, she said that a gentleman named Angus — she did not know him by any other name — had put it on her finger, and told her to wear it. The Chief said I must decide whether she lied or not. If she did lie she must go to prison, if she did not, I must answer for the crime of giving away a valuable jewel which did not belong to me. Breach of trust, I think he called it. Florence, do you know what I did? My darling, can you imagine what course I pursued?"

"I am not sufficiently versed in the sinuous ways of mankind to even give a guess," was the disdainful answer.

"I went with the Chief to the home of the young la— girl I mean, and there she, too, claimed me as her Angus."

A look that would have wilted me if I had not been honest and truthful, flashed from my wife's blue eyes. It was like lightning on a summer afternoon after a shower.

"Of course, dear, I repudiated her, and her story," I continued.

"Yes, it is so like a man."

I began to think that Florence had seen much of the world. Perhaps her father had not been all that she could have desired.

"But when the Chief swore that if I did not acknowledge that I gave her the ring, he would lock the girl up, and hold me as a witness, I saved her and myself, and a terrible scandal."

"How? No doubt you would save yourself. Men generally do."

"By a falsehood, dear, and I think it a justifiable one under the circumstances. I said that I had loaned her the ring."

"And a few minutes ago you said that you were a man of truth," in a sarcastic tone.

"And I still claim to be, Florence."

"Have you told me all? Have you made a full confession?" she then asked.

"I have told you all, dear."

She looked at me with a suspicious eye. I did not think that it was worth while to go into minute particulars respecting all that was said or done at the house. It is always best to avoid trouble and misunderstanding if possible, and women are so unreasonable over little matters.

"And this *thing*, this girl, escapes all punishment because you shielded her?"

"Yes, Florence," I answered, very humbly.

"And the mean thing wore my diamond for several days?" my wife asked.

"So I understand."

"Eh, I shall never put it on my finger again without an expression of disgust. I will soak it in ammonia to take away the stain. How dare you do such a thing?" Florence asked.

"I am doing what I believe to be right, Florence. Heaven knows how painful it is to me, for I love you, dear, and had I been the one to have been so honored as to receive such a token of your confidence no power on earth should have taken it from me."

She seemed to be meditating on all that had been said, but at last she raised her head, and remarked, —

"I can hardly believe you, and yet you seem honest and sincere."

"O Florence, trust me, dear. I am a young man of good moral and religious character."

I thought that I would hurl that sentence at her head, and see if it would not have a good effect, but, to my surprise, she did not appear to notice it. I am afraid that a majority of girls do not reverence pious young men, unless they can waltz, and drive a horse with one hand, and eat ice cream and oysters at all hours of the day and night, to the everlasting ruin of their digestions.

"Now, what do you propose to do?" my wife asked, after a long pause, during which I could hear Mr Kebblewhite, still in the dining-room, roar out the highly entertaining and instructive ballad of —

"Cease, rude Boreas, blustering railer."

"What would you have me do, Florence? You are my wife, but a wife who was obtained by deception on one part, but not fraud on mine. I would have made all clear had I been so permitted. The gentleman, the lord, the coward, who was to have married you, is miles away from the city by this time, and he will never return to claim your hand. If he did a horsewhip should honor his shoulders from my hands, or those of your brother.

"This evening, Florence, at seven o'clock, or thereabouts, I saw a young man leave the Melbourne club-house. I had but a glimpse of his face and form, and must confess they were wonderfully like mine. He was assisted into a light vehicle, and told to make for Gelong with all speed, and never return again to this city, as he had disgraced himself, and the Belle of Australia, and all her numerous friends. He was addressed as a lord, and one of the parties who acted as his escort was called Mr. Mattocks. After his lordship had been driven off, the gentlemen conversed together for a few moments, in an undertone, and, when they turned to enter the club-house, saw me for the first time. One of them, to my amazement and surprise, addressed me as the Earl of Afton, and claimed to have been the early friend of the father of his lordship, — the old earl. It was then that I learned that I was to have married you at three o'clock in the afternoon, but that I had thought better of it, and fled, or made the attempt, and returned. Just as though I would fly from such a dear, lovely little girl as you, when there was a prospect of making her my wife. Both gentlemen reproached me in bitter terms for my perfidy, and then I discovered that Mr. Mattocks was at one time a suitor for your hand, and still had hopes if I was out of the way. I thought them what we call cranks, or lunatics, and so passed on to meet a fresh one in the person of Mr. Murden. Now, dear, do you wonder that you made the mistake that you did? and that all your sweet kisses were intended for another? and that the dear hand which I prize so much would have been valueless to the man called the Earl of Afton? O Florence, take pity on me, and pardon me, for had you not been so beautiful, had I not loved you the first glimpse that I obtained of your dear face, I would have braved death sooner than give my hand where my heart did not also go. You are my wife, but only in name. Can you pardon me for my deceit?"

She looked at me as I held out my arms, but still she clung to the back of the chair, and did not change her position.

"List ye landsmen hall to me,"

came from the dining-room in a roaring tone, and how I pitied that poor Frenchman, unless he was drunk, and under the table.

I walked to the window, and threw it up, and looked out upon the bright moonlight.

There was a balcony in front of the window, and near that balcony was a stout tree of the she-oak variety, such as furniture is made of. For a moment I surveyed the scene before me, and inhaled the perfume of the fresh air. While I was standing there I heard a neighboring clock in a steeple toll the hour of one in the morning.

"Good-by, Florence," I said, returning to her side, and offering her my hand.

She did not look at me, or turn her head. She seemed to be dreaming, for all the signs of life that she showed. I waited for a moment, and then again spoke.

"Will you let me take your hand, Florence?" I asked. "I am going away, and we may never meet again."

She did not answer me, or raise her hand, or make a sign to repulse me. She did not even turn her head, or look at me.

"If you can pardon me in time, Florence, I shall feel blessed. I now restore to you your freedom. In a little while you can procure a separation, and marry one whom you can love, honor, and esteem. I shall feel very wretched when I hear of it, if I ever do, but, if your future happiness is dependent upon it, I shall remain content."

Still no word or sign that she heard me, no token of relenting or pity. Her face was set, and her eyes fixed.

"When I leave you, Florence, I shall go I know not where, and return I know not when. I am poor, and as proud as yourself, and if I am not an English nobleman, I am at least an American gentleman, and should feel humiliated to take advantage of my position, or wonderful likeness to the man you loved, to bring reproach upon your name. Good-by, Florence, once more, O my darling, good-by!"

I knelt at her side, and kissed her little hand, but there was no sign of relenting, and if there had been the parting would have been more painful than it was. I returned to the window, took off my dress coat, and threw it to the ground, for I did not dare to leave the house by the stairs and front-door, fearful of meeting some one of the family, who would demand an explanation of my nocturnal wanderings, and, alas! what could I say more than had already been said? One glance I cast around the chamber, and saw how beautifully it was furnished, with its blue silk bed-spread, blue satin covered furniture, blue damask draperies, and oil paintings on the wall, and a blue decorated marble mantel clock on the marble chimney piece. All this I saw, and then I heard the roaring of Mr. Kebblewhite, as he continued to howl, —

"Sing the dangers of the sea,"

showing that he had not yet escaped from the ballads of Great Britain, and gone into snug quarters for the night. One last glance I cast at my wife, and saw that she had not moved from her fixed position, that she had not turned her head, or appeared to be aware that we were to be separated forever, or until God's own time when we should look on each other's faces once more, but whether in heaven or on earth He alone could tell.

"God bless you, Florence, O my wife," I muttered to myself, closed the window from the outside, and, as I did so, I thought that I heard a fall, as though some one had stumbled, but I paid no attention to it, and the next moment I seized one of the branches of the tough tree, and dropped to the ground, for the bough did not break, but let me fall very gently, and when I reached the earth I found a pair of arms thrown around me, clasping me in an embrace that was like the coils of the South-American python, and fully as resistless.

I would have struggled with the person who had so suddenly seized me, but I had been taken at a disadvantage, and was nearly powerless to move, and as for shouting, I did not mean to do that, and bring upon my devoted head the great wrath of a man who could sing all night, drink all night, and had pistols and a nulla near at hand, to be used with deadly effect upon the person whom he supposed to be a noble son-in-law.

I turned my head, and saw the set, determined face and glittering eyes of Mr. Murden, the Chief of Police, whom I supposed home and a-bed long ago.

"Well," I asked, "what in the devil's name are you doing here?"

"Holding your lordship until you promise not to make a noise, and to cease struggling," was the brief answer.

"Oh, release your hold of me, for you are cracking my ribs, and I don't like a man's embrace at any time."

"Promise, my lord."

"Oh, bosh, Murden, you know that the lord business is all played out, and it is no longer a joke. Let up on me, and I 'll promise anything you ask."

"Even to walking back into that house, and returning to the room where you belong?"

"No, sir, not if you should press the life out of me. So go ahead, and do your worst," I said most determinedly.

He released me from his tight embrace, and stepped back, so that he could have a better look at my face, and watch its expression.

"My lord," he said, "I see traces of tears in your eyes, but tears are not always the sign of repentance. Why have you left your young wife at this hour of the night, and in this mysterious manner?"

"Because I am a man of honor, and will not stain my good name by pretending to be that which I am not. I am the husband of Miss Kebblewhite, but only in name, and no earthly power shall tempt me to claim her as my wife, unless she is satisfied to take me as I am, a person without title, and without fortune."

"My lord," said the Chief, with a mocking smile, as he removed his cap, and bowed low before me, "if one of my men had stood before me, and related such a yarn, I should have told him that he was a liar, and unworthy of the police force, but as you are a nobleman, and my superior in rank and fortune, I will simply say that I understand your motives, and will take all the means that lie in my power to frustrate them. I suspected something of this nature, and have waited outside of the house to thwart you in the gross wrong which you contemplate."

"What wrong do I contemplate?" I asked, astonished at his words.

"I overheard your pretended confession to Mrs. Kebblewhite while I was in the hall. We policemen sometimes have to be listeners. You told a pitiful tale, and any one but a man accustomed to all kinds of cunning and turns would have believed you. I did not. I saw through your scheme, and determined to defeat it, for your sake, and the sake of the young lady whom you have just forsaken on some mean and cowardly pretext. It won't wash, my lord, so I give you fair warning."

"I suspected that you had played the part of an eavesdropper, and had listened to a private conversation, Mr. Murden, Chief of Police, but I am at a loss to understand you, when you accuse me of meanness and duplicity."

"I will explain, Earl of Afton," speaking in a sarcastic tone. "Since you have been in Melbourne you have made some rapid conquests of the young ladies who reside here. I know all that has transpired in the last three weeks, and, if you had the least shame in your lordly nature, you would blush for your evil deeds. But as you are incapable of doing so, we will let that pass. Among all the women you met none fascinated you so strongly as Miss Kebblewhite, and the girl Kitty. The former you did not dare to insult with infamous proposals, so you talked to her of marriage, and thought that familiarity with such a sacred tie, would render her less vigilant. You were defeated, and then attempted to shirk the wedding. I put a spoke in your wheel, and made you perform your part of the contract to the letter. The girl Kitty was in the market, and you bought her. Of that I have nothing to say as long as you were a single man. You lavished money on her, and of that I do not complain. If ever a man regarded his mistress as something a little better than a dog, you were the person; but I swear to you, my lord, that if you go near that girl tonight, or any other time, if you speak to her, or make appointments with her, I will arrest you both, even if the lieutenant-governor should issue an edict commanding me not to do so. Do you understand me now, my lord?"

"O my God!" I gasped, and clung to the tree by which I had descended from the window, and then the tears, which I had so long restrained, burst from my eyes, and ran down my cheeks in torrents.

The Chief stood before me, proud, defiant, and scornful. He thought that I was playing a part, and that he was checkmating it at every turn.

"Heaven," I gasped at length, "are you a man, or a high-toned devil, fresh from the deepest parts of the infernal regions, sent on earth to drive me mad with your base suppositions? Wretch, do you believe that I could leave the presence and company of that pure angel, my wife, for the atmosphere of a mistress? If I had a pistol I would shoot you like a dog for even hinting at such an abomination."

"But as you have no pistol I am likely to live for some time to come. Other men have done the same thing, and of more distinguished rank than yourself. Even Frederick the Great" —

"—— Frederick the Great!" I cried impatiently.

"With all my heart. He's no friend of mine, and probably has been damned for many years past. If not, he deserved to be."

"Mr. Murden," I said, as soon as I could recover my composure, "to you and your devilish craftiness am I indebted for all the misery, and all the unhappiness, I am likely to experience for many long years to come. You have this night woven a web around me that I could not break through, try as I would."

"I should think not," was the complacent rejoinder. "I weave webs to stay, and not to break."

"A few hours ago," I continued, "I was happy in the thoughts of the future, of earning a fair living by my talent and industry, if not in one business at least in another. I was heart whole. I had never loved any other woman except my mother, and I did not desire to. I met you on my way to the theatre, and you were pleased to call me a lord, and to relate to me something which I knew nothing about."

I paused, and strove to keep back the emotion that would surge from my eyes as I thought of all that I had suffered at the hands of the man who stood before me, with a half-smile on his lips, disbelieving every word that I uttered.

"Devil that you are, you made me do some things that my soul abhorred. I thought that I could save that poor girl, and still extricate myself from your toils, but in saving her I lost myself."

"Bah, my lord! did you think so poorly of me as to suppose that I would arrest Kitty? It was a game of bluff, and I held a full hand, and you did not even have a pair. I called when I was ready, and you did not respond. That is all."

"Then you brought me here, to this elegant mansion, and I was received as the wandering bridegroom, with open arms and every demonstration of pleasure and respect."

"Certainly, why should you not have been? It is customary in all well-regulated society to treat the bridegroom with honor, unless the old man has especial objections to him. Now my father-in-law was so anxious to get his daughter off his hands, that he got drunk before the wedding, and when I put in an appearance, wanted to kiss me, and to swear eternal friendship, while my mother-in-law declared that I was not good enough for her child, and, in her anxiety to get us out of the house, and started on our own account, fell down-stairs, and broke one of her legs, and could n't visit us for three months. There are some bright episodes on earth, my lord, after all."

"When I would explain everything," I continued, not noticing his long harangue, "you blocked me at every step, and would listen to nothing, or permit others to. You know the result. God of heaven! I am married to an angel, and must live apart from her. I love her, and can never see her, or speak to her. There does not exist in all the regions of the civilized world a more unhappy, desperate wretch than I, and to you am I indebted for all of it."

"Of course you are. I was bound to give you a lesson, and I have accomplished my object. I determined to show you that the people of Melbourne could be as sharp as the nobility of England. I have put a stop to your *amours* and flirtations in this city at least. If you love your wife, I am rejoiced at it, but why you should leave her at this hour of the morning is beyond my comprehension. **Lovers do not act** that way, **my lord, and** you know it."

"I give it up," I sighed. "There is no power but a revelation from heaven can convince you that I speak the truth."

"Not unless backed by reliable and responsible witnesses, my lord. But now we understand one another. Go your way, if you want to. I have no power to detain you more. Wander where you will, do as you will, but go not near that girl Kitty, or there will be trouble, as sure as my name is Murden. Her house is watched, and will be for several days. Go, my lord," and he stepped back and one side, and removed his cap as he bowed. "Go, and leave a ruined and broken life behind you. You have crushed the sweetest flower in all Australia, and I hope you will be d—d for it."

"O Mr. Murden," I cried, "if you would but believe me. If you knew how much I love my wife, if you would but comprehend my delicacy," I pleaded.

"Blast your delicacy," was the rough rejoinder. "It won't wash here in Australia. I know something about it, and have heard of it in a dozen different cases. But I have had my say, and have done with you and your love affairs. Good-night, my lord. Remember my warning."

He put on his cap, and walked off in one direction, and I in another, but, as I left the extensive grounds that surrounded the house, I turned, and took one farewell look at my wife's chamber. It was still brilliantly illuminated, but there were shadows flitting back and forth, from window to window, and, with a sob of pain, I turned into Victoria Parade, and plodded along until I saw a hansom, with the driver fast asleep on the box, standing on the corner, waiting for a belated customer like myself. I did not know where the Hen and Chickens, my chop house, was located, but I determined to find it, and leave the city as early as possible in the morning. The clock struck two as I awakened the cabman, and told him where to take me.

"No short commons for me, yer know," he said. "I vants a crown to take a swell like yer at this 'our, yer know."

"All right, you shall have it. Drive on. I shall be locked out," I said.

"No danger of that, sir. They is hall nighters at the 'En."

He drove on through the rough, deserted streets, and not a soul did we encounter, except an occasional policeman, and some huge bullock teams, drawn by eight and ten head of cattle, on their return trips to the country for wool and hides, and other produce.

In ten minutes we pulled up near the door of the Hen and Chickens. We could not stop just in front of the hotel, for a large covered wagon to which was attached four horses, blocked the way. I paid the driver his crown, and even then he had the impudence to demand *pourboire*, or a glass of beer, and, as I was too miserable to refuse, I told him to go into the bar, and get what he wanted.

As I entered the tap-room I saw the head waiter seated at a table, and drinking beer with a man who was evidently the driver of the team standing at the door. He was dressed in coarse woollen garments, trousers tucked in high boots, and a broad-brimmed felt hat thrown back from a face that was unmistakably Irish, but with such a good-humored expression that I was quite attracted by it.

The head waiter jumped up, and came toward me as I entered.

"'Ad about given yer hup, sir, for the night," he said. "The chambermaid 'as been in 'ere a dozen times to ax for yer, and to see that yer vos hall right for the night. She is spoons on yer by a great deal, and she never vos so afore; but I told 'er that yer vos a swell, and not the kind of game that vould stoop to 'er, and she jist said I vos to mind my hown business, and not to meddle vid 'ers. But yer is hall right now, and vot did yer think of the play, and the Belle of Australia? Ah, she 's a rum one for good looks, I 'm told, and it 's said that a big swell vos to run in 'arness vid 'er. Vill yer 'ave somethin' 'ot or cold, beer and a bit of cheese?"

During all this conversation on the part of the head waiter, I had been examining the face of the Irish stockman, until at last he grew restless under my scrutiny, and said, —

"Well, young feller, yer will know me agin, I 'm after thinking, begor."

"No offence, mate," I replied. "I was just wondering whether you would join me in a pot of half-and-half, and a bit of bread and cheese."

"Sure I will if yer honor will stand the trate," was the reply with a grin.

The head waiter brought the bread and cheese and beer, and then joined us.

"Is that your team at the door?" I asked of the stockman.

"Sure it is not, but my employer's, sur, bad luck to him for a miser."

"Do you leave the city tonight?" I asked, thinking that I saw a way to escape.

"Faith and I do, in less than half an hour, if I can get through wid me beer by that toime."

"Where are you going?" I asked.

"To the master's shape run, about tin miles from Ballarat. We pass through Slabtown, and have an aisy journey of it, for we goes in the night, and avoid the hate."

"Ballarat? Is n't that the place where gold is found in such large quantities?" I demanded.

"Shure it is, sur, when yer is in the luck. But, begor, all a'n't in that way at all. But some makes a stroike once in a while. There was Pat Maguire, he had the divil's own luck."

"What will you charge to give me a lift on the way to Ballarat? I want to go there, and try my luck in the mines. I am an American, and a stranger here."

"An American? Whoop! do yer think I 'm a hathen to ax yer a penny for all the ridin' I can give yer? Shure yer welcome to go wid me, and to stay on the run where I look after the shape as long as yer want to, and no money shall it cost yer. But yer can't go in thim clothes. They be too noice."

"I have others. I will go with you, but shall insist upon paying my passage."

"Faith, yer may insist all yer want to, but Orish Mike is not the buy to take money from an American, now yer belave it. I has a brother there, and nine fust cousins, and, perhaps, yer knows 'em. They is in a place called New York, and all doin' well, wid lushin's of whiskey every day, and but little to do. Whoop! but don't I wish that I was there, and perhaps I shall be some day. Who knows?"

The head waiter and Mike exchanged significant looks, and then I told the former that I would run up to my room, change my clothes, leave in his charge all the best that I owned, and pay him for taking care of them until I returned. If I never returned, he might keep them, for which generosity the man expressed many thanks.

The proposed sudden departure was no cause of surprise to the head waiter. He was accustomed to it, and made no objection. He went with me to my chamber, helped me assort my clothes, and dress in gray flannel shirt and trousers, wide-brimmed hat, California boots, and spurs, and belt containing revolver and bowie-knife. The change of costume I thought would disguise my appearance so much that no one would recognize me. The poorest of my wardrobe, with towels, brushes, and hammock, I resolved to take with me, and the head waiter carried all down-stairs, and put them in the cart. I gave him a shilling for his trouble, paid for my refreshments, and then, in the goodness of his heart, the waiter filled my large pocket flask with brandy, and I was ready, and so was Mike.

"Come 'ere agin, sir," cried the waiter, as we mounted the wagon. "Hol-ways glad to see yer. Vot shall I tell the chamber-maid, sir?"

Mike awoke the horses, and we were off, so I did not have to send a message to the girl.

Through the avenues of Melbourne we rumbled, over the rough streets and roads, across the bridge that spans the Yarrow, out into the country, and on the dry, dusty thoroughfares we plodded our way; and, while I sat with head bowed on my breast, and tears fast falling from my eyes, how little I thought that in the mansion I had so recently left there was bustle and confusion, and that lights flashed from many windows, and that in the richly furnished chamber I had entered as a husband, there was lying a young, pale-faced girl, clutching wildly at the cool night air, moaning, and tossing her fair head from side to side, and finding no rest on the soft pillows, her eyes parched, and from which no tears would flow, begging and pleading in incoherent tones to her mother, who knelt by the bedside with trembling hands and bitter sighs, for pardon, for love, and the return to her arms of her young husband, while through the streets of the city hansoms raced from place to place, and three men, all sober from the effects of wine, but drunk with rage and passion, armed with pistols and rapier, went from club to hotel, from billiard saloon to free-and-easy, dance hall to cellar, in every place that a wild, thoughtless nobleman would be likely to frequent, in search of the man who had unwittingly ruined the happiness, the mind and the reason of the Belle of Australia; but neither in dance hall, nor in free-and-easy, in hotel or club house, did the angry men find the object of their search, and, as a last resort, Mr. Kebblewhite routed out Mr. Murden, the Chief of Police, and, in tones that were wild, and trembling with passion, demanded his aid in arresting, and bringing back to his house, the young nobleman who had insulted his daughter, and the whole tribe of Kebblewhites, and a reward of one hundred pounds was offered to the man who should be so fortunate as to lay his rough hands on my shoulder, and claim me as a prisoner, as the reason, health, and happiness of the newly wedded wife depended upon the prompt execution of the order. But of this I was blissfully unconscious, for had I known all I should have returned to the mansion, and by my presence soothed the unhappy Belle of Australia, and, perhaps, even then there would have been pardon and happiness for the young wife and husband. But I did not know all that was transpiring in the city, and so rode onward, and left civilization and comfort, ease and plenty far behind me, and I did not again see the city that sheltered my love for many a long and dreary day.

"BAD LUCK TO YER, YER SPALPEEN!" ROARED MIKE AS HE ROLLED OVER THE TRUNK OF THE TREE.

PART VI.

A JOURNEY, AND A MOUNTED POLICEMAN'S HALT. — THE NOISES OF THE FOREST. — A CUP OF TEA AND THE KANGAROO. — THE QUAKER AND HIS QUESTIONS. — OLD WEBBER AND HIS BLOOMING DAUGHTER. — AN INDUCE- MENT. — MIKE GIVES ME A SOLEMN WARNING.

WHILE Mr. Anderson Kebblewhite, and his son, Mr. Judson Kebble. white, and Monsieur Allete, were searching every public and private resort in Melbourne, with vengeance in their minds, and murder in their hearts, and while the white, stern-faced Frenchman was uttering the most fascinating of oaths, in a strange mixture of English and his native dialect, vowing that he would plunge his sharp-pointed rapier in the breast of the noble lord who had dared to trifle with the honor and fair fame of the Belle of Australia, the pride and delight of her father and friends, I was journey- ing through the suburbs of the city, past handsome villas, low drinking tav- erns, stockmen's shanties, sheep stations, native's huts, of grass and branches, scrub and swamp, tall trees, and extensive farms, occasionally meeting a mounted policeman, who eyed us sharply, but suffered us to pass unchallenged, and all that time I had not exchanged a word with Mike, my companion. He had seen that I was in trouble, and, with a delicacy peculiar to the sympathetic people of his race, had not interrupted the flow of my grief, or attempted to make me converse. But, as the horses trotted on, and all signs of the city began to disappear, and the country to grow wild and uncultivated, Mike lighted his pipe, handed a bottle toward me, and said, —

"It's a sorrowful load yer is carryin' in yer breast, mate, so take a sup of this, and sa if it won't lighten the spell that's on yer. Whiskey for the man what's had a misfortune, and tay for them what don't need cheerin'. Come, mate, rouse up, and be a man. Yer is young, and there's more lasses than one in the world, and, faith, wid yer swell looks and face, divil a fear but that ye 'll find anither gal what will jump into yer arms, and put her pritty head on yer shoulder. Bedad, don't I know all about it. I 've been there as often as any buy of my inches, and Orish Mike is still unblessed by praist and the troubles of a wife. Whoop, get up thar, yer blunderin' hold idiots, what don't know no more than to go to slape while walkin' in a road that is na deep in dust, except in the winter when it is waist deep in mud and water. Away wid yer, or we won't be home for a wake."

The last remarks were addressed to the horses, who desired to walk, and go to sleep, instead of moving onward at a steady trot.

I took a little sip from the bottle to please Mike, and it did delight him.

"Whoop! that does me good," he cried. "No more sorrer for a woomin, if it's one that makes yer face look like the winding shate at a wake. Begor, chere up, and it's lots of fun we 'll have afore we raches the shape run, where I has the charge."

"Ah, Mike," I said, "I shall never smile again. My heart is broken."

"Bedad, but that's a mistake ontirely now. If yer heart was broken it 's under the ground yer 'd be, and the daisies growin' at yer head, and all yer relations fightin' for yer property."

"But I have no property."

"So much the bitter. We can be more sociable loike. If yer had money ye 'd not be talkin' wid the loikes of me."

"There you are mistaken, Mike. I like a man for what he is, and not for what he is worth."

"Do yer? Well, it's a mighty queer place yer has come to thin, and it's not many yer 'll find to kape yer company. But tell me, mate, is yer sorrowful 'cos the lass has shipped yer, and taken anoother?"

"No, Mike, it 's not that."

"Has yer married her? or has she dided?"

"She is not dead, Mike, but I am married to her."

"And has she gone off wid anoother man?"

"No, she is incapable of such a crime."

"And yer has not gone off wid anoother woman?"

"No, Mike, far from it."

"Then, bedad, yer jist bate me; but of wun thing be sure, jist as true as the pole points to the nadle, or the nadle points to the pole, I jist don't know which, yer may count on wun thing, and that is yer two will come together agin, no matter whar yer may be."

"Do you think so, Mike?" I asked, really hopeful under his rough consolation.

"Sure, I know it, sur. A wooman is a strange sort of crature, arter all. If she runs from her hoosband wid anoother man she is always ready for to be forgiven, but if he runs away wid anoother wooman divil a bit will she let up on him. Now, yer has not offended her finer sensibilities, as they call it, and she has not woounded yers, and so there will be a re-union at some time, be sure. A wooman can draw a man all over the globe if she wants to. Sure one drew me to this country, and bad luck to her."

"How was that, Mike?"

"Well, sur, loight yer pipe, and I 'll tell yer. Yer see, sur, I 'm a *lag*."

"A what?" I asked, for I had never heard the word before.

"A *lag*, sur. Sure, I spake the word as plain as pussible."

"Yes, but I do not know what a *lag* is. I am new to Australia."

"Yer must be, sur, not to know what a *lag* is. I thought everybody knew what a *lag* is. The country is full of 'em, sur."

"Possibly, but I do not know all the terms you use here. Recollect I am from America."

"True, sur, and God bless yer honor for comin' from a land where a man can vote, and get elected to the highest office the furst year he lands, and for ivery vote he casts, he gets lushin's of whiskey, as me brother writes. But a *lag*, sur, is a *convict*, sure."

"And you are a convict?" I asked, with a square look at the frank face, and broad grin, extending from ear to ear.

"And why not, sur? There 's plinty of 'em round here."

"But you are at large. You are free to do as you please."

"Not quite, sur. I 'm not quite free as yet, 'cos I 'm a ticket-of-lave man, and the police kape an eye on me. But next wake, plase God, me time will be up, and I shall be fray to go whar I plase, and do what I plase, and the bloody traps, bad luck to 'em, can't lay wun of their dirty fingers on me. I reported to the office in Melbourne yesterday for the last time, and that's what sint me to the city wid a small load of wool, and to git a stock of tay and sugar for the run and the min. Whoop! and won't I be off to other diggin's next wake. I 've had enough shape runnin' to last me for all me ioif."

"But you have not told me why you were transported, and how a woman drew you all the way from Old Ireland to this country," I said.

"True for yer, sur, I have not, 'cos I kapes that for the last, as it 's the wust of all. Yer see, sur, I was transported to this God-forsaken country for havin' a little crack at a landlord."

"Do you mean that you shot at him, Mike?"

"That 's what I do mane, sur, and a moighty mane man he was. Yer see he kept puttin' up the rint, and I determined to put him down, and one night I peppered him from behind a hedge. Lord, sur, yer would have died laughin' to see him jump. Me gun was loaded wid small shot, and they all hit him below the belt. He jist clapped his hands behind him, and scrached that loud that yer could have heard him a mile. Will, sur, I was looked arter by the buys, and kept out of the way of the bloody peelers, but wun night I got word that me gurl wanted me to come to her cabin, and I wint, and the furst thing I knowed the purlice had me by the arms and the neck, and I was locked up, and convicted, and that 's the way a wooman drew me to this country, bad luck to 'em."

Mike lighted his pipe again, took a sip from the black bottle, whistled to his horses, and, after offering me a drink, which I declined, once more continued,—

"Now, sur," he said, "when yer go back to Amerikee I want yer to take me wid yer. Faith, but it 's a nice helpmate I 'll be for yer, and no wages asked for, and I 'll be the best friend yer iver had in this wourld, man or wooman."

"You forget, Mike, that I am poor, and have but little hope of making money just at present. I am going to Ballarat to see if I can find a lucky strike in the mines, or at least to look about, and see what I can do to make a living."

"Divil doubt but that ye 'll have the illegant luck. I see it in yer face. Yer was born under a lucky star, and will be a rich man, and live wid the wun yer is now lavin' miny and miny a year to come. I wants no wages till yer can be ready to pay me, and, let me whisper in yer ear, I 've a hundred puns in the bank at Melbourne, all of which I have arned since I 've been a ticket-of-lave man, now eight years, for I was sintenced for tin years, and all that money yer can have, and no questions axed, as long as yer want, to do wid jist what yer plase, and yer shall be the capen, and I 'll be a plane man, and do yer biddin', from crackin' a head to diggin' for gould. Oh, it is illegant times we 'll have, and when yer is rich we 'll go to Amerikee, and ye 'll run for alderman or mayor, and, O Lord! won't we live on the fat of the land, and won't I make the lads from Limerick vote for yer ivery time, and as often as is necessary. Sure ye 'll be as rich a purson as old Kebblewhite, the mane old divil."

"Mr. Kebblewhite?" I repeated. "Do you know him?"

"Know him? Sure, don't I know him. He 's me master, and owns me shape run, and fifty thoosand acres of land, and twenty thoosand as nice shape as can be found in all Victoria. Sure I ought to know him. I 've worked for him eight years. Oh, but he 's jist lushin' rich, he is, and owns more stores and more wool than any man in the city."

"Do you mean Mr. Anderson Kebblewhite, Mike,— a stout, red-faced man?"

"The same, sur. He lives on Victoria Parade, in a big house, and has a nice darter. O my, a'n't she the stepper, and the beauty? I seed her on the strate, and it seamed that her little foots did n't touch the ground, for she 'd jist skim over it. She 's called the Belle of Australia, and no wonder, for there 's not anoother lass in these parts that can hold a candle to her. Faith, but I wish yer could have sane her. Yer would have sighed wuss than yer do now, and, the divil fly away wid me, but yer two would have made a nice pair, she all goold and white, loike the pale rose at sunrise, and yer a little brown, loike a stately gum-tree at sunset. Ah me, but she 's not for the loikes of us, as I heard that she was married yesterday to a big swell from the Ould Country, and I 'll bet me hundred puns that he makes her heart ache afore he 's done wid her."

I turned away my head to prevent Mike seeing the tears that would start to my eyes, as I thought of Florence, and our singular marriage. How little the Irishman suspected that I was the "swell," as he called the bridegroom, who had wedded the Belle of Australia, and was now flying for his life, and in search of happiness far away from the lady he so dearly loved.

"Let us hope that she will be happy, Mike," I said, as soon as I could command my voice.

"Yes, sur, wid all me heart. Sure, if her father is a mane old kermuggin, the nice young gurl is not to blame. But now I hopes he 's satisfied.

He always wanted a *suction* of the harastocracy for his son-in law, and now he has him."

Mike had made a slight mistake in a word, following in this respect his employer, but it was not worth while correcting him. He was so honest in his opinion, that it was better to let him have his own way.

"And to think," continued Mike, "that old Kebblewhite should be sich a rich man. He's jist picked up goold by the shovelful; and, arter all, *he was only a lag loike me.*"

"What?" I asked, turning on Mike so suddenly, that he dropped his match, and nearly broke his pipe.

"Sure he was a *lag*. I thought iverybody knew that. He kapes it mighty close, and I heard that he was afeared his swell son-in-law would hear of it, and so skip out. But it sames that he did n't. Oh, the old feller was given twenty years, him and an old servant what he has, who is called Harry. They was fust-class bugglars, and cracked a bank, and got nabbed. Old Kebblewhite behaved hisself, and got a ticket-of-lave the fust year or two, and he went on a shape run, and saw what was what, and then he started for hisself, and grew rich, and then he bought and sold wool, and made more money, and he kept buying land, and more shape, and stores and land in the city, and when his time was out, that was twenty-six years ago, he was jist bustin' wid wealth. He married a nice wooman, a real lady, I 'm told, who was poor, and had n't any friends, and so was glad to take even an old *lag*, but I 'm informed that he 's a good husband to her, and loves his darter, and no wonder that he does, for she 's worth lovin', and a credit to any man."

I had lighted my pipe while Mike was relating this wonderful piece of family history, and now I could understand some of the mystery which had surrounded Mr. Kebblewhite and me. I could comprehend why the Earl of Afton, if there was such a man, had failed to keep his engagement, even if he had any intention to do so. The story of transportation for burglary had reached his ears, and he had fled at the last moment, fearful of casting a blot upon the honor of his house by wedding the true, pure-hearted daughter of a convicted felon. This was the cause of Mr. Murden's surmises and questions, of Mrs. Kebblewhite's delicate inquiries at the hour I made my revelations; and now all was plain to me, why Mr. Kebblewhite desired to form an alliance for his daughter that would raise her out of the ranks of ordinary society, and lift her and her family up to a height that no other merchant in Melbourne could expect to obtain. But his ambitious schemes were frustrated by the very person whom he had counted on to do the work.

The daughter's beauty had done its part, but pride had proved stronger than love, and the lordly suitor had left the city, and I, in some singular manner, had taken his place, and wedded the girl who was to accomplish such a miracle for her family. Did I regret it? No, a thousand times no. I would have married her, loved her, and protected her, if I had been a duke instead of only an American citizen, poor and unknown. Her father's previous history would not have made the slightest difference to me. It was Florence whom I loved and respected, not her wealth and surroundings. She was the first one that I had ever admired and really loved, and I felt that she would be the last. How I prayed that night that God would soften the stroke that had fallen upon her golden head, that God would heal the wounds which now lacerated her heart, would dry up her tears, and once more bring smiles to the pale, unhappy looking face, so beautiful in its girlish beauty on the night that she had placed her little hand in my own, and pledged her heart and herself to be mine forever. Had all the world been against her I would have stood up and loved her, and clung to her only the more closely. But she had repudiated me in the first moment of disappointment, she had turned upon me as soon as she found that I could not lift her up to the position to which she aspired, and when I would have had a kind word for a last farewell, she had not responded by a look or gesture, but had let me go forth into the night without hope or forgiveness. All these things I thought of, and how long I thought of them I do not know, for I was aroused by the voice of Mike asking, —

"Well, sur, what is yer thinkin' of now?"

"The Belle of Australia, Mike."

"Well, sur, I 'd not think of her at all, 'cos she 's beyond yer rach. She is married, and yer must not think of married ladies, when a good-lookin' feller loike yerself can foind plinty of single ones what would jump at yer loike a kangaroo at a dog, or a native black at an opossum. Come, sur, tell me what yer think of me offer. Will yer take me wid yer, and let me sarve yer?"

"I don't know what to say to your proposition, Mike."

"Then say 'Yes.' Yer shall niver repint it. Yer sa, sur, I 'll drive the tame to the shape run, stay me time out, and thin jist pack up me traps, and come to yer at Ballarat. I 'm only tin miles from the mines, and wun of the buys will take me over some day. I 'll find yer, and thin we 'll go in for a fortune, and a good time. I 'll sind for me money, and yer can use it jist as yer say fit, divil a bit do I care as long as yer take care of it for me, and let me go wid yer to Amerikee."

"No, Mike, you keep your money just where it is. Do not remove it from the bank, for I would not touch it on any account. I have a little of my own, and will make that answer until we can look around, and see what we can do in mining."

" And ye 'll take me, sur?"

" Yes, Mike, we 'll link our fortunes together, and see if we can't make some money in the next six months."

" Whoop! go long wid yer, yer slapin' brutes. Sure we is both rich men from this moment. There 's luck wid yer sure as my name is Orish Mike. But, bedad, who is ridin' loike that at this hour of the mornin'? It 's a mounted trap as sure as I 'm a Christian."

Mike's surmises were correct, for a mounted policeman, horse and rider covered with dust and foam, drew up alongside of us, and checked his steed.

"Halt," he cried. " I wish to see what you have on board, and to ask a few questions."

" Sure, yer can look wid all ver eyes, and yer can ask as many questions as yer plase," Mike answered.

" I intend to," was the gruff rejoinder. " When did you leave Melbourne?"

" About two o'clock, I think," Mike answered.

" Have you seen a well-dressed gentleman on the road, traveling on foot or in a carriage? A young man, good-looking and smooth-spoken?" the policeman asked.

" No, sur. Me mate here and me has seen no sich purson."

" Stand up, and let me see you both," was the sharp command.

" Faith we will sur, if it will plase yer. Stand up, mate, as the gintleman directs. We nade not be ashamed of our good looks, aven at this hour of the mornin', when we has not had our bath or clane linen, or barber to comb our hair."

" None of your jesting with me, Mike. I know you, and you know me."

" Faith, it 's none but good yer knows of me, and miny a chop of mutton, and hot damper, I 've given yer, Mr. Larry, and miny a sip out of the bottle on a dark, rainy night, when yer has been scoutin' for bushrangers."

" True, Mike, but I have no time to recall old times. There 's the devil and all to pay in the city. The swell that married old Kebblewhite's daughter has cut and run, and we must find him. A hundred pounds to the officer who secures him," the policeman cried.

" And must I have a crack at him if I should mate him on the road?

Sure, a hundred puns is much money, and I 'd loike it. Begor, I has me old musket here in the wagon, and it 's loaded wid six fingers, and I could blow the head off of man or baste, if I wunce drew on him."

"Not for your life," was the stern command. "He 's a big lord, and a little luny, it is said. He 's to be treated with the utmost respect, but he is to be returned to the city. The Chief wants him. He has sent out twenty men to scour the roads, and find him. Whom have you with you, Mike? Draw a match, and let me see his shape and make up."

Mike drew a match, but it did not ignite readily, and, while hunting for another, he continued the conversation, while I sat silent on the seat, dreading an exposure.

"Is it for forgere, bugglary, or murder, sur?" asked Mike. "Sure it must be a bad crime that makes so hot a chase. To the divil wid the matches, I 've no more, I don't think."

"No matter, Mike. I see your mate is a rough-dressed fellow, and so won't bother you. Go on if you want to. I must go as far as Webber's, and wait until daylight."

The horseman turned to resume his gallop, but Mike stopped him to ask a question.

"Sure, sur, yer don't tell me if it 's bugglary, murder, or decaivin' of the fair sex," he said.

"I think it must be the last, Mike," laughed the officer. "The swell married the Belle of Australia last night, and it is supposed that the happy couple had a quarrel, and separated. They will sometimes, you know. At any rate he left the house, and can't be found, and now old Kebblewhite, his son, and that Monsieur Allete, all want him, and the Chief worst of all. A hundred pounds to the man who lays hands on the swell, but no violence. He is rich, and is no burglar. He is a young fellow that has been playing the deuse with half the girls of Melbourne. Just like some men, Mike. Now you have had enough of women, since you know what they are capable of. Eh?"

"Yer 'd better belave it, sur."

"Well, solong. I must be off. Hope I shall meet with that hundred pounds before daylight."

He waved his hand, struck the powerful black horse with his spurs, and was off, riding as easy as a *ranchero* of California.

I uttered a sigh of relief as the policeman disappeared in the bright moonlight, in a cloud of dust. Mike spoke to his horses, and we moved on. The driver sat silent for a long time, seemingly cogitating over some matter which he was trying to elucidate. At length he lighted his pipe, took a pun at his bottle, and then looked me squarely in the face.

"Yer honor," he said, "that was a narrow squake for yer, and no mistake. If the matches had n't gin out he 'd 'a' knowed yer."

"What do you mean, Mike?"

"Jist what I say, yer honor. Yer is the swell what was married to the Belle of Australia last night."

I made no reply.

"I thought it was —— quare that a swell like yer should walk into the Hen and Chickens, change his clothes, and go out wid me in this old tame. Ah, sur, yer has done wrong to lave a young wife the night yer was spliced to her, and not let her know whar yer was goin'! Go back to the lady, and kiss her, and tell her that yer is sorry, and will niver do so no more, and then love her till the poor little thing will think she 's in paradise, and that yer is the boss angel of her little heaven. Oh, don't let the poor bird flutter her wings, and bate them against the scornin' world, with no husband to stretch out his hand so that she can perch on it, and find rest when he whistles. Don't be hard headed when I know that yer heart is riddy to break wid the love that yer has for the young bride, and that yer tears has sprinkled the road all the way from Melbourne loike a rain in spring. Come, yer honor, let me turn the heads of the bastes, and, although I 'll lose time by the token, I 'll bate the lives out of 'em, but I 'll take yer back to the city afore daybreak, and to the white arms and swate face of yer wife. Come, yer honor, let me entrate yer to listen to a man what has been drawn all the way from Ould Oireland to this murderin' country."

He had stopped his horses, and made a motion as if he would turn them in the direction of Melbourne, but I quieted him by a gesture, which he did not fail to understand.

"No, Mike," I said, "I must not return to the city at the present time. It would be death to me, and no use to my wife. She married me under a misapprehension; she made a mistake, a dreadful one for her and me, but it is now too late to remedy it."

"Sure, people are makin' many mistakes of a loike nature, but they don't disciver them on their weddin' night, as a gineral thing, for their eyes is so blinded wid love that they see nothin' but sunshine and flowers, ice krame and cake, a swate smile, and unlimited letters of credit on the stout old bank of love, what was never known to be shaky. Oh murder, be a man and a husband at the same time, and let me return yer to yer home, and the Belle of Australia."

"Mike," I said, "I would give this island, or continent, if I owned it, to be with my wife at this moment, and think the exchange a cheap one."

"So would I," was the muttered interjection.

"But it must not be. There has been a mistake, and I could not rectify it, do all I would. She supposed that I was a lord, when I was only a simple citizen of the United States."

"And a blanked soight better than all the lords in Ould England, or any other country, except Oireland, do yer moind. Of course I must except Oireland, and yer don't moind if I do?"

"No, Mike, I do not care what you do, as long as you do not betray me, or turn back."

"Betray yer? Bedad, if a man should offer to do that I 'd brake his skull wid my shillalah, or shoot his blessed head off wid me musket. But I 'd loike to turn back. Think of yer wife, and her love for yer."

"No, Mike, a thousand times no. When she found that I was not a lord she would not even give me her hand to say a long farewell."

"The divil she would n't. Will, now, it runs that way wid some woomen. Only to think of that now. Will, will, who would have thought it? Did yer squaze her a little, yer honor?"

I disdained to notice this remark.

"Squazin' does wonders wid some of 'em. They goes all to pieces under a nice, hearty squaze, if yer helps it along wid a few kisses, providin' yer has not bin atin' onjuns. Love and sintiment and kisses don't go hand in hand when a man has been scoffin' onjuns. The woomen thinks there 's no true love about a man what wants to kiss her after atin' a peck of 'em. Will yer honor let me smell yer breath? It 's not jokin' I am, for sure I know every turn of a wooman's heart, as well as I know the faces of me shape, and, do yer moind, every one in twenty thousand has a different look, jist loike humans. Ye 'll see for yerself, if yer come to me run, and stop for a few days."

Mike did not insist upon testing if I had partaken of the savory and high-smelling vegetable, but turned his active mind to other matters, of more importance.

"Now yer sa, sur," he went on, "if yer won't go back till the proper time, we must do all we can to kape it secret loike, so the traps won't foind yer. When yer gits to Ballarat yer will be swallowed up wid the rist of the miners, and no one will ax who yer is, or what yer is about, or care a blank about yer, at all, at all, unless yer makes a stroik, and thin they 'll flock around, and ax yer to put up the beer. But I 'll be there, and look arter yer, so have no fear. But what is yer front name, so that I shall know what to call yer?"

"Angus."

"Hangus? The divil! what a name. It would answer for Ould Oireland."

"Why, Mike?"

"Because they *hang us* in that country even for lookin' a landlord in the face, and axin' for a redooksion of the rint. But I 'll be moighty careful, and not make two words of the name while I 'm wid yer at the mines. The buys would think it was a reflection on 'em, for more than half of 'em should be hanged, and the rist should die natural deaths, under the hands of student doctors."

And from that time Mike always called and spoke of me as "Hangus," during the many months we were together at the mines, and in Australia.

"Ah, how I wish we were goin' to the city instead of the shape run," Mike said, after he had remained silent for a few minutes. "But we 'll go there sum day, and thin I 'll see yer, and the Belle of Australia on yer arm, jist walkin' around Victoria Parade of an arternoon, as happy as two kittens, and as handsome as birds of paradise, and all the men a takin' off of their hats, and bowin' low, and all the woomen a jist kartesin' and smilin' at yer, and me near yer, all riddy to bang over the head the fust pusson what did n't pay yer proper respect, and say there was none loike yer in the whole kintry."

We rode along for a quarter of an hour, Mike being too much occupied with the beautiful and enticing picture he had conjured up, to indulge in conversation, but once in a while I could see his right arm raised in the air, and tremble, as though he was mentally whacking some unfortunate person over the head who had refused to pay court to my beautiful wife, and proper respect to myself.

We were now in a wild and unproductive part of the country, with some dense woods on either hand, and high, rocky hills in the distance. Occasionally we would pass an open space, where the trees had been burned down by the careless use of fire by the native black fellows, and then again we rode through scrub and swamp, where the road was soft and muddy, and badly cut up.

"In a few minutes we 'll foind a noice clarin', where there 's runnin' water, and a place to bile the kittle, and we 'll have a pot of tay, and a bit to skoff, for I 'm that hungry that I could even ate mutton and damper. I must water the bastes, and give 'em a little rest, for we can't rache Webber's afore eight o'clock, and we 'll have to stop there till the hate of the sun is over, for it 's that powerful that it would melt the heart of even old Kebblewhite, and that 's putty tough, now I tell yer."

As Mike ceased speaking, I heard, far off in the hills, the loud wailing and sobbing of some person or animal, and then, in the woods on our left, a confused yelping and barking, like the howling of a pack of dogs that were afraid of some formidable foe.

"For Heaven's sake, what noises are those, Mike? I never heard anything like them in California or South America."

"No, I should think not," with a tone that was almost boastful, to think that Australia could produce something entirely different from any other part of the world. "They is funny noises, a'n't they? Well, I 'se heard 'em enough to tell yer all about 'em, and it 's little I mind 'em now, though the time has been I 'd think the inhabitants of a village churchyard had broke loose, and was trying to spake to each other on the coldness of the weather, and the backwardness of the sason. Do yer moind that cuss what is hickcuppin' like a drunken man? Will, that is a burd, and it 's called the laughin' jackass, jist because jackasses don't laugh, but brays. He sints the mornin' air, and, as he can't slape, is tryin' to wake ivery livin' thing that will listen to him. He 's a bad lot, he is, and no man or baste respects him."

"And the howls on our left, Mike, what are they?" I inquired.

"Sure, them 's dingos, or wild dogs, and divilish bastes they is vhin they gets near a shape run. They 'll kill a whole flock of a night, and sit thousands of 'em to runnin' that wild that there 's no gittin' control of 'em agin. Eh, they is a bad lot, too, and wusser than the burd. Sure, I doses 'em with pisen ivery month, and so kapes 'em down. They is loike the wolf and the dog, and not the good qualities of aither. Hear 'em now. Yer 'd think they wus comin' for us, but divil a bit of it. They knows bitter. I 'd loike a shot at 'em wid me old musket, but there 's no chance of that, wid the scrub so thick yer can't sa a hand afore yer. But here we is, Mr. Hangus, and if ye 'll set still I 'll have the ladin' horses off, and tied up, in no time, and then build a fire. Here 's a putty spot, and there 's water there jist at the foot of the rock. It 's a spring, and all the stockmen in this part of the kintry knows it. Kape still, yer bastes. Do yer smill the water, and want some? Will, all in good toime.'

Instead of sitting still I got out, and collected some dried branches of the gum-tree, and started a fire, and soon had a good one, the wood burning like hemp, so full was it of resinous matter. In the mean time Mike had watered the horses, by the aid of buckets, and filled a tin teakettle, and put it on the flames, and sat down with his back to a bit of scrub, and his face to the fire, while I sat opposite to him. The bright light awakened a flock of parroquets on a gum-tree, and they chattered and shrieked in a discordant manner at being disturbed of their slumbers, while a fat opossum came out of his place of concealment, in the topmost portion of the tree, and looked down at us with his sharp little twinkling eyes, and wondered what we were up to, and if we had any business relations with him that were of importance, and worth his remaining at home. The dingos drew nearer and nearer, but did not show themselves, although it was evident from their barks and growls that they knew of our presence, and wanted to take a look at us, and see if we had any spare provisions. The laughing jackass continued its discordant screams, and then had for a companion in its mirth a solemn owl, that tooted out grave remonstrances every five minutes, at regular intervals, while old parrots, with immense beaks of iron-like toughness, gray with age, and red-eyed like drunkards, damned all creation in their native tongues, and the laughing jackass breed of birds in particular. The cold, clear moon was at its full, and looked down on us with evident satisfaction; the stars twinkled with mirth, and the cool air from the hills, sweet and ladened with balsams, fanned the flames, and drove all the smoke from our faces and persons, so that we could see each other, and not inhale the smoke at the same time.

"Now this jist suits me," said Mike. "Ah, how nice it is to have a companion in yer jarneys through life, one that yer can rely on in ivery kind of wither, and one that will share the crust wid yer, if yer has one. In a few minutes the taykettle will sing like an ould grandmither cooin' the fust born of her darter on her brist, and imaginin' all sorts of bright futures for the wee thing, in which poverty and unhappiness will have no lot, for we all think our own will be under the protection of the fairies, and that goold will be in their pockets, and lots of sinse in their heads. But when the day of trial comes, when pain"—

He did not finish the sentence. To my surprise and horror a huge, hairy form, with sharp, peaked head, large, fierce eyes, stout, short arms, immense legs, and long tail, with one bound jumped from a clump of scrub directly toward us, and, in its flight, hit Mike such a clip over the head with its tail, that he rolled over a log, and then just touched me with its hind legs, and sent me sprawling toward the hot fire and ashes.

"Bad luck to yer, yer spalpeen! May the divil fly away wid yer! May all yer relations be damned, and hung by the neck at the same toime. Holy Moses, but it 's kilt I am, and the vagabond gone off a laughin', wid his long tail a shakin' loike a wither vane in a norther! Now, who 'd 'a' thought the old scamp was thar?"

"What was it, Mike?" I asked, as soon as I could gain my feet, and draw my revolver, ready to fire at the terrible monster, if I could get sight of him.

"What was it? The divil! I thought even a child would have knowed that it was an old-man kangaroo, a wild baste that 'il rip yer bellie out of yer quicker than a butcher can open a pig. Eh, but what a rap he fotched me wid his tail. It felt like a waddy in the hands of a black fellow. But, God be praised, he did n't but jist touch yer wid his hoind legs. They can kick loike a mule, and scratch loike a foightin' wooman. The ould divil, he 's been here arter water, and jist waited for a chance to git away. If yer iver mate one, and he backs up agin a tra, and opens his arms, loike as though waitin' for his swateheart, jist kape away from him, unless yer has a gun, and knows how to shoot. He 's all ugliness then, and a match for a dozen of the best dogs that iver hunted for mate. Will, put yer pistol up, ye 'll sa no more of the ould divil this noight, I 'm thinkin'."

I was about to do so, when Mike suddenly said, —

"Stay a moment, Mr. Hangus. Do yer mind that opossum that is lookin' down on us from the gum-tra? Will, let us sa if yer can put a shot in him from here. They is moighty good atin', and I 'd loike a taste of steak broiled over this fire, and so would yer, if yer only knowed how good they is."

I suspected that Mike only desired to see what kind of a shot I was with a revolver, and made the opossum an excuse, but I had no fear of disgracing my early training, as I had shot at a mark day after day in California, with a revolver, the same one which I now carried, — a heavy Colt, and one that had been owned by my father.

I threw up my arm, and did not appear to take aim. The cap cracked, there was a loud report, and the opossum fell to the ground with a bullet through its head.

"Will, holy Moses!" was the exclamation of Mike, but his remarks were suddenly cut short by the appearance on the scene of a new actor, who sprang into sight as quickly as the old kangaroo. Where he came from I did not notice or know, but there, standing before us, was a tall, thin black fellow, with only a cloth around his loins, a long spear in his hand, and a boomerang tied to his back, while his breast was scarred in deep seams, rough and repulsive to view, and showing great disfiguration in his youth for the purpose of producing such beauty spots, and he was as vain of them as a lady with a little piece of plaster on her face, to contrast with the delicate whiteness and purity of her skin.

The black fellow picked up the dead opossum, threw it over his shoulder, and would have made off if Mike had not sprung upon him, seized his thick shaggy hair, and jerked the native first one way and then another, and, finally, drew him to the fire, tripped him up, and then threw him down, and banged him over the head with a club, or waddy. The black fellow did not appear to care any more for the blows than a prize fighter cares for the tap of a woman's fan. He pointed to the opossum, and said, —

"Me."

"No, yer black thief, it 's not for 'me,'" roared Mike. "If yer head was not so hard I 'd broke it for yer impudence."

"Me," was the response, and the fellow looked with longing eyes at the dead opossum, which the blacks of Australia love above all earthly things, and will hunt in a very ingenious and patient manner, and can always tell whether the brute is at home, or has wandered off for a foraging expedition. No matter how high the tree the black fellow can ascend its trunk, and track his prey to the very top.

Mike did not respond to the last word of the black, but drew a knife, and skinned the game in a very expeditious manner, the native seated at the fire, and watching every movement of the progress with longing eyes and hungry stomach. He did not seem to bear any ill will for the cruel blows which he had received, or appear to notice them, although they would have crushed the skull of a white man, of that I am convinced.

As soon as the opossum was dressed, Mike cut off what he desired, and threw the rest of the carcass, entrails and skin, to the native, who gave a grunt of satisfaction, put the flesh and other parts on the ashes, let them remain there for a few minutes, and then devoured the disgusting mass in a revolting manner, such as would have shamed a hungry dog.

Mike paid no attention to the native. He had seen hundreds of them, knew their ways, and just how far they were to be trusted without fear of treachery and deceit; and, to do the black fellow full justice, I should state that he paid no attention to his entertainers. He gorged himself, and did not care if we noticed his disgusting eating. He was not at all modest, as far as I could judge by his actions.

In a few minutes after the opossum was dead, Mike had roasted some of the best portions on a stick, salted them, made a good pot of tea, put some hard tack on a paper (the native tried to steal the bread, and got another rap in consequence, which he regarded with perfect indifference, as before), and then we fell to with good appetites, and devoured all that was before us. But there was plenty of tea and sugar and bread in the wagon, intended for the sheep run, and the men looking after it.

"Tell me," said Mike, as we sat over our pipes, after the feast, "was that shot of yers a lucky one, or was it premeditated ontirely?"

"Oh, I can shoot very well," I replied. "I don't vary much when I fire."

"Holy Moses, if that is what yer can do right along, yer can bang most any of 'em round here, and some day I'll let yer have a shot wid me ould musket, jist as a reward. Sure 's there 's no gun in the country that can stand afore her, when she 's well pinted, and held stidy."

To show that his boast was not an idle one, Mike brought from the wagon an old rusty musket, that was wheezy and shaky, with a monstrous bore, a barrel that was near six feet long, and spliced and plastered with tin and iron, screws and nails, and a flint lock that was as large as an old-fashioned door knocker. I shuddered as I thought of the danger that would overtake a person who should dare to hold it, and fire it with an ordinary load of powder and shot.

But Mike was delighted with the weapon, and would not have exchanged it for the best rifle that was ever made. Of course I did not tell Mike that I had no desire to endanger my life by firing the musket, for it would have hurt his feelings, but I handed it back to the good fellow with the remark that it looked as if it could kill more ducks than any other weapon of its kind in Australia.

"True for yer, sur," was the satisfactory exclamation. "I 've sane it done, sur, toime and toime agin on the Darlin' and Murray Rivers."

We could see traces of daylight. The moon began to shimmer like silver, the stars appeared to be sorry for their levity through the night, and so were going to bed, and have a good sleep until the next evening. More birds joined in with their discordant cries, and the dingos were seeking their caves and holes to rest until darkness again appeared.

In the mean time Mike had been at work in the wagon, and when he came again to the fire, he said that he had made me a nice bed out of some bagging and blankets, and, as soon as we were once more under way, I had got to lie down, and have a good sleep, for I needed it, and would feel like a new man when we reached Webber's.

We hitched up the horses, and started, leaving the black fellow, with his feet to the fire, full to repletion, snoring like a New-York alderman, at the Union Square Hotel, after a city feast.

10

"Now, sur, jist git on the noice bed I 've made yer, and may slape drive away all care, and may yer drames be as pleasant as those of a young gurl wid her fust lover, or a wooman what is to have a new silk dress. I 'll call yer whin it 's toime. I 'm not slapy, and will look arter the road, and the taime, and smoke me pipe in quiet and meditation, and think of the goold we 'll pick up some toime or other, plase God, when no shape tindin' and tamin' will be naded on me part, or worry on that of yer own. Lay down, sur, and slape, before the hot sun comes out, and burns up the air, and makes it harder to draw yer breath than the cork of a beer bottle what old Webber has had on hand for a twelve-month."

I was too tired to remonstrate, and so lay down, and shut my eyes, and tried to see the face of Florence in the darkness, and to imagine what she was doing just at that particular hour. Dreaming, I supposed, of the sad mistake that she had made in giving her hand to a man whom she did not love, or even esteem, and thus thinking, I fell into a sound sleep, in spite of the rough road, and jolting of the team, and the last thing I recollect was whispering a prayer for the welfare of my little wife, and her future happiness.

When I awoke the sun was shining, and the heat was something to be remembered, as we were passing through thick woods, where not a breath of air penetrated. For a moment I could not realize where I was, but, as I raised myself up, and looked around, I heard the hum of voices, and saw that Mike had a companion on his seat, and that he was the most singular-looking man I had seen while in Australia. He was dressed in the habiliments of a Quaker, broad-brimmed gray hat, low crown, a gray coat, buttoned to his chin, gray trousers, and a shirt-collar that was once white, but time, dust, and perspiration, had changed its color to one that was unknown to chemists or to painters. For a while I remained quiet, and listened to a conversation which was not very instructive, except as far as the answers of Mike were concerned, and those were original, and, at times, very evasive and peculiar.

"Is the young man that thou hast for a mate a godly person?" asked the Quaker.

"Faith, sur, I think he is, for he can sware loike a bushranger," which was a little imaginative on the part of Mike, as I had not used profanity but in a very mild form, and offensive to no one.

"It is a pity that one so young should not fear the Lord. Verily it is saddening to my soul," groaned the Quaker.

"Don't let it wurrow you, sur, for I don't think that me mate fears the divil himself. He's bound to the mines, and he 'll nade somethin' beside goodness to take him through," Mike answered.

"Has he much worldly goods dost thou know?" asked the Quaker, as he turned, and glanced at me, and I saw through my half-closed eyes that he had a thin face, shaped like a hatchet, the lankest form outside of a living skeleton, and the longest arms and legs that were ever put on such a grotesque body.

"I don't know what yer mane by goods," Mike answered. "I s'pose he is as good as most min."

"Thou misunderstands me, friend. I mean has he much wealth, — that is to say, riches?"

"Divil a hapenny to his back, or in his pocket. Sure, what would a man go to the mines for, if he was rollin' in wealth? Ah, it's jokin' me yer are."

"No, friend, I never joke. I'm traveling around the country collecting money for a meeting-house for the friends, and I thought he might contribute, verily I did."

As the Quaker spoke, he turned his head so that Mike could not see his face, and I never saw such a devilish leer on a person's countenance as that same Quaker had on his. A grin so repulsive and sickening, that I wanted to get up and kick him into the road, and leave him there to plod to his destination on foot.

"It's no use axin' me mate for a penny. He's dead broke, and shut up shop for a moonth, and won't rasame cash payments till his ship comes in, and she has a head wind and sa to contind wid. Let the lad alone, and don't bother him in his poverty."

"Has thy young friend lived a moral life?" asked the Quaker. "Is he to be trusted with large sums of gold and of silver? Has he ever committed crime thinkest thou?"

"To the divil wid yer and yer questions!" roared Mike. "What is yez givin' me on such a run? Is it sour beer yer is puttin' afore me? What is yer drivin' at?"

"Be not riled, my dear friend," said the Quaker. "I asked out of sympathy, for, perhaps, I could help thy mate. He has a nice face, and a frank one, and he should have noble sentiments, and a bold heart; a man that would make a good policeman, or a terrible bushranger."

"He's not that koind of mate, I tell yer!" roared the indignant Mike. "He'd not take a penny what did n't belong to him. A perloceman, indade. To the divil wid yer perloceman!"

"With all my heart," responded the Quaker, with a second grin, that was as slimy as the first I had noticed. "I do not think that all policemen are good. I don't believe that Mr. Murden, the Chief of Police of Melbourne, is honest as the day is long. Dost thou?"

"I don't know. I've heard him spoken of as bein' a smart officer, and that he's tracked many a bushranger to a stout prison, and kept them in it as long as he plased. I've mit him once, but I'm not on callin' terms wid him," and Mike grinned.

"—— him!" ejaculated the Quaker, in a sudden burst of passion, and, as Mike turned in astonishment to look at the "friend" who had uttered such a worldly sentiment, the Quaker's face changed as if by magic, and the cold, calm smile passed over it. "Such is the violent language that I have heard uttered by the worldly people, when speaking of Mr. Murden," the Quaker said, in an apologetic tone. "I know him not, and do not wish to. He is a man of war and blood, and we deal not with such. But dost thou know where he is, friend?"

"In Melbourne, I s'pose. How should I know? I don't kape track of the traps unless they comes to me run for a bit of mutton, and sup of tay."

"Then he is not on the road, thou thinkest?"

"He may be for all I care."

"And hast thou met many mounted policemen on the trail the past night?" the Quaker urged. "The roads are not too safe, and I have heard that Black Dick and Slipper Sam are once more on their old beats, and taking many a pound of gold from the honest miners, and the industrious merchants. The police should look after them as soon as possible, and stop their depredations."

"Faith, I've met but one mounted trap all the night, and he went on to Webber's to stop over on some business that was argent, I think. If Dick and Sam are round it's many a fat shape I'll lose durin' the summer, but if they'll let me alone they're wilcome, and I'll not open me eyes very wide whin I foind the skins hangin' on a tra. Will, praise God, there's Webber's, and we'll be there in no time, and I hope ye'll stand the beer for the ride."

"Excuse me, friend, but I do not drink aught but water, and, as I see some flowers that I wish to gather, I'd even alight here, and thank thee for thy kindness and information," and, without waiting for the horses to be checked, the Quaker jumped over a wheel, and landed in the road, and, with a wave of his long, skinny arm, plunged into the scrub, and disappeared.

"Mike," I asked, "did you ever meet with that fellow before?"

"Ho, yer is awake, Mr. Hangus, is yer? I 'm plased yer has had a noice slape, and feels better. We is near Webber's, and there's the fat Dutchman in front of his house. No, Mr. Hangus, I niver mit the Quaker spalpeen afore, and I niver want to agin. He's not a clane man, or I 'm a sinner. He pumped hard, but the water did n't come to the spout worth a penny. Whoop, yer fat Dutchman, aNve yer is, wid yer big moouth, and bald head. Faith, yer grows younger wid years, and richer wid the days passin' over that head what looks loike a pumpkin gone to sade."

The Dutchman withdrew his pipe from his mouth, waved it in token of recognition, put it back between his lips, and did not respond by word to our arrival. He simply glared at us with his little gray, pig-looking eyes, and puffed on serenely.

But as soon as I jumped from the wagon, and went to Mike's assistance in unharnessing the horses, the whole demeanor of the man changed, and from a placid Dutchman he become a raging mountain of quivering flesh. He dashed down his pipe, glared at me in speechless horror, until at last his pent-up feelings found vent in three short words, but they came from the deepest of chests:—

"Vel, I 'm —— !"

As I had never before seen the man, I paid no attention to him, supposing that he was angry at Mike for his somewhat familiar remarks when we drove up, but, as the Dutchman continued to breathe hard, and to inform us that he was "——" we gave him some of our attention as soon as we had removed the harnesses, and turned the animals into a corral, where they could get water and barley, with a handful of hay. We walked toward the house, but Webber, the landlord and owner of the premises, obstructed our path, and, pointing to me, said, —

"Vel, I 'm ——, but he's comes here back, in spite of I tell him not for to."

"What is the matter wid the old porpuses?" demanded Mike, surprised at our reception.

"He comes here last night that ever vos," the Dutchman cried, still pointing to me. "He me slaps on der back, on der head, on der arm, all over me, and he says in a tone all loud and all laugh, 'Vel, Dutchy, gibs us some beer and some coffee, and let's see that putty darter vot yer has here all by yerself,' and he say, 'Be —— quick as ever yer vos about it, 'cos I is in a hurry.' And I says, 'I gib yer de beer, and de coffee, and de bread, and I my frou sends to vait on yer,' and den dat same bad young feller, dat is standin' dar right afore me, says, 'Yer frou may go to —— and yer, too, for all I cares one d— bit, it's de darter vot I vants to see, the pride of old Webber's heart.' Does ding it I stands, ——— ?"

He shook his fist at me, and turned so red in the face, that I thought he would fall to the ground in a fit of apoplexy.

"Don't be a fool, yer old blubberer," Mike said. "Sure, the gintleman has been wid me, on the road, all night, and how could he be here? Answer me that now?"

"He calls for mine Katrine," the Dutchman cried, "and she, like de fool big dat she is, comes, and den afore mine eyes, by damn, dat young feller puts his arm her waist around, and kisses her on de mouth more ten times afore I could open my lips, and tell him to stop dat. It vant right to do such dings, and de peoples lookin' on. He do dat, and he is not ashamed, much."

"Sure, Hangus, what does the old fool mane?" demanded Mike, a little puzzled.

I knew what it meant quite well. My shadow had been here before me, and, true to his noble instinct, had been making love to the Dutchman's daughter, and quite successfully, it seemed.

"Katrine," screamed the enraged father, "go and lock in a room mid yerself, as fast as ebber you can, for de bad young feller is here, and he is wuss den ebber he wus,——— him; and tell yer mudder to bring de long gun vot I shoots de kangaroos wid. I fixes him if he any more of his little games comes on vid me."

"Vy, fadder, vot is the matter vid yer now?" asked a rather sweet voice, and a flaxen-haired girl, with deep-blue eyes, a form that was rather stout, and far from sylph-like, came from the house, attracted by the row. "Yer makes more noise enough to vake de dead right up," the young girl said, and then, as she caught sight of me, she blushed a rosy welcome, and very deliberately walked up to me, put her arms around my neck, and kissed me three times right on my lips, before I could recover from my astonishment and surprise at her rude proceeding.

"Gott in hebin," groaned the Dutchman, "did I ebber see any ding like dat afore in mine life, all de time? Oh, by ———, var is mine gun vot shoots off?"

"Yer goes in de house, and draws de beer for mine friend, and just mine yer own business, yer old fool. Yer dink a young girl no vants a lover all de dime? Bah! gets out of dis, 'cos I vants to kiss him some more, right off."

"Gott in heben, does right I hear?" groaned the Dutchman. "My Katrine kisses a stranger, and tells her old fadder to git out. Vel, vel, and she is not to him married a bit."

"Vel, how can I, ven yer stands dar starin' at us? Ve vant to do some courtin', and ve don't want yer lookin' at us. Get out, I tells yer. Go for der beer. Come, mine friend, we has a room all to ourself, de same as last night, and ve talks of love all de time."

The Dutchman picked up his pipe, put it in his mouth, took it out again, and, in a bewildered sort of way, asked,—

"Vil yer marries her right off now, and no mistake, and I takes yer home, and does vel by yer?"

Katrine spared me the pain of a refusal, for she motioned to her father to go in the house, and put up her hand before her face to hide her blushes, as she led me into the building, while Mike followed close at our heels, and muttered,—

"By the powers, but this bangs Banagar. Will, the loikes of that I niver saw afore, and niver shall agin. O Moses, the old roarin' Dutchman has become a lamb, and me mate gets more kisses than all the buys that iver crossed the threshold of the house."

Thanks to the kindness of Katrine, we had a nice breakfast, but nothing could induce me to partake of it without the presence of Mike, for, although the landlord's daughter was rather pretty, yet she was also demonstrative, and I did not care to be a party for breach of promise, or to follow in the footsteps of the noble lord who had made love to the girl just to occupy a spare hour, and had then left her, promising to return as soon as he could, and kiss her some more, and talk of their future life.

It was useless to deny to the girl, or to Webber, that I was not the one they had entertained the night previous. I had tried that argument in a gentle way, but it had been laughed at, and so Mike no longer protested that he had brought me all the way from Melbourne. I learned, however, that my shadow had met two strangers at the house, and that, after a conference with them, they had all gone off together on horseback, at about three o'clock in the morning, and that Lary, the mounted policeman, had stopped at the house for a few hours, and then turned in the direction of Ballarat, after making some few inquiries. It seemed that, for reasons of his own, Webber had not mentioned the arrival or departure of his three guests to the officer, which looked a little mysterious, until Mike hinted that the old Dutchman did not tell the traps all he knew unless his information was of no importance, and that he had golden reasons for keeping silence regarding the movements of people who had no known business, and went and came at pleasure, but always sure of powder and lead and provisions, when they had the money to pay for them; and it was also certain that Webber's sheep were never killed, his horses run off, nor his cattle injured in any way by the black fellows, or the bushrangers, who still thronged the country, and intercepted miners on their way to the mines, and returning from them, striking sudden and fierce blows when least expected, so that the only safe method of conveying gold or bills from Ballarat to Melbourne was by the government escort, which went back and forth, too strong to be attacked by even the bold ruffians who frequented the roads, until driven into new quarters by the mounted police.

The hot day passed in idleness, if I except the violent love which Katrine would persist in making, in spite of my coldness, and attempts to hold her in check. The noble lord who had carried her heart by storm, had made the poor girl believe that he was a victim of her charms, and a more happy girl than she was, under the circumstances, it would have been hard to find. I pitied her, and would have undeceived her, but every time I attempted to do so, she would smile at me, and tell me to be a good boy, and not to talk such foolish "dings." Old Webber did not regard me in a favorable light, but, as I refrained from kissing his daughter more than I could help, he did not talk of shooting me with his kangaroo gun, and even hinted, in a moment of confidence, that if I would marry Katrine, I could have a share of his run and business, but I told him that I was too poor to marry, and that I would think of it while at the mines, and let him know the result.

Toward sundown, after a good sleep, we hitched up the horses, and started on our journey. I saw tears in Katrine's blue eyes as she kissed me, and whispered that I must come back as quick as ever I could, and that she would wait for me a long time, and always be true and tender, and then she put in the wagon a box of refreshments, such as we should want, and stood by her father's side, and cried until we were out of sight, and how much longer I never learned.

"A noice gurl," said Mike, as we struck the rough road, and jolted on. "Begor, if she had made love to me in that way, I'd have yalded in no toime. But the female cratur is peculiar, and there's no accountin' for it. But I did envy yer the kisses, for it was a waste of good material, as yer did not same to care for 'em. Whoop along wid yer, and don't go to slape."

We jogged along through the night, sometimes sleeping and dozing, past the flourishing village of Slabtown, over steep mountains, and through deep ravines, and shallow streams, meeting black fellows, and a few suspicious characters, but were not disturbed until the third day out, when Mike, just at daylight, stopped his horses at a place where half a dozen trails led in various directions.

"Here we will part for a few days," he said. "I must go to me run, and look arter me shape, and be riddy to lave the place this wake. Take some grub and a bottle of water, yer gun and a blanket, the powder and lead, and kape on this road what yer sa, and ye 'll git a lift in the course of an hour to Ballarat. I 'll take the rist of yer truck, and bring it wid me, whin I come over, and I 'll be all fra and no longer a ticket-of-lave man, the nixt toime we mate. It 's better yer should go fust, so that yer can look around, and sa what is best to be done. Lave word wid the purlice station where yer is, and I 'll foind yer sure."

He held out his hand, and his eyes watered, as he continued, —

"The holy saints have yer in their kapin', sur, and don't lave the baten road, as yer vally yer life, don't yer do it. It 's death to be lost in the bush, and don't forget it for a moment. Solong, me mate, and do take care of yerself."

He waved his hand, and was gone, and I turned and pursued my way toward Ballarat, only ten miles distant, and I should have reached the town in three hours' time if I had not left the beaten road, or trail, for the bush and scrub, the very thing Mike advised me not to do, as I valued my life, and the very thing that I should not have done unless acquainted with Australian life, and its treacherous woods and bush, and vast salt and verdant plains. But I was young, and thought that I could pick my way through dense forests, and scorned the idea of being lost if I did not wander far, and there is where I made a grave mistake, and one that I always remembered while in Australia.

"OH, ———! MEIE SCOOTIE! YOUE FIGHTIE! CHINAMAN MUSTIE GOE!"

PART VII.

ON THE ROAD TO BALLARAT. — A SHORT NAP, AND A LIVELY BLACK-
SNAKE. — LOST IN THE BUSH. — AN AUSTRALIAN CRY FOR
HELP. — THE TORTURED CHINAMAN. — A RESCUE. — AN
ENCAMPMENT FOR THE NIGHT. — A FLYING CHI-
NAMAN. — THE BLACK FELLOWS AND
THEIR FEAST. — A TERRIBLE
VISITOR. — ON THE
TRAMP.

AS Mike and his team of four horses left me, standing in the road, with the thick forests and scrub on each side, the dust of the trails as fine and light as corn-meal, which it resembled in color, with not a soul in sight, I felt more depressed and miserable than at any time since I left Melbourne. To be sure, the forests were alive with the chattering of parrots and parroqrets, and the discordant cries of the laughing jackass, and once in a while a bird of paradise, with plumage of gold and silver, and tail like a rainbow, flew over my head, and mocked me with a shrill whistle, or croak of contempt, and circling high in the air were vultures and carrion birds, examining each bush and cleared space for a dead bullock, or the remains of a miner, some one who had strayed from the trails, and become lost in the bush, and then yielded to despair and a lingering death. I felt that in the disappearance of Mike I had lost the only real friend that I had in Australia, and very bitter were my reflections as I strapped my blanket over my shoulder, slung my flask of brandy and water bottle around my neck, took my repeating rifle in my hand, saw that it was all ready for use, and then plodded on, with the high peak of Mount Muninyong for a guide, and a firm determination to reach Camp Reserve, Ballarat, before the hot sun should make traveling impossible.

It was no use to mourn over the departure of Mike. He had promised to join me in the course of three or four days, or a week at the farthest, and, with a heart as light as I could command, I started on my lonely route, and thus hour after hour passed, and I saw no sign of the mining district, nor did I meet with a single person of whom I could make inquiries as to the distances and location. By ten o'clock the heat was so oppressive that I determined to enter the woods, and seek rest under the shade of the trees, and remain there until some team or footman came along to give me a lift. I was not in the least alarmed but that I should reach Ballarat before night, although I thought that Mike had made a bad mistake, and that the distance to the cross trails was more than twenty miles, instead of being only between ten and fifteen.

The shade of the trees was grateful. There was no dust there, and the sun could not penetrate the gloom. I threw off my load of equipments, took a moderate pull at my bottle of water, lighted my pipe, had a good comfortable smoke, thought of Florence, and wondered if she ever gave me a single pitying consideration, and then went to sleep, as I might have expected, if I had given the matter a second thought.

When I awoke it was long after two o'clock, as near as I could judge. The heat was still intense, and not a breath of air was stirring. Even the screaming parrots had retired to the deepest part of the forest to escape the sun and glare, and not a leaf trembled, as I sat up, and rubbed my eyes, and wondered how it happened that I had fallen asleep when I intended to be very wakeful and alert, and felt a little ashamed of my lack of vigilance, but, as I turned my head to see that my rifle was where I had left it, and that my revolver was in my belt, I saw a strange movement in a she-oak, not more than ten feet from me, and then from the foliage was thrust a huge, black head, with open mouth, a quivering tongue, and fierce, blazing eyes, that seemed to be watching my awaking, and to be very angry because I had stirred, and was disposed to get on my feet.

"That's the devil, or a near relative," I thought, as I noted the mysterious head, and forked tongue, and then, as the neck was thrust further and further from the foliage, I saw with intense disgust, and some uneasiness, that a monstrous black-snake was coiled around the trunk of the tree, and was watching my movements with much curiosity, mingled with rage, and an evident determination to make a more minute inspection of my person, and if I had not been awakened by some good angel, just at the proper moment, I should not now be writing my history, and thinking of the past with mingled regret and happiness, for the reptile, although not considered venomous by the people of Australia, is a powerful biter, has teeth like a saw, and an embrace like an anaconda's, crushing the life out of a sheep, colt, or calf, as easily as a man can crush the shell of a hen's egg, when in a hurry to take an early train, and breakfast at the same time. The snake had seen me sleeping, and glided up the tree to take a more accurate observation from its elevated perch, and also for a leverage when disposed to make a sudden attack, which is a characteristic of the reptile when hungry. It had determined to strike with its powerful jaws, sudden and sure, a blow that could not be resisted by man when off his guard, seize me by the arm or head, and then drag me to the she-oak, and crush my body in its folds, until ribs, bones, and flesh were one mass of bruised and bloody jelly, with no semblance of mankind and humanity left, after the powerful folds were removed, and the remains had fallen to the ground, quivering but lifeless, a disgusting sight, and one well-calculated to make even the bravest of men tremble with fear and horror. This was the first large black-snake I had ever seen, and I must confess that I derived some little pleasure, now that I was awake and alert, in watching its movements, and the rapid play of its head and shining neck, the swelling of its muscles, and the fiery eyes, and white teeth. As I remained quite still, the snake became more and more emboldened, and at last darted its head toward me, thus exposing more than half of its body, which was as large in circumference as a stout man's thigh, and about fifteen feet long, as near as I could judge from where I sat.

Apparently disappointed that it had fallen short in its deliberate attack, it hissed at me like an enraged gander, and then drew its body back to the tree, and once more swayed back and forth, and snapped its jaws together like those of an enraged bull-dog, while its breath, as it hissed, was like the foul odors from an *abattoir* that had not been thoroughly cleaned through the hot summer months. Every movement that I made was looked upon as a defiance, and a corresponding threat on the part of the reptile, and while it watched me so fixedly I think that I felt a little of its terrible fascinating power, and even began to regard its threats as quite harmless and playful, and not disposed to injure me, even if it approached within striking distance.

But all at once I realized that I was in danger. It seemed as though some good angel had prayed for me, and that her prayers had been answered, for I shook off the weakness that was overpowering me, and turned my head to look for my rifle, although I held it in my hand, and knew that it was there, yet did not feel quite certain of the fact. A terrible hiss escaped the snake when it saw that its spell was broken. It shook the foliage of the tree as though a whirlwind was passing over the forest, and even the stout trunk of the she-oak bent while the struggle was going on, a struggle in which rage and disappointment were mingled and displayed, like the antics of a wild beast, when deprived of its prey, or a spoiled child, when refused a plaything.

"We have had enough of this," I muttered half drowsily. "I think that I will give the black devil something to be angry at."

I raised my rifle, took a hasty aim at the moving head, and fired. The ball struck near its eye, and passed completely through the skull, and in an instant I was nearly covered with falling leaves, with dead branches, and twigs torn from the oak, and then the whole body of the monster was unwound from the tree, and launched at me, with open mouth and chattering teeth.

I had seen the tail uncoiled, and expected some such assault, but nothing so powerful, yet, as a mere matter of precaution, I stepped back, and nearly behind the cedar-tree, at the foot of which I had been sleeping. The head of the reptile struck the trunk, and then, before it could regain its former position, I sent a ball down its capacious throat, and retreated to see it die. The scene was a fearful one, and for a rod in extent the bush and scrub gave evidence of the struggle of the terrible monster. Whole branches were mowed from the trees by the snake's tail, and one would not have believed that so much strength could have been excited by so small a body.

But at length the contortions ceased, the eyes lost their fierceness, the jaws no longer snapped, the tail to quiver, and only the muscles twitched, as if still alive; and hardly had I noticed all these things, when there was a fierce cawing overhead, and a flock of vultures alighted on the trees, and seemed to anticipate a rich treat in the disgusting object before them, and several, more bold than the rest, even alighted on the ground, and picked at the dead snake's eyes, as though anxious to partake of the real delicacies, or the *bonne bouche* of a feast, before the others had a chance to dispute their rights.

I was anxious to hasten away from such a scene, for it was sickening. Once more shouldering my traps, and taking a sip of brandy to remove the taste of the snake's breath, I started for the road, and walked ten minutes before I made the discovery that I was not going toward the trail, but in some other direction, and that I had wandered from the path, and was likely to be lost in the bush, the very thing Mike had cautioned me against, and which I had determined to avoid. I stood still, and thought of the matter, so that I should not be frightened, then started in a direction that I knew would lead me all right; but ten minutes brisk walking, with the perspiration streaming down my face and neck, under the intense heat, showed that I had not struck the right trail, and that I was nearly lost, even if I was not quite, and yet I could not understand how such a thing had happened, after all of my precautions to go straight back to the road I had left in the morning. But the encounter with the snake had so flurried me that I had not noticed the land marks, and I was likely to pay for my folly, unless I was remarkably lucky, before sunset.

Still I was not frightened or nervous. I determined to keep cool, to think of some pleasant subject, instead of the dense bush and forest, and straightway my thoughts went to Florence, and I wished that she was happy, and would pray that her young husband might be extricated from his dangerous position, and I laughed aloud at the absurdity of the thought, as though Florence cared where I wandered, or what I did, as long as I held aloof from her, and did not claim her hand, and then I whistled, and pushed my way through the scrub, stopped and took a sip of brandy, and once more went onward, and looked up to see if I could get a view of the sun, or of Mount Muninyong, so that I could shape my way, and, while I was thus employed, I heard some one give the Australian cry, a plain, full "co-ey," long drawn out on the last syllable, so that the sound floats in the air, and traverses more space than any other word that the shepherds or stockmen employ. Mike had taught me its use that very morning, and I had practised it until I was perfect in sounding the call, and now I used it for the first time in all seriousness, and then waited for a response. It came at length, full and hard, and, with a responsive cry, I dashed forward in the direction

I supposed the sound had come from, stopping every few minutes to get an echo, and finding that I was on the right trail, and nearing the person who was in distress. Over fallen trees and rotten stumps, through bushes and scrub, until at last I reached a clearing, where fire had at one time done its work, and there, yelling and groaning, swearing in pigeon English, and Chinese characters as big as tea chests, was a Chinaman, fast bound to a tree, with arms and feet so firmly secured that to free himself from the bands of vines and withes, used instead of ropes, was an impossibility. But the bonds were not the only torture to which the celestial was subjected, for in the middle of the clearing was a gigantic ant's nest, more than six feet high, and at least four feet in diameter at the base, the home of the ferocious soldier, or bull-dog, ant, the most rapacious and desperate of all the insect tribe, capable of devouring a dead bullock in a few hours, and picking the bones as clean as the inmates of a poor-house, where short rations are common, if the commissioners are of a prudent nature, and care more for the money of their constituents than the health of those whom they have in charge.

Already the ants had scented blood and flesh, and I saw with horror, that hundreds of them had swarmed over the Chinaman, and were feasting on legs and arms, face and neck, and drawing blood at every bite, and, as the attacks became more and more severe, the struggles of the poor wretch grew frantic, and his pigeon English of the most mixed character.

"Oh, ——— !" he yelled, "bitee likee dogie. Bitee likee hotee fie. Takee offee. Dammie alle busherange! Co-ey. Comee quickee, somebodie, or Chinaman muste goe."

I did not delay a moment in rushing to the rescue of the poor fellow, whose tortures must have been intense enough to turn the brain of a sane and healthy man in a short time, even if there had been life left at the end of an hour's duration of such misery. I dropped blanket and rifle, drew my sharp-edged bowie-knife, and with a few strokes cut the withes that bound the Chinaman, seized him by his long and thick pig-tail, dragged him to the edge of the woods, out of the course of the ants, and then beat the insects from his flesh with blanket and bush, with hands and feet, sparing not even the celestial's shins, as I kicked at the bull-dogs that would not let go their hold, so fierce were they after once tasting blood. All this time the Chinaman was aiding me with words, if not with hands, for, as I trampled the ants under foot, and thrashed them with bushes, like a farmer's boy in a hay field, when attacked by hornets, he continued to chatter, and found an astonished listener.

"Ah, date bery goodie. Noice Slingisman; note alle same busherange. Noe kickie shinie tooe harde. Berrie goodie youe. Alle gonie nowe. Holde upe, I telle."

Not until I trampled out the life of the last of the ants that were on the person of the Chinaman, did I relax my endeavors, and, even after I had killed all, made the celestial remove his blue jumper, to be sure that no ants were between that and his skin, and all this while the fellow's almond-shaped eyes were fastened on me in a strange, stupefied sort of glare, as though he had seen me before, but could not tell where, or just under what circumstances, or else was wondering what could have induced a "foreign devil" to lend a helping hand to a poor and despised Chinaman, who receive as many cuffs in Australia as they do kicks in California.

"Now, John," I said, "off with those blue dungeree trousers. Be quick. We must make clean work of it, and then get out of this place as soon as possible. Come, move," seeing that the fellow was looking at my face with more attention than his own injuries.

"Ah, noie, can'te doie datie. Meie modiste manie, youe knowe. Noie takie offe trousie fore manie. Allie rightie nowie. ———— busherange."

Seeing that the fellow was not suffering any further inconvenience, I did nor insist upon his removing the large and flowing garments which he wore to protect his legs, and make him an ornament for decent society, but gathered up my traps, and sought safety in a hasty flight to a different clearing, where there were no ant's nests. But even as we started to move in another direction, the savage bull-dog insects were getting ready to make a fierce and more concentrated attack on us, for they swarmed from their gigantic home in thousands, and sent out scouts in all directions, to call in the laggards and warriors, and to consult as to the best method of dealing with the common enemy, and obtaining a good stock of food for the colony. As the bull-dog and soldier ants are about an inch long, and as hard as iron, the noise they made in swarming was like the flapping of pigeon wings at a noted resort for the birds, or the humming of a country school in summer time.

I was tempted to give them a dose of fire, but feared to spare the time, as I hoped to get out of the bush before the sun set, and already it gave tokens of leaving us before many hours, and in total darkness it would be useless to attempt to travel in the woods.

I soon found a clearing, and then stopped, unloaded, and turned to have a good square look at my companion. He was like all the rest of his race,— almond-eyed, smooth-faced, about thirty years of age, stout built, very muscular for a Chinaman, dressed as they all dress, with blue blouse and trousers, celestial shoes, and long and very thick pig-tail, the latter hanging down his back, and braided, with a blue ribbon to keep the ends from working loose, and all the rest of his head, except the queue, shaven quite clean, as if the operation had been but recently performed by a barber. I saw that the man's face was still blotched from the bites of the ants, and that there was some blood on it, and knew that he must be suffering, although not a sign of pain and uneasiness did he manifest, except by his constant watching of all my motions, and a surprised look in his dark, half-closed eyes, as if he was a little suspicious of me, and waited to see what my next move would be on his account. But I did not pay much attention to his grunts, and wandering glances, as all Chinamen are a little diffident in the presence of strangers.

I gave him about half a wine glass of brandy. He drank it like a heathen, with a gasp, a sob, and a gush, and then rubbed his hand on his stomach, and said, —

"Dat bellie goode," and grinned like an idiot, an exasperating grin, which made you feel like kicking him.

I wet a cloth with the brandy, and washed the bites and blood away from the fellow's face and neck, and that must have relieved him, but still he could not keep his eyes from my face, and once he muttered, —

"Bellie strange dis manie."

"What is strange, John?" I asked.

"Noie John. Meie Gin Sling," was the answer.

At least it sounded like Gin Sling, and I won't swear that it was or was not, but as Gin Sling came as near to what he called himself as anything I could think of, he ever after went by that spirited and liquid name, and, as he did not repudiate it, I am satisfied that he was content, and thought that a high honor had been conferred on him by his 'Melican man associate.

"Bellie strange," repeated Gin Sling, still looking at me, after he had said that he felt very well, and that the wounds did not smart as much as one would suppose.

"What is strange, Gin? Out with it."

"Youe."

"Me, Gin? What is there strange about me? I cut you loose, and saved your life, for in an hour's time the ants would have picked your bones quite dry. I would have done the same for any one," I said.

"Ah, bute youe sitie stille and seee meie tied upe. Youe once saye, 'Noie kille John. Lete goie, or tiee upe. Hie notie worthie muche. Letie goe.'"

"I said all that, did I, Gin?" I asked.

"Yesie, bute de udder dammie busherangie say, 'Kille John Chinaman. Hee noie usee to onie bodie. Heie ruinie de workie people.'"

I wondered if my *bête noir* had taken part in the persecution of the Chinaman, and had saved his life as far as having him tied up was concerned.

"Are you sure that I am the person who said, 'Let him go,' Gin?"

"Yesie, yesie," with many nods, and a wise, half-cunning look in his dark eyes. "Meie sure allie timee youe de manie. Noie foolie Gin Sling."

"Well, Gin, you are mistaken. I am not the one. I never saw you before, and had no part in persecuting you."

"Alle rightie, sir. Meie dinke alle samie. Youe sete on tree, and seeie de udders lookie alle over meie for goldie duste."

"Did they find any, Gin?" I asked, with a little more interest.

"Noie," with a grin, and a cunning look in his eyes. "Meie goe from Ballarate for citie, and dis mornie dree menie sayie, 'Stoppie, you dammie Chinaman, and gibie use allie youe golde dustie, or we puttie ballie in youie headie, youe coppie-colorede sonie gunie;' and I saye, 'Meie noie goldie, meie poore manie,' and dey takee meie in de woodie, and lookie alle over clothesie, and no finde duste or monie, and denie twoe bigie menie wantie to killie meie, bute youe saye, 'Noie, lete John goe,' and de udder menie saye, 'Dammie, hee noie goodie anie howie. Noie one carie for Chinaman. Tiee upe, and leavee heree for de buggies."

I could now understand him. The Earl of Afton, I suppose, or my double, as I have said, had left Webber's two days before in company with some suspicious characters. The party had met the Chinaman on the road, and determined to rob him of all his possessions, but, as they had found nothing, the two desperadoes had taken him to the bush, and tied him up, about the time that I had laid down, and went to sleep. Had I been half an hour earlier, I should have met the party on the trail. They had tied the poor fellow near the ant's nest for the purpose of having some sport, and witnessing the Chinaman's contortions, as the ants bit him, but the sound of my rifle, as I fired at the snake, had disturbed the calculations of the two ruffians, and they had made off, under the impression that a number of mounted traps were on the road, or that some miners were out from camp, looking for stray cattle.

"What did the men say when I told them not to hurt you?" I asked, for I saw that the Chinaman was as big a crank as to my being some one else as the more enlightened people I had met.

"Oh, the twoe uglie menie saye, 'Youe jiste shute upe, or wee fixe youe

The Belle of Australia.   161

likie Chinaman,' and youe laughe, and takie alle samie onie jokie, and saye, 'De debbie youe willie. Youe bettie notie if youe knowie whate goodie for youselfe.'"

It seemed that his lordship was not in the least afraid of the bushrangers, and I began to respect him for his courage. But what he was doing with them puzzled me. Unless he was very careful he would find himself in a worse position than when he left Melbourne in such haste, to avoid marriage. If the police once laid hands on him in company with noted bushrangers, it would require some high interest to get him out of his difficulties.

"Gin," I said, very slowly and distinctly, "I was not the person who was with the bushrangers. I would not be with them. I am a good man," and I hoped this would convince him, but it did not.

"Yese, ———— goodie! Alle righte nowe. Youe comee backe, and savie lifee Gin Sling. Nowe meie paye youe for alle. Youe takee in welcomee. Meie goe and gete moree."

He gave his thick pig-tail a flirt, unbraided it with a rapid motion of his hands, and from the mass of hair dropped a razor and comb, a piece of cloth, a stick of something like caustic, a bag containing ten sovereigns, and, most wonderful of all, a thin wash-leather purse, at least ten inches in length, and as large round as a stout man's thumb, containing at least three pounds of gold dust and small nuggets. Gin Sling had beaten the bushrangers, for he had secured his treasures so carefully in his cherished pig-tail that the ruffians had not thought of searching it, and, rather than give up his gold, he had determined to lose his life, or to run his chances of a rescue.

"Youe takee alle," Gin Sling said, as he put everything in my hands. "Youe save meie lifee. Nowe takee, and keepe. Youe dammie goodie, meie knowie, bute meie noie leavie youe morie. Alle righte. Chinaman havie heartie as big as Slingisman annie timie daye."

"Gin," I said, "I don't want your property. Keep it, and when you go back to China you will be a mandarin.'"

"Noie, wille note takie. Alle youe. 'Noughe said aboute it."

He looked so determined that I had hard work to make him understand that I would not take his money on any account. Then he showed disappointment and dejection, and seemed undecided what to do with his treasures. At last his almond eyes brightened. He had hit upon an idea.

"Alle righte. Meie keepe fore youe tillie goe Ballarate. Thene youe takie alle. Date farie."

He braided his hair once more in so skillful a manner that I could not detect the treasures which it contained, and, after he had concluded, I looked to my revolver and rifle, saw that the charges were all right, and that my knife had not lost its keen edge. By that time it was near four o'clock, and the woods began to appear dark and sombre, and the birds and animals to show themselves in the cool of the evening, after their long *siesta* during the hot hours. We should be moving, but I did not know in what direction to go to find the trail. I had become completely lost as to all points of the compass.

"Gin Sling," I asked, "do you know where we are?"

"Oh, yese, in der bushe."

"Do you know in what direction we should go to strike the road that leads to Ballarat?"

"Meie noie strikie nobodie," was the reply. "If I doie badie Slingisman hite backie, and saye, '———— ratie eatie Chinaman.' Noie, meie noie strikie folkes unlese meie cane lickie."

It was useless to expect assistance from Gin Sling. He either did not understand me, or was cunning enough to pretend that he did not, so that he would not be forced to take any responsibility in the difficult task of finding our way out of the bush, and gaining the right road. I knew that people had been lost in the woods, and wandered around in a circle for days, and at last had died, within sound of their own homes, dazed and bewildered by the fact that they were lost, and did not know which way to turn, or how to regain the hidden trails.

Down went the sun behind the tall trees, and darkness was almost upon us. I thought it useless to attempt to move until daylight, for we could accomplish nothing, and should get more tired and bewildered stumbling over fallen trees, and through dense scrub, beside running the risk of being bitten by a diamond or whip snake, the only two poisonous reptiles in Australia, of the crawling species. I determined, therefore, to remain where I was until the next day, and then make a renewed attempt to escape from our imprisonment.

"Gin Sling," I asked, "are you hungry?"

"Meie bellie hungie. Alle same Chinaman begger. Eeatie muchie nowe, if havie."

Just at this moment a fat white rabbit entered the clearing, and sat up, and looked at us with as much astonishment as its little pink eyes could assume. I fired a rifle shot at it, and the poor little timid thing sprang into the air, and fell dead.

"Oh, ————, bute date goodie," and like a hungry dog the Chinama fell upon the carcass, and, with the aid of my knife, commenced stripping off the pelt.

"Gin," I said, "we shall have to remain here all night."

"Alle righte. Where youe staye meie staye. Makie fie, and habie meatie for grubie. Blerie goodie meatie."

We gathered some dead branches, and made a fire, for the Chinaman had a stock of matches and a lot of cheap tobacco in some mysterious pockets of his blouse, and, by the time the sun had set, we were feasting on broiled rabbit, and making a very fair supper, for I had a few cakes of hard tack and a pinch of salt, in my packages, which Mike had insisted I should take with me, in case I wanted a lunch on the way to the mines. Gin Sling ate like a person who had fasted for a week, and when we had concluded our repast every vestige of the rabbit was consumed. Then, with a small allowance of brandy and water, very precious because I did not know when I should see any more, I spread my blanket near the fire, and lighted my pipe, while Gin consoled himself with smoking some of the vilest homemade cigarettes that ever turned the stomach of a well man, and caused him to yearn for fresh air, and a stringent death penalty on all who indulged in such profanation of the art of smoking. But Gin was not educated up to the art of using good tobacco, and was as happy in his ignorance as some people who claim to belong to the land of Christians and churches.

The stars came out, and twinkled as though rather glad that we were in such comfortable quarters; the moon shed a little light in the open space where we sat on opposite sides of the fire, a thick bit of scrub, and a gum-tree just back of Gin Sling, and a high bush of flowering acacia in my rear, sending its fragrance all around us, and even overpowering the stench of the tobacco which Gin was enjoying after his hearty supper. In the trees that surrounded us on all sides the old gray-headed parrots scolded at each other, and rebuked the giddy and thoughtless parroquets, which were coquetting a little on some she-oaks, and mocking their elders for their propriety, acting very human in this respect, while once in a while a sly, quiet opossum would slink down from a gum-tree, and glide off to pay his respects to a female neighbor. A stately white owl, on a tall cedar, tooted out doleful complaints because the moon in its brilliancy interfered with its nocturnal pursuits, and far off in the distance the dingos were howling, and calling to each other for a friendly ramble in search of sheep and helpless cattle. Once in a while a snake would glide out of the scrub, and, seeing the fire, would hiss its displeasure, and retreat in the thickets, with no disposition to cultivate our acquaintance, when backed by flames and smoke. The insects began to hum, and sharpened their beaks for the feast that they saw in store, as soon as we should sleep, and prowling near us, but keeping out of sight, an animal called the "hairy tail," a species of Australian panther, small, but compact, and a good fighter, when aroused, growled ominously, as though gathering courage for an attack, yet did not like to commence one, for fear the fire would take a hand, and decide the contest in our favor. But I had no fear of it, with a huge revolver at hand, and a repeating rifle at my side, and Gin Sling seemed to have no cares after his hearty meal, except the fear that his tobacco would give out, and he should not be able to obtain another supply at some convenient point in the bush. His confidence in me was so unbounded that he was like a child in his careless simplicity.

Thus we sat and smoked until near nine o'clock, Gin Sling chatting in pigeon English, not forgetting to damn all bushrangers, as he thought of the outrage that had been perpetrated on his celestial person, and I was just about to nod, and let my head fall upon my breast, tired and oppressed by the labors of the day, when there was a humming noise in the air, like the flapping of swan's wings when rising from a sheet of water, and whiz came a spear from out of the scrub, passed over the fire, just grazing the fat, black, plump pig-tail of Gin Sling, and buried itself in the trunk of a gum-tree, some two feet from the ground.

For a moment there was a breathless silence, and then, as Gin Sling real'zed how narrowly he had escaped a sudden and **violent death, he gave** one spring, shouting as he did so, —

"Oh, ———! meie scootie! Youe fightie! **Chinaman muste** goe."

I saw the form of the celestial, as though it had taken wing, dart through the air, **his** body almost **horizontal, his feet** covered with coarse wooden shoes, **his legs** extended like **a pair of shears** half opened, his arms outstretched **as a skillful diver about to make a** plunge, his queue erect and stiff, resembling a cat's tail when suddenly confronted by a war-disposed dog, **and then my friend the Chinaman had** disappeared behind the thick bit **of scrub,** and all was silent for a while, but if I had died the next moment, from the thrust of a spear, I could not have prevented the shriek of laughter that escaped me, so much was I amused at the sudden flight of Gin Sling, and so comical was his disappearance.

But, even while roaring with laughter, I did not neglect all proper precautions for **my own safety.** I had seen something of Indian life in California **and Oregon,** and knew that a camp-fire was a bad place for a person **who was ambushed, so,** with a quick movement of the body, I rolled under the shelter of the acacia-bush, and awaited further developments, and did not have to wait long. From out the shelter of the forest came six black fellows, with terribly scarred breasts, and scant clothing, spears and boomerangs in their hands, and heavy waddies and nullas hung around their necks, and trailing after them came a *gin*, or old female, the wife of one of the black fellows, and on her back she bore a load of game, and some packages, which I could not make out, and over her shoulder was the tail of the black snake that I had killed in the afternoon, and which she was dragging along the ground for the purpose of forming the basis of a rare old gorging feast, such as the natives of Australia indulge in when they have an opportunity, and the supplies.

I could have killed the whole of them, and escaped unhurt, I verily believe, if I had opened fire, but the black fellows did not seem hostile, or to care for my presence. They knew that I was under the acacia-bush, but they did not come near me, or threaten me with their spears, as they might have done, so I concluded that they had made the attack on the Chinaman through accident, or else with the idea of frightening us from the fire, so that they would not have the trouble of rubbing two sticks together for the purpose of producing a blaze.

The blacks laid aside their weapons, the *gin* dropped her load, the men gathered wood, and made a roaring fire, and then the old woman threw the body of the snake on the flames, and the odors of burning flesh were soon as obnoxious as the fumes of Gin Sling's tobacco. By and by one of the dirtiest of the tribe made a movement as though to sit down on my blanket, and, as I did not care to have it stained by the filth on his person, I got up, and went toward him, revolver on the cock, determined to shoot if there was the least sign of hostility.

But there was none. The natives merely grunted a welcome, and pointed to the burning snake, as an invitation that I could share their disgusting meal, or that I had killed it, and they were greatly obliged to me for the trouble that I had taken in their behalf. I jerked the blanket away from the fellow, and he did not show signs of resentment. He seemed to take it as a matter of course from a white man. I did not then know that the blacks, so near a mining camp, were not always dangerous, but that those in the remote districts did not hesitate to spear a man, or to crack his skull with a waddy if the humor seized them, and there were no mounted police near to revenge the murder by killing ten natives to one white.

As the black fellows were so well disposed, I did not molest them, but gathered all my property, and placed it near me, so that they could not

steal it, and, as one old fellow came near, after I had sat down, I said,—
"Ballarat."

He understood me, and pointed in a direction the very opposite from the one I should have taken, and then nodded, and repeated the word, and pointed a second time. He seemed to comprehend that I was lost in the bush, and wanted to find the way out. An Australian black fellow can find his way through the densest of scrub and the darkest of woods, and not lose his course, and can track a child's footsteps over a plain, or through a morass, and never drop the scent for a moment, so when the old man gave me the direction, I took my bearings, and determined to follow his course in the morning, unless I was murdered in the night, which I certainly did not expect to be, unless appearances were deceitful.

Presently the black-snake was done to a proper degree of crackle and tenderness, for the old *gin* had attended to its cooking personally, and knew that her repututation depended upon this, one of the proudest moments of her life, and when she pulled the remains from the ashes, and asked her friends if they had ever seen such a delicate tid-bit, there was one universal grunt of approval, and they fell upon the meat before them, as the alderman falls upon the turtle soup, which the tax payers settle for. It made me almost sick to see the brutes gorge themselves. There was enough for all, and, as they tore off large pieces of the white flesh, I will confess that it did not look so bad as one might have expected. After all, is the flesh of a snake much worse than civilized tripe or pig's feet?

But, although an Australian native can eat enough at one meal to cause even an Esquimau to turn green with envy, there is a limit to his capacity, yet some people have doubted it. In this respect the younger and more vigorous eaters gave out first, like impulsive youths who did not know how to husband their strength, and then the elderly men dropped off one by one, until only the old *gin* was left, and she continued to pick a bit here and there, a little back-bone, or a delicate slice from the stomach, a sip of brain, or a thread of entrails, like a sweet young lady who is examining the contents of a box of bon-bons, and knows not what to choose, there being so much richness before her. The old woman's face was so dirty, that even a New-York street-cleaning contractor would have thrown up his job in despair, but it beamed with oily satisfaction as she licked her fingers, and sighed to think that she could eat no more at that time, much as she would have liked to. They all sat around the fire, and chatted in their guttural tongues, but sleep was stealing over them, and one fellow, whose stomach was distended until it looked like the bass drum of a musician on a dress rade, dropped his head upon his scarred breast, and snored so loudly that one of the younger members of the tribe got out of patience, like his white and Christian brethren, and jabbed his grandfather in various parts of his body with a small spear, only partially awakening the old man, and causing him to utter curses at his relative, in the choicest of Australian dialects.

"Alas," I thought, as I reposed on my blanket, under the shade of the acacia-bush, "how very human and natural that action is. It proves most conclusively that we are all descended from one common origin, with the same desires, the same antipathies, and similar persecutions for all who make night hideous by snoring. Only substitute sharp, white elbows for a spear, and the likeness is complete, and can be accepted in our world, on a brass bedstead, in an elegantly furnished chamber, or in the bush of an Australian forest, with the ground for a resting place, and naked natives as actors."

The moon was low behind the tall gum-trees; it had passed its zenith, and was hurrying toward the horizon as though fearful it would not be on time to meet an important engagement in some distant part of the world. The wind sighed mournfully through the tree-tops, the owl hooted in more cheerful tones, as it thought of the feast it was to enjoy as soon as darkness stole through the forest; the parrots and parroquets were still quarreling, but in more subdued tones, as if tired of domestic wrangling; the dingos were making lively work for some stockman's sheep, far off on the plains, as they were all yelping in chorus, trying to get up a stampede of the timid animals, and answered by howls of defiance and rage from the domestic dogs, which have no love for their wild relatives, and fight them on all occasions, unless the odds are too great; the savage "hairy tail" had not yet deserted our neighborhood, but lingered near, and sniffed the good things that sent forth their foul odors from the fire, and grumbled and growled as he saw morsel after morsel disappear down the throats of his enemies, and feared that his share would be but small when moving time arrived; the fire burned low, and was not replenished, each native being too full for active exertions; the shadows flickered over the clearing as the trees bent their boughs, and the flames danced up with expiring efforts, only to sink down, and make the dim light a little more dense, and, while I was more than half inclined to nod, and trust my life to an unseen power, I saw a sight that sent a chill to my heart, and made me shrink still further under the shelter of the acacia-bush, and to drop my revolver, and clasp my hands in a vain attempt to remember a childhood's prayer, for moving slowly into the dark, open space, where the natives were nodding and sleeping, glided a hideous phantom, something so terrible, that I would have cried out, and fled, had I not been powerless to move hand, foot, or tongue. I made an attempt to grasp my revolver, but could not do so, and, with eyes distended, and limbs shaking, watched the unearthly visitor as it approached, — a skeleton, with ribs of fire, streaks of flame on breast and face, eyes that were like burning coals, cheeks that were ever changing and flashing, as the thing moved, with blue flames issuing from mouth and nostrils, and arms and hands covered with shining, will-o'-wisp light, that trembled, flickered, and went out, only to re-appear more vivid than ever, and, as the phantom waved its hideous arms around its fiery head, and uttered a groan so unearthly that even the owl was frightened, and flew to other quarters, where such devilish visitants would not disturb its nightly meditations and repose, I wanted to shriek, but could not: I wanted to fly, but my limbs refused to obey my will, and so I was forced to remain, and fancied that I could feel the sulphurous and fiery breath of this fiend from the infernal regions, for it did not look like anything earthly. If his satanic majesty resembled the skeleton that was before my eyes, I resolved to be a sincere Christian for the remainder of my life, for I had no desire to meet such an object in the next world, and determined to avoid it if possible.

"Uoogh! uoogh! uoogh'" groaned the midnight visitor, and up went its arms in rapid gyrations around its head, and sparks and flames seemed to fly in the air, and to play around the naked skeleton, and to fall to the ground, and run along the dry leaves, then leap back to the terrible being, as if for a parting embrace, and a benediction, before dying, and disappearing from sight.

One of the sleeping black fellows leisurely opened one eye, and glanced around. His gaze fell on the skeleton of fire, and, with a yell that could have been heard even by the quarreling dingos, a mile distant, he gave a mighty bound over the scrub and disappeared in the bush.

His cry awakened the remainder of the natives. They supposed at first that their companion was suffering from an attack of indigestion, or a mild form of night-mare, and, as they roused up to rebuke the fellow who had disturbed their rest and dreams, and, possibly, to whack him over the head with a waddy for his rudeness, their eyes sighted the terrible apparition. There was a sudden and general rising of the whole tribe. Even the old *gin* staggered to her feet, and rubbed her gummy eyes, and looked her terror and astonishment.

"*Nackietite!*" was the exclamation from every mouth, as near as I could understand the word, and I may be wrong in leaving off one or two syllables, but I suppose the real translation is, "Well, the divil has got us at last, sure," and over the scrub went every black fellow, showing his heels and feet in the air, as he made a most wonderful plunge, head first, for a point of safety.

All but the *gin*. I suppose that her womanly delicacy prevented her from plunging into the bush in the presence of a stranger, or, perhaps, she was too full for a lively, standing jump, such as her relatives had accomplished. But of one thing I was assured, she could scream the heads off of her companions, and not half try, like a delicate young lady, who can't speak above a whisper in company, and yells like an Apache warrior when she encounters a mouse in her bed-chamber or on the stairs. The sharpest locomotive whistle in the country could not equal that old hag's yell, as she made an effort to jump, but, being over-weighted, could not, so clapped her hands upon her extended stomach, and waddled off, as fast as she could, to find her friends, leaving spears, boomerangs, waddies, and bundles near the fire, thinking only of personal safety, and not of personal property, and through the dry bush I could hear the natives plunge, uttering the most dismal howls as they thought of the hideous devil that was after them, and likely to devour them, and then all sounds died away, except a low, chuckling laugh, a sort of grunt of satisfaction, and, looking toward the terrible visitor, I saw that the fire which had bathed its whole mass of ribs and bones had died away, and a voice that I was familiar with said, —

"Blackie fellie muste goe, Chinaman staye. Notie muchie —— foolie 'boute meie. Hi yah!"

"Gin Sling, you wretch, is this you?" I demanded, springing toward him, and as much surprised as I was pleased to see that the terrible visitor was flesh and blood, and my friend the Chinaman.

"Oh, yesie, meie comee backie to lookie arter youe. Lordie, howe blackie fellie runnie whenie seie meie," and he laughed as heartily as a Chinaman ever does, their laughter consisting of a series of chuckles, grunts, and strangling sensations, as though a fish-bone was lodged in their throats, and then the fellow proceeded to tell me that he had fled but a short distance, and, after his panic had subsided, returned, and saw that I was not killed as he feared was the case, and then determined to scare the black fellows who had frightened him so badly. For this purpose he had taken from his pig-tail the stick of Chinese phosphorus which had attracted my attention when he first unbraided his queue, a caustic that resembles the same kind of fiery compound as is used in this country by match makers, but is more vivid and strong, and much more easily applied to the skin, leaving no scars, or black marks behind. He had annointed himself from head to foot, even taking the trouble to remove trousers and blouse to make a more hideous appearance, waiting patiently until the moon had disappeared behind the trees, and the natives were partly asleep, before venturing upon his ghostly mission, and even then he feared that he would frighten me away as well as the others, if he should be so fortunate as to escape a shot from my revolver, of which he had a wholesome dread. But he had determined to risk all for the sake of having a little quiet Chinese fun, and had succeeded beyond his most sanguine expectations.

"Nowie gibbe meie a ittie drinkie of rume, and thene takie sleepie tille lightie. Blackie fellie noie comee backie heree noie morie. Too muche runnie for datie."

He had a pull at the brandy, and a sip of water to help it down, and then extinguishing the fire, so that it would not attract other wanderers, we went to sleep, and slumbered until sunrise, and the screaming of the birds, the chattering and scolding of the parrots, and the hoarse calls of the birds of paradise awakened us. No one had visited us during the time we had slept, and, as we had no toilets to make, we were soon ready to move, and endeavor to find a trail that should lead us to safety.

The spears and boomerangs were lying just where the black fellows had left them. There were also half a dozen waddies and nullas, but we did not need them, so left everything, and were about to start, when I kicked one of the packages which the old gin had borne upon her back when she entered the clearing, trailing the snake, the night before. As the package, covered by a mat of dried leaves, did not yield to my energetic movements, in fact it rather hurt my toes, reminding me of the people in civilized countries, who kick at hats on sidewalks, on the first day of April, and then hobble away on one foot, convinced that a mistake had been made somewhere, and damning the boy who invented the trick, so I uttered an exclamation that sounded like a blessing, and then stooped down, and examined the article that had excited my ire. I tore off the leaves, and then stood and looked at the package in such astonishment that I could not speak, for there, lying at my feet, was a nugget of gold, the like of which I had never seen before or since, for purity and beauty of form. It was as large as a man's big fist, and resembled it in many respects, with not a speck of dirt or quartz to be seen on the surface. It was a lump of pure gold, without alloy, and could not have been more precious if it had just come out of a refiner's crucible.

"Gin Sling," I said, "look here, and see this nugget."

The Chinaman approached, saw the nugget of gold, and fell down, and touched his lips to it, as though it was a sacred idol, and he was the most devout of worshipers.

"By ———," he cried, "nebbe sawe de likie aforee. Youe riche nowie. Hi yah! blackie fellie leavie, and runnie 'waye. Alle youe. Niggies no comee backie, and if they dide noie habbie."

I lifted the treasure from the ground, and examined it in every part. Although so small, it was very heavy, and I judged that it weighed about twenty-five pounds, troy weight, and afterward I found that I had made a neat guess, it weighing just twenty-five and one-half pounds, or three hundred and six ounces, troy, containing twelve ounces to the pound. It was valued at twenty dollars an ounce, amounting to the neat sum of six thousand one hundred and twenty dollars, but, owing to the peculiar formation of the nugget, I sold it for much more to an agent of the Melbourne Geological Society, as a rare curiosity of gold formation, one that had never been equaled or excelled in any respect. But of this I shall have to speak hereafter, and in its proper place.

I did not lose time, but hunted for more nuggets, hoping that I might find an additional one, thus affording another illustration that a man's passion for acquiring wealth never ceases, for an hour before I should have deemed myself rich if I had had five hundred dollars in my pocket, in addition to what I had in the Oriental Bank. But no more lumps of gold were found, much to my regret, for I wanted riches for the sake of the dear young lady I had left in the city, and whom I hoped to win if I should be lucky at the mines; and here was a windfall that was well calculated to encourage me to persevere, for I did not expect to see the natives again, and certainly I hoped I should not, for I calculated that the gold would do me more good than the barbarous blacks, who could not know the value of the nugget, and had probably picked it up in some dry water course. Ah, if I could have induced the black fellows to pilot me to the spot where they had discovered it how I should have rejoiced. But there was no hope of that, so wrapping the precious treasure in my blanket, and tying the ends of the latter so that the gold would not escape, or be seen, I slung the burden over Gin Sling's shoulders, took my bearings, and once more commenced my journey, and how happy I should have felt had I but been sure that I could find the trail.

I followed the direction that the old black had given me, tramped along sturdily, and with hope, the Chinaman chattering like a magpie, and condemning to everlasting punishment all bushrangers, black fellows, and

"Slingismen" who took a fancy to punch a celestial's head if just in the humor.

On we went, over trees that were so decayed that it was dangerous to step on them for fear of snakes and ants, skirting scrub, and dodging under branches, disturbing animals in their forenoon naps, and receiving many a hiss from an angry snake, and guttural toot from a blinking owl, until at last I was forced to stop and consider whether I was on the right course. If I was not, my lump of gold would be a cheap exchange for the correct road, if we could find any one willing to make the trade.

Gin Sling looked at me as we stopped, and wiped the perspiration from his brow. He saw that I was troubled, but his face lighted up with a grin, as if to encourage me not to lose all heart.

"Noie fearie," he said. "Wee comee oute alle rightie. Seeie, youe waitie ittie whilie. Meie goie upe treeie, and seeie whate I shalle seeie."

The idea was a good one. He selected a gum-tree that was at least two hundred and fifty feet high, the monarch of the forest in that vicinity, with branches that extended almost forty feet from the ground. The Chinaman removed his blouse, so as to refrain from soiling it, kicked off his thick shoes, and up the tree he crawled, in a style that would have made even a black fellow, the most expert tree climbers in the world, feel envious. Up he went, hardly pausing to take breath, until at length the top of the tree was gained, and I awaited with a trembling heart for his verdict of life or death to us. He looked long and anxiously in all directions, and I began to feel that death stared us in the face, when he uttered a dinner-gong-like laugh, and shouted, —

"Alle rightie nowie. Seeie Ballarate, de roade, and alle dings plainie. Dis waie. Youe notie for surie."

He pointed in a direction a little to the right of the one which we had been pursuing, showing that the old black fellow had given me the right course, but that we had deviated from it, as all people do who have no fixed object to steer for. Our right feet had taken a little longer pace than our left, and thus, in the course of time, we should have been wandering around in a circle, and surely lost, like hundreds and thousands of people in similar circumstances, not only in Australia, but this country.

Once more I took bearings, and this time determined to keep well to the right, and, when Gin Sling descended, I asked him how far we were from the road, and was delighted to learn that it could not be more than half a mile, and that Camp Reserve was not more than two miles from the spot where we were stopping.

"Alle rightie nowie. Comie onie," said Gin cheerfully.

We resumed our journey, and in an hour's time saw sunlight shining through the woods, and then heard the crack of a stockman's whip, and a hoarse voice roaring at cattle, the bark of a dog, and the whinnying of a horse, and the whistling of some light-hearted person, possibly a miner on his way to the city, with enough gold-dust in his buckskin bag to make things lively for a while, when he would again return to the mines, and labor for more, and repeat his useless enjoyments.

"Gin Sling," I said, as we halted on the edge of the wood, but still out of sight of the road, "don't mention the gold nugget."

"Alle rightie; meie noie ——— foolle. Chinaman sabie muchie sometimee," and the fellow showed his teeth, and grinned.

We felt thirsty and tired, and, for the last time, took a pull at the brandy and water, and then, refreshed and encouraged, we stepped from the woods into the road, and were met by a mounted policeman, who sat on his horse in the middle of the trail, and was whistling to relieve the monotony of his long, dull, and dusty beat, at the same time keeping a bright lookout for all who passed him, going to Ballarat, or in another direction. We came upon the man so suddenly that we could not have avoided him had we been so disposed. But we were tired, and needed rest and water, and so I put on a bold front, and astonished the mounted trap by our unexpected appearance from the forest; and strange-looking objects we must have been, covered with dust and dirt, our clothes torn in many places, and that peculiar look on our faces which people have after being lost in the bush for several days, a look half of despair and half of terror, as though fearful that the human beings you met were enemies, and had some designs on your life and fortunes, and half inclined to run away from the dearest of friends, and this sensation usually lasts several days. But we had not suffered enough to feel all such effects, or we should have avoided the policeman, and his cheerful whistle.

"KITTY, MY POOR CHILD!" I CRIED, AS I LAID A HAND VERY GENTLY ON HER HEAD.

PART VIII.

BALLARAT AND ITS MINES. — HOW THREE OLD PIRATES SOLD A CLAIM AND MYSELF AT THE SAME TIME. — HOUSE-CLEANING MADE EASY. — A NEWSPAPER'S ACCOUNT OF MY WEDDING. — MISS KITTY STUCKLY MAKES ME AN UNEXPECTED CALL, AND WANTS TO TALK OF LOVE, BUT I DECLINE TO LISTEN. — THE ARRIVAL OF MR. MURDEN AT MY SHANTY IN THE NIGHT, AND WHAT HE SAID.

AS the Chinaman and myself struck the road, close to the mounted policeman, he gave us a glance, and then laid his hand lightly on the carbine which he carried at his saddle bow. We would have passed him with but a nod and a word, but the man was not disposed to let us go without a few questions, which might prove of interest to one in his calling.

"Hullo, mate," he said, looking me all over, and ignoring the Chinaman, as being of no account, and hardly worthy of notice; "not so fast, if you please. I want a word with you. Where did you come from?"

"From the bush, where we have been for two days, and hard work we had to find our way out. Thanks to your gentle whistle, as sweet to our ears as the tones of vesper bells to the Sicilian, we have struck a trail, and want food and water as soon as we can get them."

"None of your chaffing," was the response of the stately policeman. "Never joke with a police officer when he is on duty. If you want a drink take one from my canteen, and in welcome," and, as he spoke, he handed me a water-bottle that held about two quarts, from which I took a long and refreshing pull, and then passed it to Gin Sling, who followed suit with quiet alacrity, to the intense disgust of the officer, who said, —

"You might have let that heathen wait until you reached the camp."

"And see him suffer?" I asked.

"It is not much matter if he did. There are too many of these fellows in the mines at the present time, and not one in a dozen pays a tax. The copper-colored rascals look so much alike that we can't tell them apart, and when we go for their taxes one license answers for twenty, as they pass it from hand to hand, or else burrough in their claims like squirrels. They are a bad lot, buy nothing, spend nothing, live on nothing, and take out of the country all that they can steal or earn, blast them! I don't like them, and no one does."

This was the prevailing opinion of the Chinese at the time, and I do not think there has been a change of sentiment for the better since I was in Australia. They were disliked by miner and stockman, shepherd and laborer, policemen and officials, but, even while the officer was thus expressing his true sentiments, Gin Sling was listening with unmoved face, but at his flat, puggy nose was placed a thumb, and four fingers gyrated in the air, like a saucy boy in our cities some years since, when such a movement of the thumb and fingers expressed doubt and contempt, distrust and defiance. In fact, I think that it is even used at the present day by some men, for I recently saw a grave and dignified professor put his thumb to his nose, and whirl his fingers, to show his disgust at some question asked him by a friend.

But, while Gin Sling was thus gravely poking fun at the policeman, whose back was turned, he did not let the official catch him at such ambiguous practices, but dropped his hand like a flash when the officer looked in his direction.

"Have you seen any suspicious-looking horsemen near the bush?" asked the officer, whom I now discovered was Larry, the same man who had overhauled Mike and myself the night we left Melbourne.

"No, we could not very well see horsemen while we were in the bush," I answered.

"True, but men sometimes leave their horses at the edge of the scrub, and enter the bush on foot. Three bushrangers are in the neighborhood, — Black Dick, Slipper Sam, and a young fellow we can't locate. He must be a new man, as we never heard of him before."

As I had not seen the persons described, I was about to resume my journey, when the officer again stopped me with a question.

"Have you seen a young and genteel-looking swell on the road, or in the bush?" he asked.

"No, we have seen no one," I replied.

"All right, only I'd like to meet him. Send me word if you see such a swell, and I'll do a favor for you some time."

"What is he wanted for?" I asked.

"Oh, blessed if I know. Some confounded woman scrape, I believe. There's a reward for his arrest, but, if taken, he's to be treated with great respect and kindness. Fed on champagne and fruit, I suppose. The force is going to the devil, there's so much kindness shown to Chinamen and prisoners."

He was about to trot off to patrol his district, when I asked a question.

"Shall I have to obtain a license to mine for gold?"

"Yes, five bob a month, and payable in advance, at the mining office, where you will be allotted a claim, and you can work it for all that it is worth, clear down to the world underneath us, if you want to, but most people are satisfied with striking a reef of rocks, and stopping there. But don't attempt to dig gold until you get a license. It might cost you all the dust and nuggets you gathered. If you expect to make your fortune at mining take the blessing and good wishes of a policeman, for even small things are not to be despised in such a case."

He laughed, and rode off, leaving me to infer that mining was not such a profitable business as I had anticipated, but, with the nugget of gold already in my possession, I felt that I could afford to meet a few disappointments, and yet not feel very poor, even at the end of a year.

"Youe seeie, alle folkes hatie Chinaman," Gin Sling said, as we trudged along. "Allie causie wee livie cheapie, and noie drinkie rummie, and raisie devilie."

As I did not understand the question that had been raised at that time in

Australia, I marveled at the policeman's dislike, but afterward found that the celestials were a little tricky in paying their taxes, but the white miners were not immaculate in that respect, and took every occasion to cheat all who belonged to the government, and land grabbers seized on every acre of available territory, and laughed at the officials who meant to be as honest as possible, consistent with a full pocket.

About ten o'clock we struck Camp Reserve, and passed down Sturt Street, looking to the right and left for a stopping-place. Gin Sling was well acquainted in the Chinese quarter, but he said that it would not suit me, and that I must keep away from it. Some men there, he said, would steal the teeth out of my head, unless I kept my lips locked up with a padlock, and threw the key down a deserted shaft. At last I saw a rough house, that looked a little neater than the rest, and on a sign the information was given that travelers could have good beds and board, on reasonable terms. I found that a stout English woman kept the place, and that, while she was willing to receive me, if I would pay by the day, and in advance, she was decidedly opposed to making a tea-box of her quarters to accommodate Gin Sling, and the only way that I could satisfy her was to say that the celestial was my servant, and that I could not remain unless he was permitted to do so. I said that he could sleep on the floor in my room, and eat as best he could, until I found a place to pitch my tent, and go to mining, the method that all miners adopted unable to erect a shanty.

"Now, Gin," I said, after we had taken possession of a room that was about six by six, destitute of bed or chair, "do you stay here, and take care of the gold, and let no one steal it from you, while I go and get a license to mine, and see where we can locate."

"Bellie goodie. Meie doie," and, taking possession of my revolver and rifle, he sat down, and prepared to watch the precious deposit.

I found my way to the office where licenses were issued, paid a tax for Mike, Gin, and myself, said that I did not know where I should sink a shaft, so did not want any allotment just then, but would look around. There were a dozen men in the room, some waiting for allotments, others to transfer their claims to new-comers. As I was leaving the office, a battered, piratical-looking sailor touched me on the arm, and said, —

"Was yer lookin' for a good claim, mate?"

"Yes, that is just what I am looking for," was my response.

"Well, mate, I has a claim that is jist rotten with richness, but yer see I 'se hurted my right hand, and can't work, and the doctor says I must go to the city, and get into a hospital, where a bloody old saw-bones can have a look at it, and my mates they wants to go with me, 'cos they has got a good many shots in the locker, and they don't want to work all their days in this blasted old hole."

Alas, I was fearfully green as to the tricks of the Ballarat miner. A week later I should have laughed at the old pirate, and left him to attempt swindling some one else, but now I stopped and listened, the very thing I should not have done.

"Yes, mate," said the dirty, grisly old scamp, "we has a claim that is forty by forty, and a shaft that is down twenty feet, and we can jist scoop up the gold nuggets and the dust every time. We a'n't doin' much now, since I hurted my hand, but we has all we wants, and there goes with the claim a nice shanty, that won't leak unless it rains very hard, and it has three bunks in it, and a table for the grub, and pots, and pans, and chairs, and everything. It 's jist like a royal palace, it is now, I tell yer."

"And what is the price for all?" I demanded.

"Well, mate, the whole is worth twenty sovs, but you can have it for ten."

"Let me see your license," I said.

He showed it to me, and also the allotment to mine on lot one thousand and eight. I went to the clerk, and asked if the papers were correct, and if the old fellow owned such a mine. He grinned, and said that everything was correct.

"You are in a hurry to be rich, a'n't you?" the clerk asked, still smiling.

"Yes: why?"

"Oh, nothing, except seeing you buy a valuable piece of property. O Jack, Jack, you 'll kill some of us before long," and the clerk laughed and winked at the pirate, who turned his back, and was gazing at the mining camp, as though much interested in such a show of industry as was spread all over the plain.

"Come and look at the plant, mate," whispered the pirate. "The clerk is a joker, and likes his laugh, but when he sees yer wuth millions he won't grin so much, I tell yer."

I was not really suspicious that I was being sold, and the reason was because I did not feel in immediate want of money, but still was determined to be rich as soon as possible, and wanted to purchase a claim where a shaft had been sunk, and thus save time and labor.

"Come with me, mate," repeated the old pirate. "I 'll show you the Bank-of-England Mine."

"Why did you name it such a high-sounding title?" I asked.

"Oh, 'cos the parties what owns that 'ere mine will be able to buy out the bank, if they works it long enough. It's jist bustin' with richness, that mine is."

The claim was on Sturt Street, some distance from the rest of the miners and shafts. Two other villainous-looking scoundrels were seated at the door of a shanty, engaged in a game of all fours, at a shilling a game, and when pirate number one said that he had offered the whole establishment for ten sovereigns, the two others dashed down their cards in a rage, and vowed that they would n't submit to such a swindle. They would have twenty sovs, or not a penny. The first pirate said that his hand was bad, and he must go to Melbourne, and have it looked arter, and it was devilish hard on a pard, which had done as well as he had by his mates, to have to stand in the gap, but the two rascals were firm, and took me out to see the shaft, and the windlass to draw up the dirt, and the heavy bucket, and the nearness to the stream, and the abundance of shafting wood that was close at hand, and at last one old scoundrel said that he would not sell at any price, as he wanted to make a few more thousands before he knocked off work for good, and become a swell in some great city, so that he could have his grog, and his pipe, and his bit of land, and a tidy lass to keep him company.

Upon this the first pirate set up a howl, and said that it was a bloody shame, and that his hand would drop off with the dry rot unless he had relief, and his old friends to take care of him while he was on the sick list, and then the obstinate pirate said he would n't be hard-hearted, and he 'd sell for twenty sovs, and not a penny less, and then the others agreed that the sum was low, and that they would n't take anything different.

"Let me see a specimen of the gold that you have taken from the mine," I said, and this demand, instead of staggering them, seemed to brighten them up, for one of the pirates went to his bunk, and took out a bag, and showed me three or four pounds of nuggets. This looked like business, but, as the old scamps had made so much talk, I determined to retire, and not buy their property unless I could do so at my own price, and on very liberal terms.

"Look you, mates, I said, "I don't want to take such valuable property from you, so will let some other person buy it. I will look around, and see what I can find in another quarter."

The faces of the three men changed. I was not so green as they had supposed.

"Oh, take the mine for ten sovs," all cried, with one accord, when they saw me moving off.

"No, I don't want it," was the reply, as I edged away from them, as if indifferent.

"What will you give for it?" was the next humble question.

"Five sovereigns," was my cautious answer.

"Sold: it's yours," all shrieked, in chorus, as though they feared that I would decline, and not come to the scratch.

I saw the game then, but, as the shanty was worth something, I did not think that I had been swindled to any great extent, and had no doubt but that I could get my money back when I wanted to sell. I went to the office, and had transferred to me, in proper form, the Bank-of-England Mine, and, as the clerk handed me the document, and I paid the pirates, he laughed, and said, —

"You're the tenth person who has bought the mine in the past two weeks, and I've no doubt but that you'll get as sick of it as the former proprietors, in the course of a few days."

"But there has been considerable gold taken from the mine," I said.

"Not even a penny worth," was the response. "It's a sell, and those three old sharpers will again take possession when you leave, renew their papers, and dispose of the mine to some other new-comer. They have not done a day's work for months, and they do not need to. They get enough to buy rum and tobacco, and that is all they care for."

"But I saw a bag full of nuggets. They showed them to me, and said they came from the mine," I cried.

"The nuggets were manufactured ones, made for this market, and used to salt mines with. There was not a shilling's worth of gold in the whole lot," was the frank communication.

"But it seems to me that the police should protect new-comers," I remarked.

"We should have to employ a thousand men to do that. The best that we can do is to prevent miners from jumping each other's claims. Then we come down on them like a thousand of brick, and make the law felt, even if we have to shoot a few jumpers. Hope you will have better luck next time, and that you will keep your eye peeled on the chances. Good-day."

As I walked out of the office, a little ashamed of my verdancy in being swindled by three such vile old sinners, I saw the pirate whose hand was rotting off, raising a pot of beer to his mouth with the very hand that was so bad, and all three of the villains bowed to me, and drank to me, and then roared with laughter, and told every person in the ale-house how nicely they had swindled me, while the old fellow whose hand was so bad that it was liable to decay, unless medical attendance was promptly resorted to, waved that member in a free and hearty manner, to show that he had recovered its use in a miraculous manner.

Of course I did not show any of the vexation that I really felt. I would not give the pirates the satisfaction of supposing that I was disappointed in my purchase, so passed the fellows in silence, and left them carousing in the saloon, drinking bitter beer, and making plans for catching new greenhorns as soon as I got tired of my bargain, and abandoned the claim and shanty. To be sure, I had paid but little for both, but that was the secret of the financial success of the gang, for, had they asked a large sum, the would-be purchaser might have made inquiries, and had his eyes opened at the attempted fraud.

I found Gin Sling carefully guarding the nugget, and the few articles I had left in his charge, and when I told him that I had bought a claim, and a shanty, he nodded his head, and said, —

"Bellie goode. Goe nowe."

"No, Gin, we will go there tomorrow, and clean up the place, and get it in order, to commence work in the course of a few days. But I'm afraid that we sha'n't find much gold in the mine."

"Noie cane telle. Alle luckie. Wee seeie by by."

I had dinner, and received some congratulatory remarks from those whom I met on the Bank-of-England Mine, and there were many laughs as I was asked what I should do with the gold that I took out of my claim, while the landlady, who had taken quite a fancy to me, expressed her firm intention of scalding the old pirates if they ever came near her residence, and then rebuked me for not confiding in her, like a mother, before I made a move toward business. I answered all in good nature, never lost my temper for a moment, and at last had the satisfaction of seeing the current of opinion change, and to hear some hard-faced, John-Bull-looking men declare that it "was a bloody shame, and that the police should stop such business as to allow new-comers to be swindled."

As we were very tired, and the afternoon was excessively warm, Gin and I had a nap, and, after a refreshing sleep, I went through the town, and learned the art of mining, as far as I could in the short space of time that I had to spare. I found that all shafts were sunk until a ledge, or reef, as they called it, was reached, and, if gold was not found on the ledge, the shaft was abandoned as useless, and all labor was lost, and the unlucky speculators had to locate a new claim, and try once more, unless funds, or credit, gave out.

The ledge, where the largest nuggets were found, sloped toward the stream, and, while in some places a depth of four feet only would be required to reach it, yet, twenty feet from the spot, it was necessary to dig down thirty or forty feet, and even as deep as eighty or a hundred feet, where water was found, and had to be pumped out to permit the miners to work with safety. Most of the shafts had buckets going up and down, the owners being too poor to buy pumps, and slow, laborious work it was to keep the mines from overflowing. All grumbled at their blasted luck, as they called it, and only in three or four instances did I find men who would acknowledge that they were making good day wages. Such a thing as a ten-pound nugget had not been seen for many days, so they all said, although some of two or three ounces in weight were met with occasionally, and fine scale dust, such as I had mined in California, was almost unknown, except on the banks of some of the streams, or in the dry diggings, near the foot of the hills.

When I went to sleep that night it seemed to me that Florence was a long distance from me, and that I should never overtake her, but still I dreamed of her, and must have called her name in my sleep, for Gin Sling, in the morning, said, with a grin, —

"Youe talkie alle timee 'boute onie gallie, and wante to kisse, and shee noie lete. Youe comee China withe meie, and meie findie ittie gallie, footie noie bigie thane babie. Youe likie kisse alle daye," and Gin smacked his lips, as he thought of the dark-eyed females of his country, whose feet, if of the first families, are so small that their owners cannot walk without assistance, and such deformity is called beautiful in the eyes of Chinamen, but the women don't pinch their waists.

After breakfast we went over to my new purchase. The pirates had moved out, and taken up their quarters in an ale-house, waiting for events. Gin looked very grave as he glanced at the property, at the shaft, and the little prospect there was for gold. But he noticed that I was not in good spirits, and did not make any comments except to say, —

"Noie goodie. Notie worthie a ———."

I tried the bucket at the shaft, and found that it was in fair order, and that the notched stick of timber, to enter and leave the mine, was safe. I went down twenty feet, and, by the aid of a candle, saw that no one had worked the mine for months. The shovels and pick-axes were rusty, and half-covered with *débris* that had fallen, and then, suddenly, an idea entered my mind that was worth adopting.

"Gin," I said, speaking so low that he could just hear me as he leaned over the windlass, "lower the big nugget down. This is the place to conceal it until I am ready to use it. No one will ever think of looking for it here."

"Alle rightie," was the answer, and down came the lump of gold, still wrapped in the blanket. I covered the precious treasure with some old sailcloth that I found at the bottom of the shaft, and then spread a layer of dirt over all, sent the tools to the surface to be cleaned from rust, and once more rejoined Gin. Then we took a survey of the shanty, and saw that it needed soap and water, and plenty of them, before I should dare to inhabit it, for I feared contamination.

Gin understood the art of house-cleaning. He got out a big pot, filled it with water, made a fire in the rough fireplace, just out-of-doors, stripped off his blouse, shook out his pig-tail, gave me his bag of gold, and begged me to keep it for him, and to do what I pleased with it, until he called for it, pitched out-of-doors all the old dunnage that the pirates had left, — tables, chairs, and bunks, — hunted up a bar of soap, and a brush, and said that he would scrub everything clean while I wandered down the street in search of furniture, such as we should require, and a few dishes to use upon the table when we took our meals.

While I was looking up odds and ends, I saw a substantial building, and a large sign on it, giving notice that it was a branch of the Oriental Bank, Melbourne. Before the door stood an armed policeman, and, on asking him if the institution was all right, he said that it was as good as the Bank of England.

"Not the mine of that name, but the mother of all banks in England, the old lady herself," and the officer grinned, and I had no doubt but that he recognized me as the unfortunate purchaser of the mine with the substantial name.

"Have you got out enough gold to make a deposit so soon?" asked the officer. "If you have you have done better than the former owners. It is a sell, and don't you waste time on that mine. It is no use."

"Well, I shall give it a fair trial," I said. "I am in no hurry to leave it. I like the place, and intend to stay there for the present, at least."

The officer laughed as I walked into the bank, and saw that it was quite an extensive establishment, with bright scales and massive safe, and a serious-looking man as cashier.

"What are you paying for gold this morning?" I asked.

"About eighty shillings an ounce, if pure," was the answer.

I emptied Gin's gold-dust on a sheet of white paper. The cashier went all over it with a magnet, and then examined each nugget with great care, for fear of fraud.

"I will give eighty shillings an ounce for it," the cashier said. "It is pure, and a good lot."

"If I leave the money on deposit will you allow me interest for it?" I asked.

"Yes, I will allow you ten per cent if it is left on deposit longer than a month," was the satisfactory answer.

"Take it," I said, and the dust was weighed out, and I found that Gin had three pounds and a half, or forty-two ounces, worth about eight hundred and forty dollars. I took out a certificate of deposit in my own name, with the understanding that I could transfer it to the Chinaman at any time, and that he would be paid as readily as myself. I determined that Gin should not lose his hard-earned gains by gambling (a vice that no Chiman can resist), if I could prevent it.

Then I went and purchased some rough but decent chairs, a table, some dishes, coffee and tea, pots, knives and forks, tin pans, three palm-leaf mattresses, blankets, pails, and dippers, and, by the time I had completed my bargains, and shipped them to the mine, it was twelve o'clock, and everybody was out of the bowels of the earth, and eating dinner, such as they could obtain.

I found Gin with an assistant in the person of a young Chinaman. He had picked him up in the course of the forenoon, and set him to cleaning. They had made a visible improvement in the shanty. The bunks were torn down, the walls and floors scrubbed clean, not a trace of dirt to be seen anywhere, excepting the deep stains of weather and decay, and Gin was hard at work with hammer and nails, putting up a shelf here and there, hooks and pegs to hang clothes, a closet for dishes, strips on the roof to keep out the rain, if we should have one, new boards on the sides of the imposing shanty, so that inquisitive people could not see what was going on inside, and, while working, he was driving his countryman by words and actions to make greater exertions in his labors, shooting at his head all sorts of pigeon English, and a mixture of guttural sounds, that reminded me of an eager boy, who wants to talk when his mouth is full.

Where the lumber came from I did not know, but I think that Gin compelled the young Chinaman to go and find it, and bring it to him. He might have stolen it, or he possibly got trusted. I never heard the full particulars, and received no bill.

"Gin," I said, as he stopped to rest for a moment, "where did you pick up your countryman?"

"Oh, hee bellie goodie manie. Meie knowie hime muchie. Noie paye for alle dis workie. Gibe hime grubbie, dat alle."

I could well afford to do that, and he had a square meal at the boarding-house, and by sundown all of our furniture was in place, the table set, our few clothes hung up, the mattresses spread on the floor, candles lighted, a good pot of tea ready, some hard tack, and a can of preserved meat opened, and we were all ready to commence housekeeping in earnest, or just as soon as Mike made his appearance, and he could be looked for any day. The Chinamen would not sit down to the table with me, although I invited them to do so. They preferred to wait, they said, until I had concluded my frugal meal. They evidently felt that I was some person of importance, and I fear that Gin Sling romanced to his companion when telling of my remarkable deeds in the forest. At first I did not know but that the Chinamen had concocted a little scheme to steal the big nugget, and murder me, but then I thought Gin would not have intrusted to me all his savings, and asked for no account of the same, and I was the more persuaded that no harm was intended by his covering the mouth of the shaft with some logs which had been hauled to the mine by the previous owners to keep the sides of the shaft in place in case the depth required it.

"Tomorrowe," said Gin, as I rose from the table, "meie builde once ittie roome fore youe. Den bellie goode fore alle."

I liked the plan, and said that I would find some lumber. It would give me a room to myself of an evening, or when I wanted to read and write. The expense would be but a trifle, and three of us could build the annex in a day.

We moved from the boarding-house that night, and took up permanent quarters in our shanty, and, after we had lighted our room with candles, it did not look so bad and uninviting, and I rather felt proud to think that I was the owner of such a unique establishment. Gin Sling and his friend wanted to run over to the Chinese quarters, and see some of the disciples of Confucius, and, as I had no objection, off they went, and I was left with my pipe, and a late Melbourne paper, *The Boomerang*, which my landlady had given me just as I took leave of her. I did not expect to see in the journal anything that would interest me, but I spread it on the table, and the first article that my eye fell on was the following: —

The Belle of Australia.

"MARRIAGE IN HIGH LIFE. — We learn that the young and wealthy Earl of Afton was **united in holy wedlock last evening to the beautiful and accomplished daughter of our affluent and respected fellow-citizen, Anderson Kebblewhite, Esq., wool merchant, Collins Street. The lady has been known for the last two years as the Belle of Australia, and she is justly entitled** to that flattering distinction, as her beauty is **something** to be remembered for many years if seen but once. The wedding **was quite** private, only the immediate family friends **being present.** This announcement will cause some **heart-aches in our city, when it is read by the young gentlemen,** who have **followed in Miss** Kebblewhite's train ever since **she entered** society, some **two years ago, and numerous** have been the handsome offers which the **young lady has received, but to** all she turned **a deaf ear,** until his lordship arrived **here in the frigate** *Carrysford,* **a passenger and** friend of **Lord** George **Pollock, the captain, last from Hong Kong, China,** just four weeks since. **This is quick matrimonial work, but proves that love is impulsive, and not to be restrained by society's formal demands** for delay. The earl **is only nineteen years of age, and has an income of three hundred thousand pounds a year, beside castles, lands, and jewels, all of** the **value of** two or **three million pounds sterling. He is the sixth Earl of** Afton, we believe, **and has a mother living, the dowager Countess of Afton, but no brothers or sisters. This** wedding **has made a great sensation in the city, and is considered the best match of the day, for** while **the noble** bridegroom **has** birth, the bride has great **beauty,** more than enough **to counterbalance her husband's rank** and wealth. **Thus** another tie is formed **of** flowers and **gold, silk and happiness, to bring our** prosperous colony **nearer and nearer to the mother country. Our reporter** was not able **to see** the bride, **as the wedding was private, but one of the servants said that she '**looked **'eavenly,' and no** doubt but **that she did, still it would have been a** little more in **accordance with our free institutions if the doors of the** mansion had been **thrown** open, and the press invited **to enter, and take a few** notes of the **dresses,** the bridal-chamber, **and other matters which would** interest our fair lady readers. Neither is it **just such treatment as our** reporter is accustomed to, to have the outer **door slammed in his face, when he asks a few** pertinent questions of a very **uncivil man servant, or butler, as the** people of Victoria Parade now **call any human being clothed in livery. We do not want a** bloated **aristocracy in Australia at any time. We** can get along without it, **just at present, and for years to come, and we will** state, for the information of whom it may concern, that the threat to set a bull-dog on the **person of a** gentleman of the press, **did not cause a** particle of fear in the heart of a man who has faced the enemies of Her Majesty, God bless her! in more ways than one, and is ready to do so again, if necessary. Our citizens like fair play, and will sustain the press in protecting the liberties of the people, even if they have to wade through blood knee deep to accomplish their object. We do not mention this matter because we care to participate in the festivities of a wedding in high life, but simply as one of our rights, and will have them, regardless of uncivil menials, or threats of bull-dogs. Where there is news to be had we shall endeavor to obtain it, regardless of expense, and so we dismiss this wedding in high life, with the wish that the young couple may enjoy the future as they have the past, and, when they visit England, will exert their influence for some modification of the postal laws, so that a newspaper, as valuable and useful as ours, can be sent through the mails at half the present rates. The Earl of Afton is called a very handsome young gentleman. We were presented to him at the governor's reception, and would have explained to him many things that relate to the welfare of Australia, but his lordship was wearied by the bores who surrounded him, and only gaped and yawned as he saw that they were determined to talk him to death. It is a little singular that some of our well-meaning people do not know enough to take a hint when in the presence of first-class society. However, we have been reliably informed that his lordship reads our valuable journal every morning at the breakfast-table, and no doubt he has noted our able leading articles, and reflected on them, and will avail himself of the knowledge which they contain to be used hereafter in the House of Peers. Our old-fashioned contemporary, always a year behind in news and enterprise, never yet enjoyed the distinction of being perused by a real earl, at breakfast, or at any other time. We shall still keep the price of our journal at one penny a single copy, or one pound ten shillings a year, in spite of the expense which we are constantly adding to our establishment, to produce a paper second to none in the world. This may cause our poor, spiritless contemporary to squirm, but talent and enterprise will succeed, and we shall be found willing to give an account of the lady in her boudoir, her dresses and toilettes, as well as the grave complications at the government house, by a fractious ministry, disappointed and angry at being foiled in an attempt to rob the people of their rights. Papers in wrappers can always be had at the counting-room."

"THE VERY LATEST. — SOMETHING MYSTERIOUS AND REMARKABLE. — Just as we were going to press, at three o'clock this morning, a report reached our office of so remarkable a nature, that we sent a special messenger to a free-and-easy, where our reporter was presiding, to summon him to the office for active service. There was no time to lose if we would keep at the head of the journals of Melbourne. It seems incredible, no doubt, but the young Earl of Afton suddenly and mysteriously vanished a few hours after his marriage with the handsomest lady in the country. He disappeared, and no one knew where he had gone, or his reasons for going. Our reporter was instantly despatched to the mansion of Mr. Kebblewhite, to learn the full particulars of this unhappy affair. He saw that the house was all blazing with light, and that people were moving back and forth, as though much excited, while every few minutes a hansom dashed up to the front-door, and some one alighted, and went into the mansion for consultation, and then re-entered the carriage, and was driven off at a rapid gait. Our reporter, sheltered by a cedar-tree, and thus out of sight of the inmates of Mr. Kebblewhite's house, knew that it was useless to apply at the front-door for information, so skipped around to the rear, and saw one of the young ladies connected with the household, holding the important position of chamber-maid, or assistant seamstress. She was questioned very closely by our reporter, and told that she need not say anything to implicate or criminate herself in any way, but that she must speak the truth, and be very quick about it, if she would save much trouble to herself, and the whole family. Upon this cheerful assurance the young lady said that she had been stationed at the head of the front stairs, to indicate to his lordship the room he was to occupy, and that at a late hour — she could not be assured of the precise time, although questioned very closely on that point by our reporter, who has attended many sessions of the police court — his lordship came up-stairs, all smiles and blushes, but when he saw the young lady who acts as assistant seamstress, or chamber-maid, his smiles suddenly ceased, and he looked at her fixedly, without saying a word, for several seconds. Then he sighed deeply, put his arm around her waist, and kissed her several times in rapid succession, before he let up. The young lady was so astonished at this remarkable act of a nobleman on his bridal night, that she did not offer the least resistance, and could not have screamed if he had kissed her a dozen times more, only she was fearful her 'missus' was looking through the keyhole. Then his lordship slipped a sovereign in her hand, and told her to keep mum (and she always should), and she showed our reporter the sovereign, and told him the date that it bore, but refused to let him take the coin in his own hands, even under a sacred promise to return it the next day, and then a still more solemn obligation to hold it but for a few minutes. The young lady's word can be implicitly relied on, as she has been in the country for fifteen years, and her sentence expired some three years ago, having been transported for setting a house on fire, in the hope of burning her father and new step-mother. Upon being asked, quite candidly, what she supposed was the real cause of his lordship's sudden disappearance, she blushed quite vividly, and hesitated, but our reporter pressed the question home to her, and then she thought that the young earl had suddenly felt as though he had made a mistake in marrying so hastily, and before he had looked around a little, and seen some young ladies, who might not be rich, yet had just as much beauty as some other young ladies who were wealthy, and that after he had seen her, and kissed her, he felt that there was no longer any happiness in this world for him, and he had fled the house, and committed suicide. Upon being asked if the earl had ever seen her before, she said that she had at one time met him in the hall, and that his lordship had looked at her quite fixedly, and then stumbled over a dust-pan, and said a wicked word, a method which noblemen have of paying a compliment to women whom they like. Upon being further pressed the young lady said that the word sounded like 'damn.' She was quite certain that his lordship was sober when he came up-stairs. He had been drinking freely, but he could walk straight, and talked quite nicely. She had freed herself from his embrace as soon as she thought of the keyhole, and she saw him enter the proper chamber, and she had listened at the door for half an hour, or more, she could not tell which, and she heard low talking, but could not make out any words, and all at once her mistress tumbled down, and she ran in, and saw that his lordship had fled through a window, and that her young lady was lying on the floor, nearly speechless, and crying out that she 'wanted her mamma.' Of course there was a tumult, and a doctor was sent for, and Mr. Kebblewhite and his son, and Monsieur Allete, searched the whole city to find his lordship, and punish him, and we are glad to know that they did not, for we want no lynching in Melbourne, or blood shed. The law is sufficient to protect the highest, and the lowest, the rich and the poor. The press must frown upon such meditated violence, no matter where it comes from.

"After squeezing the young lady quite dry, our reporter visited several of the houses situated on Victoria Parade, and, after hard ringing and pounding on the doors, was enabled to arouse the inmates, and put questions to them as to the disappearance of his lordship. Most of the neighbors did not seem pleased with the Kebblewhites, and so told our reporter to go to a hotter place than Australia, and that the whole tribe of Kebblewhites might follow, for all they cared. As it was near four o'clock in the morning, it is probable the good people felt a little annoyed that they were not invited to the wedding, and so have a chance to read their names in print. We thank our fellow-citizens for answering our reporter's questions so plainly, but the elderly party, who emptied a pail of slops on his person, will be looked after if he is ever before our police court, and his whole record, from the time he was transported until the present period, will be brought to light.

"Of course our reporter found our able, efficient, courageous, and gentlemanly Chief of Police, Mr. Murden, in his office, and smoking a choice cigar, from the store of Cabbage & Growem, Russell Street, first door on the right. He was asked for all the facts connected with the case, and he said that he was not prepared to furnish them just at that time, as such information would defeat the ends of justice. We can assure the citizens, however, that the Chief has his eye on his lordship, and could put his hand on him at any time, if it was really necessary. His lordship has not committed suicide, and there are twenty mounted police on his trail, and they will be heard from in due time. The Chief says his lordship had one peculiarity which was not generally known. After he had drank three bottles of champagne, or more, he was liable to be troubled with aberration of mind, and not to know where his home really was located, and to mistake other peoples' wives for his own, and to deny that he was a lord, but still no alarm need be felt. He was married to the Belle of Australia, and that lady is now the Countess of Afton, whether he returns to the Kebblewhite mansion or not. Our efficient Chief of Police will give our reporter the first information that is received, and our citizens can be assured that as long as we have as active, as brave, and as gentlemanly a person as Mr. Murden for Chief of our police force, no wrong-doer will escape punishment, whether he be nobleman or plebeian.

"We hope to have a few more facts in time for an extra this forenoon, but can't promise, as our reporter, tired and wet, is now drinking unlimited quantities of gin and sugar to keep out the cold. Of course, after this, we shall raise his salary five shillings a week, thus making him the munificent donation of fifteen shillings a week for his services, and they are worth it. Hereafter he will be able to dress so as to mingle in the best society, and will be *comme il faut* as regards costume, which, for the information of our contemporary, as it neither understands French, nor the best of Queen's English (God bless her), means that our reporter will be about as good as they make them, and able to hold up his head with the best in the land, at the governor's house, or private residences.

"In the mean time we tender our sympathies to Mr. Kebblewhite and his distressed family, and especially to that young wife who has thus early realized how hard is the road to happiness when a coronet is in perspective. No steps, we hope, will be taken for a divorce until after a full explanation, and, in the mean while, we offer our columns to the lady, the noble lord, or the father, for a full and free discussion of the merits of the affair, reserving to ourselves the privilege of writing quite freely for or against either party, and, in the mean time, our paper will be sold for one penny single copy, or at the usual yearly rates, and advertisements inserted on liberal terms, with displayed head lines."

When I had finished reading this delectable piece of scandal, my pipe was out, and my happiness, also, for I could have shed tears of vexation at the manner in which Florence's name had been introduced by the reporter of the paper. It was evident that the affair had created an intense excitement in town, and that I was looked after quite sharply by the police, and others, but I did not anticipate that any one would discover in me the noble lord who had made so much trouble in the city. How my heart beat for my poor little wife, and I wondered if she suffered much on my account, and if she was really ill from mortification and grief? and then I remembered her beauty and her grace, and I could see her sweet smile as she looked up in my face on the night of the wedding.

While I was musing over my misery, and the unfortunate publicity of my kissing that confounded chamber-maid, and wondering why she should lie so outrageously about the number of times my lips met hers, when I was ready to swear on the Bible that I had kissed her but once, and then under a slight aberration of mind, the door opened unceremoniously, without the formality of a knock, and in walked an old man, bent, wrinkled, and gray, and none too clean.

"Evenin', mate," he said. "I 'as called in a friendly way, 'cos yer is a neighbor of mine, and I makes it a pint to call on all the green ones, and give 'em a little bit of adwice. Yer 'as got a bad claim, but don't yer be put hout as long as yer 'as me to adwise yer. A bit of 'baccy vould n't be bad jist now, and a little sumthin' to drink vould not be amiss, but don't yer trouble yerself. I 'll take rum or beer."

I gave him a piece of tobacco and a pipe, and a glass of beer, and my caller made himself at home in a very cool manner.

"Yes," he said, although I had not addressed him, "as yer say, I'm the oldest miner at Ballarat. I vos 'ere ven the fust gold vos taken hout, and I 'elped to do it. A little more 'baccy, please, and another glass of beer. Thank yer, sir. 'Ere 's to yer, and my respects, and all that."

MINERS' SPORTS.

He blew out a cloud of smoke, and then resumed the thread of his remarks: —

"Lord, vot times ve did 'ave, to be sure, ven the gold vas fust diskivered 'ere. Ve took it hout by the pound, and I 'as made as much as a 'undred puns a week, and my mates as much more. O Lord, the fortunes vot ve has squandered. Three times I 'as 'ad all the money vot I vanted, and three times it 'as gone. Ve used to jist go to a store, and clean it hout, and then pay for heverything vot ve smashed. Did yer notice the 'Digger's Rest' place, jist to the right of us? Vel, sir, me and my mates 'as jist gone up there of a hevenin', taken all the champagne vot the cove 'ad on 'and, and then set the bottles up, make believe they was ten-pins, and ve vould throw bottle arter bottle at 'em, and smash 'em to the right and left, and the miner vot did the most damage vos the best feller. I 'd like some of that vine now, sir, to treat yer vith, and some of the money, too, vot the sport cost me."

He reached out his hand for more tobacco, and then left me, after borrowing a shilling until the next day. He did not return the money, but was a frequent visitor to my quarters after that introduction. But his story, as I afterward learned, was true. He had been just so extravagant.

After the old miner had left me, I sat all alone, and smoked my pipe, and so the evening passed away, and was thinking of retiring for the night, when some one knocked very lightly at the door. Wondering who my caller was, I got up and opened the door, and saw a woman standing before me, in the dark, with a shawl and veil on shoulders and face. She did not speak, but stood there looking at me very attentively.

"Have you made a mistake in the place?" I asked, as I raised the candle, so that I could get a view of my visitor's face, and wondered if it was young and handsome.

"No, Angus, I 'as made no mistake," was the reply, and, to my surprise, the veil was brushed aside, and I saw before me the pretty face of Miss Kitty Stukely.

I started back, and could only look at the girl, and wonder what sent her to Ballarat, and what evil genius had brought her to my shanty, the very person whom I did not wish to see, situated as I was, with the suspicious Chief of Police likely to drop in on me at any time, and to accuse me of breaking my word.

"Yer do not treat me, Angus, as though yer vere glad to see me," said the girl. "Yer do not even ask me to enter yer 'ouse, yet I 'ave come many miles at yer request."

"My request, Kitty? Surely you have made a mistake. I sent you no request," I cried.

"Vill yer let me enter the 'ouse?" she asked, "and I 'll soon prove that yer sent for me, or I should not 'ave dared come."

I motioned for her to enter, and she came in, and threw off her shawl, and sank down on a chair with a weary sigh. She looked tired and distressed, and I felt a pang of pity for her unfortunate condition.

"I vould not 'ave come, Angus," she said, "if yer 'ad not sent for me to meet yer. But now that yer did vrite for me to come, I hexpected that yer vould be glad to see me."

"Kitty, my poor girl," I cried, "I did not send for you. I never saw you until the evening I called with the Chief of Police. There is some strange mistake in the matter."

"There ha'n't no mistake in the matter at all," she replied, while a tear trickled down her face, and she could only keep back her sobs by a powerful effort.

She put her hand in her bosom, and took out a letter, stained and frayed.

"Read that," she said, "and see if I 'as made a mistake."

I read the note,—a few lines asking her to meet her dear friend Angus at Webber's as soon as possible. It was dated four days before, and I must confess that the writing closely resembled mine, so much so that unless I had known most positively that I had not written it, I should have supposed that I was the author.

"Vell?" she asked, after a long pause.

"Kitty, I did not write this note. Some person who resembles me did, but I am not the one."

"You are married, Angus?" she asked in a low tone, and with a gasp.

"Yes, Kitty, I am married."

"And yer fled from yer vife the wery night yer vos vedded?" she continued.

"That is a matter I do not wish to discuss with you, Kitty."

"Vos it because of me, Angus?"

"It had nothing to do with you, Kitty."

"Vos it 'cos yer loved me better than yer vife? Hanswer me that, Angus."

I felt a thrill of indignation at the question, and was about to express it, when I saw that the girl was sincere in putting the interrogation, for her eyes were filled with tears, and her pretty face was troubled.

"Kitty, I love my dear little wife with all my heart, and all my soul, and be assured that I do not love you, that I never have loved you, and never can."

She uttered a faint cry, and a bitter sob, and fell into a chair, and laid her fair head on the table. I waited for her to recover her composure, but made no attempts to console her for my blunt, plain words. At last she raised her face, and, although she showed how much she suffered, said,—

"Yer leaves yer vife on the night of yer veddin', yer sends me a letter to meet yer at Vebber's, and yet yer say yer don't love me. I don't hunderstand it. Can yer hexplain?"

"Yes, Kitty. I am not the person who has made love to you. It is somebody who resembles me, but I am not the man. Of that be most thoroughly assured."

"And yer hexpects me to believe hall that?" she demanded, in an indignant tone.

"Yes, Kitty, I expect that you will, because you are a sensible little girl, and know that I would not deceive you."

She gave a sniff of scorn, and tossed her head. She was not convinced by my words, I could see that very plainly.

"Angus," she said, trying to speak calm and firm, although it was with an effort, "I met Mr. Murden, the Chief of Police, the night yer was married. 'E told me that yer vos vedded, and 'e 'inted that yer might come and seek me, and that if yer should I was to refuse to see yer, and he made some strong remarks in case I did. I promised that I vould not let yer 'ave a hinterview vid me if yer come to my 'ouse that night, and 'e vent avay satisfied that I vould keep my vord. I vos wery unhappy, until the next mornin' ven I sees by the paper that yer had cut and run for it, and left yer vife in the lurch. I felt quite 'appy ven I reads hall that, and I vos still more pleased ven I gets this letter from yer to come to Vebber's. I 'as but little money, Angus, but I knows that a great swell like yer vill 'ave enough for me ven I sees yer, so I takes the mail coach, jist as soon as I could, and starts, and ven I gets to Vebber's a bold, flat-faced Dutch girl says that yer is 'ers, and that I 'as no business to go around the country a lookin' for men, and she vould n't 'ave me in the 'ouse, but I learns that yer 'as gone on to Ballarat, vid a man named Mike, and I follows in the next coach, and ven I gets 'ere I axed and axed, and at last I finds yer, and 'ere I am, Angus."

"And here you must not remain, Kitty. No money could induce me to give you shelter for even one night. You must go," and I spoke firmly.

"Leave yer?" she asked, in tones a little louder than necessary.

"Yes, Kitty."

"But yer sent for me, yer know."

"No, Kitty, I did not send for you. I have told you that I did not several times, and you will not believe me."

She uttered a wail, and wrung her hands. I dreaded a scene, but now that one must come prepared for it.

"Angus," she cried, falling on her knees, and clasping my hands, "do 'ave pity on me, do love me a little. Please not send me avay from yer, Let me stay 'ere, and be vith yer. I vill vait upon yer, do yer 'ousework. take care of yer if yer is sick, and love yer hall the time, and never be un 'appy if yer vill but smile on me. I knows that I am a poor girl, and a'n't vorth the love of a swell like yer, but yer von't never find no one vot loves yer like me. Don't turn me avay from yer, Angus. I'm poor, and I 'as not dosh enough to takes me back to Melbourne, unless I valks, and that vould not be safe for me ven so many bushrangers is round. They vould not respect me, if they should meet me in the road. Let me kiss yer 'and, Angus, and bless yer for being kind to the un'appy girl vot did not love no one till she met yer at Jobber's free-and-heasy. Yer knows the night, don't yer, Angus? I did not hexpect a swell like vot yer vos to take notice of me, and ven yer did, I thinks that life vos more pleasant for me, and that the sun shone brighter, the flowers looked sweeter, and that hevery one vos more 'appy. Yer taught me to love yer, and now let me teach yer 'ow to love me. I'm a poor girl, Angus, but I is rich in 'avin' a varm 'eart, and its varmth is hall for yer."

She held my hands, and kissed them in the most tender manner, and I could not release them without exerting all of my strength, and, as soon as I did succeed, she clasped my knees, and held me fast, so that I could not break away from her firm embrace.

What to do I did not know, yet I was just as firm in denying all knowledge of the girl, as when she first entered the hut. I would not yield, be the temptation what it might. I had a wife, a dear little wife, and as long as the union was undissolved I would revere her, and be worthy of her, even if she repudiated me, and did not respect me. I loved her, and it was useless to attempt to supplant that love while her face was ever before me, glorious in its beauty and innocence. Yet here was a poor girl, kneeling at my feet, and begging for a word and smile, simply to make her happy. It was hard, but I had to be firm, and do what few men of my age would have done. It made my heart bleed, but the sacrifice had to be made, and the quicker the better.

"Kitty," I said, as sternly as I could.

"No, no, do not speak to me in that tone," she cried. "I can't endure it. Be kind to poor Kitty, and remember that she 'as traveled night and day to join yer, thinkin' of yer love and yer 'appiness. Let me rest at yer feet until I am assured yer vill take me to yer 'eart."

"Kitty, you poor child," I cried, as I laid my hand on her head, and put an arm around her waist, lifting her to a chair, "you must be calm, and listen to me as attentively as you can. I am not the person who made love to you simply to occupy a leisure hour. Be assured of that. I am a poor man, have come here to seek my fortune, and hope to find it in time. If I was the person you suppose, do you think I would be in this miserable hut, wearing these rough clothes, and prepared to search for gold in mud and water? It is absurd, and your good sense should teach you different. There is a man who is said to resemble me, and he is called an earl, and very rich. He has caused all this trouble, and all your unhappiness and mine. He is young and thoughtless, and thinks it sport to play with a woman's heart. I do not, Kitty, and you should see the difference between us without this long explanation. Trust me, Kitty, and be assured that I speak the truth. Come, be a good little girl, and clear your eyes of tears, and then smile once more."

"And vill yer love me?" she asked, looking up, hope once more beaming on her bright face.

She did not believe a word that I said. I could see it in her eyes. She thought I was lying to her.

"Do not talk of love to me, Kitty," I said. "Let me be a friend to you, one who will advise you, and be kind to you, but not a lover. Do not speak of love."

"I don't care vot yer calls it, if yer vill only love me," she answered, and I sighed to think what little progress I was making in trying to set things right. Every instant I expected the two Chinamen back, and Mike might arrive at any moment. How could I explain to them the presence of the girl? She must leave the hut, and I would find her comfortable quarters until the next day, and then ship her home by the mail carriage, which made the run between Melbourne and Ballarat in ten or fifteen hours, according to the condition of the roads, and darkness of the nights, and will of bushrangers.

"Kitty, you can't remain here tonight," I said. "You must be under the protection of a good woman, who will take care of you, see that you have some supper, and a good night's rest. I will furnish you with the money to return to the city, and pay all your expenses here. This is the best that I can do for you, poor child, but do not talk to me of love, for I swear to you that you can have no place in my heart. My wife alone occupies it, and ever will."

She uttered a loud wail, and shed more tears, and begged, but I was firm, and at last got her calmed down until she agreed to go with me to the boarding-house, and remain all night, under the protection of Mother Higgins, as the boys called the old English lady who carried on the establishment.

We set out, Kitty half-crying and half-begging me to once more take her into favor. It was eight o'clock when we reached the house, and I took Mother Higgins aside, and asked her as a favor to me to give shelter to Kitty, and to see that all her wants were supplied, and to look to me for payment of her bills.

Mother Higgins sniffed, as though she smelled something disagreeable, and then she looked at me, and sniffed some more, and glanced at Kitty, and sniffed louder than ever.

"I know what you suspect," I said; "but I swear to you that your suspicions are unjust and cruel. Would I be likely to come to a lady like you if there was wrong? This poor girl has made a sad mistake in coming here in search of a lover. She has not found him, and is in distress. Will you not let your big, motherly heart expand for one unfortunate?"

She sniffed worse than ever, but finally consented to take charge of Kitty for the night, and give her a shake-down in her own room, and would also get her a good supper, and a cup of tea. This was all that I could expect, and I thanked the old lady for her kindness.

"Humph," cried Mother Higgins, as she rubbed her nose with a bit of tallow from the candle she held in her hand, and looked at me, and then at Kitty, in wondering surprise, "I 've been married three times, and am now a widow woman, and open to a good offer, and I 'll say this, that you are the most wonderful man I ever saw, or you are the biggest hypocrite. I don't know which, but time will tell."

"I hope that time will convince you that I am just what I seem, an honest young man, of moral and religious character," I replied.

I thought that would have some effect on her, just as I had tried it on my wife, but Mother Higgins only snorted harder than ever, and told me not to give her "sour beer," or any more of my gab, for she really believed I was as big a devil as any of 'em, and none of 'em were any too good for this world. She knew: she had tried three men, and she doubted if either was in heaven, or likely to get there. Most of them, when alive, cared more for swipes than they did for her, and, in fact, she rather hated men, after all, only she really had rather have twenty men boarders than one woman, as the latter were always grunting and groaning about the house, and turning up their ridiculous noses at the grub, and wanting to wash in the kitchen at all hours, and to put on irons just at the most inconvenient moment. In fact, she did not care for the whole human race, man or woman, and thought the world would be better off without either. But still the old lady patted me on the shoulder, and said I was a good boy, and she would be a mother to me as long as I was in the mines; that I must be careful and not make love to every girl I met, for I had such a look as would induce the fools to think I was in earnest.

"Good-by, Kitty," I said, when ready to go. "I hope you will have a good night's rest. I will see you in the morning, and arrange about your passage to Melbourne."

"Good-night, Angus, and God bless yer. I believe that yer means vell by me."

She gave me her hand, and put up her lips for a kiss. Mother Higgins sniffed, and turned her head. I kissed the girl, and left the house, and, as I was leaving, I thought that I heard the old lady mutter, in a doubting tone, —

"Humph! Moral and religious character is he. Well, they all like to kiss the girls if they do put on high-peaked airs."

The Chinamen had not arrived at the shanty when I returned, so I lighted my pipe, and sat down and had a smoke, and when Gin and his friend did come back it was nine o'clock, and time to turn in; but I was not sleepy after the adventures of the evening, and once more I took up the *Boomerang*, and read the account of the wedding, and the report of my escape from the matrimonial bonds, and there was no chance for me to write to the truthful journal, and set the editor right as to my motives for leaving so suddenly, and I could not even send a line to Florence, and deny the monstrous story that the chamber-maid had told, and I blamed myself for doing as I had done, and promised to be more careful in the future, if I had a chance to meet a smiling little girl at the head of a pair of stairs.

"Alle Chinaman saye dise noie goode minie," Gin remarked, as he removed his heavy, wooden-soled shoes, and kicked his countryman for making so much noise when he knocked over a chair.

"I have heard the same thing before, Gin," I remarked, a little impatiently.

"Stille, onee verie wisee Chinaman saye hee dinke somie golde rounde herie. Hee saye diggie, and seeie whate youe shalle seeie. Berrie wisie manie datie Chinaman. He drinkie morie teae, and seeie morie thingies, thane any manie meie ebber seeie," and Gin went to bed with his companion.

I had put out the light, and was just dropping off to sleep, when a loud rap at the door started me.

"Gin, get up, and see what is wanted," I said.

"Noie meie goe therie. ———— bushrangie arter Gin Sling."

With a muttered anathema on the courage of the Chinaman, I got up, lighted a candle, took my revolver, and went to the door.

"Who is there?" I demanded, in a stern tone.

"Open in the name of the law," was the reply, and, throwing back the bolt, I opened the door, and in stalked Mr. Murden, Chief of the Melbourne Police, booted and spurred, and covered with dust and perspiration, as though just from a long ride over the dry roads and trails, and the look he gave me as he entered was not a pleasant one, for I expected trouble, and found that it had come upon me before I was ready for it.

"IS IT A YANKA TRICK YER SPAKE OF, BUYS?" CRIED A FAMILIAR VOICE.

PART IX.

MR. MURDEN EXPRESSES HIS OPINION QUITE FREELY. — KITTY'S DISAP-
PEARANCE. — THE NUGGETS OF GOLD, AND HOW MUCH THEY
WERE WORTH. — A SALE OF THE MINE. — MY WIFE AND
HER FATHER, AND HOW THEY WENT AWAY. —
A SCHEME TO CAPTURE FLORENCE AND
HER FATHER BY BUSHRANGERS.
MIKE WANTS TO FIGHT
SOME ONE.

THE Chief of Police of Melbourne did not wait for an invitation to enter my humble quarters. He stalked in as though he had a right to come and go where he pleased, and at all hours of the day and night. As the door opened I caught a glimpse of two mounted officers, and that one of them held the horse that the Chief had just dismounted from, covered with foam and dust, like its rider. Mr. Murden raised his cap as he entered, and looked at me in a curious way, as though rather puzzled to see me in my rough, miner's garb, for I had not removed my clothes when lying down, and the two Chinamen, who dreaded the sight of a trap's uniform as they did a boy with a live rat tied by its tail, sat up on their mattresses, and turned more sallow than ever from fright, for they feared imprisonment, and punishment, for some former invasion of the mining tax, which they hoped had been forgotten by the police.

The Chief stared at me long and minutely, and I returned his fixed glance without flinching or speaking. At length he said, —

" We have met again, my lord."

" So it seems. To what am I indebted for this unseasonable visit ? " I demanded.

" Can you ask, my lord ? "

" Yes, and very emphatically," I said.

" Do you remember our last meeting, my lord ? Think for a moment before you speak."

" I do. It was an unhappy one for me, and I hoped never to have the pleasure of seeing your face again."

" You are complimentary, my lord," with a short, sneering laugh.

" I do not mean to be. I speak just as I feel. You promised to no longer molest me, and yet I see that you have followed my trail, and run me down, for what purpose I know not."

" You shall soon be enlightened. You must return with me to Melbourne, and to the countess, your lawful wife."

" Did she send you to arrest me, and drag me into her presence ? " I asked, and for a moment I trembled, and felt a little faint, at the anticipation of meeting her.

" She desires to see you," was the short answer. " A reward is offered for your return. Did you know it ? "

" So I have heard. You naturally wish to earn the reward," I said, in a bantering tone.

A dark flush showed itself on the Chief's face, but he could command his temper, and did.

" I have no desire for the reward, but I wish to make an unhappy lady happy, if it is in my power to do so. My lord, you will return with me."

" I shall not do so unless you have a letter from the lady saying that she forgives my deception, and desires to see me. Have you such a letter ? "

" No, my lord, I have not," was the prompt response.

" I did not suppose that you had."

" Nevertheless, my lord, I trust that you will go with me. You have caused much distress in a good family, and now you should make all the reparation in your power. That can be done by returning with me without delay."

"And you still think, wise Chief that you are, that I am the Earl of Afton?" I asked, in a bantering tone.

"My lord, I know that you are. I have followed you foot by foot all the way from Melbourne here. I kept just in the rear of the girl you wrote to, asking her to join you at Webber's. You were suspicious that I would be on your trail, and sent word to Kitty, by an old Quaker, that you would meet her near Ballarat, on the road, somewhere between this place and the cross-roads. I thought it was a blind, and did not fall into what I supposed was a trap. At Webber's I had learned two things, — that you had been seen talking with two suspicious persons, and then I also learned from Webber's daughter that you had arrived at her father's in company with an Irishman, a fellow called Mike, whose ticket-of-leave has just expired. I got information that you had made love to Katrine. Nay, man, don't frown at me in that manner. It is true, and you know it. I am aware of all that has transpired since you left the city. I trailed you to the cross-roads, and then lost sight of you, but I suspected that you had gone to your father-in-law's sheep run, where Mike has charge. I paid it a visit in the night time, for I did not desire to give you warning. I found Mike, but he was closer than the bark of a she-oak-tree, and pretended to know nothing about you, except that he had given a lift to a poor young fellow, who had left him on the road, and gone he knew not where, but he thought to some sheep station, to find work, but in what location he could not imagine. You are paying strict attention to all that I say, my lord?"

"Oh, yes. It interests me to see what an immense amount of trouble you have taken to earn that hundred pounds. I would have given you more to let me alone, and let my name die, and be forgotten, as I hope it will after a while."

"All that will happen in good time, my lord, if you continue your present disgraceful career. I am not working this thing for money, but for fame. I would not accept a penny for what I have done, but I will receive a grateful woman's thanks for saving her husband from numerous follies, such as he is old enough to avoid. I am responsible for your marriage, and, as I am thus responsible, I mean to hold on to you by the powerful arm of the law until you cease to play the madman, and make Irishmen, miners, and stockmen's daughters the objects of your idle life. When this is done we will separate, and not until then."

"Go on," I said. "I feel quite interested in your struggles for my welfare. Have you more to say?"

"Yes," the Chief cried, in a burst of passion. "In spite of being baffled and misled, I followed, and traced Kitty to this shanty, and here she is. My lord, you promised me most faithfully never to see that girl again. Have you kept your word? Answer me that."

"Yes, as far as was in my power," I replied.

"Then why did you write to her, and ask for an appointment?" the Chief demanded.

"I did not write to her, and did not ask for an appointment," I said, boldly and calmly.

"My lord, you should weigh well your words. The letter Kitty received I read before it reached her hands."

"Then you tampered with her correspondence, and opened a letter in an unlawful manner. It should cost you your commission, Mr. Chief."

"I run my risk for the sake of the public good. I suspected that I could find you through the girl. My surmises were correct. I watched for letters, and found the one you sent to her. It was unmanly, my lord, and is not to your credit, after your pledges."

"Mr Murden," I said, as calmly as I could, "the girl has made the same mistake that you have. She sought me, I did not seek her. She has been here this evening, and I need not tell you that from the bottom of my heart I pity her, and would help her in her hour of trouble, if I could do so in a manly manner."

"She is with you, and you must give her up," was the stern command of the Chief. "I shall take her from you."

"She is not with me, but under the protection of a Mrs. Higgins, a good and kind woman, who keeps a boarding-house in this place."

The Chief nodded, and then glanced around the room, as though expecting to see Kitty.

"I know whom you mean. She is a good-hearted woman. But you will permit me to search your room. I wish to be positive, my lord, that Kitty is not here."

The Chief took the candle, and with a motion of his booted and spurred foot indicated to the Chinamen that they must get up. They responded with alacrity to the command, for they knew that if they did not a kick would hasten their movements.

"Lift up that mattress," Mr. Murden said to the Chinamen, in a harsh tone.

Gin Sling obeyed, but I am sure that he said something wicked in his native tongue, for he did not dare to swear in English to the officer.

The Chief examined the floor long and earnestly. He suspected a trap in the badly fitted boards, and that I had concealed the girl beneath them. He went over the walls, and then, feeling satisfied, put the candle on the table, and looked at me a little puzzled.

"Are you satisfied?" I asked, for I had remained standing all this time.

"Yes, that the girl is not here."

"I have convinced you that I spoke the truth. Now let me further prove to you that I am not the person you think I am," I said.

"You will have a nice time to do that, my lord," with a grin that was very provoking. "Did you, or did you not, marry Miss Kebblewhite?"

"I did marry the lady. I do not deny it, and very proud I should be of the fact under other circumstances."

The Chief shrugged his broad shoulders, and smiled.

"Go on," he said.

"Do you think that if I was a lord, and had all the money that a lord is supposed to possess, that I would be here, in a miner's costume, and consorting with Chinamen?" I demanded.

"Noblemen have queer freaks. You are not the first who has led a wandering life, and associated with the scum of the earth," motioning to the two Chinamen, who were listening with wonder depicted on their yellow faces, yet did not dare to move or speak.

"I have heard of such insane freaks; but did you ever know a noble lord to write to a young girl for an appointment, and when she came put her under the care of an honest woman, so that she could be returned to her friends in the morning?" I demanded.

The Chief thought of the question a few seconds before he asked, —

"You have done all that, my lord?"

"Yes, sir, I have done all that, and have nothing to feel ashamed of as far as that young girl is concerned."

"I don't think that I ever heard of a nobleman acting as you say you have done unless insane, and blank me if I don't believe that you are," was the blunt exclamation.

"No, Mr. Murden, I am not insane, but I am honest, and try to be good. Of that be assured."

"Oh, stock it," was the reply, as though such words grated on his ears. "Don't preach, my lord, or I swear I shall suspect you of worse crimes than those which you are supposed to have committed. Whenever I hear a man prating of his goodness and virtue, I always tell my officers to watch the fellow, and see what lay he is on. As a man of the world you have no occasion to act a part. Be natural as you can."

"I am not acting a part, Mr. Murden, but I am trying to render myself worthy the wife I have deserted."

"Well, my lord, don't play it too fine, for, as a general thing, I don't believe that wives want perfect husbands. One who can lie a little, just enough to cast a shade of doubt on his lodge-night operations, is the man who is worshiped in domestic circles, not the one who reads prayers three times a day. The fact of it is, women like a little of the devil in mankind, because it agrees with their ideas of what they would be if men. You follow me, my lord?"

"No, I do not. I am too much in love with my wife to entertain those odious ideas for a moment," I said, a little proudly.

"Time will cure you of all such weaknesses, my lord. You are not the first one who has been in love with a wife, but you are the first one who refused to return to a wife as charming as the Belle of Australia. You will go back with me, my lord?"

"No, not until a year has elapsed will I appear before her. Then she will have learned to forget me, or to appreciate me for what I am."

The Chief shrugged his shoulders, his favorite protest.

"Your masquerading may have a design in it," he said. "I do not pretend to understand the whims of the quality. They are so mysterious that even a police officer can't spot them. But I will talk to you on this subject tomorrow. I have ridden all day under a hot sun, and am tired. I need rest. I can't endure as much as formerly. In the morning we will discuss the subject of your return to Melbourne. Have I your lordship's word that you will make no attempt to avoid me until then?"

"Certainly. I am here to stay, and to win a fortune, if possible. God grant that I shall."

"Your good fortune lies in Melbourne, and there I hope to see you soon. Your wife is far from well, and would welcome you most cordially, forgive you very cheerfully, and forget the greatest insult that can be inflicted on a woman, desertion on her bridal eve."

"She would welcome me as the Earl of Afton, I suppose?" I asked, a little bitterly.

"Of course, the countess should welcome her husband by his title. I don't know if people in high rank say 'duck,' and 'sweetness,' or simply 'my lord,' and 'my lady.' I used to call my wife 'old woman,' and she was accustomed to it, and rather liked it, but when she retaliated, and called me 'old man,' I thought it was time to stop, and return to first principles. Well, good-night, my lord. I will see you in the morning, I hope. Shall I kick the Chinamen out of the hut?"

"No, they are useful to me, and I have need of them. They are honest and industrious."

"You do not know them any more than you do the people of Australia. I tell you there is treachery in every glance of the fellows' eyes, in every movement of their hands. Keep them at a distance, if you know what is good for yourself. If you desire, I will leave one of my men here tonight to see that no harm happens to your lordship," the Chief said. It was evident he did n't love Chinamen.

"It is unnecessary, sir. I rescued one of the men from a terrible fate, in the bush, the other day, and I do not think he has forgotten the act quite as soon as this. I will run all risk, and, even if the Chinamen are as bad as you represent, I have a revolver to defend myself."

"Bah!" with an expression of disgust, "do you think the fellows would face you and your revolver? They are not of that kind. They attack in the rear, and use an axe or hatchet. I know them as well as I know the tricks of the black fellows. Come, my lord, be advised by me."

"Please do not call me a lord again, Mr. Murden. I am plain Angus Mornington, and do not wish to sail under false colors. As such I married my wife, and as such she must receive me, if she ever does."

"As you please, sir. But I will see you again in the morning," and then the Chief bowed, and left the shanty, and the terrified Chinamen laid down, and whispered in tea-box Chinese, and I once more went to sleep, and did not awaken until long after sunrise, and then I found that Gin Sling had arose, and got breakfast, and that it was waiting for me, with a nice pot of tea, and some hard-tack, and broiled mutton, the latter obtained from a fellow who hawked sheep through the camp, and made a profitable business out of it, as he stole most of his stock.

After breakfast the two Chinaman went to work on the annex of my hut. I bought a deserted shanty near mine for a song, tore it down, and removed the best part of the rubbish to my claim, and, after the celestials had got to work, went over to Mrs. Higgins's to make arrangements for Kitty's return to Melbourne by the noon stage.

To my surprise Mrs. Higgins did not respond to my good-morning with as much cordiality as she had exhibited the night before. In fact, she looked cross.

"How is Miss Kitty this morning?" I asked, with a winsome smile, and not a particle of guile in my heart.

Mrs. Higgins gave a sniff that could have been heard all along Sturt Street, and then expressed her opinion very forcibly.

"I said last night," she cried, "that you were either a fool or a hypocrite, and that time would show which. Time has shown."

"My dear Mrs. Higgins," I began, but the lady silenced me with a sniff that was like a steam-whistle.

"Don't dear me. I 'm an honest woman, thank God, and keeps a respectable house, and when I take people in 'cos other people want me to, and when those other people put on a soft look, and talk smooth, they can't come it over me but once, now I tell you," and there was a whole volley of sniffs.

"Will you explain what you mean, dear Mrs. Higgins?" I asked, quite humbly.

"Yes, sir, I will. I said I 'd be a mother to you, but I take it all back from last night. I 'll not be a mother to the likes of you," and there was a terrible sniff.

"Why, what have I done?" I demanded in astonishment.

"O Lord, hear him ask what he has done! You did n't come back to this house about nine o'clock last night, and say that you must see your Kitty without a moment's delay? You did n't rouse her out of bed, and catch her in your arms, and kiss her, and say that you had made a mistake, and did n't meet her just where you expected to? Oh, no, you did n't do all that, and then carry the girl off to a rough cart, and drive away? Oh, no, Mr. Innocence. Of course you would n't do such a thing," and her sniffs were something terrible to an honest, timid young man like myself, who thought that he had found a true friend in the motherly landlady, for had she not noticed me above all of her lodgers?

"Yes," she continued, her rage increasing as she talked, and thought of the great wrong she fancied I had done her, "I put confidence in your smooth, gentle ways, and your smooth, nice face, and your quiet, polite manner, and I thought that if ever there was an angel of a young man that you were one, and yesterday if you had asked me to be your own, true, hard-working wife, I should not have hesitated one moment to put my womanly trust in your keeping, and to have reposed my modest head on your breast, and found that rest that only a good, quiet woman like me can expect to find in one of your sex. But, bah! you are all alike. False as Satan where a female with a pretty face is concerned; and now let me tell you,

you mean, deceitful scamp, that if you should go down on your knees I would not marry you, so don't ask me. I 've had three husbands, and I know what men are capable of, I do."

"Do you mean to tell me that Kitty is gone?" I demanded, almost bewildered at the information, and the tirade of abuse.

"I mean to tell you that she is gone, as you well know, and she is where you well know, and for what purpose I don't wish to know. So there now."

"The man who took her away resembled me, did he?" I asked, still bewildered.

A scornful sniff, that knocked all preceding sniffs into a cocked hat, was the answer, accompanied by the words, —

"It was you, and there 's no use talking about it. Go away from me, and don't speak to me again."

"Yet, Mrs. Higgins, you are mistaken. It was not me, I do assure you most faithfully."

"And a pretty time I had of it this morning," she said, "when Mr. Murden called on me to see the girl, and found that you had run away with her. He swore awfully, and galloped off with a black tracker to find the trail. He said that you was the biggest liar on the face of the earth, and, faith, for once I agreed with him, for I think that way myself. Well, well, I 'm ready to believe anything of men now. Drat your impudence, what do you mean by insulting a respectable woman, who works hard for an honest living, and who has buried three husbands, by coming here with your innocent ways, and your smooth words, and making my home a place for your mistress? I 've a good mind to shake you as ever I had to eat my dinner. Get out of here, or I 'll scald you."

Mrs. Higgins was getting angry, and she had reason for her rage, if she really believed me capable of all that she charged. The Earl of Afton had played a mean trick, and I could not defend myself, strive hard as I would.

"The Chief has gone in search of me, has he?" I asked, after a moment's pause.

A sniff, and an angry look.

"He need not have gone far to find me, Mrs. Higgins. I did not leave my shanty from eight o'clock last night until an hour since, as I can prove by the two Chinamen, who slept in the same room with me."

"And do you think that I 'd take a Chinese heathen's word any sooner than I 'd take yours? You have only to lie, and they 'd swear to it for half a crown. Such testimony don't go down with me, now I tell you, so go along about your business, and don't come here with your innocent airs any more, or I'll hurt you. You'd corrupt a girls' boarding-school in a week's time, if you had your way."

She turned her back upon me, and was about to resume her usual hard day's labor, when I said,—

"At least you will let me pay for the trouble the girl occasioned you last night."

"You tossed me four sovereigns last evening when you went away, and that is pay enough. I'd scorn the money, but you might use it for a worse purpose than giving it to a hard-working woman, who has lost three husbands, and is as honest as the day is long, and wouldn't marry a fourth unless he was more moral, and better than you in every respect. But go your way, you good-looking imp of Satan, and don't provoke me, or I shall get mad. I have trials and temptations enough every day of my life, without standing here, and seeing your looks of pretended surprise, corrupting my servant-girls, leading them into temptation, and I know not what. I am a woman of few words, as all of my dear, dead husbands frequently used to say, and I never spend my time talking to man or woman, especially the latter, for they are too mean to live, some of them, and are just as bad as the men, only they won't own it, more is the shame for them, and if I had my way, I'd find a place for all of them good-for-nothing huzzies, mighty quick," and then Mother Higgins paused to take breath, and I put in a word.

"Please, my dear friend, don't think me as bad as you would make me," I said, very humbly.

"Don't dear me, sir. I'm not one of your dears, I'd have you to know. I'm an honest widow woman, and have buried three husbands, and you needn't think that you'll be the fourth, I can tell you. Now, there. Get out of my sight."

There was no more to be said, and, with a muttered malediction on my double, who was causing me all this trouble, and intense annoyance, I turned to leave the house, and had the satisfaction of hearing two stout Irish girls utter shouts of disparagement on account of my guilty conduct, yet both of those girls were on probation, and had been taken by the really good and motherly Mrs. Higgins, in hope of saving them, and of ultimately marrying them to sedate and elderly miners.

I returned to my hut and Chinamen in no enviable mood, and all day long labored at the addition to my shanty, and by night it was all ready for occupancy, washed and dried, papered with some old illustrated journals, and it had quite a gay and comfortable appearance when my bed was made up on the floor. I had now determined to remain at the mines, for I saw two or three chances to make money, and I needed a home, even if gold-digging was not a success. But I should require Mike's assistance to carry out my plans, and waited for him quite anxiously. If all other schemes failed I resolved to cut and haul timber for bracing the deep shafts, as it brought a high price, and was scarce.

Several days passed, and we were kept busy cleaning up the rubbish around the hut, building a cooking-house, and fireplace, and constructing a bathing-hole on the banks of the stream, so that I could take my bath after the labors of the day, and feel all the better for it. My Chinamen were not as fond of the water as a Japanese, but I made them wash, although sometimes they shirked and lied about it.

In the mean time the three pirates used to visit us regularly every day, and sit on a log, and smoke, and banter us for not working the mine, and after they tired of such pleasant amusement, they would go to the nearest alehouse, and get drunk, and boast of their rascality. Still Mike did not put in an appearance, and I began to feel a little worried about him, as bushrangers were reported on the road, and doing a lively business in robbing all who were not strong enough to resist an attack.

"Gin Sling," I said, one morning after breakfast, "how much longer does that Chinese friend of yours intend to remain here?"

"Hee goie nowie s'posee youe noie wante."

"Then let him go, for we have no more work for him. How much shall I pay him for what he has done?"

"Notie. Hee likie meie, hee likie youe, and hee workie ittie nowie. Hee goie workie wide Chinaman againe."

The friend of Gin took his departure after breakfast, and then I determined to bring to light my big nugget, and have it in the bank before night, for I did not know how soon Mr. Murden might return, and make trouble for me, as I knew that he would not accept my assurances that I had nothing to do with the abrupt departure of Kitty. Mr. Murden was a very good man, but he was as obstinate as Mrs. Higgins about some things. He thought that he could not be wrong.

I sent Gin down the shaft, and told him to dig thirty or forty buckets of gravel, and send them up, and when I gave a whistle, he was to load in the nugget, and then come to the surface. While I was working the windlass, and emptying the dirt, the three old pirates came along, as usual, and sat down on their accustomed log, and almost went into convulsions of laughter when they saw me laboring, **and looking over the gravel, as** I emptied it, in the hope **of** seeing the color of **gold,** or a small nugget.

I paid no attention to the fellows, and **all their harsh words did not pro- duce a** reply. Then one **of the** pirates went to **the "** Digger's Rest," and returned with some beer, and **a fresh supply of** tobacco, and then drank to my health, and to my exertions, and said some profane things, **and** blew clouds **of** smoke toward me, and laughed, and wanted to know if I would **sell** out cheap, and to let them know when I got tired of such stupid play. **Even Mother** Higgins, who, I think, had a little motherly feeling for me, **after all her** harsh words, came toward the shaft, and looked at me **kind** of sorrowfully, **as** though she wanted to make up, and be good friends, but **when** I smiled **at her in a pleasant way, she** gathered her petticoats around her, and **sidled off, but stopped long enough** to say,—

" Now, Mr. **Angus, don't be a fool any longer. I know you are wicked and** immoral, **but still** you might **reform, and then, perhaps,** I 'd **listen to you.** I 've buried three husbands, **and neither of them would take advice when living, and** you see the consequences. **They 're dead, but, perhaps, the** fourth would outlive me, **and I should** leave **him all of my money," and** with this shot she **was off.**

" Vell, **of all the cussed fools that ever I did see,"** one **of** the pirates **said, and** just **then I gave the signal, and the** big nugget was loaded into **the** bucket, and **I made a seeming effort to draw** it to **the** surface, **pretending** that it was much **heavier than it really was.**

" He 's **got a bite, Jim," said the** old ruffian who had sold me **the claim.** " He 's cotched **a gudgeon, or a vhale."**

I **said** nothing, **but drew the** bucket up, and emptied the nugget **on the ground, a** big **shining lump** of solid gold.

" **It 's a whale this time,** mates," I cried, as I lifted up **the treasure. and carried it into** the shanty as quickly as possible.

" **Hullo! vhat** in the devil **are you** doin' vid that?" roared **the** three ruf- **fians, and came toward me, and three** more surprised pirates were never seen.

" That 'ere belongs **to us. Ve only left it** there **to keep till ve** vas **ready** for it. Jist yer hand **that over, or the vust for yer, now I tells yer."**

" Yes, it 's hours," **they all roared together. " Yer jist give it up to us. Ve** von't stand any of yer **bloody games on us."**

They would have entered the hut, and seized **on the** nugget, **but I had ex-** pected all that, **and** was prepared for it.

" Mates," I **said, as I stood in the doorway, and** raised my heavy revolv er, "if you dare to enter this shanty, or to cross the threshold, I'll shoot you dead. Mind what I tell you, for I'm in earnest. Gin, go for a trap, and tell him to come here immediately, and help escort a big nugget to the bank. Run for it, and let no one stop you."

"Meie offe," was the answer, and away he went, although one of the ruffians did attempt to intercept him, but failed, for Gin was like an eel in his movements.

"It's a bloody Yankee trick, a —— mean Yankee trick, and yer a rascal to take adwantage of three 'onest men, vhat are hold and poor, and 'as no money but that 'ere nugget to get 'em in a 'ospital."

"Is it a Yanka trick yer spake of, buys?" cried a familiar voice. "Wi'l, here's a rael ould Oirish one, and, bedad, I hopes yer loikes it. Take that, yer beggars, and that, and that, and thin tell me if yer loikes it as will as the Yanka trick that yer spake of?"

There was a whistling sound in the air, some solid blows, and I saw a stout stick flourishing around the heads of the three pirates, and then prolonged howls, as the old ruffians tumbled to the ground, and, as they attempted to rise, were helped along by several vigorous kicks, that must have hurt, for Mike wore heavy boots, and the toes were sharp, and very thick.

"Do yer want some more of the same kind, yer dirty spalpeens, that insults a true-blooded American, that honors the country by comin' here at all, at all? Git out wid yer, afore I commits bigomy, and murders every blessed one of yer. Don't stop to spake, but go, for I can't restrain my shillalah when once it gits to workin', and I'm jist spilin' for a fight, for I have n't had one since me time was out, some tin days ago. Whoop, let me git at 'em agin."

But the three old pirates had taken the hint, and gone, as fast as their legs could carry them, to the ale-house, and then related the wonderful news that I had found a nugget as large as a barrel, and worth at least twenty thousand pounds, but, as most of those present thought the fellows drunk, or lying for a purpose, no notice was taken of them, and this was fortunate for my plans, for, as soon as I had welcomed Mike, I told him to run to the tax-office, and take out claims, each side of mine, one in his name, and the other in that of Gin Sling.

"And who is Gin Sling, sur?" asked Mike.

"A Chinaman, who is working for me," I replied, although it was no time to answer questions.

"A hathan, sur?"

"Yes, but a real good fellow, and one you will like. Now run as far as you can. Here is the money to pay for the tax. Remember, Gin Sling. Don't forget."

"Sure, I'll remember. It's a very spirited name. One don't forget the gin. Faith, I wish I had some now, for it's tired I am. But I'm off, and, if yer honor would jist sa that me parsonal property is taken from the tame, and give the lad what brought me here a little drop of somethin', I'll tell yer all about meself when I return," and he was off.

I helped unload the team, and found my hammock and clothes-bag all right, and that Mike had among his effects the long, rusty musket that he thought so much of, and which he had promised I should fire some day, as a great personal favor.

I gave the driver a drink of beer, and something to eat, and learned that he was a shepherd on Mr. Kebblewhite's run, and that Mike had delayed leaving his place until the last moment, because a party of bushrangers, some four in number, had raided on the sheep, and killed quite a lot, just out of pure wantonness. Mike and the others had laid in wait for the fellows, assisted by an old Quaker, but had not been able to encounter the robbers, and, as they appeared to have left that part of the country, Mike packed up, and joined me.

While I was talking with the stockman a mounted police officer returned with Gin Sling, and offered to escort me and the nugget to the bank. The man was astonished at the lump of gold, and declared that it was the purest specimen of the kind that he had ever seen in Ballarat.

I packed the nugget in a blanket, on the Chinaman's back, and walked to the bank, and astonished all who saw it by demanding that the gold be weighed, and estimated as to its value.

"Do you mean to tell me that this came out of the Bank-of-England Mine?" asked the cashier in astonishment.

"That is what I mean to say," was my reply, and I spoke the truth.

"Well, some people are born lucky, and you are one of them," the cashier said.

"Oh, that is a mere baby to what I intend to find," was my careless reply, but I must confess that I had no idea that my words would come true. I was only bluffing a little for the benefit of those who had laughed at me so heartily when I purchased the mine.

All the bank officers left their usual avocations to question me, and to examine the nugget. They were delighted with it, and seemed really pleased with my good fortune, and not a man present said a disagreeable word about my being a Yankee. After all we do like to congratulate a person on his good luck, almost as much as we like to learn of a dear friend's misfortune, and loss of money, and influence in the political world, and, when every one had guessed the weight of the nugget, the old miner came in, the same one who had borrowed several shillings of me, and forgotten to return them, as his memory was failing him quite fast as respects money matters, but still he could remember many things that were not of near so much importance as returning loans.

The old fellow pushed his way to the front rank, looked at the lump of gold in silence, wiped his mouth with the back of his hand, for his agitation caused drops of water to fall from his lips, and then he said, in slow, deliberate tones, as if to impress each one within his hearing of the truth of his yarns, —

"I 'm an old man, and if any one 'as a bit of 'baccy about 'em, 'e can't do better than to bestow it on me, and a glass of beer or rum, but I prefers the last, if it is all the same to yer, 'cos on an occasion like this peoples should be generous, and all that. Thank yer, sir, yer is wery kind. Now the rum. Vait must I? All right, sir, but I 'opes yer 'll make it two glasses vhile yer is about it, for the information I 'm about to impart is wery waluable, and no one hever 'eard the story afore now. It 's just goin' on for ten years, sir, since I 'elped find the ' Velcome Nugget,' in this wery camp, and I 'll tell yer all about it, sir. Yer see, I vos down in the mine, and I seed it fust, and I jist sit right down, and could n't speak for a full 'our, and if some one vould give me a lush of rum I could talk much better than I does now, as it 's dry work."

"Oh, clear out, old chap," said the cashier of the bank. "We have heard your lies for the last five years, and you never tell a story twice alike. You never saw the ' Welcome Nugget,' or lent a hand to mine it. Git out," and the old man was waltzed out by a trap, in spite of his protestations, but, just as we thought we had got rid of him, and when we were all patting the nugget, and guessing at its weight, the old miner once more edged his way through the crowd, and took up his position near me, and again resumed the thread of his discourse, only interrupted by being turned out of the room by the policeman.

"Yes, gents," he said, "as I stated afore, I could n't speak afore an 'our or two, I vos so surprised, but I called for some lush, and my mates kinder thought I was faint-like, and they sends me down a nip of rum. I vish some of yer gents vould do the 'andsome thing by me at this time. I could go on vid my sermon a little more lively if yer vould."

"Officer, run that old fraud out of the room," roared the cashier. "We have no time to fool with him. If he won't go, kick him out. He will corrupt the whole of us with his outrageous lies."

The trap run the old fellow out once more, and then returned to feast on the sight of the nugget.

"Ven I fust seed the 'Velcome Nugget,'" a familiar voice cried, and, on looking up, we saw that the old miner was perched on the window, outside, holding on by his hands, and looking in on us, in a very benevolent sort of manner, as though he had no animosity toward us for our cruel treatment to him. "If any gent vill be kind enough to give me a small piece of 'baccy, and a glass of rum or beer, rum preferred, if jist as handy, if not, beer vill do. Thank yer, sir, but that's not the kind of go vot I vants," for some one threw a sweet potato at his head, and it just missed him, and came near breaking the glass.

"Clear out, you old liar, or I'll have you locked up in jail," roared the cashier, and the trap started to haul the miner down, but the people outside the building began to enjoy the fun, and would not let the officer interfere, and it was not worth quarreling over, so the old chap held on, until one of the bank officials asked him if he would clear out for a shilling.

"Yer jist try me, that's hall," was the response. "A good von, yer know. But I'd rather tell yer hall about the 'Velcome Nugget,' if it's hall the same to yer, and I von't charge yer heny more, except some von vants to give me a little piece of 'baccy, and a lush of rum, or 'll take beer."

"Take the shilling, and be off," some one said, and the veteran put it in his mouth, and vanished.

The nugget weighed just a little over three hundred and six ounces, or most twenty-six pounds, and was valued at twenty dollars per ounce, but, as the lump was a great curiosity, the cashier said that he would give me seven thousand dollars for it, in our money, but I told him I thought I could do better, and then a gentleman came forward, and said that he would buy it for a historical and natural history society, of Melbourne, and, after a little banter, I was offered ten thousand dollars for the prize, and as this was more than its intrinsic value I closed with the bid, received my money, placed it on deposit at an interest of ten per cent, bought a draft for two hundred pounds in my mother's name, and felt quite satisfied with my day's work. I afterward learned that the nugget changed hands at a large advance, and I think that it is still in Melbourne, and if it is not there is a facsimile in one of the institutions, and an account relating all the facts as to the finding, but I think the black fellows could have told a different story. However, I never heard of them, or that they made a complaint of their loss, for the native black is a wanderer, here today, and on the sea-coast or in the interior tomorrow. Ever moving, and restless, without homes or huts, they go where the most food is to be had, and remain until the stock is exhausted, caring nothing for wealth or clothing, and taking pride only in their boomerangs, their spears, nullas and waddies.

By the time I returned to the hut Mike had arrived from the tax-office, with all necessary papers, and I found quite a crowd assembled around the shaft, and all discussing the wonderful luck which I had experienced, and then the laugh changed, and the old pirates were objects of derision, and so badly were they ridiculed that they packed up what few traps they had, and went to other mines, where their little game was unknown.

Of course a hundred miners, as soon as they heard of the lucky find, rushed to the tax office to take out claims next to mine, but found that they had been forestalled, and were compelled to accept of lots some little distance off. But I had what I expected, cash offers for Mike's and Gin Sling's claims, and from one hundred pounds the bids went up to five hundred pounds each, and on that basis I sold, took my cash, and put it in the bank, and let that go on interest also. Thus in one day I had banked fifteen thousand dollars. I began to feel that the firm was able to hold up its head, and, in honor of the event, I told Gin to go and buy materials for a good dinner, a dozen bottles of ale, and also such fruit as he could lay his hands on, for we would do no more work that day. Then I listened to Mike's wonderful adventures with the bushrangers, his desire to be with me, and his sense of duty that kept him looking after the sheep of his employer. While telling Mike of my being lost in the bush, and of finding the Chinaman tied to a tree, I forgot to mention all about the nugget that the blacks had left behind them when they fled. I did not think it desirable to let the story have too large a circulation, and Gin had received a hint to keep his mouth closed. A Chinaman can keep a secret much better than a lover, or a young woman. Even a cork-screw can't draw out of him what he does not want to be known, so I had no fear of his talking too much.

"So the hathan is to be wid us?" asked Mike, as soon as he had learned all the particulars of my adventures.

"Yes, Mike. Gin is a useful fellow, and can work as hard as the rest of us. You will like him."

"P'aps I shall, sur," was the cautious answer; "but I'd loike him better if the cratur had some little religion in him. He's a hathen, anyhow, and blank a hathen that's no religion."

Mike got over his prejudice after a while, and he and the Chinaman were good friends, although Mike always called Gin by the name of "Hathen," to show that the celestial was not quite up to his standard in matters of theology and salvation.

While Mike and Gin prepared dinner, I wrote to my mother a long and minute account of my travels, my landing at Melbourne, my sudden marriage to a beautiful young lady, who supposed me somebody else, my misfortunes, because I resembled an English nobleman, of Scotch ancestors; how I had been traduced, and made to suffer, on account of that mysterious person, and asked her to write to me fully and frankly why two men, of the same age, the same name, yet one an Englishman, and the other an American, could look so much alike that one was constantly being mistaken for the other. I also wrote her that, what was still more singular, the father of the nobleman had been the first lieutenant on board the line-of-battle ship *Asia*, and that I knew my parent had been first lieutenant of the line-of-battle ship *Ohio*, and that I had heard him speak of lying at Naples, alongside of the Englishman, for more than two months, or until he thought that both ships would get aground on the beef-bones thrown overboard. I said that I should remain in Australia at least three years, that I had done well so far, and sent her a draft on the Oriental Bank in hopes that she would use it to her advantage, and that I would send her more money just as soon as I learned that she had received my draft, and answered my letter. I hoped that she would approve of my conduct in leaving my wife on the evening of my nuptials, considering that Florence had wedded me through a great mistake, but that I loved the lady very dearly, and hoped that in time she would love me, but that I was not sanguine, and should avoid her until she sent for me, and forgave, and acknowledged me as her husbsnd, without feeling mortified at her choice.

All this I told her, and many other things which I knew would interest her, and, before dinner was ready, I had mailed my letter, and saw it go out in the midday coach, dashing along the dusty road on its way to Melbourne, and from thence by steamer to England.

Our dinner was a great success. The mutton chops were not as tough as some that we had had, the tea was no more smoky than I had drank before, the fruit was about as hot and wilted as one could expect in the mines, and the hard-tack was venerable, and a little inclined to be weevily, but this, the Chinaman said, was an advantage, because you could get more for your money than you otherwise would. But the ale was good and lively, and, the first bottle Mike opened, two-thirds of its contents flew over Gin, and covered him with foam, until he looked as though he had been through a typhoon in the China Sea, and was hopelessly shipwrecked. The only regret expressed was the loss of the ale, and a wet rag soon restored the Chinaman to a proper state of cleanliness.

"Did yer moind the smooth-tongued Quaker, Mr. Hangus?" asked Mike, while we were at dinner. "The divil that rode a pace with us near Webber's?"

"Oh, yes. What of him?"

"Will, he's bin on the shape run for a wake past, and said he'd help tackle the bushrangers, but when we'd go for 'em wid him in company, sure there was no findin' of 'em. But what puzzles me ontirely is that I saw yer one day, Mr. Hangus."

"Me, Mike?" I demanded, astonished at the information.

"Yes, sur. Sure I sung out to yer to come to yer friend Mike, but yer only laughed, and took to the woods; and why did n't yer spake to me, Mr. Hangus?"

"It was not me, Mike, but the person who is supposed to look like me. Do you think I'd refuse to speak to an old friend like you? I have not been absent from Ballarat."

"Will, now, it puzzled me, it did. I could have sword it was yer, Mr. Hangus. But, as yer say that it wa'n't, I'm bound to belave yer. But the loikeness was wonderful. Bedad it was," and here the subject was dropped.

In the afternoon we received many visitors, and all were interested in the big nugget. We had many offers to sell the mine, but I declined them all, as I did not wish to swindle people too outrageously, out of revenge for the small sell that had been put on me. But I will say, in this connection, that the two claims adjoining us, and which I sold at large figures, did turn out very well, and netted the proprietors a handsome profit, so they had no cause of complaint.

That night I slept in my old hammock, in the annex, and left Mike and Gin the dining-room to themselves. I could hear them talking, and boasting of their countries, until long after ten o'clock, and then I went to sleep, and, as usual, dreamed of Florence, and that she was pleading for me to return to her arms.

The next day we worked rather languidly at the mine, but did not see a speck of gold, and so on for days and days, and at length I began to grow weary of always bracing the shaft, as it grew deeper, of pawing over dirt, that did not contain gold, of hoisting up gravel and mud, which were worthless, and I really began to debate whether I had not better sell out, and try a new location, when an incident occurred that set the whole camp in motion, and produced the greatest excitement that was ever known in the mining region of Ballarat.

One morning I had gone to the bottom of the shaft with Gin, leaving Mike to do the hoisting. I did not feel very good-tempered, for I saw week after week pass over my head, and no addition to my fortune, while there was constant expense to feed all three of us, and a certain sum that I had agreed to pay Mike and Gin, as long as they remained with me. The wages were satisfactory to both of them, higher, in fact, than was paid at Camp Reserve, and the work not half as hard, but I could not operate alone, and needed the assistance of both men.

I took up a pick, and struck a spiteful blow on the gravel, and felt the point of the tool touch hard rock, a substance we had been looking for for some days past.

"Hollo, Gin," I said, "we are down to hard pan, and now we shall see if we are to find gold."

I withdrew the pick, and caught a glimpse, by the dull candle-light, of a yellow color, that looked like gold. I stooped down and felt of it, and held my candle close to it, and worked away the dirt and gravel, and, by Jove, it was gold, and a big nugget at that, so large that I could only say to Gin, who was stoping, with his back toward me, —

"Wee catchie muche golde at laste, Gin."

It was my pigeon English, and he turned to grin at my efforts, but he saw a sight that made his almond-shaped eyes start almost out of his head, for there, lying at my feet, was a nugget that seemed to exceed in size all nuggets ever heard of before or since, yet it was not half uncovered.

Gin uttered an awful howl of joy, fell on his knees before the lump of gold, and "chin-chined" to it, just as he would have done to Joss, one of his heathen gods.

"What is the matter, yer hathen?" asked Mike, who was listening at the windlass, and did not know what to make of the tumult.

We did not return any answer, for we were scratching away the dirt, with naked hands, and as though we feared the nugget would vanish from our sight unless we tore it from its long resting place, and held it firm.

"What's the matter, Mr. Hangus?" again cried Mike. "Is the hathen hurtin' of yer?"

"O Mike," I said, "we have found the grandmother of all nuggets. Don't say a word, but come down the ladder as soon as you can."

"Whoop, divil a word will I say at all, at all. The grandmother of 'em all, did yer say? O murder! but a'n't that noice?"

"Stop your noise, you lunatic," I shouted. "You will have the whole camp on top of us if you keep on that way."

"Not another word will I say, sur," was the response. "The grandmother of 'em all. Poor ould grandmother. Faith, she's rested in her bed a long time, and now let's start her round doing good."

Down the ladder he came, and found us on our knees, scraping away the earth, regardless of the skin and nails on our hands. Mike joined in with a will, and the three of us soon had the monster exposed to view, and such a sight I never saw before or since. It was a mass of bright, shining gold, as large as a ten-pound shad, and about the same form, long and flat, with head and tail like a fish, and fins on sides and back, with a few white specks of quartz, which looked like scales. It was a singular formation, and showed the intense heat to which it had been subjected at one time, when the earth was convulsed with internal fires, and an upheaval had occurred which produced the peculiar metal called gold, a metal that men have worshiped, and women adored, for thousands of centuries, and will be reverenced for centuries to come, unless the tail of a comet knocks us out of time to eternity.

We sat around that inanimate nugget, and just worshiped it, and rubbed it with our hands, and talked to it as though it had been a living being, and then we lighted our pipes, and puffed away in silence, and looked at each other with greedy eyes, as if we feared that a conspiracy was being mentally formed to spirit it out of sight, and so lose the results of our lucky find.

"Faith," said Mike, knocking the ashes out of his pipe, and getting on his feet, "I thinks that if we stay here long there'll be murder in our hearts, and all for a lump of gold. Let me out of this as soon as yer plase, for I want no more thinkin' in this dark hole, wid the hathen's eyes lookin' loike a tiger's, and his hands a workin' loike a kangaroo's hind legs, when pushed by dogs, and its back is agin a tra. Up I go, and don't stay here any longer, Mr. Hangus. Go wid me, and let the hathen load it in the bucket."

I could hardly bear to part company with my treasure, but did, after a long and affectionate glance, and climbed up the ladder, and then had to drink a wine glass of brandy to steady my nerves, and quiet my imagination, for I was all of a perspiration, and as weak as a child. But we gained strength at last, and slowly hoisted the nugget to the surface, and when it was safely landed Mike could no longer control his feelings, but let them find vent in one general howl of delight, and a dance that would have driven wild with envy half the boys of Tipperary.

Mike's yells attracted the notice of all the people at work on the adjoining claims, and they flocked to our place in crowds, to see what was the trouble. Their sensations when they saw the gold found vent in exclamations of astonishment and delight, and some few of envy, but the majority of the miners, carried away by enthusiasm, yelled themselves hoarse, and the shouts sent every mounted trap to our claim in hot haste, thinking that a Chinese war had again broken out, and that the celestials were being murdered by infuriated miners.

"Form a procession, boys," shouted one man, who had a claim which I had sold him. "Fall in, lads. We'll escort this nugget around the camp, and then to the bank," but just at that moment the old miner put in an appearance. He had been disturbed, in the "Miner's Rest," by the noise, and now came, as fast as his tottering limbs would permit, to take his usual share in all the public celebrations.

"Coves, hall," he shouted, as soon as he learned that a nugget had been found.

"Who in thunder do you call coves?" asked one brawny miner, and he threw a decayed orange at the ancient miner's head, but it missed him, and landed full on the flat face of a Chinaman, much to his astonishment and indignation, for the juice made him look more yellow than ever.

"Vell, then, gents hall, if that suits yer better, although I 'as seen the time ven cove vas good enough for me. That vos ven ve found the 'Velcome Nugget,' and, as I 'as never told a soul about it, I vill jist relate hall the circumstances as they took place," and the old miner mounted on a barrel, the better to get off his speech, and to overlook the crowd. "Vell, gents hall, ven I fust seed the 'Velcome Nugget' I vos that surprised that I could n't stand, and so I jist sets down"—

"As you do now," some one said, and over went the barrel, and the miner with it, and he was heard of no more until we got to the bank, then he once more came to the front, and began to relate his story, but I gave him a shilling, and a piece of tobacco, and he went back to the saloon, and told lies all the evening, to the intense amusement of his audience, who filled him so full of beer, that at last he swore his Welcome Nugget weighed one thousand pounds, and that he knew where there was another just like it.

"Fall in, boys," cried the miner who was disposed to boss the procession, and who was really a clever fellow. "We goes with the nugget to the bank."

The suggestion was adopted. The miners dropped their tools, one man ran to his shanty, and brought back a drum, another had a banjo, a third a trombone, on which he could not play, yet produced the most hideous sounds ever heard outside of the Chinese quarters; some got hold of penny whistles, and blew on them until their eyes started out of their heads, and one fellow seized on a tin kettle, and pounded it until the bottom fell in, which he did not mind in the least, but banged on sides and every available part, until the whole thing fell to pieces. Even Mrs. Higgins came over to us, and sniffed, and said that if I was not immoral she would kiss me, but that her reputation would not suffer such a strain, and so she must decline, which was quite good on her part, as no one had asked for the chaste embrace, or even thought of it. But Mother Higgins was a peculiar woman, and was not so much offended with me as she pretended. I believe that she would have married me had I pressed her to accept my hand, then and there, before all the miners. But I did not.

We extemporized a litter, on which the nugget was placed, and, with Mike and Gin at the handles, and I at the head, marched through Camp Reserve, down Sturt Street, up Lydiard Street, through the principal mining camps, the procession constantly receiving additional recruits, until at last we halted in front of the branch of the Oriental Bank, where a strong detatchment of police kept the crowd back, and prevented it from overrunning the outer room of the institution, and frightening the officials out of their wits. To enable all to see the nugget the miners were formed in some kind of order, and walked past the treasure, and the various comments that were made on the lump of gold would fill a book of the size of BALLOU'S MAGAZINE, small type.

But at length all had seen the "Old Grandmother," as it was called, and many returned to their labors, while others lingered around, and talked over the matter, and then adjourned to ale-houses, and drank more beer than was good for their heads or stomachs.

Mike, Gin, and myself were admitted to the bank with the nugget, and waited impatiently to see it tested, and to know its value. The officers did not have enough weights, and were compelled to send to the branch of the bank of Australia, and borrow all the troy weights it owned, before the scales would balance, and then, amid a silence so profound that it was painful, the cashier read off the figures, — one hundred and twenty-eight pounds and six ounces, or fifteen hundred and forty-two ounces, and worth, as the bank officer stated, the snug little sum of near thirty-one thousand dollars, and he said that he would allow me that for the nugget, and take it without further questioning. But I concluded, as it was the largest mass of gold that had ever been found in Australia, except one, the Welcome, it was worth more than that as a curiosity, so told the officers to lock it up in their vault, and I would think the matter over, and decide what to do with it in the course of a day or two. It was just as well that I came to that decision, for a consultation of the bank officials and a few gentlemen took place immediately, and then I was offered just an even forty thousand dollars for the nugget, and I accepted the bid at once, received my money, paid it back to the bank, and had it go on interest with the rest.

I do not know where that wonderful nugget is now. Those who purchased it took it to Melbourne, claimed that they had dug it out of their mine, and gave lectures on gold, and its formation, and exhibited the treasure at the same time. The admission fee was one shilling, and some days the owners made as much as one hundred pounds by their enterprise. It was carried to all the principal places in Australia, Sydney, Gelong, Adelaide, Bathust, Port Phillip, and other cities, and finally sold to the British Museum, although I will not state positively that such was the case, as the sale had not been effected when I left the country, but negotiatious were being carried on at a large advance from what I received.

I began to feel that I could hold my head up, and that I was not such a bad match for Mr. Kebblewhite's daughter, after all. I had over fifty thousand dollars in the bank, and it was growing every day, at the rate of ten per cent interest, beside the one hundred pounds in the bank at Melbourne. Well, fortune had favored me, and I resolved that my dear, good-hearted mother should share in my prosperity, and I again wrote to her in full, and sent another draft, for a thousand dollars. She might not need it, but women can get away with an awful sight of money, if they set their minds seriously on the subject, and give their whole attention to it.

"I tell yer what it is, Mr. Hangus," said Mike at supper, "yer has the divil's own luck, and it 's me opinion that things will come around all roight in time. But we must wait wid patience, and we 'll sa what we shall sa. Now, sur, I 've a hidea."

"Hee hase a hideae. Bellie goodie. Wee wille heare ite," said Gin, who had a little fun in his disposition, even if he was a Chinaman.

"Shut up, yer hathen, and don't interrupt one of yer Christian betters when he spakes. Now, sur, I 've heard that when yer find one big grandmother of a nugget, yer is apt to foind two or tra grandchildren near the old lady, to kape her company loike. Begor, I belave that 's so, and what if we should foind more nuggets in the Bank-of-England?"

"I have heard such a report, Mike, but it don't seem as though luck could strike us many more times."

"Meie knowe onie Chinaman whoe makie fortunee in onie moone," cried Gin, but Mike wanted to monopolize the conversation, and was not disposed to listen to the heathen just at that time.

"Kape that big mouth of yern shut while I 'm spakin', yer hathen. It 's wisdom ye 'll hear fall from me lips if yer listen. Now, it 's me opinion that luck is loike an Australian freshet, all fuss and fury, and if yer swim wid it all roight, but if yer try to stand agin it down yer go. It is soon over, but if we take the water when it 's on the run we shall land on a bank, or in a tra-top, quite safe. We is swimmin' wid it now, and whin the flood is done and gone, we want to be high and dry, and that remoinds me that I 'm dry now, so pass the tay, yer hathen, and don't talk to me iny more about yer Confusiones, after listenin' to me, for I can bate all the China philosophers that iver ate rats, or roasted poor puppies, and sarved 'em up at the big fastes."

"Onie ——— liee!" cried the Chinaman, indignant at the reflection cast upon his people.

"Don't yer ate shark-fins?" demanded Mike, in a lordly way, as though he could floor Gin in a moment, and by a pertinent question.

"Yese, blerie goodie," and Gin smacked his lips at the recollection of the feasts he had enjoyed.

"And don't yer ate burd-nists?" persisted Mike, leading the heathen on, in a quiet manner.

"Yesie, datie nicie alle timie," was the confident answer, as though he knew what he was talking about.

"And now answer me this, yer hathen, and none of yer shyin' off. Don't yer ate the dirty slugs what is found on the sa-shore?'

"Datie blerrie goode alle timie. Meie cooke somie fore youe, if youe gete," was Gin's kind answer.

"Don't insult me, yer ignorant barbarian," roared Mike. "I 'm a Christian, and ates Christian food, and drinks Christian whiskey (whin I can get it), and yer should know that min loike me don't take to rats and puppies the same as the hathen of yer ould country, what has 'em on their tables at all times of the day, cold and hot, the dirty pigs."

Gin made a gesture of contempt at such a reflection on his people, but passed the tea, and let Mike talk until he was tired, and then we went to bed with the firm resolve to find those grandchildren nuggets, if they were in our mine, and to commence next day the laborious search.

But the grandchildren were bashful, not like grandchildren of our own flesh and blood, but such as are made of precious metal, and refused to exhibit themselves, although we toiled day after day, in searching for them. We did not work hard, and I did not enter the mine at all, unless it was to give directions how to stope. I was getting above such common labor, but still I worked the windlass, and answered all questions that were put to me by wondering visitors, and also declined all offers to sell the Bank-of-England Mine at a price that would have made me think I was rich at one time.

But at last the grandchild arrived, and Gin had the honor of welcoming the little stranger. It was a magnificent specimen of gold, nearly pure, and weighed eighty-five pounds, or one thousand and twenty ounces, and I may as well say that I sold it as a specimen for twenty-five thousand dollars, and there was no fuss over the trade either, on the part of the buyers.

After that I hired Gin Sling's friend to come and work for me, and to tend the windlass, and to do the cooking. I was growing rich, and did not propose to hurt myself with hard labor. I saw a chance for quiet speculation, once in a while, in certain articles, and I did not fail to take advantage of every turn to increase my wealth. I wanted Florence, and I supposed that I could obtain her through money, and it looked as though the latter would not stand in my way unless I met with some misfortune, or my bank should collapse.

In the mean time I had not heard a word from Mr. Murden, or from Melbourne. The parties who had purchased the three large nuggets claimed that they dug them, so their names went into the papers instead of mine, and thus the Kebblewhites did not hear from me, or know where I was. Once in a while I would receive a report that a gang of bushrangers were seen near a Mr. Smith's run and house, but that the rascals always took to the bush when the mounted police put in an appearance, and so escaped. As the fellows never came nearer than ten miles of Ballarat, none of us paid much attention to them, our gold being safe, and sent to the city under armed escort, so strong that the bushrangers did not dare to attack it.

The wet season of July had set in, but, except when it rained, the weather was pleasant, and the country assumed a most beautiful appearance. The trees looked greener, the grass sprung up with marvelous rapidity, the wild flowers covered the plain, the acacias were all in bloom, and filled the air with perfume, the roses were sweet, and nodded a welcome from every highway and garden, and violets and tulips struggled for supremacy with modest rivalry. The dry water-courses were now full of life, and the streams rolled and tumbled toward the Darling or the Murray, as if glad of the chance to seek a wider sphere of usefulness, where they could see the world, and mix with it, and enjoy life by giving vitality to the thirsty soil through which they passed, blessing every one in their onward course, and at last losing all individuality by mixing with the deep-blue ocean, and then twisting and turning through Bass's Straits, until dashed upon the bleak shores of New Zealand, or Japan, thence rebounding, and crossing the Indian Ocean, or taking a look at the China Sea, and a fierce typhoon.

On the tenth day of July we found the third nugget we had looked for so long. The last of the grandchildren came to light, and our mining was about over. It was near ten o'clock in the forenoon when Mike came upon it, at the depth of forty-five feet, and just ten feet, by stoping, from the spot where the old grandmother had been found. We took the good luck quietly, and made no demonstration whatever, but carried our precious treasure to the bank, and had it weighed. The bank officials had now got so accustomed to my appearance with a nugget, that they simply said, "What! another? How long do you intend to keep this thing up?" and put it on the scales, and called out, "This is only a sixty-five-pound nugget," and treated it almost with contempt. But it weighed seven hundred and eighty ounces, and was the fourth largest nugget ever produced from the mines of Ballarat. I sold it for eighteen thousand dollars, as a specimen, and some one proposed to give it to the lieutenant-governor, and the scheme would have been carried into effect, I think, but just at that time the governor gave a *soirée* one evening, and promenaded with the good-looking wife of a merchant of Melbourne, and did not even offer his arm to the wife of the gentleman who wanted to make the presentation speech. She was old and fat, and had a mustache and chin whiskers, and the handsome lady was beardless, and lively. Perhaps the governor never knew what he lost for the want of a little attention. The proposer, early the next morning, after the party, in a wild sort of manner, as though he had passed a sleepless night, withdrew his subscription, and would give no reason for such a singular course, but he was properly punished, for he was an applicant for the office of the ninety-ninth readjuster of the public lands, at a salary of five hundred pounds, and nothing to do except hear the squatters swear once a month, that they were ruined. The husband of the handsome lady obtained the prize, and the beauty received marked attention at the government house until the opposition said some hard things on the subject, and the governor had to banish her to a less exposed place, and call in the evening.

The same day that the last nugget was found, a party of capitalists combined to purchase the Bank-of-England Mine, and made me a handsome offer, but I said that I wanted five thousand pounds for the mine, and should hold it until I obtained that sum. Then they agreed to buy it at that price, if I would take some stock, but I did not care for stock in that mine, although there was a bare possibility of more nuggets being found, but I considered the chances a little weak from what I knew of mining in Ballarat. But, after a long and spirited conference, I sold the mine for five thousand pounds, or twenty-five thousand dollars, all in cash, and the papers were passed, and I no longer had a home, and yet, rude and humble as it was, I did not like to leave it, for it had sheltered me so many months, and there I had experienced the only happiness I had known in Australia, the happiness of thinking that at some distant day Florence would acknowledge me as her husband, and love me with a little of the devotion that I felt for her.

I determined to keep my people together until we returned to Melbourne, for all had been faithful and true to me, and I would not cast them off. I could afford to pay them their wages, even if they were not employed, for I was worth near two hundred thousand dollars, and it was not lying idle by any means. I hired quite a respectable house, and had Gin and his friend, whose name was Ah Sugar, to look after my welfare, and to do the cooking, while Mike bossed the two, and made himself useful in various ways.

One day Gin came in, his face looking like a scraped pumpkin, with a candle in it, on a dark night. Such as country boys delight in at the fall of the year.

"Ah, meie seeie bellie putte gallie, and shee looke at meie, and laughie. Meie dinkie date sheie falle in lubie wid meie," he said.

"Shut up, yer hathen," roared Mike. "What would a gurl fall in love wid the loikes of yer for, whin there's a buy loike me around?"

I went to the window to see the lady Gin had alluded to, and the sight of her face almost made me stagger, for there sat Florence, looking pale and sad, in a carriage with her father, and Monsieur Allete, the Frenchman. They had stopped the vehicle opposite my house, and were asking some questions of a gentleman who was connected with one of the banks. The party did not suspect my presence, and I dodged back so that they could not see me, but still I kept my eyes fastened on the dear, sweet face of my wife, and could only, by a powerful effort, prevent crying out, and rushing into the road to meet her, to fall down on my knees, and beg her to look kindly upon me, if but for a moment. But no, she would repulse me, and upbraid me, and that would render me more unhappy than ever, for my love was too strong to be met with indifference.

How handsome she was as she sat there in her carriage, apparently indifferent to all her surroundings, and not noting the questions her father was asking and answering. She was very pale, and her face had lost some of its fullness, but there was the same clear-cut features, the large blue eyes, and the wealth of golden hair falling over neck and shoulders, burnished by the bright sun, until she looked like some sweet saint who had visited the earth for the purpose of showing that the great hereafter was one of angels and perpetual joy and beauty. How I remembered the last time I had seen her, on her bridal eve, and the manner in which I had left her.

At last the carriage drove away, toward the best hotel in the place, and I lost sight of the vision, and all seemed dark and drear, and when Gin came to call me to dinner, I did not hear him until he had spoken several times, and then astonished him by saying that dinner could be cleared away, for I wanted none. He thought I was ill, and brought me a pot of hot tea, but tea could not cure a wounded heart, and all that day I remained in my room, and tried to crush out the love that was devouring me. But it was useless, and at dark I wandered out, and toward the house where I supposed Mr. Kebblewhite and daughter were staying, and then I learned, to my great surprise, that the whole party had started homeward at sundown, intending to reach Smith's place, and pass the night.

"Good Heaven," I thought, "if they should be attacked by bushrangers what would be the fate of Florence?"

I turned to go home, and start in pursuit, when a man's hand was laid on my arm, and a voice whispered, —

"Vot 's yer little game now, old feller?"

"Who are you?" I demanded, shaking off the man's hand, and fingering my revolver.

"Oh, don't yer know a cove ven yer sees 'im, cully? Vot is yer arter 'ere?"

By the light from a saloon I saw that the speaker was the old Quaker who had ridden with Mike and myself on our trip from Melbourne.

"Say," whispered the Quaker, and, although dressed in that quiet garb, no longer used Quaker language, "vot is yer doin' 'ere at this time o' night? Vere is the boys? and is they hall ready?"

"The boys are all right," I answered at random, and anxious to learn some news.

"Does they know that old Kebblewhite and gal vill be on the road to-night?" the Quaker asked.

"Yes, they said something about it. Where will the boys meet them?" I demanded, with an anxious heart.

"Near Smith's, the stockman's place. It vill be a rich 'aul, now I tell yer. Twenty thousand pounds ransom, and no mistake, and then ve is hoff to other climes. I 'se sent a man to tell the boys, and means to foller in a little vhile. Vill yer show up vid us, or is yer on another lay?"

"I expect to be with you," I answered, and most assuredly I did hope to be there.

"All right, my friend. I thank thee for thy kindness to a poor old man, who wants a little money to build a meeting-house for his order in the city. Heaven will bless thee, and thy friend, Aramena Meully, will remember thee in his meditations," and this was uttered in a whining tone, because a policeman strolled near us, and was listening to our conversation quite attentively.

The change was sudden, and the long, lank form, with the straggly arms, and huge feet, shuffled off, but I could not help looking after the fellow, and wondering what had come over him so suddenly. At one moment he had used the slang of the lower class, and the next the pure and simple words of the Quaker. What could be the meaning of such a change of base? And then I recalled the time he had rode with Mike and myself in the team, when we stopped at Webber's, and the daughter of the latter had mistaken me for her lover, and kissed me to the indignant surpise of her father. It also flashed across my brain that Mr. Murden, the Chief of Police, had spoken of meeting a Quaker on the road, that Kitty had received a letter from his hands, and that Mike had alluded to the same person, when lying in wait, on the run, for bushrangers, and that all attempts to capture them, while he was in their company, had signally failed, as though some warning had been given to the desperadoes to keep them out of the way. It was singular, to say the least, and I jumped to the conclusion that the Quaker was a sham, but the policeman merely said, —

"I think that 'ere Quaker is a rum one," and passed on, toward the Chinese quarters.

It was evident that Mr. Meully had mistaken me for some other party, and that he was acting two parts in the town of Ballarat, where he had been sent as a spy.

But Florence was in danger, and how could I aid her? The police? No. The superintendent would not detail a man in my behalf, on such evidence as I presented. I must act with what force I could rally at short notice. Mike and my two Chinamen. They must aid me, and now was the time for them to show their friendship.

I ran to the house, and entered like a whirlwind, to the astonishment of all three.

"Mike," I said, "my dear little wife is in danger, and we must go and fight for her."

"Yer wife is it?" he demanded, starting up.

"Yes, Mike," breathless with haste.

"I thought she was in the city, sure I did."

"Don't ask any questions now. She is in danger, and we must fight to save her from the bushrangers."

"Foight is it? Whoop! I 'm the man for that, now moind yer, and I 'll bate the loife out of all the ——— bushrangers in this divil's own country if they touch a hair of her blessed head. Whoop! up wid yer, yer hathens, and get some blood in yer hearts, for the master's wife is in danger, and we is the buys that 'll save her. Give me me shillalah, and me ould musket. I 've got 'em, and now I 'm riddy. Whoop! come on yer hathens. Amerikee, Ould Oireland, and the land of rats and puppies foriver! and if yer iver felt loike havin' a real good foight, now is the time to show it, for Orish Mike will lade the way, and yer nade not fear to foller him! Whoop! yer hathens, this night yer shall sa how one of the real ould stock from Limerick can handle his stick and his gun, for the sake of Mr. Hangus's pretty wife. Hit me, somebody, or 'll bust!"

THERE WAS A TREMENDOUS REPORT AT MY SIDE, A SHEET OF FLAME AND SMOKE.

PART X.

A DISAGREEABLE NIGHT RIDE. — FINDING THE TRAIL. — THE BLACK TRACKER. — THROUGH THE BUSH. — THE BUSHRANGERS' CAMP. — THE SUDDEN ATTACK. — A HAND-TO-HAND BATTLE. — THE CHINAMEN'S BLOOD DELIRIUM. — A VICTORY. — THE HIDDEN TREASURE. — FLORENCE RECOGNIZES HER HUSBAND, AND IS VERY FAR FROM BEING SATISFIED.

WHILE Mike was expressing his determination to smash all the bushrangers in Australia into everlasting smithereens, as he expressed it, the two Chinamen did not seem enchanted at the prospect of an all-night's tramp, and, perhaps, a savage fight in addition, as one would suppose. They exchanged a few words with each other, in their native tongue, and then stared at Mike as if under the impression that they saw a first-class crank before them, and, as he continued to flourish his shillalah in close proximity to their heads, they dodged around the small room, and uttered many exclamations of wonderment and alarm.

"Mike," I asked, as soon as he became calm, "do you know where Smith's run is?"

"Sure, I do, sur. It's tin miles from here, and old Smith was a *lag* once, but now he's a rich man, and a mimber of parliament, and the divil knows what, and he has tin thousand as noice acres of land as can be found in the country, and foive thousand shape, and lots of other animiles. I know the place well. It's offen I've been thar."

"Well, we must start for his run at once. I have heard that a gang of bushrangers is on the road, and that it intends to capture Mr. Kebblewhite and his daughter near Smith's run. We must prevent them."

"Wid all me heart, sur; but I don't care much about ould Kebblewhite. Sure it would n't hurt him if the bushrangers jist laid their paws on him for a little while."

"But, remember, he is the father of my wife, and I must do all that I can to save him."

"True for yer, sur; but could n't yer get the gurl better if the ould one was out of the way?"

This reasoning of Mike's was so original and wicked, that I did not care to adopt it; and then we sat down for a moment, and laid out our plans for our campaign, the Chinamen listening with patience and calmness as we adopted them. We thought that we might pick up a mounted trap or two on the way, and secure their aid, but of that there was no certainty. We should have to depend on ourselves, perhaps, and when I thought of Florence, and her danger, it seemed to me that I could endure any risk, and encounter any odds, if I could but show my love for her, and prove to her satisfaction that I was worthy of her hand. But, while I was so eager for the encounter that I expected, I did not intend to neglect any precautions that a prudent man would be likely to take. I knew that bushrangers fought like pirates, with a halter around their necks, and that they were desperate men, and cruel as they were determined, and that if we failed to conquer them by surprise, they would show us no quarter. When we went forth we went with our lives in our hands, and expected rough treatment. Mike had no fear as long as he had his old musket and club, while I depended on my heavy revolver and rifle to do some powerful work in case of necessity.

"Gin," I asked, "will you go with us, or stay at home?"

"Wee goe," was the reply. "Chinaman fightie likie debble whene hee noie runie. Yese, wee goie."

"What do you want to fight with, Gin?" I asked, pleased at his reply.

The Chinaman took from a box two enormous knives, curved and heavy, like a farmer's sickle, the backs nearly an inch thick, while the edges were keen as a razor. I had never seen the weapons before, as the Chinaman had kept them secreted, as they did all of their valuables. They were dreadful looking instruments, and capable of taking off a limb at a blow, and as clean as a surgeon's knife, in the hands of a skillful operator.

"Can you and Sugar use pistols?" I asked, as I felt of the edges of the knives.

"Noie wante pistol. Wee usie udder dings muche bettie pistol. Hite bushrange hee thinke debbie gote hee," and Gin Sling's eyes looked perfectly fiendish, as he run his bony fingers over the edges of the knives, and then, for fear they were not sharp enough to inflict deadly wounds at the first blow, produced a whetstone, and proceeded to put a little more keenness to the terrible weapons.

I remembered Mr. Murden's warning, when he had paid my hut a visit, about the time I first arrived at the mines, and how he had cautioned me that the Chinaman's method of attack was not an open one, but a sudden assault, with axe or hatchet, and I began to think that there might be some truth in his words, for here had I resided in the same quarters with the two celestials, and never suspected for a moment that they owned such formidable and murderous-looking knives as they now displayed for the first time, and I must confess I felt a little singular for a moment, as I thought how many times the Chinamen might have murdered me while I slept, and dropped my remains down a deserted shaft, where they would never have been discovered, as no one ever entered them, and time and dust filled them up, or, if too dangerous, the police hired some one to shovel in some of the refuse matter that was lying around the camp, for when a miner deserted a shaft, he felt too much contempt for the mine to make it safe, and, consequently, accidents were of frequent occurrence, especially when drunken men attempted to reach their homes by short cuts across lots, during dark nights.

But I dismissed the hideous idea that Gin Sling and Ah Sugar would be guilty of such terrible ingratitude as to have even thought of taking my life, and I believe to this day that I am right, and that Mr. Murden was wrong, although he would never acknowledge that such was the case, and always considered that I run a great risk in consorting with the celestials, with no one but Mike as a companion, but I never heard that a Chinaman at Ballarat committed deliberate murder of a white man, although in the celestials' quarters there were some bloody frays, and death might have resulted from them, but no one cared enough to investigate the details, and even the police turned a deaf ear to many reports that might have been investigated, and guilty parties punished.

"Gin, do you know how to use those knives, in case we have a lively fight?" I asked, and the Chinaman smiled a terrible, blood-curdling smile, and simply said, —

"Youe seie. Meie cute de debble oute deme bushrange," and he gave his knife a swing that would have lopped off an arm.

I did not pay much attention to this boast at the time, but remembered afterward, for I was preparing my arms, and seeing that they were carefully loaded, and that I had powder, balls, and caps in abundance, and that my bowie-knife was in good condition, while Mike was loading his beloved musket with a miscellaneous assortment of slugs, fine shot, and a bullet as large as a crab apple.

"The saints help 'em if that hits 'em," said Mike, piously, and I thought that the Lord would have to protect the one at the breech of the gun as well, and I mentally resolved to get behind a tree, and remain there, if Mike should persist in discharging that old musket, while I was near him. To have expressed a doubt of the goodness of that gun would have set Mike wild with indignation, so I remained silent.

As the roads were in very bad order from the heavy teaming and rains, it was thought best to hire a one-horse covered carriage, so that we could keep out of sight, and, in case of more rain, dry at the same time.

I sent Mike to a place where I knew such a carriage could be obtained, a sort of an express wagon, and then set the Chinamen to work putting up luncheon and drink in baskets, and, by the time we had packed all that we needed, Mike was at the door, and we piled into the cart, after locking up our premises, and were off.

Luckily the night was clear and crisp, no rain having fallen for a day or two, but we had to proceed at a walk most of the distance, owing to the gullies in the roads, about as hard traveling as could be found outside of California in the wet season. We met but few teams, as all had hauled up for the night, but once in a while we encountered a lumbering wagon, drawn by ten and twelve yoke of oxen, and it was hard work for even such a string as that to get through the mud, and for miles, in the stillness of the night, we could hear the sharp snap of the stockman's peculiarly formed whip, all lash, and very little handle, and then the fierce roar of angry voices, and strong profanity, as the cattle got stalled in some deeper quagmire than usual.

Once we met a mounted policeman, and asked if he had seen Mr. Kebblewhite and daughter, and he reported that he had, just at sunset, and that no bushrangers had been heard of for several days, and it was thought that the gang had separated, and gone toward the Murray. Only two persons had been found murdered in the last week, and that was considered good evidence that the roads were more fully protected than ever.

It was about twelve o'clock, I judged, when we suddenly pulled up to examine something that was lying on the side of the road. It was white enough to attract attention, and required investigation. Mike jumped out, and picked up the object that had caused us to halt.

" It is nothin' but a bit of rag, sur," he said, in a disappointed tone, and was about to throw it away.

" Let me see what kind of a rag, Mike. Gin, light the dark lantern, and we will take a look at it."

The lantern was lighted, and handed to me, and the rag proved to be a white linen pocket handkerchief, and in one corner I saw the name of Monsieur Allete. I jumped from the wagon, and examined the ground carefully, and saw that my worst fears were realized. There were tracks of the carriage drawn by two horses, which I had noticed that very day in front of my house, and which had contained Florence, her father, and Monsieur Allete, and there were marks of horses' feet, as though mounted men had suddenly dashed from the scrub and bush, and taken the lady and gentlemen by surprise, for there were no evidences of a struggle, or any signs of bloodshed, in the thick mud.

" Mike," I said, " we need go no further at present. The villains have captured the lady and her father."

" Sure, I wish 'em joy of ould Kebblewhite. They 'll wish they 'd let him alone, for a maner man niver lived."

I was too much grieved to rebuke this fling at my father-in-law, for all my thoughts were of Florence, and her fate. Could I save her? and how?

By the aid of the lantern I was enabled to study out the whole situation. The bushrangers had waited in ambush at an angle of the road, where the scrub was thick, and, warned by some one who had kept track of Mr. Kebblewhite's movements, had made a dash, stopped the team in the dusk of evening, caused the occupants to dismount, and follow the robbers into the forest. I could see that there were six horsemen concerned in the affair, that the animals were not well broken to such work, for they had danced around, and splashed the mud in all directions, as though restless, while not one of the horses had on a shoe, a sure proof that they had been taken from some stockman's run, in a half-wild state. I could even see the place where one of the bushrangers had dismounted, and then helped Florence on his horse, while the two other prisoners had been compelled to step into the mud, and wade to solid ground the best way they could. It was at this point the Frenchman had dropped his handkerchief, like an old campaigner, in hope that some one would find his trail, and rescue him. This he had done unobserved by his captors, or, if they had noticed the act, they had been in too much of a hurry to pay any attention to it. It is quite probable, however, that Monsieur Allete had chosen his own time, for an old and experienced bushranger is as sharp as a native black fellow, and takes no great risks when he is on dangerous ground, or thinks the traps are on his trail.

I followed the track of the horsemen into the scrub, and saw that it led to the thick brush, and was then lost to view in the darkness. There was nothing to do but wait, and I need not say how heavily the time dragged by, nor how impatiently I wished for dawn. At least a dozen times I was determined to start on my own account, and seek the retreat of the bushrangers, but a moment's reflection showed how useless such a measure would be, and how helpless I must be in a forest of which I knew almost nothing. I should be lost and bewildered before I had proceeded a mile, unless some one undertook the task of acting as guide. For this important duty I trusted to Mike, as he said we were on part of Smith's run, and that he had tracked wild cattle in this very bush, and thought that he knew enough of it to prevent going far astray. But that did not trouble him so much as following the trail of the robbers, and so take them by surprise, and before they would have time to commit any of their devilish acts, for he did not think that they would proceed to extremities until they had rested, or daylight appeared, to see what their prisoners were like.

If the bushrangers were in search of money, they would seek it on the persons of their prisoners, and, if in a good-natured mood, let them escape without bodily injury, as they had been known to do, or else held them for a heavy ransom, but I could not hope that the gentle, loving little Florence would be thus kindly treated. Her beauty would not melt the hearts of Slipper Sam, and his fiendish companions. A price was set on their heads, and they knew it, and were also aware that one crime in addition would have but little effect on the verdict of a jury; that death was just as sure to end their careers, as though they saw themselves standing under a halter, or with a rope adjusted around their necks, or else a lucky shot from the carbine of a mounted policeman would do the work, for no quarter was asked for or expected when bushrangers and officers of the law met at close quarters. It was for Florence I feared, and I would undergo all risks to save her from a fate that made me almost wild when I thought of it, and more than once that dark night did I pray mentally for her welfare, and for daylight, so that I could move onward in my search, and hope of a speedy rescue.

"Oh, if I only had a black feller what I knowed," muttered Mike. "He 'd take us to the spot loike a burd, and not turn his head one way or anoother, but land us right down on 'em. But it 's useless to wish, for the feller is now slapin' under the la of some scrub, and will not open his dirty eyes till the sun is up. Many is the good turn he has sarved me, and many is the shape what was all broken down wid the rot, has I gave him for a noice little fade. Ah, if wishes would do any good, sure it 's in Ould Oireland I 'd be at this moment, or else in the land of the fra, with a mighty good glass of whiskey in one hand, and a bloomin' wife in the other. But cheer up, Mr. Hangus, by the blessin' of Heaven we 'll come out all roight yet, and the darlin' will have her own agin."

Mike stopped his harangue to light his pipe, and, after listening to the heavy breathing of the two Chinamen, who were in the wagon fast asleep, he was about to resume his speculations, when a dark, thin, naked form glided out of the scrub, and said,—

"Ah!"

"Give me the bull's-eye, Mr. Hangus," Mike said, "and don't fire for the loife of yer, till I sa what kind of a divil it is that is near me. It 's a black feller or a baste, and I don't know which."

As I opened the slide of the lantern the light fell upon a naked native, who was squatting beside Mike on the damp grass, and appeared in no way startled at being discovered.

"Holy Moses!" cried the Irishman, "but yer have only to spake of the divil, and he appears to yer, Mr. Hangus. I 'm murdered if it a'n't the black tracker what I was tellin' yer of. The thaef of the world must have seen me face, and heard me swate voice, whin I loighted a match for me pipe, and come straight for me, for the vagabonds can sa as well in the dark as at noonday, although yer may not belave it. They can come and go loike the cats, and are jist as quiet. What brings yer here, yer black son of the divil?" asked Mike, turning to the native, and speaking thus pleasantly to him.

"Back," was the answer, short and sweet.

"Ah, I thought so. Yer would smell terbac if yer was miles away, and a miner was smokin' on the top of Mount Muninyong. Mr. Hangus, we must hold on to the feller till daylight, and it 's most here. We can do it by a dose of rum, and numberless pipes of tobacco. He 'd smoke his blessed head off if he had the chance, and niver lave yer as long as yer gave him a pipeful. It 's in luck we are, if the thafe will only stick to us, and do his duty, and I 'll break his ugly head if he don't, and that 's no idle boast, for their skulls is loike bull's, and nade a stout club and strong arm to crack 'em. If yer don't belave it, take me shillalah and try it. Fetch him a heavy one roight on the crown of his head, and ye 'll sa that he won't so much as wink. He 'll think yer is foolin' wid him, or else crackin' the bastises that 's in his hair. They is the divil's own for standin' up under a blow, and sure, if I had a skull loike one of 'em, I 'd be the bist man at all the wakes and fairs in Ould Oireland, and care nothin' for a dozen buys at the same time. Hit him a good one, Mr. Hangus, and it 's complimented he 'd be, for the harder yer struck the better he 'd loike yer, and have the more respect for the power of yer arm. Faith, I 'se sane two big fellers stand up afore each other, and fust one would whack over the head, and thin the other, a dozen blows or more a pace, before they 'd yaild, and it would n't as much as give 'em a headache, and only a few drops of blood would foller the wake of the clubs. We used to match 'em at me run, to sa the fun, for it made us think of ould times in Oireland, whin we was at the wakes and fairs, and every buy was as good as another, until he was proved not to be, and thin he 'd fall back, and wait till he was ripe, and could play wid a stick loike an ould hand. Ah, will, thim days is passed, and I 'll sa 'em no more, but it was innocent reckeration for the buys, and kept 'em at home, and out of diviltry, and thin the whiskey was good, and a man could n't drink enough to hurt him, even if he was full of it, and I wish I had some now."

I handed Mike a flask, and he took a good pull, and then said, —

"And where was I, Mr. Hangus?"

"Breaking heads, and drinking whiskey," I answered, anxious to hear the man talk, so that my thoughts might be diverted from the painful business of the night.

"True for yer, sur. Why, for a dead shape, or one what had dieded from some disease, yer know, for we would n't give noice mutton to the loikes of thim fellers, what prefers their mate a little strong, yer know, jist so it won't hold togither, and is all tinder-loike and juicy, I have sane this black divil butt wid a ram, and a big one at that, and the ram did n't hurt him if he struck fair, headfust, but the horned brute was cunnin'-loike, and would dodge one side, and hit him on the shoulder, and the black would claim a foul, and yer 'd have died a-laughin' to see 'em as they came together, and rolled over and over, and yer could n't tell which was the most surprised, the ram or the black. Ah, it was great sport for us, whin we were a little homesick-loike, and there was no whiskey within fifty miles, and the ta was out, and the run hot enough to burn the brains roight out of yer, and the dingos was troublesome. Yes, that used to cheer us up a bit, attoimes, and now, Mr. Hangus, will yer jist hit him a stunner, and sa that I spake the truth, and pass the flask, for the ground is damp, and I 'm feared that I 'll take a bit of cold, settin' here on the grass."

I declined the invitation, for I did not want to injure the poor black, yet it is quite probable that if I had banged him over the head with a club that I should not have hurt him in the least, for I have seen them receive terrific blows from each other, and never flinch, or appear in the least damaged.

I gave the black fellow a pipe, and a glass of rum, and he settled down to real enjoyment, while Mike by words and gestures endeavored to explain the service we required. But the fellow smoked on, and only grunted out a few English words, such as he had picked up among the stockmen, and I regret to say that most of his vocabulary consisted of expressions that would not be admitted in good society, and in the presence of ladies of an æsthetic and sun-flower turn of mind. We could not speak his tongue, and even Mike acknowledged (a rare thing in an Irishman) that he only knew a few words, and those not of a scriptural nature.

But the black fellow smoked, and held out his pipe for a fresh supply of tobacco, and swallowed the smoke, and strangled under its influence, and gasped and groaned, and altogether had a terrible time of it, but all the same he enjoyed every moment, and every whiff, and seemed to express by his actions that if he ever had a boss evening it was when he fell in with such sincere friends as we had proved ourselves to be. And then he would motion for more rum, but that was a prohibited article, after the first glass, as we wanted him sober and not drunk, and, while the black can endure much tobacco, he is not steady under a deep cargo of rum.

At last we saw glimpses of daylight, and very thankful we were, for I had not been able to restrain my impatience, but had paced back and forth in the damp grass, and listened to all the animal sounds that abounded in the deep and dark forest. At last the dingos gave a final howl of disgust at the appearance of light, and went to bed, and then the parrots and parroquets commenced grumbling, and soon hundreds of birds were skimming along over the tree-tops, in search of that early worm, which economical fathers are continually holding up to their sons and daughters as good, wise lessons, in season and out of season, just as though human beings wanted to get out of warm beds in the winter for the sake of giving point to a very old and very stupid moral, which no one obeys unless obliged to by the stern law of necessity.

In fifteen minutes it was light enough to see a trail even in the dark woods, and by this time the black fellow had smoked so much tobacco that I feared his stomach would turn, and revolt at the sight of a pipe, but it did not, for he wanted more when I insisted that we should be on the move. I could no longer control my impatience. The Chinamen were awakened, and yawned, and looked as though they had been kneeling before one of their gods all night, and he had not answered their prayers to their perfect satisfaction, while Mike, after a short pull at a wicker flask, said that he was all right, and ready to fight at a moment's notice.

"Ask the black fellow if he will follow the trail for us, in case I pay well for the trouble, — a bottle of rum, and a pound of real plug tobacco," I said, as I knew that such gifts would be considered a fortune by the native.

And now commenced some of the most extraordinary pantomime that was ever witnessed on the stage of real life. Mike used tongue, arms, eyes, hands, and feet in the effort to make the native understand what was wanted.

"Do yer sa this now?" said Mike, with a gesture of the thumb and fingers. "We go follie now, right off, catch ———— bushrangers. Do yer understand phat I 'm sayin' to yer, black divil that yer are?"

Mike run away with the same idea that many other people do who endeavor to converse with one that does not speak or understand English. He thought that if he shouted loud enough, and broke his words into little pieces, and scattered them all around the person whom he addressed, there was no doubt but that a perfect understanding could be arrived at, and if not, it was no fault of the speaker.

"Rum, yer divil," yelled Mike, "and bacce, bacce, bacce. Sa, a big pace. All yer."

The native grunted, and reached out his hand for the prizes, but he was not destined to secure them until he had performed his part of the contract, and at last, by showing the black fellow the footprints of the horses, and the trail in the scrub, he comprehended the work that was required of him, and signified that he would do what was desired, but he must have a drink as earnest money, and that he received, and then coolly going to a piece of scrub took from it a spear, boomerang, and waddy, weapons which he hid the night before, for fear we might consider his visit hostile if he appeared before us armed.

We took the horse from the wagon, and hitched him to a tree, and drew the vehicle to the cover of some high scrub, and, once more examining our arms to see that they were in good order, followed the black, who, with head down, and trailing spear, trotted along, neither turning his face to the right nor left, never puzzled or confused, and just as confident of finding the resting-place of the bushrangers, as a business man, who lives in New York, is confident of meeting his merchant neighbors at the nearest free lunch at one o'clock every day except Sunday.

On we went, through scrub, and in some places where the trees were large, but not dense, the native leading, I close at his heels, and the two Chinamen in a dog-trot, which they can keep up for hours, swinging their ugly-looking knives, and having all the appearance of two men who wished that they were well out of the affair, yet did not feel like turning and running for it.

For an hour we tramped and toiled along, as noiselessly as possible, avoiding dry sticks, and rotten logs, yet never uttering a word above a whisper, until at last the black tracker raised his hand, and signified caution, and then we knew that the trail was getting warm, and that we were not far from the camp of the bushrangers.

"Mike," I whispered, "if we come to a brush, and I am sure we shall, do you think we can depend upon the Chinamen?"

"Divil a bit do I know, yer honor. If they was pin'd up, and had to foight, it's hathens they'd be wid their bloody sharp knives, a-choppin' and a-slashin' the loif out of a body, and hittin' a man whin he was down, and losin' their heads as they hacked a feller all to paces. It's demons they is whin they can't run, but for a rale square foight I suspicions 'em, I'm afeared."

"And the native — will he lend us a hand, do you think, Mike? He looks like a stout fellow."

"Divil a bit, yer honor. As soon as he pints out the thaves of the world, and gets his rum and bacca, he'll return to the wagon, and stale all we left thare, and it's not much he'll git, for I hid phat we did n't bring wid us But it's his way, and there's no help for it."

"So we must depend on ourselves, Mike?"

"That's about the soize of it, yer honor, and we'll make the thaves squale if we gets at 'em, so don't be so sorrowful-loike. Sure, we is good for any six of 'em, and lave out the Chinamin ontirely. If they helps, so much the better, and if they does not, we'll do the best we can. If I gets a fair crack at 'em wid me musket, I'll blow the divil out of 'em, now be sure of that."

"Hist," said the black tracker, and he pointed with his spear to a bit of scrub, and just beyond it we saw a light smoke ascending, and mingling in the morning vapors that were arising from the bushes and swamps.

"Bushers," he uttered, that being about as near as he could pronounce bushrangers, and then held out his hands for the prizes.

"The hathen will go no furder," whispered Mike. "He's not disposed to risk the noomber of his mess for us, and who can blame him? Give him the rum and bacca, and let him go. He's kept his word, and we'll kape ours."

I relieved Gin of one of his flasks, and gave it to the tracker, and also a plug of tobacco, and, with no more concern than if we had never met, the black turned, and retraced his steps, and did not even look behind to see if we had moved from the place where we had halted. Bushrangers or miners, it made no difference to him. One was as friendly as the other, although, perhaps, as a general thing the robbers were a little more kind when they wanted a favor, and very ugly when they did not require one.

It must not be supposed that we were standing in an open space when this conference was going on. That would have been very poor leadership, for we did not know how many pickets were lying in the bushes, and ready to give an alarm if we advanced. No, we stood under the shelter of a thick she-oak, and did not move from it until the black was out of sight, and we had matured our plans.

Those plans were soon made. We were to crawl on our hands and knees, difficult as the task might be, through the scrub and bushes, until we could get within range of the ruffians, if ruffians were really there, as we supposed they must be, and then let events take their course, governed entirely by circumstances, but under no consideration were we to retreat if we saw that Florence was a prisoner. That was settled quite firmly in my mind, and in the mind of Mike, while the Chinamen said but little, but listened hard enough to make up for lack of conversational powers.

After these preliminary measures, we dropped on our hands and knees, and crawled, Indian-like, toward the smoke, and our movements appeared to excite the utmost astonishment in a couple of laughing-jackass birds, that sat on a cedar-tree, and derided us in no measured terms for our snake-like contortions, while an old-man kangaroo, all covered with scars, and driven from his harem by some younger member of the family, looked at us in such amazement that he took a few playful leaps in our direction, and then stood still, and dared us to follow him, or even to fight him in a regular stand-up battle, in which he should have the privilege of using his hind legs if necessary.

THE OLD-MAN KANGAROO.

But we paid no attention to birds or animal, crawling on as carefully as we could, and at last gained the scrub, went through it, and then saw that we were close to a burnt clearing, and that there was a fire near the centre, and around that fire sat six of the most desperate ruffians that I ever saw, outside of a penitentiary or a slave-ship. They were all busily engaged in cooking their breakfast, as the smoke and smell of burned mutton tainted the morning air, while on the ground, near the fire, was the carcass of a fat sheep, showing Smith's run had been raided on the evening previous, to furnish supper and breakfast for his troublesome neighbors, the bushrangers, and as one scoundrel would cut off a strip of flesh, he would place it on a stick, and broil it on the coals, and, when about half done, would tear it from the skewer with his strong teeth, and let blood and fat and burned flesh mingle with the juices of the meat, and run down his face, thus rendering it more repulsive than ever. Dirtier it could not be. All were engaged in the occupation of eating, and the sheep was fast disappearing under their combined attacks; but their savage onslaught on the mutton did not occupy my time and attention. I was looking for Florence, and at last saw her under the shelter of an acacia-bush. There was some regard for her comfort, for she was seated on a blanket, and on a leaf for a plate was a huge piece of half-broiled mutton, sprinkled here and there with ashes and coals so as to give it piquancy and relish for a delicate young lady's appetite, but as Florence did not appear to have hunger for a sauce, the mutton remained untouched, much to the delight of a vulture, that perched over her head, and hoped he would have a chance at that which was so coldly rejected.

As soon as I saw that Florence was alive, and to all appearances uninjured, I glanced around to see if Mr. Kebblewhite and Monsieur Allete were near, and found that the two men were very securely lashed to trees, hands and feet, and even necks, so that they could not turn their bodies or heads, and yet they had not been gagged, a strong threat being suffcient to keep them still, if disposed to make a noise, which they were not, as they knew it would be useless.

More wretched-looking beings than Mr. Kebblewhite and the Frenchman it would have been difficult to find all through Australia, just at that moment. They had been tied to the trees all night, they had been dragged through the bush and mud, they had had no chance to wash, and the insects had preyed on their faces and hands until they looked like patients from a small-pox hospital, wandering around in a delirium of fever. The Frenchman could give vent to his sufferings in a language that the robbers did not understand, and so cared nothing about, while every time Mr. Kebblewhite spoke in tones of remonstrance, he was emphatically told to "shut up," and the order was enforced by anything that happened to be near at hand, a bone, a club, and once a quart tin pot, that a bushranger had just drunk out of, and, therefore, had no further use for it.

All this time, while I was scanning the camp, and locating the people who occupied it, I did not lose sight of Florence, who sat with bowed head, trying to forget the misery and degradation of her situation, she, the Countess of Afton, as she supposed, the petted daughter of a rich and influential Melbourne merchant, yesterday traveling in her father's private carriage, and indifferent to all of her surroundings, every wish of her heart gratified, her slightest will law in her household, and now the prize of the most hardened ruffian who should claim her, and back his claim with determination and strength. Good Heaven! what a change, and no wonder she sat upon the blanket, to protect her *petite* form from the damp earth, with her fair head bowed upon her little white hands, and wished for death, or a speedy deliverance from her miserable condition.

How I pitied her, and longed to take her in my arms, and kiss away the tears that were falling from her eyes, and to tell her that her husband would share her fate, welcoming death if it was by her side. But I knew how useless it would be, and that I should neither save Florence nor myself by such a rash course, and once, when it seemed as though I must make a dash for the clearing, and encounter all six of the ruffians, Mike laid his hand on my arm, and warned me that I was getting too excited for the leader of an expedition where coolness and presence of mind were required.

"Wait, my buy," he whispered, "and don't yer do it, for the loif of yer. It's death and damnation to the rist of us. The toime will come if yer bet kape cool, and wait till I get me ould musket in place, to blow the bloody heads off of the spalpeens. Look at 'em now, a'n't they beauties, wid their darty faces, and their darty paws?"

"If I was only free, and had a pistol in one hand, and a sabre in the other, I'd make short work of some of these dogs," Monsieur Allete muttered in his native tongue, but loud enough for us to hear. "The beasts, the cowardly ruffians! How I'd like to punish them!"

"Keep quiet, Johnny Crapeau," said one of the bushrangers, a powerful man, with enormous shoulders, and a face as dark as a Spaniard's. "Don't get excited, you frog-eater, for it won't do any good, and it would be a little more respectful to the company if you would use English when you wish to express your feeling."

The speaker I supposed to be Black Dick, whom I had heard of several times, for whose head a reward of one thousand pounds was offered by government, dead or alive. He had been a broker's clerk, in London, and transported for life, for forgeries. He had escaped to the bush some two years before, and had led a most eventful life, defying capture, and gathering a band of men around him as desperate as himself, and committed murders and robberies in every section of the country.

"I 'll give five thousands pounds if yer vill release us, and let us go free," Mr. Kebblewhite said. "Only think, five thousand pounds for our freedom, and the money shall be paid to yer jist as soon as I can reach Melbourne."

"We knows a trick that is better than that," remarked another bushranger. "We means to have more money, and we has it in our hands afore you gets out of this, now I tell you."

"How much?" demanded Mr. Kebblewhite, while Florence raised her white face, and listened with eager interest to the conversation.

"Twenty thousand pounds, and not a penny less," was the reply, and a shout of laughter was the response to a deep groan from the father, as he made a rueful face, but said,—

"Yer shall 'ave it, but no wiolence to us, and safety to my child."

"Oh, the kid is safe enough. We 'll take care that no harm comes to her. We all loves her like a sister, don't we, boys?"

"We does," roared the wretches, and then one clapped Black Dick on the back, and laughed, as though some terrible meaning was concealed beneath the words.

I made a movement to spring into the clearing, and begin the struggle that I knew must commence, but Mike laid his hand on my arm, and held me back, and whispered,—

"Don't spile all, Mr. Hangus, wid yer fiery temper, and dasire to foight. Sure I 'm not the one to hold back whin the blows fall thick and fast, but we must kape cool,— hit 'em unaware loike. There is time enough for us, if we has to wait a full hour. All that I ax of yer is to kape quiet, 'cos yer 'd miss 'em now, yer shake so much, as though yer had the ager. Be guided by Oirish Mike, and sa the rare gineralship he 'll show yer whin the time comes."

I yielded to his pressure, and listened to some of the bushrangers' conversation, although it made me almost wild with rage and fear that I should fail in saving the dear little girl who looked so wretched.

"Look a-here," growled one of the scoundrels, whom I supposed was the second leader of the gang, Slipper Sam, so called because he had a peculiar habit of slipping out of every prison in which he had been confined, and from the custody of the mounted police, whenever arrested, "yer don't mean to say that we divides all the prize money quite even, and that one cove is to have the gal and his share of the dosh too? I don't stand that, now I tell yer. The cove what takes the gal don't get the same as the rest of us. That 's fair and ship-shape. Give me the gal, and five thousand pounds, or Dick can take her, and the same sum."

"Who put up this job?" asked Black Dick, turning to his companion in crime, and speaking in a tone that was a little threatening.

"Yer did n't," retorted Slipper Sam, in a sneering way. "I did n't, and yer did n't. The Quaker planned the whole thing, and yer know it. He is willing to take a thousand puns for his share, and he shall have it, and Jack shall have his thousand, and the other two mates shall have their thousand each, and the cove what takes the gal must pay for her. I 'll stand no nonsense about this thing. A cove can't have all the luxuries, and the dosh at the same time."

For a moment I hoped the bushrangers would quarrel among themselves, and fight for the possession of Florence, as such robbers have done ever since men were vile enough to steal and murder, but the Quaker saw the storm brewing, and allayed it by a few words.

"Don't let thy evil passions arise, my dear friends," he said. "We will divide the money, and then put the girl up at auction, and the highest bidder shall take her, or we will all ask her to favor us with her smiles and kisses."

A roar of laughter greeted this rude speech, and I could hardly control my indignation, but just at that moment, away off in the direction of the hills, I heard the deep and powerful bay of a blood-hound.

"It 's Smith's dog," whispered Mike. "I know the brute well, and he 's as big as a calf, and as ugly as one of them murderin' villains. What is up, I wonder? The baste is kept chained day and night, onliss there 's trouble."

The bushrangers heard the deep bay of the Siberian blood-hound, and it seemed to surprise them, for two of them started up, and listened very attentively.

"Now, Mike, give them Hail Columbia," I whispered. "We can wait no longer. Aim well, and fire."

I discharged my rifle, and just at the same instant there was a tremendous roar at my side, a sheet of flame and smoke, a concussion that brought down upon our heads dead leaves and branches of the trees under which we were concealed, and then I caught a glimpse of Mike revolving like a circus acrobat, cart-wheel fashion, all legs and arms, in the air, as though seeking to separate from the body, and thus he whirled over and over until he brought up against a tree, and, finally, stopped, and then I heard a voice, and saw a face blackened with powder, and the voice said, —

"Bedad, there 's not in Ould Oireland, or any other country, a gun that can shoot loike that, now do yer moind?" and then I turned, and saw one of the bushrangers throw up his arms, and pitch headlong into the fire, while the other, who was standing up at the time of the discharge, presented the dreadful appearance of a man whose face was entirely shot away, and who was groping with outstretched hands for something to support his form, which swayed and reeled like a person on a ship in a storm, before he has got his sea-legs on, then, finding no support to grasp, fell all in a heap, and rolled over and over, yelling with pain and rage, blinded and bleeding, and no longer capable of offering resistance.

There was surprise and consternation in the camp of the bushrangers, and the Quaker, a long, slim man, with thin arms, and immense hands and feet, dressed in gray, yelled out, —

"The traps are on us. Each man for himself. I'm off, and advise the rest to move."

He started to run, and, as he did so, I gave him a shot with another barrel of my revolving rifle, and down he tumbled with a broken leg, and a howl of pain.

"Stand firm, boys," roared Black Dick. "We'll beat them at their own game. Fire a shot into the bushes, and I'll take care of the woman."

He discharged his pistol, as he spoke, in our direction, and then, with the smoking weapon in his grasp, dashed toward Florence, waving a long knife in his left hand.

The two remaining bushrangers poured a discharge of buck-shot in the direction we were supposed to be, but, as their aim was hasty, and we were concealed, no one was injured. I glanced over my shoulder to see how the Chinamen stood the fire, and, to my consternation and deep disgust, saw that they had disappeared, struck their colors, and fled at the first fire, and only Mike and I were left to continue the fight with the three uninjured robbers.

I should not have minded this if my rifle had not failed me just at that moment, and when I most needed it. The lock had become disarranged by the falling splinters from the trees, and one piece had lodged in the revolving part, and remained there, and no effort that I could make seemed capable of dislodging it, and restoring the gun to its usefulness. With a malediction I threw the rifle aside, and drew my revolver, and then, looking up, saw that Black Dick was near Florence, and that he was flourishing a knife, and shouting, —

"If you fire again I swear to you that I'll kill the girl, and all the prisoners. Come out of the bush, and give yourselves up, or I'll cut her throat from ear to ear."

He raised his knife as he spoke, and there was the look of a demon on his face, as he stood waiting to see if his request was complied with immediately.

"Fire one more shot," he yelled, "and my knife shall drink this girl's blood; even if it is with my last breath I'll kill her. Come out of the scrub, and let us see who is the strongest, and then we'll settle the matter."

"Wait till I load my ould Ebenazar," Mike said, "and then I'll blow him to smithereens, and be hanged to him for a bloody villain."

"Dog," I yelled, jumping from the bush, and rushing toward him, "touch but a hair of that lady's head, and you shall be torn to pieces!"

"Hullo! what traitor and spy have we here?" Black Dick asked. "Give him a shot, boys, and then I'll cut his comb at my leisure. There's only two of them, and they are half whipped already."

Luckily for me the bushrangers had not had time to load their guns, or it would have gone hard with me, but one of them raised a pistol, and I gave him a shot as I passed, and it must have touched his hand, for he dropped the weapon, and uttered a howl, and the next instant I heard Florence scream, and the bushranger had his hand on the golden hair of her head, but, as I ran toward him, he did not strike the fatal blow, but hurled the long, keen knife toward me, and, as it whizzed through the air, it struck me on the arm by which I held my revolver, and I felt the point penetrate the flesh, and then the knife hung quivering in my shirt-sleeve for a moment, and dropped to the ground at my feet. I stopped for a second to pick it up, and, almost before I had recovered an upright position, the huge bushranger was upon me, clasping my arms, and holding them to my side as though he possessed the strength of half a dozen ordinary men, and, as I felt his hot breath on my face, and saw his fierce eyes blazing with rage and triumph, I knew that my chance for life was a slim one unless I could prevent my opponent from hurling me to the ground, and stamping out my existence by means of his heavy boots.

"Now, —— you, I have you fast," the bushranger said, and as he spoke he raised me in his arms, and sought to dash me to the earth, but I avoided the fall, and bounded on my feet, and did not spend my strength in resisting his terrible efforts to put an end to my existence.

Three times Black Dick raised me in the air as easily as he would have lifted a baby, and three times I avoided the deadly fall, and clung to him with the desperate hope that I could use my pistol or knife, but I was held in too firm a clasp to work with either, but once, while I was swinging in the air, I did manage to give him a little thrust with the knife, but it only acted on him as a spur to a fiery horse, rendering him more fierce and terrible than ever.

"You would, hey?" Black Dick growled, the white foam falling from his lips, as he felt the point of the knife. "I 'll pay you for that, and other things, my lad, be assured," and once more he strove to dash me to the ground, but, failing in this, exerted all of his immense strength, and clasped me in his arms in a desperate attempt to crush in ribs and chest, and thus end the contest.

One hug he gave me, and it seemed as if all the blood in my body rushed to my head, and that it would burst with the terrible pressure. I think that if it had not been for Florence I should have wilted under that anaconda embrace, but the thought of her sufferings and danger saved me, and as his arms relaxed I once more breathed freely, and the blood receded from my brain, and I was ready for another trial.

"Jack," shouted Black Dick, "come here and give the spy a clip with your knife. He is a hard egg to crack, and I will waste no more time with him. I wanted to take him alive, and then burn him at my leisure. But I can't fool around here all day."

"I 'll see you ———, and then I won't," was the sullen response. "I don't lift a hand agin that lad for all the gold in the country."

This was a cheering assertion, and Black Dick uttered a curse so horrible, that it does not seem possible the English language could be tortured into such blasphemy.

"Whoop! I 'm comin', Mr. Hangus, with ould Ebenazar loaded nearly half full, and I 'll finish the bastes in no time," I heard Mike shout, for, so particular was he about that old kicking, worthless musket, he had stopped to load it, and nearly forgotten that I was close to death's door by his delay. He thought that I was strong enough to take care of myself in a scrimmage, where a hand-to-hand encounter was necessary, but he had forgotten that I was almost a boy, and Black Dick a grown giant, with sinews of steel.

"Don't fire, mate, I hist the white flag," shouted the man Dick had called Jack, and who had refused to aid the leader.

"All roight, throw up yer arms, and stand at rist," responed Mike, and then my opponent saw that the day had gone against him, and that if he would live to fight another time he must get out of our power, and take to the bush, and hide in the scrub, until the excitement and pursuit had subsided.

For a final effort he sought to bend me back until my spine should yield to his brutal force, but, just as he commenced the task, his eyes on Mike, who was covering his prisoners, and preventing their escape, I saw two nearly nude dark bodies, glistening with oil and perspiration, glide from the bush like spirits of the night, armed with the terrible, heavy knives I had seen for the first time at my shanty the night before.

They were my Chinamen, and they meant business, as I could tell by the angry gleam of their tigerish eyes, no longer half-closed and sleepy with opium, but open to their widest extent, like a cat's when stealing on a bird.

Without a word or a sound, bare-footed, and only wide trousers on, their bodies annointed with oil, or fat, so that an opponent could not seize and hold them, in case of a hand-to-hand contest, the Chinamen glided toward Black Dick, whose back was toward them, and all unnware of the danger in his rear.

"Look out, Dick," yelled the fellow whose leg I had broken with a rifle-ball, and who was lying near us, watching the fight with much eagerness, even if he did suffer intense pain. "The coves in the rear is arter yer."

But Dick was too much occupied in attempting to escape to hear the warning, and, while I was suffering severely, and weakening every moment from the loss of blood, for my arm was bleeding badly, I would not give the ruffian the satisfaction of asking for quarter, which I knew I could not get, nor yet release the bushranger so that he could escape, by sudden bounds, to the bush, and thus end all pursuit. But, as the fellow continued to exert his immense strength, and to bend me back, slowly but surely, expecting every moment to bear my bones crack, I shouted, —

"Shoot the scoundrel, Mike."

"Bedad, but I will, and which one shall I pop at?"

"Don't fire at me," roared the prisoner called Jack. "I 've got my hands up, and give in."

"Then, bedad, I 'll have to have a hack at the uther," I heard Mike mutter. "But if I do phat will become of me prisoners? Will yer kape quiet, yer blaggards, if I take me eyes off of yer?"

But help was arriving in another quarter. The two Chinamen glided toward us, carefully, and with timid steps, as if fearful Black Dick would turn on them, and catch them in a trap, but, as they saw that his attention was fully occupied, they quickened their paces, and, with a sudden bound, crouching and like the spring of an animal, they jumped upon the bushranger, and commenced hacking him over head, neck, arms, and shoulders, blows raining down upon the brute like the wings of a mill during a stiff gale.

Flesh and blood could not stand such an assault as that, and not turn and defend itself if possible. Dick released his hold of me, and turned, and, as he did so, I placed my revolver to his back, and fired. There was a loud report, a splash of blood through the thin shirt, and the bushranger plunged forward, only to be received on the edges of the sharp knives, which the Chinamen continued to wield, as though crazed and dazed by the smell of powder and blood. They did not mind where or how they struck, but hacked and hewed, cut and slashed, without mercy, or, seemingly, without knowing what they were doing. White foam flew from their lips, like that from an enraged boar, or mad dog; their eyes snapped and sparkled as those of a dangerous and murderous lunatic, and their yellow faces worked and writhed as if convulsed by a fit of epilepsy.

Black Dick, in spite of his wounds, struck out with his hands, but the blow was weak and uncertain, and, even as the poor wretch made an effort to die fighting, like the desperate being that he was, one heavy blow of a knife struck his wrist, and the right hand fell to the ground, and a large stream of blood gushed from the terrible wound, and then the bold bushranger, the terror of miners and police for years, fell to the earth, an oath on his lips, and defiance still in his heart, and, before he could do more than utter one bitter curse, death came to his relief. In the mean time the mad Chinamen did not relinquish their dreadful work, but continued to foam and rage, and hack at the dead body, as though they feared it would resume life, and punish them for their ferocity, and, even when I called upon Gin Sling to stay his hand, and Ah Sugar to cease his butchery, they paid no attention to me, while stout-hearted Mike, who had removed his gaze from the prisoners, to see the fight, uttered an exclamation of horror and deep disgust, and shouted, —

"Stop 'em, yer honor. The hathens is blood crazy, and don't know what they is doin'. They'll cut the body into mince-mate afore they quits, onliss they comes out of the spell. Spake to 'em, yer honor, or they 'll turn on us, for they don't know friends from foes whin they is crazed with the smill of blood."

I darted forward, caught the two Chinamen by their pig-tails, and jerked their heads backward, and then dodged one side, and it was well that I did, for the crazy devils turned in my direction as savagely as if a new foe had come upon them, and, with uplifted knives, hacked and slashed at me.

"Gin," I shouted, as I put my pistol on a level with his ear, "drop your knife, or I 'll blow the head off your shoulders. Don't you know me? Hold still for a moment, and listen to reason. Oh, would you?" as Ah

Sugar made a lunge at me with his heavy knife, and missed me, owing to his crazy blindness, and my watchfulness.

I struck the fellow so heavy a blow with my revolver barrel that he fell all in a heap, bleeding like a pig that has just received the *coup de grace* from the hands of a skillful butcher.

"Hit him agin," roared Mike. "He a'n't got no friends whin he 's on a rampage."

But there was no occasion to do so. Gin Sling saw his countryman fall, — and he lay where he fell without moving, — and, as his eyes cleared, and the foam stopped issuing from his lips, he recognized me, and made no offer to renew the attack. He rubbed his forehead, and let the knife drop from his hand.

"Alle bloode aforie meie eyes," he muttered, and then tumbled down in a dead faint by the side of his friend.

Now I was free to turn my attention to our prisoners, and those whom we had rescued. Thank Heaven, Florence was in a swoon, and knew nothing of what was going on, and had not witnessed the terrible hacking of flesh and blood, which the Chinamen had indulged in. I wanted to run to her assistance, but did not dare to, for fear that, in spite of all my exertions in her behalf, she would spurn my advances, and think I desired to plead with her on account of my services. No, I would not go near her just at present. I wou'd wait and see how she acted when she revived; but I hastened to Mr. Kebblewhite and the Frenchman, and cut their bonds, and set them free.

"Young man," said my father-in-law, "I think yer made a bloody good fight of it, and I 'd like to 'ave 'ad a 'and vid yer. Yer did vell, and I 'll not forget it ven it comes to the money part. Any time yer vants a 'undred pounds to spend do yer come to me, and yer vill get it. Do yer understand?"

I did not answer him, but Mr. Kebblewhite continued, as he wiped the dirt and dust from his face, —

"Ven it comes to money I can be as free as any von, now I tell yer. Yer has freed us, and yer shall be paid for it. Yer jist draw on me for a 'undred pounds at any time. But, let me see, vere 'as I seen that face ot yern afore? I thinks I knows it."

"You had better hurry to the assistance of your daughter," I said, not caring to enlighten him as to where he had seen me the last time.

"I vill. My poor child 'as suffered intensely, and I fears for her 'ealth. I 'll get 'er hout of this as soon as possible. But vere 'as I seen yer face afore, young man? It seems to me quite familiar like, but I can't hexactly place yer. Did yer ever borrer any money of me, and forget to repay it?"

"I think not, Mr. Kebblewhite. If I had ever asked you for money it is quite probable that you would have refused my request," I said.

"Vell, I don't know, yer know. If yer 'ad the right kind of security, I don't know but I might 'ave let yer 'ave a few pounds. But yer voice sounds like von that I 'as 'eard afore, and vere I can't for the life of me tell. Vere 'as I met yer, young man?"

"I have no time to explain all the circumstances of our first meeting," I answered, "and, if I did, you would not feel very friendly toward me, I am afraid, even if I have saved you from the bushrangers, and your daughter from a terrible fate. Suppose that you delay all questions until a more proper time, and then I may be inclined to answer some of the most important ones."

He stared at me a moment, and would have spoken again, but I turned my back to him, and he left me, and went to his daughter, muttering, and soon I faced Monsieur Allete, who had waited quite calmly until I had concluded my conversation with his friend, and then he addressed me, hat in hand.

"You are a *brave homme*," he said, "and thank you I do much very. Hope I that you escaped have all injuries. But I before have met you. Yes, sure am I. It is milord. *Parbleu*, but droll is it, to meet here you fighting the bushrangers, and giving them *assez*. Ah, well did you do. Had I a son you like much, proud I would be of him. You good man must be, milord, to save us, and your *petite femme*. Me your friend from this time. Ah, fight you well. *Sans doute, je merci vous.* Shake hands you will. Ah, good that is. I fly to madame to tell the good news to her."

"No, monsieur," I said, detaining him. "Will you please not mention to madame that I am here? Let her discover me if she desires to."

"I understand it not. But, *je ne veux pas*, if you wish. But fly you should to her arms. The *petite* has suffered much on your account, I think. Milord go on the night of his *noces*. Bad that is for him. But he explain will. Think I well of him now. Fights he like the great Napoleon, to conquer."

He shook hands, and offered me a pinch of snuff from his gold snuff-box, which the bushrangers had not despoiled him of the night before on account of the darkness, and the lateness of the hour. Then the Frenchman put on his hat, and walked toward Florence, who appeared to be reviving under the careful administration of her father.

As I passed the wretch whose leg was broken, he uttered a whimper of pain, and begged for a drink of water, but I had none to give him at the time, for the Chinamen had charge of the water-bottles, and had left them in the scrub somewhere, when they had stripped, and oiled themselves for the fight.

Mike was still keeping guard over his prisoners, — one a sailor-looking fellow, whose face I had seen before, I thought, although I could not place him, — keeping that wonderful old musket at a charge, and ready to pour its entire contents into the bodies of the men if they moved an inch without his consent, while close to him, holding his hand, and suffering intense pain, was the bushranger I had shot though the wrist on my run to save Florence. Both ruffians were not disposed to make trouble. They had had all the fighting they wanted for the day, and seemed cowed, and only anxious to save their lives.

"Mike," I said, "we have whipped them, but it was a narrow escape for us. I would not like to try it over again."

"Will, sur, I don't know but that I would. Yer sa, whin me ould Ebenazar gets started it don't want to let up for a whole hour, and, faith, did yer iver sa so illegant a gun in all your loife, sur? It shoots of itself whin once it gets started."

"What made you so long in the scrub, Mike? I thought it was all up with me at one time."

"Faith, sur, I had me oye on yer all the time, and well yer done, and I don't loike to spile a man's sport, and thought I 'd give yer a fair chance. Besoides, sur, I was loadin' me gun, and that takes time, if yer want it to do its duty loike a man."

"It's all right, Mike, but the next time I'm in a tight place, I wish you would think more of me, and less of your gun. A few minutes more, and even your gun could not have saved me."

"Faith, sur, no man could think more of anither. Ah, would yer, yer beggar? Put up yer hands this minute, or I 'll blow a hole through yer big enough to throw in a family Bible, and half a dozen prayer-books, yer dirty spalpeen."

This remark was addressed to the sailor-looking prisoner, who had dropped one of his hands to brush away a troublesome insect that had settled on his nose. But Mike did not admit of such liberties, and up went the man's hands in a hurry.

I went to the scrub where I had left my revolving rifle, found it, and soon removed the splinter from the part that had obstructed its working, and then re-loaded rifle and revolver, and was ready for a fresh attack, in case one was made.

"I knows yer, sir," said the sailor prisoner, as I finished, and was wondering what I should do with the captives and the dead.

"Where did you ever see me before?" I asked.

"I was on the old *Iowa*, sir, what brought you here. Don't you remember Jack, sir, what got a batting at the wheel one morning, and you came forward and dressed his cuts? I'm the man, sir. I knowed you at once sir, and then when Black Dick sung out for help, I did n't turn to, now did I, sir?"

"No, Jack, you did not. I am glad to see you, but not in such poor company as this. What induced you to turn bushranger?"

"Well, sir, after we got to Hong Kong I deserted, and found a hooker that was comin' here, and I shipped on her, and, arter knockin' about Port Phillip a while, I went out for a shepherd's work, and, while I was on the run, I met Dick, and he persuaded me that there was money in bushrangin', and, faith, there is; but what use is money when you can't use it? I had money but no fun with it, and here I am, and a hard course I 've got to steer for the next ten years, I suppose."

"I 'm sorry for you, Jack, and will do what I can for you, if I have the chance. How long have you been with Dick?"

"Only three months, sir, as you must know, 'cos I 's spoken to you many times, but you did n't seem to remember me, and never would own up about the old *Iowa* afore, for some reason, and Dick told me you was a swell, and not to bother you when we met on the run where you stopped with the girl."

"It was not me, Jack, that you spoke to, but some other person, who resembles me."

"P'aps so, sir, but I 'm mum if you wants me to be. I 'll swear I never seed you afore, if you wishes to get out of a scrape."

"Does any of the rest of the men recognize me?" I asked.

"No, sir, exceptin' Slipper Sam, whose face and eyes was shot away at the fust fire you give us, and who is gone to Davy Jones's locker. That 's him, sir. Jist turn him over, and see what a sight he is. He and Dick was the only ones what met the 'swell,' as they called you. But once I was sent to you on a message, and I seed you and the lass at the hut, but you would n't hail me, and so I clawed off, and never seed you agin till this minute. You was actin' with the traps all the time, was you, sir?"

"No, Jack, I was not acting with the traps, and I am not the person you think. I came here to save that young lady and her friends, and I am glad that I have done so."

"You know best, sir, what is all right and ship-shape, but I s'pose landsmen has as good a right to have a wife in every town, as a sailor in every port."

Jack was like the rest of them, — he would not believe my statement, and thought that I had been acting, for reasons of my own, as a spy, for the purpose of finally destroying his gang of bushrangers.

I did not accept of the sailor's kind invitation to turn Slipper Sam over on his back, and examine his mutilated face, for the sight must have been a revolting one, the whole charge of shot and slugs lodging in it, and tearing the flesh in every direction, and some of the lead penetrating the brain, thus causing a painful and speedy death.

"Jack," I said, "we must place you in irons, or in other words, lash you, and the man with a wounded wrist, to trees, until we can get assistance. I would n't do it if we could depend on you."

"All right, sir, I 'm willin'. Tie me where you please. I 'm rather glad that my bushrangin' life is over. It was a bloody unsartin one, and no fun to be on the tramp night and day, expectin' the traps to tumble on you every moment. My vige is ended, and now I 'm being paid off, and it will be a topsail-breeze sentence, I 'm thinkin'."

"Hope for the best, old shipmate. It shall go hard if I do not have a word to say in your behalf."

Mike and I lashed Jack and his companion, a fellow who had none of the good qualities of the sailor, to a couple of trees, tying them so firmly that they could not escape, and, while I was thus occupied, my friend Jack whispered, —

"A word with you, Mr. Angus. Don't pretend to mind what I 'm sayin' to you, but listen, and believe me, for it 's the bloody truth I 'm speakin', as sure as I 'm a sailor. You have done me a good turn, and now I 'll do you one, if you will but believe me, and it 's God's truth I 'm tellin' you, though you may not think so. Let me whisper to you, sir, and mind every word I say. Under that smudge of a fire, sir, about two feet deep in the ground, is a big box, and that box is nearly filled with gold coins, gold-dust, and bank notes. It 's the result of Black Dick and Slipper Sam's robberies for the past two years. I 've seen 'em bury their plunder there many a time, and they did n't know I was watchin' of 'em. There 's thousands of pounds, and no one knows it but me, now that Dick and Sam has slipped their cables. You take it, and keep it, and you 'll be rich. I shall never live to put my fists on it, and it 's a pity to let it lay in the ground when it can do so much good to a kind-hearted mate like yerself."

"But is there no way by which it can be restored to its rightful owners?" I asked, hardly able to give credence to the story.

"Not a ghost of a way," was the confident answer. "Dick and Sam always burnt up the bags and pusses what held the money, and dumped all in together, and it would puzzle a sea-lawyer to tell which from the other. No one can claim the dust or coin, and the bank bills are few, and of no account, if the numbers has been taken."

"Are you speaking the truth, Jack?" I asked.

"As I hope for a good watch below, sir, I 'm not yarnin'. You 'll find the treasure there all right, for no one knows of it but me now the others is dead."

"But why should they bury it under the fire?" I asked.

"Because it is the last place any one would think of lookin' over. Don't you see, the ashes is removed, the box taken out, put back agin, and then the coals is returned, a new fire is started, and who is to know what is underneath? It is not as though you broke ground every time, as that is sure to attract attention. Dick knew what he was about when he selected this spot for his headquarters. He did n't think a trap could find his way here."

"And we should not have discovered you had it not been for a tracker, who led us here. We could not have found you without his aid if we had hunted all day."

"I don't think you could, sir. We had our landmarks and courses as much as a ship near the shore, or at sea."

"And do you mean to keep this matter a secret, Jack?" I asked, in a careless tone, although I was anxious to test his story, and, if possible, to add to my wealth.

"Yes, sir. I 'll not whisper it to another man but you, not even if my life depended on it."

"Then I 'll see if your yarn is a correct one some day, when I have time. But, true or false, Jack, I 'll not forget to look after your welfare."

"Thank you, sir," and Jack dropped his head on his bosom, and appeared to dream of his early days, when he had hopes and ambition of a bright future.

In the mean time the two Chinamen had recovered from their blood delirium, and were smoking, and talking over the events of the day, one of them with a damaged head, and the other still greasy and stained with gore from Dick's wounds. They were quiet enough now, and had put their murderous-looking knives out of sight.

"Gin," I said, "go and get the water flasks. You know where you left them."

"Youe bettie Chinaman fighte likie deble whene hee wante. Seie, Ah Sugar gettie clippe frome —————— bushrange. Hee noie minde. Brave mane, Sugar. Alle samie likie meie. Wee lickie dozen mene alle samie timie."

The Chinamen did not appear to remember that I had pulled them from the dead body of Dick, and, in order to save myself, and the remains from further mutilation, had been obliged to knock Ah Sugar down with the barrel of a pistol. They had been so delirious with rage, that the past was a blank to them, excepting their hacking at the bushranger with their knives. Now they boasted of their courage.

I did not think it was worth while to hint to Ah Sugar that I had nearly fractured his skull, for Chinamen sometimes take sudden and terrible revenge for injuries, real or imaginary.

"Youe seie that blamie rascale?" asked Gin, as he arose to go in search of the water flasks. "Hee onie bade bushrange whate tiee meie upe in the bushe whene youe comee lete meie goe. Noe tiee upe morie Chinaman," and the fellow grinned as he pointed to the dead robber, and then walked off to find the water, which we all stood in need of just at that moment.

I saw that Mr. Kebblewhite and Monsieur Allete were still endeavoring to calm Florence, whose nerves had received a severe shaking, and I was just about to go to her, and offer a drop of brandy, when I heard a renewal of the baying of the hound, and this time it was quite near.

"Holy Moses," cried Mike, "the bloody baste is loose, and comin' this way, and, if he is on the trail of the bushrangers, it 's a moighty lively toime we shall have. Take yer rifle, Mr. Hangus, and shoot onliss the baste recogknizes me voice, and comes to me. He 's the divil and all his imps whin he 's on a scint."

Mike took his old gun, and I cocked my rifle and revolver, and took my position in front of Florence, to defend her if necessary.

"Vot is it now, young man?" asked Mr. Kebblewhite. "No more bushrangers, I 'ope? Remember, if yer vants a fifty-pun note at any time call on me. I 'm a man vot never forgets a favor, and I 'm not the von to let this 'ere affair slip hout of my mind. If I could 'ave got at 'em, I 'd 'ave made 'em sing small for it, but I vaited to see vot the scamps vould do. I 'm a terrible man ven I 'm aroused, as hall my relations vill tell yer, if yer ax 'em. My friend here, this poor Frenchman, vill let yer know vot I can do, if I 'as a mind. Speak hup, moorsur, and inform this young person 'ow I told yer to be calm last night, ven the gang grabbed us."

"Yes, talk much did you," the French gentleman answered, with a terrible shrug of his shoulders. "To me say you all the time, 'Don't mad much make them, or they us kill.' For the *petite* keep I quiet. Fear much for her do I. Attendez, think I. Time enough my life to give away ven they lay hand on de lady. Fight I den if die I for it. People some there is not fear de death. Monsieur Allete die not for fear ven de lady is danger in. If de fadder talk much, he fighte less den he talk. But I love de *petite*, like daughter to me."

"Yes, yes, ve knows hall that," my father-in-law said. "Give me a chance to speak vonce in a vile. I am liberal, and tells this young person to come to me for fifty puns. Ve hall hunderstands, and 'e does. Don't talk no more on the subject."

"But talks vill I," Monsieur Allete said, his calm face flushing with anger at the curt suggestion of his old friend, and the father of the young lady whom he worshiped in a manner that seemed incredible to one who knew how many snubs Mr. Kebblewhite gave him in the course of twenty-four hours. "To save de *petite* give her all dat I have. To her hair prevent being hurt, my life risk I vil. Do you that? Bah! The shentleman has much fight for us. To him give we money much. Speak have I."

"Vell, then, speak in yer hown name, moorsur, and not for Mr. Kebblewhite. I knows vot I 'm about as vell as yer does, and fifty puns is a fortune to this young man. It is quite probable that he never seed so much money in hall 'is life at von time. Vy, I commenced business vid less than that sum, and look at me now."

"Yes, I see, by gar!" the Frenchman said, with a shrug of his shoulders that was eloquence itself. "I look at you all de time, and vonder dat de *petite* father like you have. *Parbleu*."

"Not a penny more than fifty puns," growled Mr. Kebblewhite, and he turned away, with a look of determination.

He was falling in his debt of gratitude quite fast; but just at this moment Florence looked at me, for the first time, and suddenly threw up her arms, and exclaimed,—

"O Heaven, my husband!"

"TO THE DIVIL WID YER, YER BASTE OF THE WOORLD!" MUTTERED MIKE.

PART XI.

AFTER THE FIGHT. — ARRIVAL OF THE POLICEMEN, AND MR. MURDEN PUTS IN AN APPEARANCE, AND EXPRESSES HIS VIEWS. — MY OLD SHIPMATE. — SOME THINGS ARE EXPLAINED, AND OTHERS A MYSTERY. — THE HIDDEN TREASURE. — A BOLD PROPOSITION. — A WOOL SPECULATION. — FLORENCE IS OBDURATE. — SMITH'S HOME, AND ANOTHER FEMALE CRANK. — A BOLD CLAIM FOR A HUSBAND.

AS Florence uttered the soul-stirring cry of "O my husband!" I felt all my resolution weaken, and should have run to her, and fallen at her feet, if Mr. Kebblewhite had not sprung up in an excited manner, and cried out, —

"Vere is 'e? Show 'im to me somebody. Vere 's my pistols and my nulla? Let me get at 'im!"

"Faire la moue, vous stupide!" roared the Frenchman, but he might as well have talked in native Australian for all that Mr. Kebblewhite knew about French. "Quiet keep, tell you I. You are an imbecile. Nothing know you. Bah! you use not de pistols last night when de rangers bush take us. The petite has more of the courage than you. Now, call you for your pistols, and for what?"

"To shoot the man that 'as vronged my darter," was the savage reply.

"Bah! the petite has not been wronged much. The garçon is an homme brave. Fights he like a Frenchman at the barricades. He is friend mine. Speak I for him. He shall have the petite if he wants her, and know I that he loves her."

"O Angus," I heard Florence say, but just then I had to turn my back to her, and, kneeling on one knee, await the onset of the blood-hound, whose bays were growing more distinct, as he neared our quarters.

"Look a-here," Mr. Kebblewhite said, as he laid a hand on my shoulder, "is yer the Hearl of Afton, and my darter's 'usband? Jist hanswer that, vill yer?"

"Be quiet, man," I cried. "I will attend to you, and your questions, as soon as this danger is passed."

"Vot danger? There 's no danger now, is there, sence I scattered and killed the bushrangers? Vot ever does yer ludship mean? Let me see the danger, and go and meet it!" Mr. Kebblewhite roared.

"In a minute or two an infuriated blood-hound will burst upon us, and woe to the one who gets in his way. He is a tiger in his wrath, and nearly as powerful. I shall remain here, and defend Florence."

"That is right, yer ludship. Always take care of yer vife; but, as I 'as none 'ere, and as yer vill look arter Florence, I think that I 'll run hup a tree. Fight for 'er, my lud, and don't forget the fifty puns. If yer need 'elp I 'll come down, and take a 'and."

He left me, and went up a cedar-tree with wonderful rapidity, considering his age and size, and rotundity.

"Faith," muttered Mike, "if it wa'n't for the lady I 'd lave the ould spalpeen to fight it out as best he could. He 's jist fit for the saints, or the divil, and I think the last will get him. Oh, I knows him well, the ould *lag*. He is the mane one."

"Hush, Mike. Don't let the lady hear you speak disrespectfully of her father. She loves him, and he has been a good parent to her," I said.

Mike sniffed disdainfully, but just then Monsieur Allete came to my side with one of the Chinamen's immense knives. He had found it, and intended to use it, in case the dog was mad, or disposed to attack us.

"Ve vill save the petite, milord, above all other things else. Ve vill side by side stand and fight, like at Waterloo the Old Guard."

He reached out his hand, and gave my fingers a squeeze, then took a pinch of snuff, and offered his box to me, but I could not accept his hospitality just then, as a fit of sneezing would disarrange my aim.

"Don't foire at the baste till I try it wid a koind word," said Mike. "Sure, I 've spoken to the dog quite offen, and, may be, he 'll know me, I don't know. Smith kapes him chained up, unless the black fellers get at his shape, or the dingos is round, or the bushrangers is a little too fra wid the mutton. Thin he lets him go, and a divil of a row he makes of it. Holy Moses in the bulrushes! but here he comes, like a tornado, butt end foremost."

"O Angus, dear Angus, come to me, and protect me," moaned Florence, who began to be alarmed at the terrible bays which the dog uttered, and at the sudden stillness of the party that stood in front of her, while the bushrangers, who were tied up, and wounded, uttered fearful howls for protection from the savage beast, as they thought he would be likely to tear them limb from limb in his rage, unless we stopped him in his course.

"Let Angus alone, vill yer," impatiently exclaimed my respected father-in-law from his safe position. "'E 's honly doin' 'is duty, and vot does yer vant to make 'im give hup for jist now? There 'll be time enough for hall hexplanations ven the danger is past. Remember the fifty puns, my lud, or votever yer calls yerself, and if 'arm comes to my darter yer don't get the money. Call on me if yer vants 'elp. Oh, 'ow I vish I 'ad my pistols and nulla 'ere. I 'd meet the dog hall alone, and down him in a hinstant."

"Faith," cried Mike, "there 's room for all of yer. If yer want to fight we can accommodate yer. Sure, no one will take the bread out of yer mouth. But here is the dog, and we 'll sa what we will sa."

As he spoke, the huge animal, his eyes like balls of fire, and his mouth covered with foam, sprang into the clearing, and, with nose close to the ground, ran on until he found the dead body of Black Dick in his path, and this seemed to surprise him, for he sniffed at the blood for a moment, taking no notice of us, and then sat down on his haunches, and uttered a deep and prolonged death howl, a howl that was more dreadful than one of rage, such as he had expressed while following the trail.

"Rover, Rover, good, noice doggie," cried Mike, in a conciliatory tone, that he intended should be very effective, but the dog only looked at him for a moment in quiet contempt, and renewed his howls, deep and unearthly.

"To the divil wid yer, yer baste of the world," muttered Mike. "Who cares for yer anyhow?"

I heard a movement in a she-oak at the edge of the clearing, and, looking up, saw that the two Chinamen had taken refuge in the topmost branches, and were looking down on us with much complacency and independence, while, confound them, they had the two water flasks around their necks, and were taking quiet drinks, as though they enjoyed them, and the spectacle before them, at the same time.

"Let me have a shot at 'em wid me ould Ebenazar?" pleaded Mike. "I 'll bet a pound I could tumble 'em out of the tra, pig-tails and all, at the first fire. Only half a shot, yer honor."

"There are horsemen approaching us, Mike. Listen. I can hear them galloping through the scrub, and splashing in the swamp. Who can they be?" I remarked, ignoring the request, and yet full of anxiety for those who looked to me for protection.

"Begor, it must be the traps, and they has followed the dog. Sa the baste. He sabes more than a hathen Chinaman, arter all, for he don't stir from the side of the one he trailed to this spot, and he knows there 's no more fight in him. Thunder and Moses! here they comes, — the traps, six of 'em, — and don't they ride illegantly. Look at the lader, and sa him jump the scrub. Whoop! well that. I could n't have done bitter meself, and I was the divil's own buy for a staple chase in Ould Oireland, some years ago."

The six mounted officers rode into the clearing, jumping the rude obstructions as easily as circus horses leap over the low barriers placed in the ring, and, as they drew up, each policeman with a light carbine on the pummel of his saddle, and ready for immediate use, they did present the appearance of being a formidable and courageous body of men, capable of making a good fight in case of necessity, while at their head I saw the well-known face of Mr. Murden, Chief of the Melbourne Police, and the man who had given me more trouble than any other in Australia, from the day I landed on her shores, until he had met me at the mines in Ballarat, and accused me of enticing Miss Kitty from the city, by the aid of a love-letter.

"Well, it looks to me as though there had been a lively little brush here," said the Chief, as he dismounted.

"Thank 'eaven yer 'ave come," cried Mr. Kebblewhite, dropping out of the tree. "Ve 'as 'ad a devil of a row, and no mistake. I 'as 'ad fightin' enough to last me for the remainder of my life. In a minute more I should 'ave killed that bloody 'ound, yer know."

"What, while you were in the tree?" asked the Chief, with a grin.

"Vell, yes; yer see I vent up there to be hall ready to drop on 'im, and mash 'im, if 'e come near my darter. Arter ve killed the bushrangers ve 'eard the dog, and did n't know but vot 'e belonged to 'em, so got hall ready for 'im. But 'e did n't show no fight, and yer comes up, and saves 'im."

"Jist hear the ould divil lie," muttered Mike. "In a few minutes he 'll swear he did all the fightin', and we only looked on."

But Mr. Murden did not appear to take much stock in Mr. Kebblewhite's assertions, for he walked toward me, gave me a sharp look, touched his cap, and said, —

"Pray, my lord, how does it happen that I find you in such distinguished company? The last time I saw you was at Camp Reserve, and you then gave me a promise which you did not keep. You broke it in less than two hours."

"If you had returned to the mines, instead of hunting in the bush, you would have found me, and learned that I kept my word then, and as I always shall," I said.

The Chief shrugged his shoulders, and then bowed low to Florence, who came forward, and placed a hand on my shoulder.

"Mr. Murden," she said, "we owe our lives to this gentleman, who is my husband."

"I can swear to that, madame, for I saw you married," the Chief remarked, with an encouraging nod.

Florence kept back her tears as well as she could, but still allowed her hand to remain on my shoulder. But she did not once glance at my face, as though she feared her resolution would fail just when she needed it most.

"This gentleman," she continued, "and this brave Irishman " —

"Whoop! that 's ma," yelled Mike. "Thra chaers for the Belle of Australia."

Mike called for the cheers, but no one joined in with him. The police did not dare to, or could not for laughter.

"And the two Chinese," continued Florence.

"The hathens what is up in the tra. Yer can jist sa their heads stickin' out from the laves like howls," interrupted Mike.

The Chief gave him a look, and he wilted for a moment, but Florence continued, —

"We were captured last night just after sunset, and brought to this place, as the bushrangers said, to be held for a ransom of twenty thousand pounds."

"I 'd seed 'em blanked afore I 'd paid it," muttered the lady's father. "I 'd fit 'em single-'anded fust."

"Mr. Angus, or my lord, I know not which, learned of our danger, and started in pursuit. The result is before you. We have escaped outrage, and are free. For all this I owe him my deep, my heartfelt thanks, and he has them."

"And is that all, Florence?" I asked, as she paused, and withdrew her hand from my shoulder.

"God help me that is all," she responded, with a sigh, and would have turned from me, but I detained her very gently, and kissed her hand most lovingly.

She started as my lips touched her fingers, and seemed trying to be angry, but the effort was a failure. I could tell by the glance of her blue eyes, by the faint flush in her delicate cheeks, by the convulsive movement of her thin lips, that her heart was stirred by my deep love and devotion, and, if we had been alone, I could have conquered her proud spirit, for a few kisses, judiciously bestowed, does wonders with a woman who is uncertain in her mind as to which course she shall take, — be loved and happy, or rich and miserable.

"You do not hate me, Florence?" I asked, still holding her hand, and venturing on another kiss, to the intense delight of Monsieur Allete, who continued to make motions for me to keep the thing going, and not relax the kissing part even for a moment.

"I do not know my own mind as yet," she said, with a weary sigh. "I have had some hard, wicked thoughts regarding you and your conduct. But I am grateful, and let that suffice for the present. I am proud of your courage, of your struggles in my behalf, and, oh, if you were only good, I should love you as man was never loved before. But you are bad, and I want to hate you, but I don't quite."

"You have not yet fully forgiven me?" I asked, still pleading.

"There are some things a true-hearted and loving woman cannot forget, or forgive. You know what they are."

"You are unmerciful, Florence," I said. "I have suffered and endured much for your sake, and have labored day and night to win a fortune, that I might prove myself worthy of your esteem and love. But I see that it is useless. It would have been better for me had I fallen in the struggle with yonder dead bushranger; but, Florence, the thought of you, and your danger, gave me courage and strength, for I knew what your fate would be had I yielded."

"You have but yourself to blame for this coldness on my part, Angus," Florence said, with a trembling lip. "I might have pardoned your deception in marrying me, if indeed there was deception, which I have reason to doubt, had you been true to me, and not disgraced me by a clandestine flight."

"You know, Florence, that I asked your pardon for all that had occurred, but you would not grant it. You refused me even a word of consolation. Do you forget?"

"Why did you leave me on that dreadful, unhappy night so unceremoniously?" she demanded, with a proud look.

"Because I am a young man of a religious and moral character," I answered, thinking those words would crush her, but they had no more effect than when I first used them, the night I was married.

"It is false," she cried, with a fierce stamp of her pretty little foot. "You are neither religious nor moral. Did I not read in that dreadful Melbourne paper the confession of one of my maids, that, on your way to my chamber, you stopped on the stairs, and kissed her?"

"Blast that girl," I thought. "She was so proud of the kiss she had to tell of it. So much for trusting a secret to a woman. I shall know better next time." But I only said, —

"Can you believe me guilty of such a crime, Florence?"

"Yes, crimes a thousand times worse. Angus, I could have forgiven you for kissing that mean, contemptible, forward jade of a girl, — I packed her out of the house as soon as I was well enough to get out of bed, and read that awful paper, and I wanted to have her imprisoned, but could n't, so refused to give her a reference, — but when I think of other sins you have committed, my heart turns against you, and is hardened. I can never trust my happiness in your keeping; and yet I will own that I love you a little, and that I shall never love another as I do you. Of that be assured."

"Will you name my sins, Florence, so that I can defend myself from the charges?" I asked.

"You have no defence," she replied, her pretty face showing more emotion than when she commenced to arraign me. "I have heard of your scandalous doings in Melbourne. All of my female friends told me of them, as soon as you deserted me. I blush for you, Angus. At Webber's I again traced you, and find you vowing devotion to a flaxen-haired *thing*.

At Ballarat you take a bold, mean girl out of a respectable house, and run away with her. Do you deny it, Angus?"

"I do, most decidedly, Florence, and it is cruel to accuse me of such things."

"Mr. Murden can prove every word that I have uttered," my wife replied, indignantly.

"I do not wish to be called into this controversy," Mr. Murden said. "It is a family quarrel, which can best be settled by the parties most interested. Mr. Kebblewhite offered a reward of one hundred pounds "—

"Twenty-five, my friend, I think," interrupted Mr. Kebblewhite, with a wave of his hand. "And the reward was withdrawn months ago, so I sha'n't pay a penny."

"I was anxious to touch a portion of that reward for my men, and so made a rapid search for my friend's noble son-in-law. I found him at Camp Reserve, after hearing of him in various quarters, disguised as a miner. He did promise me most faithfully that he would have nothing to do with Miss Kitty Stukely, and yet, in less than two hours, he broke his word, and played a very sharp trick on an old policeman. I have no more testimony to offer, for I had no orders to arrest, and no grounds to make one. That is my share in the business."

"You hear, Angus," said my wife very softly, as though she was rather sorry the case had gone against me.

"Yes, Florence, and every word is false, excepting one portion. I did kiss your maid on the stairs, but it was while I was laboring under a slight aberation of mind, and did not really know what I was doing."

"I 've had 'em meself in that way miny and miny a time. All men is liable to 'em, miss, some time or other, married or single," interrupted Mike, and, while the Frenchman grinned, and Mr. Murden smiled, Florence did not appear to see anything laughable in the matter, but turned on me the full battery of her scorn.

"You see, Angus, how useless it is for you to defend yourself against the charges I have made against you. Prove them false, and take me, even if you are poor, for I still love you."

"Not much," cried Mr. Kebblewhite. "My son-in-law must dress my darter as a lady. If yer a'n't a nobleman, and yer a'n't got no money, the thing is hoff, yer know. I'll give yer ten pounds for vot yer 'as done for us, but Florence must 'ave a 'usband vot can pony up the cash, yer know."

"You have enough for all of us, papa," Florence said in a determined tone.

"Yes, and 'e means to keep it," was the response. "Yer 'll git a divorce, and find a swell vot 'as the brass, and I 'll give Angus here a five-pun note, and that vill be hall right, and satisfactory."

"He 'll make it a penny in a little while," muttered Mike, with a disdainful croak.

"Are you very poor, Angus?" asked Florence, once more laying a hand on my shoulder. "Have you money enough to support a wife, even in humble circumstances?"

"I am poor, Florence, and don't think I have enough fortune to support you as you have been accustomed to."

I was determined that if she took me she should do so for myself alone, and not for money, and, although I had a good large sum, I did n't know how much it cost to dress and support a fashionable young lady, so determined to be on the safe side, and say that I was poor. Let a wife imagine that you are making money, and her wants will increase faster than your bank account.

"I am very skillful at housework," Florence said, as though thinking of the future. "I can dust, I have made a bed, and once I tried a pie, but no one would eat it."

"And no von vould or could lay on the bed," her father remarked to the Frenchman, who nodded his head in acquiescence, and made a grimace, as he thought of that terrible pie.

During all this time, although we had been conversing, the policemen had not been idle. They had assisted the wounded, as far as possible, and one of them had secured the hound, and tied him to a tree, and not till then did the Chinamen descend from the she-oak, and grin a welcome to the traps.

"Black Dick and Slipper Sam are dead, sir," reported one of the officers to Mr. Murden.

"Are you sure?"

"Yes, sir, quite sure."

"Then you are in luck," turning to me. "A reward of one thousand pounds will be paid for the death of Dick, and five hundred for Slipper Sam, and one hundred for each bushranger of less note. My lord, you and your associates have made a good day's work of it."

"Then I withdraw the reward of five puns which I offered for our rescue," Mr. Kebblewhite said, in a hasty tone.

"I knew he would come to it at last," whispered Mike. "Oh! the mane baste."

"And, as I did some of the fightin', I think I ought to share the reward," Mr. Kebblewhite continued.

The Frenchman's face expressed the disgust which he felt, as he said, —

"My life, and dear all that I ho'd, owe I to milord. If poor he is, all that have I is his. He shall keep the petite for his femme. Spoken have I."

"And a very noice koind of a spach it was," cried Mike. "It does honor to yer heart, and should have come from the mouth of a son of Ould Oireland, bedad."

"Mr. Murden," I said, and a twinge in my arm began to show that I was wounded, and a little weak from the loss of blood, "I would not take a penny for the death of those men, or the capture of the living, if I never had a copper in my pockets. It would smell of blood, and the money would burn in my hands, and bring no happiness to me. Let the reward be distributed among Mike and the Chinamen. I will have none of it."

"Anoother sentiment worthy of Ould Oireland," cried Mike. "But I have no sich delicacy, and don't be afeared to offend me by givin' me the lion's share, for, sure, it 's little the hathen did at the pinch."

"We will arrange it to your satisfaction," the Chief said. "There shall be no trouble about distributing the rewards, although I could have wished that my men had had a share. But, as they did not take a hand in the fight, we must go without it."

"Sure, there was fight enough for all, while it lasted," Mike responded. "At one toime I 'd have given a few puns out of me own pocket had yer but bin near us, and ready to lend a hand. But, the Lord be praised, we won, and our reward is the greater."

Mr. Murden was about to leave us, when Mike noticed blood slowly trickling down my left arm, and staining the ground, and green grass.

"Sure," he cried, coming toward me, "Mr. Hangus is hit, and blaedin' loike a pig, and we knows nothin' about it, and a-settin' here, and chatterin' loike ould parrots. Sure, yer honor, it 's not bad, I hope?"

"A mere cut, Mike, but it needs dressing, for it has bled quite freely, and is painful."

Mike rolled up the flannel shirt-sleeve, and I saw that the point of Black Dick's knife had entered the fleshy part of my arm, and made a wound about an inch long. Luckily the weapon had not touched the bone, or cut an artery; but my escape was a narrow one.

"Come here, yer hathens, wid the water and the brandy," roared Mike, addressing the two Chinamen, who had descended from the tree some time before, feeling assured that the blood-hound would not molest, or the police arrest, them, and, in obedience to the summons, they advanced, and gave Mike the brandy flask, and a water-bottle.

"Take a sip of the sperit, yer honor," Mike said. "It will put life in yer heart, and strength in yer busom. That's right. Now we'll wash away the blood, and put on a bandage in no time."

"Let one of my men, who is something of a surgeon, attend to the wound," the Chief said. "It is not dangerous, but will render the arm stiff for a few days."

"Divil a man prisent dresses the cut but me," Mike answered, a little brusquely. "I can do it as will as any sargeon in the force, for it's sich things we is used to in Ould Oireland. Here, hathen, bring me a smokin' brand from the fire."

The Chinamen looked puzzled, but just then Florence left the side of her father, and came toward me.

"Angus," she asked, in a low, sweet, sad voice, "will you let me dress your wound? I did not know that you were hurt."

"I fear that the sight of blood will cause you to faint, but, if you wish, I shall be glad of your help," I answered, pleased at her kindness.

"I shall not faint, and I will do all that I can to relieve your sufferings, but you must never, never ask me to forgive you, for I feel that I cannot. You have been too wicked and cruel for mercy at my hands."

"Ah, miss, don't talk to the poor young gintleman in that way. Sure, he has n't a cruel bone in his whole body, and he loves yer to distraction, and ivery night he drames of yer, or some one else, and calls yer name, and mourns for yer."

Now this would have been splendid, and helped me in my wife's favor, for, when she said she never would forgive me, it meant that she was all ready to do so, if a little urging was resorted to; but poor, blundering Mike, with the best intentions in the world, and who was willing to do a little lying for my sake, as men usually are where a woman is concerned, overshot the mark, and made a complete failure.

"Whose name does he mention in his dreams?" asked Florence, as she knelt by my side, and her face assumed a most angelic expression while holding my arm.

Now if Mike had only said, "It is your own, miss," all would have been well, and my lovely little wife would have had her head pillowed on my heart in a moment's time, but, unfortunately, he did not remember Florence's name, and so uttered the very one that he should not have mentioned.

"Sure, miss, he says in his drames, 'Me own dear wife, Kitty, how I love yer.'"

"What?" cried Florence, dropping my arm, and starting up, with anger on her face.

Poor Mike thought he had not put the case strong enough, and so continued to add more testimony, —

"And it's day after day, and night after night, he spakes of his Kitty, and drames of her, and, O miss, he loves yer wid his whole heart, and don't yer iver forget it."

"No," said the indignant little fury, "I never will forget it; and yet I was fool enough to love this man in spite of all the reports that I have heard of his *liaisons*. You wretch! Don't you ever speak to me again. I want to go home to mamma."

"Yes, I shall, Florence," I answered. "When I can prove to you that I have been honest and true, and that my love for you has never swerved, and never will, then, O my darling, I shall speak to you, and you will listen to me."

"How long before that time will arrive?" my wife asked, a little more appeased, still lingering near me, as though loath to depart.

Again Mike blundered, and yet with the best intention in the world.

"Sure, miss, yer should have sane him at Webber's, if yer has doubts of his love for yer. Faith, ould Webber's darter come up to him, and put her arms around his neck, and kissed him half a dozen times, and his honor was so indignant that he could n't spake for tin minutes, and thin he said she must n't do that any more, for he was a married man, or wanted to be one, I disremember which."

"Take me home to my mamma," the trembling little woman said, and burst into a flood of tears.

"O Mike, Mike," I moaned, "you have done it now."

"Faith, sur, I think I have, but in what way is a puzzle to me. I did the best I could for yer, but the lady don't same to take kindly to yer, for some rason or other."

"If there is a mean man in this world, if there is one that I thoroughly despise and hate, it is you," Florence said, brushing away a tear, and looking at me as though she believed every word that she uttered, but I knew that she did not, because she was only jealous, and a jealous woman is lost to all sense of truthfulness, and has no control of her temper. For a while she is a fury, and cannot distinguish between right and wrong. "You say you love me, and feel proud of being my husband, and what do I find?"

"Yer find him fightin' loike a brave man for yer loif and yer liberta, and there's not miny is loike him, miss, now I tell yer," Mike said, in an indignant tone.

"You mind your own business," the lady cried. "I can manage my own affairs without your interference. I loved this man, would have lived in a fourth-class hotel with him, would have almost waited on myself, when I was not tired, for his sake. But now I have done with him. I will no longer be his wife, whether he is lord or Yankee."

"Thra chaers for the Yanka," roared Mike, who was not in the least abashed with the tirade of words, but Florence fled after one regretful glance at my face, and I could not win her back to me. She did not even look at me, and I really believe she hoped my arm would pain me as a punishment for my crimes. If Mike had held his tongue, I really think that I could have convinced her, while dressing my wound, that I was not the one who was masquerading through the country, making love to every fresh face that could be found, and promising marriage to a dozen women, and yet not coming up to the mark when time was called. But it was no use, and I could only sigh my regrets, as Mike bound on a bandage, wet with brandy, and then held my arm over a smoking brand, to take out the soreness, and heal the cut, as he said, and a very good remedy I found it, as it is much used by the black fellows to cure their horrible self-mutilations, on breast and other parts of the body.

"Shall I go to the lady, and spake to her agin, and sa if I can't move her?" asked Mike, as he put the finishing touches to my arm, noticing my deep, dejected look.

"No, Mike, you are not skillful in matters of the heart. I must trust to time, and my own exertions."

"Thin the saints help yer, sur, for, sure, yer knows no more about a woman's heart than yer do of the trails in this pace of bush. A moment ago, if yer had but held out yer arms, she would have tumbled into them, as aisy as a drunken miner falls down a shaft of a dark night. But yer lit the opportunity go by, and now where are yer? And after all I had done for yer too. O Mr. Hangus, will yer niver larn that a bold front, and a little lyin', is all that the bist of 'em wants, to make 'em think that the world has but one parfect man, and that man is her own. Will, will, I sa that I shall have much trouble in yer edication, if yer mane to run arter women instid of settlin' down to real domestic life."

Mike's assurance was amusing, and yet he was really unconscious that he had brought much trouble upon my head by his thoughtless chatter.

"If your lordship is ready we will now look over the prisoners, and see what is to be done with them," Mr. Murden said. "Of course you are willing that they should be turned over to my men, as we can take care of them?"

"Certainly, but there is one thing I wish you would oblige me in," I said.

"Yes, you have but to name it."

"You will persist in calling me a lord. I have denied it from the evening when we first met until the present time."

"And now you admit the fact?"

"No, sir, I admit nothing of the kind. I am not a lord, I have no right to a title, I don't want one, and feel content with being an American citizen."

The Chief whistled softly, and looked at Florence and her father, who were sheltered from the hot sun by some branches, cut from the trees by the attentive Frenchman.

"What name do you wish to be called by, my lord? I beg pardon, Mr."—

"Angus," was my answer. "As I told you before."

"Very well, Mr. Angus, I will respect your whim, if you will answer me one question."

"Certainly, sir. Ask it."

"How did you disappear the night you left Camp Reserve with Kitty? I followed with a tracker, one of the best in the country, and you threw me off the scent, and I never recovered it."

"And yet if you had returned to the mines, you would have found me there, for I never left them, and I have not seen Miss Kitty since the night I parted from her, and left her in charge of Mother Higgins."

The Chief whistled a waltz, and did not seem inclined to pursue the conversation. He still thought I was romancing for some purpose or other, but what that purpose was he could not surmise.

"As you please," he said, and then, looking at Mr. Kebblewhite, asked, "Have you learned your father-in-law's history as yet?"

"Yes, Mike related it to me some months since."

"I might have suspected it. He was in the employ of Mr. Kebblewhite while a ticket-of-leave man, and knew all about him. Has it changed your sentiments toward the young lady now your wife?"

"No, she is just as dear to me as the night I left her so abruptly. I still love her, and always shall, but she will not believe in me until the Earl of

Afton and I are brought face to face, and this, Mr. Murden, you must do for me."

The Chief shrugged his shoulders, and again laughed, a polite laugh, but an incredulous one.

"I can't perform miracles, Mr. Angus, and you should know it."

"You can do an act of justice, and must do it, Mr. Murden. Somewhere in this vicinity the Earl of Afton, if there is such a man, is concealed, and with him is the girl Kitty. To you I look for solving this terrible mystery."

"How?"

"Send out these men, with instructions to visit every sheep-run in Victoria, or at least in this section of the country. Let them question every stockman they meet, every native black, go from one place to another, never letting the scent grow cold, always insisting upon searching the huts of the shepherds, and I will guarantee that the noble earl will be unearthed, and placed before me, and that I shall be vindicated from some of the charges that now hang over my head."

"The undertaking is a formidable one. What reward can I offer my men if successful? A reward to a policeman is like an opiate, — it either puts him to sleep, or makes him wild to distinguish himself. If he can make more by slumbering, his dreams are serene, and if there is money in vigilance, he can keep on a trail day and night, for a week, and feel no fatigue."

"Mr. Kebblewhite offered a hundred pounds' reward for me, did he not?"

"Yes; but he supposed that you were a great lord, and had wandered off, insane from happiness. I did not tell him the cause, for, to speak the truth, I considered you a little loony at that time, and I think you are now. But you have your reasons for acting as you do, and I am satisfied. Some swells have funny fancies. Sometimes they think it cunning and pretty to chatter and grin like idiots, at other moments they dress as monkeys, and look as near like fools as possible. But you have your peculiarities, and I am satisfied. Now about the reward."

"Would your men be satisfied with a reward of two hundred pounds if they should find my 'Dromio'?"

"Yes, they would be delighted to earn the money, but it seems a pity to send my fellows scampering all over the country, when I know it will be of no use."

"At least let them try the experiment. They shall be paid if they succeed, and shall be rewarded if they do not. Is it a bargain?"

"Yes; if you are in earnest."

"Then call your men together, and state what I want of them."

The Chief did so, and all took a square, policeman-like look at me, so that they would be likely to know me again. Then they were instructed to make search for a person just like me, and to arrest him, and take him to Melbourne, and hold him at the Chief's private office until Mr. Murden ordered his discharge. No violence was to be offered, and the party was to be treated with respect. Then the men were informed that a reward of two hundred pounds was to be paid for the arrest, and that the money would be placed in the Chief's hands in a few days. If, however, the men should meet me on the road, and could not tell whether I was myself or my double, then I was to make a peculiar sign, and the traps would know that I was not the one desired, and so let me pass. This was necessary, as I should have to return to Camp Reserve to settle up a few business details, before I went to Melbourne.

"Tomorrow you can commence your search," Mr. Murden said. "Now we must take care of the dead, and the prisoners. I will send the latter direct to the city by the men who are waiting for us at Smith's, and despatch a party to bury Dick and Sam. Let them rest where they fell. There is no need of formal funeral ceremonies over the remains of two of the greatest scoundrels that have roamed the bush for years. A common grave shall hold them. Let one of the men ride over to Smith's and order the rest of the force here, and tell them to bring a couple of spades, and three or four led horses, one of them with a lady's saddle. It's no use to talk of carriages here. We can't get one through the scrub; and, by the way, tell Mr. Smith we shall all drop down on him about dinner time, so that he can be prepared. Let one of the men search for the bushrangers' horses. They must be hobbled near here. Bring them in, if you find them, and put the saddles on. I see them lying under that scrub. Better take that hound, Martin, if he will follow you. He is dangerous to have around. Tell Smith he did nobly, and to tie him up. He has his father's blood, and is the best dog in the country for a trail."

All these orders were given in an off-handed manner, as though Mr. Murden was accustomed to command, and to have his commands obeyed.

"The American gentlemen I spoke to you about, the first evening we met, owned a wonderful hound, and this is a direct descendant. Like his ancestor he is named Rover, and is nearly as good, but much more savage. Rover, this gentleman says that he is an American. Will you shake hands with an American, old boy?"

The huge animal looked at me for a moment in savage grandeur, then slowly raised one of his paws, and put it in my hand.

"Is he a Yankee, Rover?"

The hound threw up his head, and uttered a roar that could have been heard half a mile distant, and again nearly drove Mr. Kebblewhite and the Chinamen into the tree-tops with fear.

"That settles your case," said the Chief, with a puzzled look. "Rover can tell nationality as well as a human being. I never knew him to make a mistake. He is your friend now for life, and will do your bidding much better than mine. All of the blood are alike in that respect. Ask him if you are a Chinaman."

I did so. He showed his teeth, and an open mouth, like a cavern, while a howl of intense disgust broke upon our ears, and rattled off toward the mountains, awakening the sleeping dingos, and stirring to a flutter the drowsy parrots.

"Good boy," I said, and patted his massive head, and, although the policeman called the animal, to take him to Smith's, his owner, the hound refused to pay the least attention to the command, but followed me around and laid down at my feet if I rested for a moment.

"Mr. Murden," I said, as soon as he had issued his orders, "I want you to do me another favor."

"What! a second one?"

"Yes; and not difficult to grant."

"Name it, and let me be the judge on that point."

"That poor fellow, who is tied up, and looks at me so beseechingly, was once a shipmate of mine. He is a sailor, and has had hard usage. He is not a bad one, as I happen to know. Can't you let him escape accidentally?"

"Good Heaven! do you know what you are asking me to do?" cried the Chief.

"Yes, to perform a good action. Let him be carelessly guarded, and slip away tonight, and make the best of his course to Melbourne, where he can find a ship. I will see that he has enough money to support him until he obtains a vessel."

"The devil! Do you know what kind of a job you are giving me?"

"Yes, an easy one. Take all the rest, and do with them as you will, but set Jack free."

"You are in earnest in this matter?"

"Yes, quite serious."

"Well, I'll think of it, and, perhaps, it can be brought about. But it's difficult."

"I have another reason for asking," I whispered. "He has revealed to me where all the treasure the bushrangers have stolen for the last two years is hidden."

"Certain, sure?"

"I think so."

"And what do you propose to do with it?"

"You and I will share in the spoil, Mr. Murden. We will take the dust and gold, and the bank-notes you can advertise as having been found on the persons of the bushrangers."

"A devilish good idea. Your friend shall step out this very night, and we will lift the deposit as soon as you please. Name the hour."

"This afternoon. But we can hold on to Jack until we find out if his statement is correct, and to prevent his forestalling us."

"I see. You were born for a policeman. How far shall we have to travel to find the spot?" asked the Chief eagerly.

"That I can't tell you just now. Jack's yarn may be true or false. If true, no one will be the wiser. If false, you will let him go just the same? Promise me that."

"It is hard, but I promise. If the packages of dust and nuggets can be identified we should be bound to restore them to their original owners," sighed Mr. Murden.

"But that need not trouble you. All the plunder was poured into a common lot, coin and dust, and the bags and purses destroyed."

"That relieves my conscience amazingly. Cunning rascals, they wanted all evidence destroyed. They did well. We sha'n't have to advertise for owners. Ah, this reminds me of old times. I feel as though I was growing young again, when my American friends and myself roamed all over this district, and made it rather lively for the gangs of bushrangers who infested some parts of the country."

At this moment one of the officers approached us, and reported to the Chief that the bushranger who had been injured in the leg, a bone being broken, it was supposed, looked like an old offender, but no one could place him.

"Let me see him," said the Chief. "If he is an old convict I think I shall be able to give some account of him."

We walked over to the shade of a gum tree, where the wounded men had been humanely placed by the police, and there, sitting on the ground, with his back to the tree, sat the man who was dressed in the quiet, gray clothes of a Quaker, and the same person who had accosted me in the streets of Ballarat the night before, and who had given me the information of the contemplated abduction of Florence and her party, the man whom I had first seen on Mike's team, and who had left us before we reached Webber's. In fact, the wounded robber was no other than Aramena Meully, the Quaker, traveling through the mines and country, to obtain funds to erect a Friends' meeting-house in Melbourne, as he had repeatedly stated.

"Thou seest before thee a very unfortunate friend," said Meully, as we approached. "Taken captive by the blood-thirsty wretches, held by them for three days and nights, and thus prevented from prosecuting my sacred mission, I desire to thank thee for my deliverance."

Mr. Murden did not answer. He was looking very attentively at the Quaker, as though trying to remember where he had seen him before, and under what circumstances,

"I know your face," the Chief said. "I have seen it somewhere."

"Thou hast. We have met quite frequently in Melbourne, where I pursue my humble calling, a member of the small family of Friends. Wouldst thou contribute a moderate sum of money to aid our cause?"

"Jack," I asked, "is the man's story true?"

"I don't go back on a messmate to save my neck," was the firm reply.

"Can you answer the question?" asked Mr. Murden of another fellow, who was nearly dead from pain, a shot from my revolver having passed through his hand, just as he had been drawing on me, when I sprang into the clearing.

"You believes what you please," was the sullen answer.

"If thou will lend me a horse to get to Ballarat, I shall find friends there who will aid me until my health is once more restored," whined the Quaker.

"Did n't I see you at Camp Reserve last evening?" I asked.

"Thou couldst not, my friend. I was here, a fast prisoner, and much did my spirit chafe at the detention, and the unholy orgies of these bad men."

There was considerable whine to the Quaker's tones, and he overdid it a little, for suddenly Mr. Murden struck his hands together, and exclaimed, —

"Why, you blanked old scoundrel! It 's Steel Spring, boys. You have heard of him. He was discharged from prison a little while ago," and Murden danced with delight.

The policemen crowded around to get a glimpse at the face of one of the most celebrated bushrangers that ever infested Victoria, or any other part of Australia.

"Thou art mistaken, friend. I am an honest man, and a true member of the society of Friends. All Melbourne knows me, and thousands in Gelong love me."

"I recollect the old rascal now, your honor," said one of the younger members of the police. "I saw him while in prison, and on the day he was discharged. He was taken care of by a Mr. Meully, a good Quaker of Gelong, who hoped to make a useful man of him. While with him he must have learned to palaver as he does, and, after he got proficient, dusted out at his old trade. I have met the cove half a dozen times on the road within the last few months, and never suspected that he was on the fly. Yet, confound him, he always led me along to speak of the traps, and what they were doing. It is Steel Spring, sure enough. I could swear to him anywhere."

The face of the pseudo Quaker never changed so much as by the quiver of a muscle, and his eyes looked firmly at us as the charges were made. He had a wonderful command of countenance, and it stood him in need just at that time.

"Thou art all mistaken, friends," he said. "I am only what I seem, — a poor member of the society of Friends."

"Oh, stock it," cried the wounded bushranger, who was tired, and sick with pain. "Own up like a son of a gun that you are, and don't come none of the Quaker dodges here. They knows you, and it's no use."

"Vot does yer mean, yer miserable vhelp?" the so-called Quaker responded, a sudden change coming over his placid face, as well as his tongue. "If I vos as bad as yer is I 'd be the devil, or anything but a 'uman being. Yer 'as committed crimes enough to 'ang yer a dozen times and hover, vhile I 'as only acted as a spy sence I jined the gang, and never 'urt a 'umnn being, so 'elp me 'Eaven."

It was surprising to see how the fellow had changed from a peaceable-like Quaker to a fiend, and his calm, quiet words, well chosen, and correctly spoken, gave place to the slang which he had been accustomed to use when mixing with his companions in crime. He was a wonderful man in many respects, and the like was never seen in Australia, or any other land, whether we consider his low cunning, or the remarkable manner in which he could twist his thin form and legs in all sorts of shapes and grotesque figures.

"It is Steel Spring," said Mr. Murden. "No one can mistake that voice or look. We have got you again, old fellow, and now it will be a lifer, and no mistake."

"Blank yer all," the fellow snarled. "I vish that I could live my life over again. I would show yer less mercy than I 'ave in the past. But I cheated yer as a Quaker, and not von of yer smartest traps picked me up, and I a dodgin' of 'em every day. Ah, and yer call the perlice smart, don't yer? Vy, right 'ere in yer midst is a swell vot 'as been vid us for months past, 'e and 'is gal, and yer don't lay a 'and on 'im, 'cos 'e suddenly plays the traitor, and sells us hout. Ah, if ve 'ad but known it a few 'ours ago. Honly a few 'ours."

"Who do you mean?" asked Mr. Murden, with sudden interest.

"That 's the von I mean," responded Steel Spring, pointing to me. "'E and his gal 'as been vid us, and Black Dick and Slipper Sam said 'e vos all right, and keepin' hout of the vay of the traps, for some crime in Melbourne. Now 'e turns on us, just as I knew 'e vould. Ve should 'ave twisted his neck ven ve 'ad the chance."

I was not surprised at the charge, and neither was Mr. Murden. He had listened attentively to all that Steel Spring said.

"You see, Mr. Chief, that the Earl of Afton is in the neighborhood. You can find him, and, perhaps, these fellows may give you a clew;" but all that we could say would not open the mouths of the prisoners, and even Jack did not state in what direction was the hut in which my double and the girl were living, or on whose run it was.

By this time it was noon, and the dry weather still remained. The policemen had arrived with several led horses, and one with a side saddle, for Florence. The bushrangers' animals, all stolen from Smith's run, were driven in, and saddled, and while two of the officers dug a common grave for Black Dick and Slipper Sam, the rest of us prepared to get ready to start for Smith's house. I sent Mike and the two Chinamen to find the horse and wagon we had left in the bush, and directed them to drive to the stockman's as soon as possible, so that the animal could be fed, and we return home in the evening.

"Florence," I said, approaching that young lady, hat in hand, "we are about to leave here for a house where you can find some of the comforts of civilized life. Shall I assist you to mount a horse, and ride by your side?"

For a moment she hesitated, and I thought that she would relent, but the struggle was of short duration. She became hard and cold, but still did not look at me, as she said, with quiet, womanly sarcasm, —

"Your wife would be only a burden to you. Dutch and other vile girls seem more to your taste. No, sir, I can dispense with your services for the present," and she tossed her head.

"When I prove, Florence, that I have been wronged, then you will smile on me, and be sorry for this."

"O Angus, if you only could, you do not know how happy I should be," and, for a moment, I hoped that the ice had been broken, but it was not, for she remembered the evil reports that had been circulated respecting my moral character, and she froze up at once, giving her hand to Monsieur Allete, who bowed, removed his hat, and conducted Florence to her horse, and whispered to me, as he did so, —

"Courage, mon garçon. Vell all vill be some time. La petite is not en regale now just. De bath does she need, clothes clean. Vomen, de handsome vones, mind you, do desire not love to be made vhen their hair is down all, and curl not in. They vant to be sweet vhen vish dey to be sweet. Attendez."

Florence did not look quite so attractive as the evening she was arrayed in her bridal dress, but I made all allowances for a lady who had passed a night in the bush, where water was scarce, and towels unknown, and no combs or brushes within some miles. But I had seen her under other circumstances, and my love was just as devoted, and just as true, as the night I had wed her.

She passed me with a bold attempt at bravery, but there was a tear in her eye, and the pretty head was not elevated at an angle of forty-five degrees. If I could have been alone with her, and she had been dressed to receive company, I think that I might have overcome her objections, and she would have looked on me with favor. But women don't like to be bored when not debonaire, and I was wise enough to pursue just the best course that I could take, that is, let her alone, until she had recovered her spirits, and thought of the danger that I had undergone for her sake.

I watched her until she was mounted on a steady old horse, and then Mr. Kebblewhite turned to me, and remarked, —

"I don't know jest vot to say to yer. If yer is a lud, I vants to thank yer, and to say that I still thinks that the veddin' 'olds good. If yer a'n't a swell, I 'as my doubts on the subject. But, no matter vot yer is, call on me for a pun or two if yer ever needs it. I 's a ginerous man ven I takes a notion, and I do rather fancy yer, but yer shculd n't have deceived us so by givin' hout that yer vos a lud."

"You forget, Mr. Kebblewhite, that Mr. Angus did protest that he was not a swell, and that no one would listen to him. You must remember that.

He stated to me the same thing several times, but I thought that he was just crawfishing, for the purpose of getting out of a matrimonial noose, after having heard some reports which were circulated quite lively through the streets of Melbourne."

"Vhat reports?" demanded Mr. Kebblewhite, in innocent surprise.

Mr. Murden approached, and whispered in his ear a few words. What they were had a wonderful effect on the man. His red face flushed a deeper scarlet, and his lips trembled. He did not utter a word, but mounted his horse, and, with head bent down, waited for Mr. Murden to give the signal to start.

"Ride with me, Mr. Angus," the Chief said. "Here is a nice animal that I have saved for you. Now, then, all ready? Well, come on. Keep an eye on the prisoners, men."

Mr. Murden had grown very polite and affable to me since I had mentioned the hidden treasure. It was quite evident that I had secured a new and powerful friend in the person of the Chief.

"Did you hear what I said to old Kebblewhite?" asked the Chief, as we walked our horses through the scrub.

"Of course not. You whispered to him, and I do not listen when people do that."

"Well, I do. Have to, you know. It is part of my trade. When people whisper in my presence I think it is something I should know. The night you were married I heard your confession to your mother-in law, and so stood under the window ready for you when you dropped. Don't look angry. I believed that you were a swell, and did n't mean a square deal by the girl, and I was just vain enough to think that you should be made to keep your word. I saw you married, and was satisfied with what I had done, and, to speak candidly, I more than half believe that you are the Earl of Afton, but just want to have a little fun before you settle down to domestic life. You are not? Well, let it go that way for the present. But I gave old Kebblewhite an awful dig in the ribs just now, confound him."

"Indeed. By word or blow?"

"Word. I just hinted to him that there were more people in Melbourne who knew him when he was a lag than he supposed, and it wilted him, for if there is one thing that he is ashamed of, and wants forgotten, it is the fact that he was transported many years ago, and served his term, and then went in for money and respectability, and he has got both; but the stain remains, and he would give fifty thousand pounds if it could be blotted out. But people remember such things, and the higher the old fellow climbs, the longer will the disgrace be kept alive. It won't do to look closely at the record of some of our public men. There was a curious mixture sent here in old Botany-Bay times, but all that is done for now, and we have some people in Melbourne who are the equals of any to be found in the world, as honest and as intelligent, as generous and as enterprising, and the ranks are constantly increasing."

"But Mr. Kebblewhite has not yet been able to lay aside his vulgarity, or his peculiar use of the English language," I said.

"Because he commenced the upward grade too late, and he is hot-headed, and won't let his children or his wife correct him. Did you ever notice how angry people become if you set them right in the pronunciation of a word, or correct their grammar? It is a curious fact that no one will endure it from a relative, and sometimes kick over the traces when a teacher interferes. It is very human to get angry on such occasions. Mr. Kebblewhite is no exception to the general rule. Now, his son is a gentleman, and speaks like one, while his daughter is a lady, and would do honor to any station in society, even as the Countess of Afton, and, by Jove! she is as good as she is beautiful, and no wonder the young bloods call her the Belle of Australia."

"By the way," I remarked, as we rode along, the huge hound following close by my side, and looking up in my face once in a while with an expression that was almost human, "how does it happen that you are here to-day, with your men?"

"Last evening some of my people found a carriage and two horses in the scrub, and brought them to Smith's, and put them up. I intended to pass the night with the old stockman, a friend of mine, and a great friend of those young Americans I have spoken of. In fact, I believe that his name is mentioned in the same book with mine, more than once. We suspected robbery and violence, but could do nothing last evening in the scrub and marshes, so waited for daylight. At supper time one of Mr. Smith's shepherds said that several of his fattest sheep had been killed during the week, and that a gang of bushrangers was in the vicinity, but just where no one knew, so, after breakfast, we put the old hound on the trail, and he followed Black Dick's footsteps to this place, but we were a little too late for the fight, and a lively one it must have been. I wish that I had been there. That Frenchman says that you really held Dick a pretty lively tussle, or until the Chinamen came in his rear with their bloody knives, and so decided the contest. An ugly man, and he would have thought it sport to cut your throat, had you given him the chance."

"I am thankful that I did not gratify him in that respect, and yet, I will confess, had it not been for the thought of my wife, I should have been forced to yield. He pressed me pretty hard."

"Mr. Angus," said the Chief, as we trotted along, "do you know that I have been thinking of a pretty little speculation we might go into, and make old Kebblewhite get up and howl, if we succeed, as I hope we shall?"

"Will you name it?" I asked.

"Yes; but mum is the word, Kebblewhite has been making a tour all through Victoria, to find out how the wool clip is. It is short, and he knows it. Not more than half the usual supply will reward the stockmen. Mr. Kebblewhite pretends that it will be large, and he talks that way to all whom he meets. We go into the market at Melbourne, and buy all that we can get hold of at the big auction sale next week. If we get the hidden treasure we can take it, and pay for the purchase. If we don't find what we expect, we will raise what money we can, and pool in. Wool must rise, and as it goes up, we will sell, and share the profits. What do you say to the bargain?"

"I say that I will agree to it, and do all the buying, and let you stay in the background. I have some money of my own, even if we do not strike the treasure that is buried. But you are sure about the wool clip?"

"Not a doubt about it. Mr. Kebblewhite has been at work, and so have I. His notes agree with mine, and mine agree with that of every shepherd in Victoria. But here we are, and there is old Smith in front of his crazy built house, all up stairs and down, tumble here and there, liable to break your neck at any time. He thinks it is a wonder, and so do I. It is the only one of the kind in Victoria."

We drew up in front of a wooden house, gave the horses to some stockmen, to be taken to a corral, and then I was welcomed by Mr. Smith, a stout old fellow, with the baldest head that was ever seen outside of New York, and the biggest stomach, and the most benign, beery expression on his full face, which was smoothly shaved, as if he expected company, and wanted to honor it.

"Ah, Mr. Angus," he said, like a man who had known me all of his life, "we are glad to see you back again," and he shook hands quite heartily and his soft blue eyes beamed with good nature.

Now, considering that I had never seen Smith before, this was certainly most friendly, and I supposed that some of the policemen had mentioned me when they went to the house to get spades, and a new mob of horses for our party to ride.

"Hullo," exclaimed the Chief, "I did n't know that you two were acquainted."

He had witnessed the cordial greeting, and was surprised at it, even as much as I was.

"Well, I should think we knew something of each other. Hey, Mr. Angus?" and the amiable Mr. Smith chuckled and laughed, as if he had perpetrated a good joke, and wanted us to share in his amusement. "She 'll be surprised, and glad to see you, sir. She don't know that you are here, but I 'll call her."

"Good Heaven!" I thought, "I hope that there are no cranky women here," for just at this moment Florence had rode up, and seemed more than half inclined to allow me to assist her to dismount, but, for fear that her resolution to be firm should weaken, waved me off, and allowed the Frenchman to perform the act of courtesy, which I should have esteemed a great favor.

"Here, Susan, here, old lady; where are you all?" roared the stockman, who was anxious to display some real Australian hospitality, even by giving up his whole house for the benefit of his guests.

A young girl, rather pretty, and with nice black eyes, and a fine, healthy form, and good, clear skin, came out of the house, stopped for a moment to survey the arrivals, and then, with a glad cry of astonishment, as she caught sight of me, ran toward me, put her arms around my neck, and kissed me three times before I could recover sufficiently from my surprise to check her freedom. Still, I will confess, that I did not struggle very hard to clear myself from her embrace. I should have done so, but astonishment overcome me for the moment, and rendered me unconscious of the liberties that were being taken with my lips. It often happens so with men who have reveries or dreams while awake.

"O Angus," said the young lady, who I surmised was a daughter or relative of Mr. Smith, "how pleased I am that you have returned, and you won't go away for a long, long time, will you, dear?"

This was decidedly embarrassing for a young man who was in love with his own wife, and, while he might have endured the indignity had she been some miles distant, it would not answer in her presence, and while I was all ready to assume a severity that is very becoming to young men, I stole a glance at Florence, for I dreaded the effects of the exhibition on her. As I half expected, and feared, she showed signs of rebellion.

"How dare you put your arms around my husband's neck, and kiss him right before my face and eyes?" Florence asked, her pretty countenance showing some of the rage that swelled her little body, until she looked as though she was six feet high, and stout in proportion. "Take your hands off of him this instant! I am ashamed that one of my sex should be guilty of such disgraceful conduct!"

The attention of the company was attracted at this singular spectacle, and by the words. All were looking at us in astonishment, Smith staring until his eyes were fixed as those of a painter's lay figure.

"Your husband?" stammered poor Susan, for that, I learned, was the girl's name, "your husband?" she repeated. "Why, this gentleman is engaged to marry me, and has been for two weeks past."

"O Heaven!" gasped Florence. "Take me home to my mamma. O father, this is too terrible for me to endure, and just as I was all ready to pardon him, because he looked so sad and repentant, for his past crimes. But this is a little too much for one woman to overlook, and now my mind is made up. Never will I see him again. This I am firmly resolved upon. Nothing shall change me."

This was hard news for me, but what could I do or say to such a little fury?

"Do you mean to tell me," asked Susan, who began to get angry also, and she released me from her embrace, for which the Lord made me truly thankful, and walked straight toward Florence, and then those two handsome young women looked at each other with all the scorn that females can usually throw into their eyes and faces when jealous of each other, "do you mean to tell me," repeated Miss Susan, "that this man is your husband?"

"He is my husband, my lawful husband, and I hate him, and I hate you, and I want to go home to my mamma."

"Angus," asked Miss Susan, turning to me, and speaking with forced calmness, "is this lady's story true?"

"Quite true. She is my wife, and I assure you that I love her dearly," I answered very frankly.

"Then what did you mean by coming to this house, and saying that you loved me?" asked the young lady, with a dangerous look in her eyes.

"There you are mistaken," I replied. "I never saw you before today, and I never visited this place until now."

Both women uttered incredulous cries of doubt, rage, and intense hatred, and I wished that I was once more fighting bushrangers, in the mines, on the trail, or anywhere except in the presence of two young girls who had made up their minds not to be convinced of my honesty, and all the witnesses in the world would not have shaken their faith in their own ideas of right and wrong.

I looked a little foolish and weak, I know, and, perhaps, a shade or so guilty, but how can a man appear different when a strange woman will persist in kissing him, and claiming him, and a young and pretty wife is standing near, ready to believe all the evil she ever heard of you, and to remember none of your virtues, if you should happen to have any?

"Do you mean to say that you never spoke to me before today?" Miss Susan demanded, and her fingers worked a little nervously, as though she was getting ready to scratch somebody, and her black eyes looked through and through me.

"I must persist in repeating that you are a stranger to me, as I am to you. Loving my wife as I do, I am incapable of such conduct as you charge me with," I said.

"Somebody has got to be killed before a great while," Mr. Smith roared. "I'll load my gun, and have a shot at the meanest liar in the country, and, although I'm a member of parliament, and should respect the law, blast me if I don't smash all the laws for the sake of punishing a man who is married, and comes here to make love to my wife's sister, and promises to marry her, and spoons with her until the girl's head is turned. Just wait until I get my gun. Only wait."

He would have gone for it, but Mr. Murden stopped him, and just at this moment Mike and the two Chinamen drove up to the house, with a horse that was half starved and unsteady on its legs, for it had neither eaten nor drunk since the night before, at Ballarat. This attracted attention, and gave Murden a chance to appear as my protector.

"GOOD HEAVENS! MAMMA, THERE'S TWO OF THEM; AND WHICH IS MY HUSBAND?"

PART XII.

THE BURIED TREASURE.—A BOX OF GOLD.—THE RETURN TO BALLARAT. —SELLING OFF.—FAREWELL TO THE MINES —A BIG SPECULATION IN WOOL.—A HASTY SUMMONS.—FACE TO FACE WITH A LORD AND A DOUBLE.—MY MOTHER'S ARRIVAL, AND HER STORY.—TWIN BROTHERS.—FLORENCE MAKES HER CHOICE, AND IS HAPPY.—GRAND EXPLANATIONS.—MR. KEBBLEWHITE OPENS SOME WINE.—MIKE'S CAREER.—A GENERAL CLOSING UP.—THE END.

FOR a moment hostilities were suspended, to witness the arrival of Mike and the Chinamen. But the lull was only temporary. They had nothing to offer that was new; and, as soon as the poor suffering horse had been led away to get a feed of barley, Mr. Smith again expressed a firm desire to kill somebody, and that somebody, as near as I could understand, was me.

"Smith," said Mr. Murden, as soon as he could lay hands on the stockman, and calm him down a little, "you keep your paws off of guns, and let me explain matters. We have been old companions for many years, and I never deserted you, even when you wanted friends. That you very well know."

"That's true," was the sullen response. "But this is a little too much for human endurance. I thought as much of that fellow, and his swell ways, as I would of an own son. He has been here quite often, and made love like, like — mad," and, as Mr. Smith could find no other word, the comparison was not so bad after all, for most lovers are insane.

"There has been a great mistake here," the Chief said. "I want to see fair play, and will state that Mr. Angus was married to Miss Kebblewhite nearly a year ago. I was present at the ceremony, so there can be no dispute on that point."

A wail from Susan, and a smothered oath from Smith, who looked his anger.

"But I have reason to believe that there are two men in the country who resemble one another in all respects, and each has been mistaken for the other time and time again. One is called Angus Mornington, Earl of Afton, and the other is called Angus Mornington, an American, and my friend, for the sake of old friends."

"Which is this one?" asked Smith, pointing to me, looking still sullen and angry.

"Hang me if I know," was the blunt response, "but I can prove that this gentleman has not been out of the mines of Ballarat for the last ten months. Mike, come here, and bring the Chinamen."

The Chief asked them if I had been absent from my home during all the time they knew me, and they did not hesitate a moment. They swore that I had not, and that I could not have left the place without their knowing it.

"The Chinamen will lie on all and every occasion," Smith said, with a look of contempt. "I do not count them as of any importance, and an Irishman will lie when it suits his convenience," a remark that enraged Mike so much, he offered to fight Smith on the spot, for the mere love of it, and to vindicate the honor of "Ould Oireland." Smith did not mean it, but he was an Englishman, and prejudiced, and angry at the same time. Peace was at last restored between the two, but the ladies looked at each other without relenting.

"To think that I do not know who is my own husband," sobbed Florence. "Here is a person who has made love to his Kitties, his Webbies, h'"

Susies, and I don't know how many more, and, oh! how I hate every man in the world, and I 'm very unhappy. Take me home to my mamma as quick as you can."

"And I 'll never believe in a man again to the longest day of my life, and I hate the whole race of them, and I wish they were all dead, and then," after a long pause, " that they would come to life again, and be better than they are now. That is what I wish."

And then, wonderful to relate, those two women, who a moment before had desired to scratch out each other's eyes, actually embraced, and mingled their tears, and entered the house with their arms around each other, leaving me out in the cold, with no one except Mr. Murden and Mike to take pity on me, for Mr. Kebblewhite and Monsieur Allete followed the ladies.

"I 'll give you the benefit of a doubt," Mr. Smith said, as the girls disappeared. " I will take the assertion of Mr. Murden as a correct one. I 'm a plain, old Australian stockman. Come in and have some dinner, and don't so much as look at Susan again, if we are to be on friendly terms."

I accepted the invitation, and sat down to a well-filled table, but the ladies did not appear, and I saw no more of them until afternoon, just as the Chief, Mike, and myself were ready to set out in search of the buried treasure. Then Florence came to the door, looking much better, after a nap, a bath, and clean clothes.

" Florence," I said, for I was alone with her for a moment, " next month will be a year since we were married. On the anniversary of that event, I shall come to you, and ask you to be my wife in earnest. If I can prove that I am better than you now suspect will you listen to me, darling?"

" Have you used the same arguments with your other loves?" she asked, with a little curl of the lip, and a toss of her pretty head.

" You are cruel, Florence, and unjust, but I forgive you, and hope for your love as soon as proper explanations are made. Will you let me take your hand, and kiss it?"

" Yes, if that will do you any good," and she gave me her hand. " I owe you that scant courtesy for your rescue of my friends and myself."

" Will you think of me, dear little wife, while I am absent?" I whispered.

" I have no doubt but that I shall hear enough of you to keep you fresh in my mind," with another toss of her pretty head, and a provoking sneer, that was far from becoming to such a handsome face. " If you continue as you have begun, all Australia will ring with cries of detestation at the mere mention of your name, and fathers and brothers will hunt for you as the police now seek for bushrangers. Why could you not be good? Is it so hard for a young and rich man to pursue a correct path?"

"I do not know, Florence. I have never been rich. I have had temptations placed in my way, and such as few men could have resisted, and yet I can safely assure you that I am good, and wish that you would believe me. I should be much happier than I have been the past year, for I love you, and only you, and it was for your sake I fled the night we were married."

"I do not believe you. I do not think that you are speaking the truth. You suppose that I can be deceived as easily as your Kitties, your Webbies, and your Susies. I am young, but I have seen much of the little world in my circle of life, and I don't know who I'm talking to, and wish that I had never seen you, and what did you come to Australia for to cause so much unhappiness? Before I saw you I never had a moment's care. Oh, what trouble men are!"

"I am going now, Florence. Will you let me kiss you good-by, dear?" I asked, growing more bold.

"No, sir, I will not," very decidedly. "How do I know whether you are my husband, or the other man? The wretch!"

"I can tell you all the particulars of our wedding, dear, if that will satisfy you. Will you listen to me?"

"No, sir, I do not care to hear you."

"Then good-by, dear, and may God bless you," I said, with moistened eyes, and fervent lips.

I turned and walked toward the saddled horses, and waved a farewell to Florence, but I do not think that she saw it, for her head was bowed down, and she was clinging to a tressel, on which some roses were growing, and scenting the air in every direction.

Mr. Murden had explained to Smith and the rest of the party, that it was necessary we should scout around the country, and see if there were more traces of the bushrangers, and I had taken leave of the gentlemen, and thanked Mr. Smith for his hospitality, but he looked at me a little suspiciously, and evidently did not take much stock in my assertions. Susan I did not see. She kept away from me, and I was glad of it, on her account, and my own.

Mike had secreted a spade, although he did not know for what purpose, and, by a steady gallop, and a brisk walk, we were at the bushrangers' quarters by three o'clock. The grave of the dead robbers was just as we had left it, the fire was still smouldering, and no one had been on the spot since we departed in the forenoon.

"Now where is the place?" asked the Chief, anxious to commence work at once.

"Here," I answered, taking the spade, and turning over the ashes.

"Under the fire?" asked the Chief.

"That is what Jack says."

"Well, I should never have thought of that spot. But give Mike the spade, and let us see what we shall find."

Mike flung aside the ashes and earth, and dug down two feet, before he struck a box that was about one foot square. It gave us hope that Jack had not told an idle romance after all, and he had not, for we excavated the package, although it was not an easy task, as it was heavy, wrenched off the lid, and there before us were gold coins, doubloons, American eagles, sovereigns, and an immense number of nuggets, and pounds of gold-dust.

"By the sacrid name of Moses, and the children in the bulrushes, but this is the koind of minin' that I loike," cried Mike. "All in a lump loike a fat pig. Whoop! what a haul for us."

"Shut your mouth, you wild Irishman," said Mr. Murden, who was as excited as Mike and myself. "Do you want half a dozen mounted men to gallop here, and spoil the sport? Come, let us look over the treasure, and estimate how much there is."

But we had no time to do that before night fell, and we were just superstitious enough to desire to get out of the woods before dark. We did not want Black Dick and Slipper Sam disputing our prize, if they could revisit the earth, and I don't believe that one of us would have gone after the gold in the night time, for the whole of it.

"We must pack this box on one of the horses," Mr. Murden said. "It is a devil of a load, and weighs near three hundred pounds, but one of the animals will have to take it. We can't get a cart in this scrub, and I don't like to leave a portion of the treasure until tomorrow. There may be other people who know the secrets of the bushrangers as well as Jack."

"I will tell you what we had better do," I remarked. "Let Mike go to Smith's, and get the horse and wagon we rode in from Ballarat. He can then meet us on the road, and by means of the team we can get the treasure to Camp Reserve. Tomorrow I will take it to the bank, have it weighed, value estimated, and deposited, and take drafts on the principal house in Melbourne, then, when I come to the city, I will bring your share, draw the money, and hand it over. It won't do for you to take charge of the gold. Suspicion would be excited."

"There is no other way that I can see. There must be twenty thousand pounds in that box, and I can't manage it. Do as you suggest. I trust to you in every particular, and believe that my confidence will not be abused."

"Then take the bank notes, and put them in your pocket, and hint that you found them on the prisoners, and you will get much credit with the respectable people of Melbourne, and you need not care for the other classes."

"And don't forget the reward, Mr. Murden," pleaded Mike. "I don't want to lose me thousand puns."

"You shall have your share, Mike, just as soon as I get back to the city, and make my statements and affidavits. I'll send the prisoners on to Melbourne tonight, and Jack shall be among them, but we can drop him on the road in some manner. Then he can make the best of his way to Port Phillip, and from there get down to Sydney in a coaster, where he will be quite safe, if he but keeps his mouth shut, as he must do, if he would save his neck."

"Give him a hundred sovereigns out of this box to start him in life. It is more money than he ever had in the world, and much good may it do him," I said, and counted out the gold.

"Just as you please. It will all go to the grog shops, but that is not our lookout," and Mr. Murden put the sovereigns in his pocket, but he did give them to Jack, and kept his word, for the old salt was accidentally left unguarded, when near Melbourne, and he did some good walking through the scrub and woods, until he reached the city, and from thence he went to Manilla in a ship, and I never heard of him again, but, dead or alive, I shall always think well of poor Jack, who remembered an act of kindness, and returned payment a hundred-fold when he had an opportunity.

It was hard work getting the box of treasure on the back of one of the animals, but we succeeded after several attempts, and lashed it with ropes and spun-yarn to the saddle, and then, while one of us led the horse, and Mike steadied the package to prevent its slipping, we retraced our steps toward Smith's residence. But I cast one last look around the place before we started. There was the grave of the bushrangers, the spot where I had struggled with Black Dick, the resting-place of Florence under the acacia-bush, the trees where Mr. Kebblewhite and Monsieur Allete had been secured, and passed a very bad night, and then I turned and thanked Heaven that I had arrived in time to save Florence from what would have been worse than death. I never saw that spot again, but I could easily find it, even at this late day, unless the dense scrub has over-run the clearing, and hidden from sight the solitary grave of the robbers.

When we were about a mile from the public road, I sent Mike to the house for the team, and with instructions to the two Chinamen to remain with the stockman until the next day, and then make the best of their way to Camp Reserve. I did not desire their presence until the gold was disposed of, or encounter their inquisitive eyes, while handling it.

We waited at the edge of the scrub until Mike made his appearance, then transferred the box to the wagon, and were ready to start.

"Now, Mr. Murden," I said, as we shook hands at parting, "you will do all that you can to aid me, and relieve me from the embarrassment under which I labor, and prevents me from receiving the love of a dear little wife?"

"Tomorrow half a dozen of my best men shall commence the search, and I assure you it shall be a very patient one, and a very thorough one. I will map out every sheep-run in the district, and every stockman's house. If there is a twin-brother of yours in Victoria I will find him," and Mr. Murden smiled as though he had uttered a joke, but it was no joke to me, much as I had suffered in the past year.

"There is some one who bears a remarkable resemblance to me in the country. I saw the man who is called the Earl of Afton leave the Melbourne Club House the first night I met you. His two friends supposed that he and I were one. You can solve the mystery, and satisfy Florence that I am worthy of her, and then I shall be perfectly happy."

"For how long?" asked the Chief, with a low laugh, as though he had heard just such protestations before.

"All my life, or as long as God spares us for each other, and the world," I said earnestly.

"Amen. I begin to think that you are what you represent, — a real American sovereign, as you vainly call yourself, instead of a wild, adventurous, love-making nobleman, with more money and time than he knows what to do with. Well, old fellow, I must be off, and start my prisoners on their journey. The sun is nearly down, and we may have rain tonight. I shall be in Melbourne the day after tomorrow."

"And I shall be there in the course of a few days, and will call on you."

We shook hands, and, as he turned away, asked, —

"Is there any word that you wish to send to your wife? No? Well, I 'll give you a lift if I can. I have watched the lady, and can tell that she loves you, and will drop when the proper urging is applied. But her confounded pride and disappointment are a little too much for her just now. From a countess down to the wife of — Well, never mind. Don't get angry. You are worth a dozen of the modern earls, although, to tell you the truth, I 'd give ten thousand pounds just to have plain and common 'Sir' as a handle to my name. It makes people respect and look up to you. Au revoir."

He touched his horse with a spur, and cantered off, and, with the box of gold in our possession, with rifle cocked, and revolver all ready for action, while Mike's terrible gun rested across his knees, loaded with eight fingers of powder and shot, we jogged along the rough road, but did not meet with any one who was strong enough to dispute our possession, and at eight o'clock reached our hut, just as the rain commenced to pour down in torrents.

We got the box into the shanty, and sent the horse home by a miner who wanted a job, and a drink, and then had a fire started, covered the treasure with blankets, prepared a good supper, locked up the house, and went to bed, and slept soundly until eight o'clock the next morning, for we were both very tired, having hardly closed our eyes the night before.

The rain had passed away by daylight, but the roads were in a terrible condition, full of holes and gullies, slush and mud, yet I managed to get my treasure to the branch bank, and had the dust and nuggets weighed, and all the gold coin valued, and then found that Mr. Murden and I were about eighteen thousand pounds better off than we were the day before, but out of the amount I gave Mike five hundred pounds, and he nearly went crazy with delight at the good fortune that was pouring into his lap, and more than once declared that I was the best man that ever lived, with some rare exceptions, and those were to be found only in Ould Oireland.

In the course of the next day I had made up my accounts, sold my shanty, and all the comforts which it contained, went around and bid goodby to the many friends I had made, and then found that with all of my lucky findings, speculations, interest money, and sales I was worth near three hundred thousand dollars, a sum that was far beyond my wildest dreams of wealth.

The Chinamen arrived in time, and reported that all the people had left Smith's for the city, and, after they were rested, and had eaten their supper, I told them that I was going there myself, and should not return to Ballarat, but that they could remain and mine on their own account, or they could go to Melbourne, where they would get the money for the capture of Dick and the rest of the bushrangers, and that I would give to each of them a gratuity of a hundred pounds, in addition to what I owed them. They preferred to go to Melbourne, and return to their beloved China, with money enough to make them rich for life, and I will here remark that they did sail for the celestial empire in the course of a few weeks, and that the last I heard of Gin Sling he was a fourth-class mandarin, engaged in the tea trade, in the Fou-Chow district, and had a peculiar habit of applying bamboos to the backs of such Chinamen as sold tea to any house except his own, and at his option, while Ah Sugar went into rice speculations, opium smuggling, and other business-like enterprises, and is a rich man, with one regular wife, and a dozen irregular ones. Gin Sling sends me once a year a half chest of real mandarin tea, and a monstrous letter, written in Chinese characters, but, as they all read just alike, I no longer have them translated, but send them to charity fairs to be disposed of as curiosities from the son of the moon, the Emperor of China. No one has yet discovered the imposture, and the charity people are satisfied, and clamorous for more letters, as they sell readily. Ah Sugar is at Canton and Hong Kong, and could be a mandarin, but does not like to pay for the title, so remains a plain Chinaman, and has thus far escaped very serious squeezing from the officials over him. I understand that he has a profound contempt for all Englishmen of low degree, especially gold-miners, when he encounters the latter.

The next day Mike and I took the mail wagon for Melbourne. He persisted in carrying his gun, but I made him draw the charge before I would allow him to enter the carriage. I did not want my head blown off by that formidable weapon in case Mike got careless or excited.

We were two days on the road, the wheeling was so bad. When we drove up to Webber's I remained in the carriage, for I did not desire to encounter Katrine and her father, the Dutchman, and have another scene. Neither of them saw me, for I covered up my face, and Mike swore that I was a sick man, with symptoms of the small-pox, an announcement that sent every one scampering away, and even Katrine, who had grown rosier than ever, in retreating stumbled up the steps, and revealed a pair of ankles that were not Grecian in shape or size, and caused old Webber to roar out, —.

"You should be much ashamed of meself, Katrine, ven de men all looks dis way, by —— !" and the girl shook down her skirts, gave a pretty little giggle, and vanished, and that was the last that I saw of Katrine for some years, and then she was married, and kept the wayside inn, in place of her father, who had been shot by a bushranger, on the supposition that the Dutchman had not dealt fairly by him, and public opinion was rather on the side of the robber.

We dashed through Slabtown, where we stopped one night, then on, until we reached the spot where Mike and I had encamped the first morning out, and where the "old man kangaroo" had played so mean a trick on the Irishman; crossing small streams by fording, over bridges that were none too secure, through dangerous and quivering swamps, past the nice country residences, and at last, tired and bruised, we drew up at the Hen and Chickens, my old inn, and were received at the door by the same old head waiter, bald as ever, his face as red and oily as usual, his hair, what little he had, as stiff and fiery as it was a year before, and he wrung his hands, and smiled, just as he did the first day I saw him.

"Mike, me boy," said the waiter.

"Jeemes, me buy," was the remark of Mike to the waiter, and, after much cautioning, Mike placed his precious gun in the hands of "Jeemes," and told him to take care of it, and then he proceeded to show me some attention.

"'Appy to see yer, sir," was the greeting. "Vil yer 'ave the same hold room, sir? It's hall ready, sir, and the chambermaid vil be delighted to know that yer 'as come back, sir, and yer clothes is hall right, sir, and the chambermaid 'as brushed 'em twice a veek, 'cos she said it vos a melancholy pleasure to 'er, sir, to do them little things for yer. They is hall ready for yer, sir, at this moment, if yer vants 'em, and vot vil yer 'ave for supper?"

"Look a-here, Jeemes," said Mike, "this gintleman is none of yer common sort. He will have a bed-chamber, and parlor, and grub in his own room. He don't ate here wid ivery one, now I tell yer that, and do yer moind me, me buy?"

"Certainly. Ve vil do vot ve can to make 'im 'appy. Got just the rooms for 'im, but they comes werry hexpensive."

"To the divil wid yer hexpense," roared Mike. "We has money enough to buy yer ould shebang, and iverybody in it. His honor can fill a room wid gould, and not moind it, or miss it."

"Bless me, yer don't say so," and the head waiter's eyes expressed astonishment.

I had my luggage taken to my rooms, and left Mike to arrange for supper, while I went in search of a hot bath, and, luckily, found a place on Market Square, and, after I returned to the Hen and Chickens, a nice meal was already served in my room, and as soon as it was disposed of, in addition to a pipe of tobacco, and a glass of old ale, I was ready for the nicest bed that I had slept in for nearly a year.

Just before I fell asleep I thought of the wonderful changes that had taken place in my fortunes since I landed at Melbourne, and then I felt a thrill of pleasure at the idea that Florence was not more than a mile from me, and that I could see her if I would only summon sufficient courage to call on her. But I was not ready for that duty just then, and went to sleep, and dreamed that my wife had been scalped by a dozen bushrangers, and that they were dividing her curls as souvenirs, while I, tied to a tree, was powerless to prevent them, and when I awoke Mike was pulling one of my arms out of its socket in the hope of arousing me.

"Murderation, yer honor, but yer has had a moighty hard toime of it in yer slape, to joodge by the way yer made the bed-clothes fly. Come, the breakfast is all riddy, and it's eight o'clock, and a bright morning for this part of the woorld, but nothin' to Ould Oireland."

I was soon shaved and dressed (not that the former operation required much time), and put on the business suit I had left at the inn, and the very one I wore the day I landed in Melbourne. It did make me feel a little stiff and constrained to put on a white linen shirt, and collar, and neatly fitting clothes, but, at any rate, I felt that I was cleaner, and more suited for the company of ladies and gentlemen, in case I should be thrown into their society, than when clothed in rough garments.

As I ate my breakfast, waited on by Mike, who would not sit at the table with me, I read an account in the morning paper of the destruction of the gang of bushrangers, and the terrible fight which Mr. Kebblewhite had waged with the robbers when he was first captured, and how he had defied them to the last, and there was some few words of praise for a miner whose name was unknown, and an Irishmen, and Chinamen, who had rendered some little assistance at the eleventh hour, but nothing to any extent, a statement that made Mike almost wild, and he wanted to go and punch old Mr. Kebblewhite's blasted head for giving out such an account to the press, but I persuaded him to keep cool, and let the story pass for what it was worth.

After a leisurely breakfast, I took my drafts to the Oriental Bank, found that everything was satisfactory, and was received with much courtesy by the cashier, who was disposed to respect a man who had so large a balance standing in his favor, and had not drawn on his account from the time he made the first deposit. Then I took Mr. Murden's half of the buried treasure, all in good new bills of large denominations, and went to the police headquarters, and found the Chief in his office, and very glad he seemed to see me, and very much pleased to have placed in his hands near nine thousand pounds, which he never would have obtained had I not let him into an important secret, and asked his aid.

"Have you received any information of the gentleman who so nearly resembles me?" I asked, after the money was counted, and locked up in a huge safe.

"Yes, and no. One of my mounted force has sent me a short despatch, saying that he was on the trail of a man and girl, near the banks of the Murray, but that he could not tell who he is, or where he comes from. He is spending his time shooting kangaroos, black swans, and ducks, and appears to have no other occupation. There may be something in it, but we must wait. There are so many sheep-runs on the Murray that it will take time to look them all up, and examine them. Courage, my boy. All will come out right I hope."

I sighed very dolefully, for when a man is separated from a young and pretty wife he is apt to be low-spirited.

"Don't sigh like that," laughed the Chief. "A man can be a devoted lover, and yet wear a smiling face. Come home with me today, and dine, and we'll drink a glass, or half a dozen of them, for that matter, of real old champagne to the health of the Belle of Australia and her husband, and then we will go to the theatre, and perhaps she will be there, and you can see her. Is it a bargain?"

"Yes, I suppose so. But it is hard not to be able to approach the lady, and speak to her," I said.

"All in good time. Let us show her that you are a true man, and love her dearly, and her woman's heart will flop towards you like a white swan to its mate. Now read the morning papers, and let me receive a few reports, and I shall be able to talk with you about that wool speculation."

A dozen officers, detectives, and inspectors came in, and reported, received instructions on some pressing matters, and went about their work, and, after all had gone, Mr. Murden was ready for business.

"Your amiable father-in-law," he said, "has circulated such accounts of the immense wool clip, that holders are anxious to realize, and ready to sell at a low price. I know that the reports are false, and that the clip will be short by nearly a million pounds. Now, take my nine thousand pounds, and put in nine thousand of your own, go to this broker (handing me a card), and tell him to buy for your account four hundred thousand pounds of wool, at the lowest market price, to be delivered in the course of a month. Put up our money as a margin, to show that you are sincere. There is a large auction sale at noon today, and the purchase can be completed at once.

We 'll give old Kebblewhite a twist, or I 'm much mistaken, and, remember, the richer you are the better he 'll like you for a son-in-law."

I took the card, and saw that the broker's office was located on Collins Street, and lost no time in going there. I met many people who stared at me rather hard, and one gentleman took off his hat, and bowed very low, and would have stopped and spoken to me, but, as I knew it would be on the same old subject, I hurried along, and found the broker, and laid my project before him.

"You are incurring some risk in buying so much wool on a falling market," he said. "I never knew it so low; but still, if you are prepared to put up a margin, I should like the commission."

"And you 'll keep the matter a secret, so that there shall be no chance for a rise on the strength of our purchase?" I asked.

"Certainly, that is part of my business," was the reply. "We can keep secrets when necessary."

I deposited eighteen thousand pounds with him, and then started on my return to the Hen and Chickens, when, just as I was turning into Russell Street, who should I encounter, face to face, but Doctor Haverley Haverley, the gentleman who had claimed me as the Earl of Afton, in front of the club house, and intimated that he was a great friend of the old nobleman, my father.

"Gracious Heaven! what are you doing here, my lord?" the surgeon asked, apparently astonished at seeing me.

"I am in the city on business," I answered.

"Shall you remain for any length of time, my lord?"

"I am uncertain at the present moment how long I shall remain," was my answer, for I had no relish for an argument.

"And when did you arrive, my lord?"

"Yesterday."

"And you did not think it worth your while to call on me, my lord?"

"What would have been the use? You would have reproached me, and we should never understand each other," I answered, for it was no use to argue with a man whose mind was already made up.

"True, my lord, I should have reproached you, for it was not acting with candor to te'l me that you could not marry Miss Kebblewhite, and then, when I had left you for a few moments to attend a patient, to go to the house, and marry her, and, after you had been united, to act so much like a simpleton as to desert her in an hour's time."

"You are candid, doctor."

"I mean to be, my lord. I have letters from your noble mother asking for information concerning you, and what can I write her?"

"I am sure I don't know," I replied.

"For nearly a year I have heard not one word concerning you, except a short letter saying that you were having a jolly time, and that you meant to keep it up, for it was much pleasanter than fashionable life. There was no date on the note, and no postmark. You did not go to Gelong, as I proposed, overland?"

"No," I said, "I did not go to Gelong."

"Then where did you go, my lord? Give me some account of your life."

"It is too eventful to be told on the corner of a street. Some time I will relate it to you with pleasure."

Just at this moment Mr. Mattocks passed us, and gave me a cold bow, and the surgeon a cordial one. He did not like me, for he had been a suitor for Florence's hand, and failed to win her.

"Poor Mattocks," the surgeon said, "he feels his loss keenly, and will never see another lady whom he can love as he did the Belle of Australia. Strange that what you do not value he would esteem as the best thing in this world. Will you take my arm, my lord, and walk home with me? My wife will be pleased to see you."

"Thanks, but I shall have to defer the pleasure, and when we next meet I trust that you will not condemn me as you do today."

I lifted my hat, and parted from the kind-hearted surgeon, leaving him standing on the sidewalk a little astonished at my coolness and indifference to an old friend of the family.

I had half a dozen low bows before I was sheltered in the Hen and Chickens, and, to prevent embarrassment, when I went to Mr. Murden's house to dine, took a hansom, and thus escaped notice.

Mr. Murden was a widower, but had a good housekeeper, one who could look after his personal comforts without the expectation of marrying him as soon as he grew old and childish, and thereby gain a husband, and a fortune at the same time. She knew the temper of her employer, and so minded her own business, and served up a charming little dinner, and we enjoyed it, and at eight o'clock took a hansom, and went to the Royal Victoria Theatre, and retired to the recesses of a private box, for Mr. Murden did not think it safe to exhibit me to the full gaze of a Melbourne audience, until a public explanation had been made regarding my conduct in the matrimonial line.

The play was a burlesque of some kind. The "Invisible Prince," I think, or it might have been the "White Fawn," I was so busy scanning the house to see if Florence was present, that I did not notice, but suddenly one of the lady actresses advanced to the footlights to sing some doggerel, and in her lines she improvised: —

> "Now I see that he is here,
> Earl of Afton, noble peer,
> He left his bride on his wedding night;
> Left her, it is said, because he was tight.
> These are the nobles we love so well,
> This is the man who married our Belle."

The lines were evidently manufactured for the occasion, and by some person on the stage, who saw me, and supposed that I was the real lord, and not the plebeian. But little notice would have been taken of the circumstance, if the singer, rather a pretty and piquant girl, dressed so that most of her form showed to great advantage through very little clothing, pointed directly at me in the private box, thus calling the attention of the audience to the fact that I was in the theatre. I don't suppose the girl really meant anything more than a fling at me, and to raise a laugh, and a little applause, but if she had thrown a fire-ball into the orchestra she could not have caused more excitement than she did. In an instant there was an uproar, and howls and hisses, yells and stamps, were so loud, that the singer got frightened, and fled from the stage.

"Out with him!" roared the audience.

"Throw him over!" yelled the gods in the gallery, and down on the stage came oranges, and other fruits, and the groans grew louder.

"Turn him out!" shrieked the people in the boxes, and the women waved their handkerchiefs to encourage the men, and seemed to enjoy the tumult.

I looked on, a trifle astonished at my unpopularity, or rather of that of the Earl of Afton, and wondered what the next move would be. The noise continuing, the manager came forward, but, before he could utter a word, an orange took him full in the face, and another struck on his shirt bosom. and left a bad stain. Then he was mad, but no one would listen to him for a moment.

"Will you go, or remain?" asked Murden. "If you will stay I'll have enough men here in ten minutes to protect you, but you will be injured very probably, and so will some others. The best thing we can do is to cut stick, and beat a hasty retreat. An Australian mob is the devil, and you can neither coax it, nor drive it, except with bayonets. Let us slip out through the stage door, and so throw the people off the trail. Come along. We have no time to lose."

And we did n't have. The audience was just roaring itself hoarse, as we slipped out of the box, and through the stage entrances, where we found the actors and actresses in a flutter of fear. We did not stop to exchange a word with them, or the manager. Mr. Murden put me in a hansom, and told the driver to be off as quickly as he could, and, while I went to the shelter of the Hen and Chickens, the Chief returned to the stage of the theatre, and assured the audience that the obnoxious person had left, and would not return, and that, now they had given expression to their feelings as true British subjects, men who would never be slaves to caste, or to rank of any kind, but loved fair play, the burlesque would go on. Then the audience called for three cheers for Mr. Murden, for Englishmen in general, and themselves in particular, and allowed the young lady with but few clothes to finish her song, and mincing walk at the same time, so I lost the benefit of that play through my resemblance to the Earl of Afton, confound him! as I said at the time.

The next morning, at nine o'clock, while I was reading a paper, giving a highly colored account of the outbreak at the theatre, an officer entered, and gave me a note from the Chief. It read, —

"*Dear Mr. Angus,* — Come to the house of Mr. Kebblewhite as soon as possible. We have got him, or got you, I don't know which, or who is who, and I 'm in a maze, and have been a blasted fool, and I a'n't fit to be Chief of Police, and I mean to resign, and turn shepherd, or hang myself, or do something desperate. Both of you must be confronted with your (his) wife, and let her decide which is the rightful one.

"Yours mystified,

"MURDEN."

"When was he brought in?" I asked the officer.

"Late last night, sir."

"Does he look like me?"

"Well, sir, I think you got here before me, and that Mr. Murden is up to some lark. If there are two of you I could not tell you apart, and no one else could. It 's some joke of the Chief, I really believe."

I dressed with care, and some little nervous haste, and then told Mike that my double had been found, and that he was to be exposed in the course of the forenoon.

"Shall I bate him, sur?" Mike asked.

"No, but you may go with me."

It was half-past ten when we drove up to Mr. Kebblewhite's house. I saw two hansoms there, and supposed that Mr. Murden had already arrived. I hurried to the door, and was met by Harry, the inside servant and butler.

"Vell, vich is vich?" he asked, with a grin. "There is von of yer in the dinin'-room, and yer go in the parlor and vait. Miss Florence vill 'ave a nice time assortin' yer over, and a-pickin' of yer hout, and tellin' vich is vich, and the hold man is in a horful 'umor, I tells yer. But arter hall she von't know if she 'as got the right von."

How I trembled as I entered the large drawing-room, which I remembered so well. I walked to the very spot where I had knelt when I was married; I glanced over the music on the grand piano, and saw that the song "Then You'll Remember Me" was on the rack; I noticed the clock, the windows, the paintings, the flowers, the carpet, and Persian rugs, and then the folding-doors were thrown open with a crash, and Mr. Murden came toward me, arm in arm with a dark young man, with black curling hair, and the very features, form, and height of myself, as far as I could judge.

For one minute we gazed at each other without speaking, and then, faint with suspense and apprehension, I sat down in a chair, and covered my eyes with my hands to hide the tears that would steal down my cheeks, but they were tears of joy, to think that I had been vindicated from all the charges brought against me.

"My God! what a wonderful resemblance to each other," cried Mr. Murden. "Don't move; don't mix yourselves up. Stand just where you are. Sit still. If you stir we shall never know who is who. Well, this beats all of my experience on the police. Which of you is the Earl of Afton?"

"I think that gentleman must be," and my double laughed, and pointed to me.

"No, it is not true. I am plain Angus Mornington," I cried.

"And I am Angus Mornington, also, but I won't admit that I am plain, for the ladies say I am not," and the other Angus stroked his light mustache, and laughed as if he had not a care in the world, except getting into difficulties, and out of them.

"How in the name of Heaven does it happen that we look so much alike?" I asked, as soon as I could speak.

"Well, Mornington, my father was a very handsome man, and a naval officer," the earl laughed, in a careless way.

"And my father was a very handsome man, and a naval officer, also. Was your mother very attractive?" I asked, and the young fellow flushed, and then laughed, as he said, —

"Let us drop personalities. It seems that you have caused me much inconvenience by traveling all through the country, and making love to every pretty girl you met. That was not right, Mr. Mornington. You should not disgrace the name. Be true to your honor, and the fair sex, if you wish to succeed in life, and be an ornament to society, like myself," and he laughed again.

This sounded well from a man who had been doing some very disreputable things all through the country, for the past twelve months, and for which I had to bear the blame.

"If you are a sample of the ornaments of society," I said, "I should prefer to mingle with those who are outcasts, for even the latter have some regard for their word, while you had rather deceive a woman than aid one."

"Don't be too severe, Mornington," laughed the nobleman, for nobleman he was. "You have injured my reputation, married the Belle of Australia, and then deserted her the very night of the wedding, which I should not have done, and I am afraid that my friends have put me down for an imbecile, and that I shall never recover lost ground. Then you send out a squad of policemen to hunt me up, and offer a reward for my apprehension, and drag me here, just as I was having the best of shooting on the Murray, killing kangaroos and ducks to the right and left, and I want to go back as soon as possible."

"Not until a full explanation is made," I said. "Clear me of all false charges, and I will willingly see you depart."

"Upon my word, I can't act as your father confessor, Mornington. I have no sins of my own, and don't know how to rebuke those which others have."

He moved toward a seat, but Mr. Murden kept close to him, for fear he would escape.

"Don't get mixed," he pleaded. "You are dressed about alike, and I can't distinguish you if I turn my head for a moment. Keep still for a while."

"A lady is 'ere vot is haxin' for Mr. Mornington," cried Harry, putting his head in at the door.

"Some of your flames have followed you here, Mornington," said my good-natured, impudent double, with a laugh. "We will retire if necessary. Don't mind us."

The next instant a lady entered the drawing room, and, to my intense astonishment, I saw that it was my mother, whom I supposed in Boston.

"O my dear boy, O my dear son," she cried, and folded the lord in her arms, while I was left out in the cold, and neglected.

"Gently, madame," laughed the lord. "Give me a chance to breathe, you know, because it 's deuced awkward to be smothered by one's own mother. Now then, try it again, if you want to."

"Mother," I said, "I am the one to welcome you. I am the one who should receive those kisses."

The poor woman came to me, and stopped, looked at us, first one and then the other, and, woman-like, began to cry to express her feelings.

"I see it all now," she said, as I put my arms around her, and kissed her heavenly face, and strove to dry her tears. "You are both named Angus Mornington?"

"That is my family name," said the young lord, with a tender look on his face, all levity being banished for the time being.

"And that is my family name, also, as you well know, dear mother," I responded.

She made a motion for the Chief to close the doors, and he obeyed, but remained in the room.

"Angus," she said, looking at me, and to the second Angus, "take each other's hands, and love one another, for you are twin brothers, as I hope for heaven."

"What!" we both exclaimed, thinking that the lady was insane.

"You were born twin brothers, and I am your mother," she repeated.

"Come, you know, that is a little rough on a fellow. Confound it, my title and fortune are involved, you know. This is a strange sort of romance to spring on a fellow, you know. By Jove, I don't know what to think of this," and the noble lord did n't look happy.

"Is this gentleman to be trusted?" my mother asked, pointing to Mr. Murden.

"Yes, I am sure of him," I cried, and the other Angus nodded assent to my words.

"Then listen to me, children," she said. "Here, take a seat on each side of me, on the sofa, and let me hold your hands."

"Don't mix 'em," cried the Chief, but no notice was paid to him.

"When I was first married to your father, Angus," patting me on the cheek, and then patting the other fellow, "he was ordered to the Mediterranean station, as the first lieutenant of the United-States ship *Ohio*, one of the largest men-of-war in the navy. I followed him in a packet across the Atlantic, and met my husband at Naples, where his vessel was lying close by the seventy-four-gun-ship *Asia*, a famous craft in the English navy. Her first lieutenant was Angus Mornington, the only son of the Earl of Afton, and called Lord Mornington, being a lord by courtesy. My husband was of Scotch descent, and was also named Angus Mornington, and a distant relative of his lordship. The singularity of the names and positions of the two gentlemen, and relationship also, made them fast friends. Lady Mornington and I also became attached to each other. My husband saved the life of Lord Mornington one night, in Naples, and thus they were greater friends than ever after that event. We all had rooms on the same floor at the Hotel de Europe, and the husbands passed what time they could with us, and thus we were two happy families. Singular as it may seem, Lady Mornington and I became mothers at the same time, at the same hour, and in nearly adjoining apartments. Her ladyship's child was a girl, but it lived only a few moments after birth, while I was the mother of twins, two stout, healthy boys, but of this I was not conscious for many days afterward, and now rely entirely upon my late husband's statement, and that of the nurse, a faithful and devoted Frenchwoman, whom we engaged at Naples, for all the events that followed. Lady Mornington was so much affected at the birth of a babe that she was almost wild with joy, and her husband did not dare to tell her that the child was a girl, and dead. He made so many objections to her seeing the baby, that at last her ladyship grew suspicious, and finally frantic for a sight of her infant, and then his lordship hit upon the expedient of borrowing one of my children, and presenting it to his wife as her own. I was unconscious of the deception, for I knew nothing of the affairs of the world for many weeks. My husband saw that it was a matter of life or death to the wife of his best friend, and consented that one of his boys should be exhibited to her ladyship, and that the deception might be kept up until Lady Mornington should recover her health and strength; but she became so devoted to the babe that neither my husband nor his lordship dared to undeceive her, and thus matters drifted on until I was able to travel, and still the terrible secret was kept from both mothers, and at last the two husbands swore never to reveal the matter as long as they lived, so that no question could arise about inheriting the Mornington title and fortune. These are the facts of the case, and it was only after my husband's death that I discovered his statement, addressed to me, unsigned, and not sworn to, with the request that I would not make it known to any one, and I should not now, were it not for the peculiar position in which you are placed. No harm can happen to either of you by what I have stated. The nurse is dead, Angus's father is dead, Lord Mornington is dead, and the Dowager Countess of Afton knows nothing about the exchange, so proof is impossible, for my lips are sealed from this moment on the subject. As soon as I received your letters, Angus, telling me of the wonderful likeness which you bore to my other Angus, I knew that you and your twin-brother were near each other, for I recognized the name, and then determined to come here, and see you both, if possible, and also be prepared to love my daughter-in-law. I took passage in a fast-sailing clipper ship from Boston to Melbourne, arrived yesterday, and have spent most of my time in discovering your whereabouts, and I should have been unsuccessful had you not told me the name of your bride. Some gentlemen directed me here, and, thank Heaven, I have met both of my sons, but one of them I must love a little better than the other, as is natural, for from this time forth one is my real son, and the other is the Earl of Afton, and belongs to another mother. It must be so, for it is too late now to exchange children, or explain matters to the world."

We kissed her hands, and my brother was visibly affected. But he did not want to lose his title and wealth, and so acquiesced in the arrangement without a murmur. No wonder. He had not known my mother's tender care, and it was natural he should not enthuse over a lady he had never seen before.

"What puzzles me," said his lordship, for so I shall continue to call him, "is this. I am one of the best of men, and my brother is rather wild, and uncertain. How do you account for it, mother dear?"

This was cool, and even Mr. Murden had to laugh, while I looked indignant.

"I do not think that a young gentleman who engages himself to a lady, and then permits his brother to take his place to save the reputation of the family, can make many boasts of his goodness," replied my mother, slightly pulling the ear of the earl, while she pressed my hand.

My brother laughed, as he said, —

"Well, I think Angus is a little superior to me in some respects. But if he had had my position, my wealth, and my crowd of flatterers, would he have been so much better, do you think? Answer that, mother," and for a moment he was serious.

"Angus was always a good son," was all the remark my mother made, for she wished to be non-committal on some points, and she was not aware of all that I had suffered on my brother's account.

"The history which you have here related, madame," said Mr. Murden, coming forward, "bears upon its face the test of truth, and if further proof was wanting — don't mix up please," for my brother was about to move his position on the sofa — "look at the two young gentlemen. I have a quick eye, and a steady one, but I can't tell the lord from the commoner, and no one can do so. Even their mother can't. Now I have abused one party, thinking he was the lord, and I have intimated to him that he was lying time and time again, and will say this, that for an out-and-out good one the commoner is the best man I ever met, except three other Americans, whom I won't mention at the present time, and I don't know but that he is their equal. I can't yet decide the point."

My mother smiled on the Chief quite graciously, for she approved of his comments.

"Oh, say something in praise of me also," laughed my brother. "You are giving the other too much of a good thing."

"I shall have to wait for a blessed hereafter before I can praise your lordship," was the answer. "To tell the truth, you have been the bête noir of my life for the past year, and I shall be glad when you leave the country."

"Well, Mr. Murden, you are not complimentary," laughed my brother, as though he had heard a good joke. "But I am going home in a short time. I determined to see something of bush life, and what kind of ruffians bushrangers were made of. I met two, one called Black Dick, and the other Slipper Sam, and Satan never painted worse scoundrels than those two men."

"They are both dead, my lord," the Chief said, very quietly.

"Are they? So glad. They promised to teach me the art of bushranging for a certain sum, and to let me do as I pleased in the mean time. They charged high, but I do not regret the experience. The first victim they practiced on was a Chinaman, and my new partners threatened to blow my head off for interfering in their business. They said that I was only an apprentice in the art, and had no voice in affairs of importance. I suppose the poor devil's bones are picked dry by this time, for he was lashed to a tree, near an ant hill. After all, the scamps did not get a penny, for he had no money."

"Yes, he did," I said. "I rescued him, and in his queue was a bag containing three pounds of gold."

"Well, Angus, I 'm glad that you are capable of such good actions. Ah, my boy, if you had been as noble in all your conduct how proud I should be of you," and the earl caressed his mustache, and looked like an innocent young man.

I thought Mr. Murden would explode in his efforts to restrain his mirth, while my mother kissed me to show how much she approved of my conduct.

"You know," continued my brother, after Mr. Murden had composed his face, "that all the fellows in the nobility line are crazy to write books, and I am as bad as the rest. I struck out for this part of the world, and can give them odds, and beat them all. But if I don't write a book, and I may be too lazy to attend to it, I 'll get you to do it for me, Angus, and I 'll publish under my own name, and you shall have the profits. I 've got lots of incidents to make a big volume. But now to more serious things. Mr. Murden, you have heard the confession of my mother, and a dear, good mother she is, I know, and all that sort of thing, but I can't love her quite as well as I do my reputed mother, who has spoiled me by letting me have everything that my fancy craved. You don't expect it, you know, do you, mother?"

She, with tearful eyes, kissed my brother, and murmured, —

"No, I don't expect it," but it cost her a bitter pang to utter the words.

"That is all right, you know. Now, Mr. Murden, I can make it for your interest to keep still about this matter. Will you do so?"

"Yes, my lord, most faithfully do I promise, but not from interested motives, or pecuniary reward."

"I don't care what your motives are as long as you keep your mouth shut. I have a little political influence at home, and can use it at times for the benefit of those I like. The office of lieutenant-governor is not beyond the reach of a gentleman like you. Think of that, sir."

Mr. Murden bowed quite low, and his eyes glistened at the prospect before him. From a simple inspector of police to the high office of lieutenant-governor was a great jump, and he knew it.

"Now there is one disagreeable duty for me to perform," my brother remarked, as he bent down, and kissed the white brow of his mother, "and that is to set Angus right with his wife. I should like to shirk the task, but can't see my way out. Somehow she thinks he is a little off color, but we can persuade her that she must not believe all the reports she has heard about him. I 'll stand by you, Angus, and, although I won't lie to any woman, I will render things to her eyes the couleur de rose, unless you have gone too far in your liaisons, and if you have I give you up," and he looked the picture of innocence.

"O brother," I asked, "does the nobility of England possess as much impudence as you, individually and collectively?"

"I am afraid that I am modest compared to some of them, Angus. Now, Mr. Murden, bring in the actors. I understand that you have a room full of interested parties up-stairs, and we must not keep them waiting too long. We will let the young lady pick out her husband if she can. Let us test her, Angus."

"It is cruel," I said. "Pray do not sport with so serious a matter."

"Oh, bosh, just as though a young woman thinks it very cruel business to pick out a husband from two good-looking fellows like you and me. Call them in, Mr. Murden. The sooner the thing is done the better I shall feel. My brother is spoony, and, if he has done some wrong, we must try and set him up, and put him on the right track," and then his lordship once more smiled, and stroked his tiny mustache.

Mr. Murden threw open the door, and left us. In a few moments we heard a rustle on the stairs, and then Mr. Kebblewhite, his son, Monsieur Allete, the maiden aunts and cousins, and, lastly, Florence, looking very anxious and handsome, supported by her fair-faced and gentle mother, all entered the drawing-room, and ranged themselves opposite to us, like wall-flowers in a ball-room.

I started forward to greet Florence, and welcome her, but my brother stopped me.

"Fair play, Angus," he whispered. "Give me a chance. Let us start square."

My dear little wife had been informed that some curious denouement was about to happen, but what it was she had not been able to learn, and now that she was permitted to look around, and saw standing near her two men, so much alike, she nestled closer to her mother, and exclaimed, —

"Good Heaven, mamma, there's two of them, and which is my husband?" and she seemed frightened.

"Can you ask that question, Florence?" demanded my brother, as he stepped forward, and extended his hands, as though to inclose the dear girl in his arms, and give her a warm embrace. He was fully capable of such a crime. "Does not your gentle heart tell you that I am the one to whom you gave your little hand? a hand that I prize above all things in this world. Speak to me, O darling, and tell me that you have not forgotten me, and never will."

I remained silent, leaning on the back of a chair. My emotion was too powerful for speech. God knows I wanted to start forward, and throw myself at her feet, and kiss her hand, and call her my own precious wife, but I was powerless to move. Had my life depended on it, I could not have uttered a word. Would some instinct of love, some tender response from her kind heart, point out the true and the false, and guide her to my arms, and to my breast?

"I do not know which is my husband, and which is the impostor," the trembling girl said, still clinging to her mother, and looking first at my brother and then at myself. "I love one of you, but it is the one I wedded, and not the one who rejected me. Oh! in mercy tell me to which do I belong? Do not torture me by this suspense. I am weak, and have suffered, oh, so much! and it is cruel to thus wound me so deeply. Be merciful, if you are men."

"Florence," said my brother, and now all levity was banished from his fun-loving face, and he took another step forward, and touched her unresisting hand, "I am the Earl of Afton, and I regret to say that I am not your husband. This gentleman is, and believe me, when I tell you, that he is a thousand times more worthy of the love of so good and pure a woman as yourself than I am. You have made a fortunate choice, sweet lady, and now let me lead him to you, and your trials are over, I hope. He loves you as I never could, for it is not my nature to be true or constant to any woman, much as I have tried. But time will cure me, I hope, of that weakness, and make me a pattern of domestic virtues."

"Is this true?" asked Florence, looking at me with startling earnestness.

"It is true, Florence. I pledge you my knightly word of honor that it is true," my brother said, very earnestly.

"And my husband has not been guilty of all the sins that have reached my ears?" demanded Florence eagerly.

His lordship winced a little, and hesitated, but he was a bold man, and a good fellow at heart, and, therefore, replied,—

"Charge them all to my account, Florence. Your husband is worthy of you, and ranks next to a saint. He is a Joseph, and your handsome face will keep him good, or I am much mistaken."

Florence hesitated a moment, and then I opened my arms, and the next instant she was held close and fast in my embrace, and her lips were kissed with a zest that made my brother wink very hard, as he realized what he had lost.

"Thra chares for the Belle of Australia, and Mr. Hangus!" I heard some one yell in the hall, and I had no difficulty in recognizing Mike's voice, but he was hustled out of sight, and pacified with a glass of real "ould Oirish whiskey." But even in the basement of the house I could hear him cheer.

"Vell, look a-'ere," cried Mr. Kebblewhite, "this a'n't jist vot I bargained for, yer know. I vanted a syphon of the nobility for a son-in-law, yer know."

"Tush, man," returned my brother, "he is worth a dozen men like me. He will never give your daughter a heart-ache, and I am sure that I should. Be content with a man, and not with a title, such as you have aspired to. Think of your daughter's happiness."

"But 'e a'n't got no money," Mr. Kebblewhite protested, beginning to grow angry.

"Then he shall have some," responded my brother. "I have more than I can use, and this very day I will draw a draft on my London bankers for fifty thousand pounds, and place it to his credit, and if that sum is not enough he shall have fifty thousand more. He shall not want for money as long as I have millions."

"That is hall wery vell," Mr. Kebblewhite said, "but 'e a'n't a lud, arter hall."

"No, but he is a man, and that is something better," responded his lordship, curtly, and did not appear to care any more for Mr. Kebblewhite, and his opinions, than he did for those of a common servant. In fact, he snubbed Mr. K. at all points. "Florence," his lordship continued, turning to my wife, who lifted her blushing face from my bosom to look at him, "do not feel angry at me for not keeping my engagement. So help me Heaven, I felt that I loved you when I asked you to become my wife. It is one of my peculiarities to fall in love with every pretty face that I meet, and to offer marriage, and then repent. I meant to wed you, but remembered in time, that my mother, the countess, had arranged a match for me with the eldest daughter of the Duke of Westchester, a nice girl, given to fairs, painting flower-pots, and petting the poor of the parish, and I knew that there 'd be such a deused row, that I became frightened, and shied the track, and this gentleman, a relative of mine, took my place, and I wish you lots of happiness, and all of that kind of thing, you know, and now who is going to stand a dozen of champagne? for I am tired of talking. It is dry work and I never gabble, unless it is to a pretty woman, and, as Florence is lost to me, I don't want to waste my time in a useless manner. Come,

Mr. K., set out your wine, and let us have a jolly time of it today, drinking the health of your daughter."

"Dear Angus," whispered Florence, "do you truly forgive me for all my hard thoughts and words?"

"As I hope to be forgiven, pet."

"And you will always love me as much as you do now, O my husband?" she asked.

"God grant it, darling. But come, dear, let me introduce you to my mother. She is here, most unexpectedly, and will love you for the sake of her son, and for your own dear self as well."

"I know that I shall love her if she is like her son," was the cheering response, and the two women fell into each other's arms, and, of course, commenced crying immediately, as they always do on such occasions.

"Vell, 'e 's a swell, arter hall, and is a relative of a hearl," Mr. Kebblewhite said. "That a'n't bad. Yer, 'Arry, put hout the vine, and let us hall 'ave a cold snack. Strip the cellar of champagne, and blast the hexpense. I 'm 'appy as any of 'em."

"Attendez," cried the Frenchman, coming forward. "Vait all of you, s'il vous plait. Speak vil I. To the young couple give I all my moneys vhen I no longer them vant. It is much, and have it all shall they. Spoken have I. Hein."

"Better and better," roared Mr. Kebblewhite. "'Arry, you willain, open hall the vine in the 'ouse. Bless me if I don't sing some sea songs for yer," and at this information the Frenchman grew pale, and there was a commotion among the cousins, and an ominous silence.

"Will you let me congratulate you, Angus?" said a soft, pleasant voice, and, turning, I saw the sweet face of my mother-in-law. "I loved you the first night I saw you, and now I love you as well as if I was your own mother. May God bless you and Florence."

"Amen, mother," I answered, and kissed the dear woman so earnestly that my wife came toward us, in pretended alarm.

"You will make me jealous, Angus," Florence said, "if you kiss my mother so fervently," but I never gave her cause for jealousy, and loved her ever. "And you will never let those mean, contemptible Kitties, and Webbies, and Smithies, kiss you again, will you, dear?" whispered Florence, "even by mistake, you know."

"Never, darling, when you are near," and the answer appeared to give her great satisfaction, for she clung to me closer than ever, and seemed as happy as a bride should always appear.

"'Ere is another voman vot vants to see Mr. Angus," cried Harry, and his lordship looked at me, and said, —

"I hope that it is not another flame of yours, Angus. You should keep them at a distance on such an occasion as this," but, by the time he had finished speaking, who should come into the room but Mother Higgins, whom I had met at Camp Reserve.

"You poor, dear boy," the good lady said, as she caught sight of my brother, and supposed that it was me, "I have learned at the police station all the facts of the case, and I came to tell you how sorry I am for my treatment of you. O you angel," and she hugged his lordship most fervently.

"Let up, will you!" roared the earl. "What the deuse do you mean, you know? It is bad enough to have a young girl put her arms around you, but when it comes to an old woman, I can't stand it, you know. Get out. You are crazy. I never saw you before."

"I think that I am the one the lady wishes to see," I said, stepping forward, and then Mother Higgins turned the wealth of her affection on me, and just gushed.

"Yes, you are the one, you dear, good young man, whom I supposed was vile. Let me kiss you. And this is your sweet wife? Oh, how handsome she is! Ah, my dear lady, you have got a treasure for a husband, let me tell you. He is an angel, if he has n't got wings. Why, the night he brought that girl to my house, and then left her in my care, and kissed" —

"What?" asked Florence, a little abruptly.

Mrs. Higgins saw that she was on the wrong tack, and backed water at once, much to my relief.

"And kissed me, a woman old enough to be his mother, because he was so glad I was good to the poor thing."

I breathed a little freer. His lordship had wisely left the room. He did not relish such reminiscences in the presence of company.

"I know what men are, dear lady," Mother Higgins continued. "I 've buried three husbands, and now I 've got a fourth, and shall put him in the ground unless he stops drinking."

Florence looked a little shocked, but Mrs. Higgins continued, —

"I know that I shall surprise you, Mr. Angus, but I 've taken the old miner for my fourth. He is out-doors waiting for me. We are on our bridal tower. He is a little shaky, but I will make him useful washing dishes, and setting the table. I shall find enough for him to do; and then, when he is not otherwise employed, he can tell my boarders all about the

'Welcome Nugget.' He loves me dearly, and if you ever come to Ballarat don't fail to patronize me, and I shall not charge you in advance, like other people."

I thanked the wife of the old miner, for I never learned her new name, and then we heard sounds of mirth in the dining-room, and the good woman pricked up her ears.

"You must excuse me," she said. "My old man is in there, and, from the noise, I know they are getting him drunk. I shall have a nice time with him, sha'n't I?"

It was even as she suspected. His lordship had seen the old miner on the steps, invited him in the house, and then filled him with brandy, and got him to tell the story of the wonderful nugget, and, while he was thus employed, his wife entered the room, seized him by the ear, and walked him out of the house, much to the disgust of the earl, who wanted some fun, and found life rather tame in the city.

We were now alone, for all the company had gone to the dining room, and I could hear the popping of champagne corks, like the irregular fire of a badly drilled military company.

"Florence," I asked, as I encircled her slight form in my arms, and gazed at her smiling and blushing face, "are you sure that you do not regret marrying me instead of my brother — I mean the young earl?"

"I will be candid with you, Angus," she answered. "When his lordship first paid me marked attention I was flattered, for all of my young friends were envious, and when he asked me to be his wife I accepted him without very much hesitation, for I thought what a proud position I should occupy in the world of fashion as the Countess of Afton. Of course I was disappointed when you told me that you were not the one I supposed you to be, and I really imagined that you were not speaking truthfully, and desired to desert me, but, O Angus, I did love you, and if you had but pleaded with me for a few moments longer, instead of leaving me so abruptly, on the night of our wedding, I should have pardoned you, and we would have been very happy together. I suffered for many weeks, dear, as a punishment for my pride, and for some days I did not know even my own mother, and only called for you, as they tell me. Then, when I recovered, I was informed of some terrible rumors regarding your liaisons in the city, and also read in the *Daily Boomerang* the disgusting statement of my maid, that you had kissed her, even at the door of my chamber, and I determined to forget you, and hate you, but I could not do either. And, O Angus, what possessed you to kiss that bold-faced thing?"

"I think, darling, that I was a little insane that night, and hardly responsible for my doings. I was torn by a conflict of anxiety and happiness, as you know."

"Well, dear, I do not want that kind of insanity in my family, so you will please be rational hereafter on all occasions where women are concerned. My maids I shall choose, if I employ any, for their work, and not for their beauty, be assured of that."

"You are not jealous, Florence?" I asked, kissing her white forehead, and smiling at the serious face, and thinking how much I loved her.

"No, indeed, but I noticed that you did not resist as much as you might when that Smith girl put her arms around your neck. You remember, do you not?"

"I did not want to be rude, dear, and she was so much in earnest, and felt so disappointed."

"Yes, I know, girls of that kind are always earnest, and it is just as well to keep them at a distance. How would you like to have me kissed in that way? and all through a mistake."

I evaded the question. It is one women always ask, and is never answered satisfactorily.

"But, pet, you know I did not make love to her, don't you?" I asked, with a smile.

"I hope that you were not the one, Angus. But, oh! the resemblance is so wonderful, and men tell such queer stories sometimes. You know they do. Don't deny it."

"But I am truthful, Florence, and would not deceive you for all the world," and I felt every word I uttered.

But she only nestled the closer to my heart, and sighed a little doleful sigh, as if she was not sure, after all, that I was not deceiving her. In fact, I think she took solid comfort in having a slight jealous pang, in the midst of all our happiness. But I kissed the clouds away, and she smiled once more.

"I am so thankful," she whispered, "that I am the wife of a true man, who loves me tenderly and dearly, and I would not exchange his affection for all the coronets in Europe."

"But you still have a title, pet. You are the Belle of Australia, remember."

"No, dear, I renounce that claim forever, and take up one more sweet and pleasant to my ears. I am the honored wife of one of America's sovereigns."

"And my queen, dear, now and forever," and the red lips of my wife were raised for a kiss.

"Ahem!" coughed some one, and, turning, we saw that Mr. Murden had entered the drawing-room, quietly as usual, as if he expected to find a burglar at work with the silver or family jewels. "Ahem," he repeated. "Excuse the intrusion, but, really, his lordship has made a brilliant speech, and toasted his relative and bride, and we all want you to respond. I was sent to request your presence as soon as possible."

"One moment," I said, as the Chief turned to leave the room. "Tell me some more as to how and where your men found his lordship."

"As I said, on a sheep-run, on the banks of the Murray, at the foot of the chain of mountains that we call the Australian Alps. He was having a jolly time, hunting kangaroos, and ducks, and had an old Chinaman to cook, and a black fellow to carry the game. He refused to come to the city at first, but, when everything was explained to him, consented, like the trump that he is. He got here last night, reported to me immediately, and agreed to meet you here at ten o'clock, and stand the exposure. I sent word to all the friends to muster in force, and keep up-stairs, and out of sight, until I called them down, and explained matters."

"Give the men who discovered him a hundred pounds extra," I said. "They deserve it."

"I will, and it shall come out of my own pocket, for being such an idiot as I am. However, it has been the means of making your fortune, so there is consolation in all things."

"And Kitty?" I asked, in a whisper.

"She was with him, as happy as a boarding-school girl, home for the holidays. She returned also, and is at her old residence, quite pleased with her life in the bush."

"What will he do with her?"

"Pension her off when he leaves for home. He won't go back to the sheep-run. Some new freak has entered his head;" and pension her his lordship did, but Kitty nearly died of a broken heart when the parting took place. She recovered, however, and married a mean sneak of a shysting lawyer, who wanted a home and her money, and he got both. She became known as Mrs. Kimball.

"By the way," whispered Mr. Murden, "the broker bought our wool at auction yesterday for about one shilling two and a half pence per pound, and this morning it has advanced five pence per pound. It is going higher," and it did go higher, and we sold at a profit of ninety thousand dollars nett, in the course of two weeks, much to Mr. Kebblewhite's surprise, for he did not make quarter as much.

"'Ere is another voman and a man to see Mr. Murden," Harry announced, with a terrible grin on his face. "They hall is comin' 'ere, I believes. The vine von't hold out at this rate."

"Show them in, Harry," said the Chief. "I will speak to them here. Who are they?"

I began to tremble, for I did not want too much happiness in one day, and I still feared complications, owing to the bad conduct of that brother of mine.

Harry ushered in Mr. Smith, and his wife's sister, the pretty little Susan. What could have sent them here? Miss Susan looked at me in a scornful manner, but Florence went to her at once, and actually kissed the young lady.

"I was down at the central house asking for you, and the officer told me that you were here, and that some wonderful new revelation had occurred," Mr. Smith said, addressing the Chief. "It seems that we wronged some one, and we have called to apologize. Susan has got over her love fit, and is all right now, but we would like to see the man that spooned her."

Just then the noble lord entered the room to call me, but, as soon as he saw Susan and Smith, beat a rapid retreat, and went back to the other guests. He did not care to face the new-comers. Susan saw him, however, and she gave a sniff of contempt, and then looked at me, and gave another sniff, and began to cry, while Florence comforted her.

"Don't grieve," my wife said. "You will get all over it in time; and don't look at my dear husband in that scornful manner. He is just as good as he can be, and live, and I half fear I am not nice enough for him. He would die before he would make love to any woman but me. It was the other one who deceived you, but he is not worth a moment's thought. I am very happy, and I wish that you were, but we poor girls can't be too careful in placing confidence in men, and let this be a warning to you, dear. I would trust no one but my Angus. He can't do wrong."

This was very cheerful news to me, and showed that Florence was improving rapidly.

Smith and Susan would not remain, although we invited them to stay. But they felt that they had intruded, and went away, and we were not sorry to see them go. It was not wholesome to his lordship to have them in the house. Susan soon married a good stockman, and now actually boasts that she was once loved by a lord, to the disgust of her husband.

Florence and I entered the dining-room, and I had to make a speech, and Mr. Kebblewhite insisted upon singing a nautical song, and, as the fun grew fast and furious, led by my brother, who seemed to take pleasure in hearing my father-in-law bellow, and in seeing him drink, Florence and I escaped to the drawing-room, and there we found her mother and mine in the recess of the bow window, and, as we drew near, I heard my mother say, —

"Well, when Angus first had the measles, he was six, and I "—

"Yes, I know, but when Florence was first taken with the whooping cough I " —

We did not remain to hear more, but fled. They were engaged on a subject dear to every mother's heart. We wandered up-stairs, and sat down in the quiet of my wife's chamber, and contrasted our present happiness with the time when I had dropped out of the window, and fell into the arms of Mr. Murden.

The only unpleasant incident of the day was when Mike, who, for a drunken man, was the most peaceable Irishman I ever saw, offered to fight "'Arry" for half a crown, because the butler said that even a "hemperor" was not nice enough for his young misses, and Mike thought that was a reflection on me, and my goodness. But Mr. Murden sent Mike home to the Hen and Chickens, and had him put to bed, but he woke up half a dozen times in the night, and frightened the inmates of the chop house into convulsions by shouting out, —

"Thra chares for the Belle of Australia, and Mr. Hangus!" and renewed doses of whiskey were needed to pacify him.

Mike came to the United States with me, and I left him in New York. He opened a large liquor saloon on Third Avenue, and, consequently, soon became an influential member of the Board of Aldermen, and now wears a gold chain, about as large as a yacht's cable, and looks forward to the time when he will be a member of Congress. He is married, and has half a dozen children, and the eldest boy, when angry, twits his parent for not being a native-born American. I often see him when in New York, and then he talks of old times, and Australia, by the hour, and actually praises the country. Last November he dined with me at the Union-Square Hotel, and, under the soothing influence of a bottle of champagne, swore that he would elect me to Congress if I would settle in his district, and take to politics. But I declined the proffered honor.

Of course the return to the city of Lord Afton made some talk, and we were both interviewed by a reporter from the *Daily Boomerang*, and our wonderful resemblance commented on, and I think the conclusion of a three-column sketch read like this : —

"The Belle of Australia, instead of marrying an English nobleman, has taken an American sovereign. It is well. Thus another silken tie has been formed that will bind this prosperous and powerful colony to the great republic. Let us hope that the happy bridegroom, when he returns home, will take some steps to inaugurate free trade, and reduce postal charges, so that the *Boomerang* can go to the ends of the earth at cheap rates. We shall be pleased to offer our columns, gratis, for a full expression of his views on married life, or the great resources of Australia, and he has permission to look over our exchanges at any time, when disposed to call at this office."

"Angus," said my brother that evening, "I shall return home in the course of a few weeks. Come with me, wife, mother, and all."

"Not for the world," responded Florence hastily, and she nestled a little closer to me.

"Why not?" asked his lordship, petulantly.

"Well, I don't want any more mistakes, if you please. The resemblance is too wonderful. No, we will remain apart for the present, or until I am better acquainted with my husband," Florence said decidedly.

His lordship laughed, and did not renew the subject. He is now a steady married man, but has not published his book on Australia, and bushranger life.

And Florence and I are happy, and the love which she inspired me, the first time I saw her, when I was forced to accept her hand, has not grown cold, nor has the color faded from her cheeks, nor the sparkle from her eyes, nor the golden shimmer from her hair, nor the sweet smile from her red lips, nor — a little touch of jealousy from her gentle heart when I am very agreeable to other ladies, as it is necessary to be sometimes.

Mr. Kebblewhite is still alive, and so is his kind wife, and both are anxious to see their grandson. Monsieur Allete is well, and sends us substantial tokens of his kindness. Mr. Murden still has hopes of being lieutenant-governor of Victoria. He is now a member of the cabinet, and liable to be pitched out at any time, by a vote of want of confidence of the house on some land question, or who shall make the governor's breeches, or repair them.

Shall we go back and review the scenes of our early years? Ah, well, who can tell what the future may bring forth? But, be it as fate may ordain, I shall never forget the kind hearts and warm friendships I formed in AUSTRALIA, and they will live forever in my memory.

THE ANNOUNCEMENT OF A NEW STORY.

ON LAND AND SEA,

OR

CALIFORNIA IN THE YEARS
1843, '44, AND '45.

BY WILLIAM H. THOMES.

I hope that all who have followed the fortunes, good or bad, of "THE BELLE OF AUSTRALIA," and "ANGUS MORNINGTON," will need no urging to read my next story, a biography of a voyage to California, in the year 1842, when, as a boy of fifteen, I shipped in the *Admittance*, of Boston, Captain Peter Peterson, and for three years, or from March 4, 1843, '44, and '45, remained on the coast, engaged in the arduous work of hide-droghing, and during that period visited every port in the country several times, from San Francisco to San Diego, and saw California as it then existed, with little trade, not much energy, handsome women, and very lazy men. The reading of Mr. Richard H. Dana's "Two Years Before the Mast," prompted the voyage on my part, and I often told the author, when alive, that to him was I indebted for three years of the hardest work, and the most careless and happy life, that I ever experienced, for there were six boys on the ship, and at times we made things lively for officers and Mexicans. I do not hope to give so graphic a picture of sea life, and California experience, as Mr. Dana has done in his little volume, but I shall describe things as I encountered them, and, perhaps, I can entertain my readers with a biography that will amuse them, even if it does not instruct to any great extent. As far as seamanship is concerned I was the equal of Mr. Dana, and afterward, perhaps, a little superior, for I have sailed under many flags, and in various parts of the globe, and occupied some responsible positions on board the finest vessels in the world, so the reader can rely on my sea terms, and the truthfulness of my seamanship. To refresh my memory I have before me the private diary of Captain Peterson, who is still alive, and living at South Boston. He has loaned the volume for the purpose of writing out a history of the voyage, and, as the doings of every day are recorded for the three years, I shall make no mistake about places or dates. I am sorry to state that my name is found quite often in the diary, and not always in terms of great praise, and for remarkably good conduct. I am afraid that we boys did try his temper, not always angelic, as I had reason to know, but he must take the bitter with the sweet, in fair part, I trust. In fact, I know that he will, for we are good friends, and what is the use of having friends unless you can abuse them a little? He used to stir me up, and now I can retaliate by giving him a lift occasionally.

WILLIAM H. THOMES.

www.ingramcontent.com/pod-product-compliance
Lightning Source LLC
Chambersburg PA
CBHW030013240426
43672CB00007B/928